Dana Thornock's

LEAN&FREE 2000 PLUS™

Dana's
COOKBOOK™

Cooking Lean – Not Extreme!

*With Special Help For Those With Diabetes,
High Cholesterol, and High Resistance to Fat Loss*

ACKNOWLEDGMENTS

- Richard Bird for his thousands of hours of brilliant and patient graphics; and his wife Beth, for her cheerful encouragement.

- Dr. Mary Beard for her medical editing and invaluable support.

- Lisa Jones for her beautiful art direction, food styling, and detailed help with recipes, shopping lists, and editing.

- Michael Lewis for his professional food photography.

- Cheryl Young and Lisa Meiling for their work with recipes and food lists.

- Judith Nielsen Crocker, Jack Lyon, Leni Davenport, and David Bird for their skilled editing.

- Elizabeth (my step daughter) for her valuable assistance in final proofing of this book.

- Colette and Caroline (my sisters) for their much-needed help with housework, cooking, and "taxi service" for my children.

- Aaron, John, Tyson, Riley, and Chase (my sons at home) for their candid input on all recipes that, with their help, taste too good to be good for you; yet they *are*!

- My husband Marty, for his continued support in all that I do; and for his kindness and love.

Front Cover Photograph:
Cheese-Stuffed Jumbo Shells with fresh green beans; and Grandma's Marvelous Chocolate Velvet Cake with fresh strawberries

THIS BOOK IS DEDICATED TO

You

*if you have ever worried about your health or your weight. You **can** do this and you'll finally have the freedom to get on with your life. I truly believe this is right. Best Wishes and Happy Eating,*

Dana Thornock

Dana Thornock

Published by
Danmar Health Corporation
P.O. Box 2000
Kaysville, Utah, 84037
1-801-546-3262

ISBN 1-56684-079-1
Printed in the United States of America

10 9 8 7 6 5

NOTICE: The information in this book is true and complete to the best of our knowledge. This book is intended only as an informative guide for those wishing to know more about nutrition, fitness, emotional and physical health, and excess body-fat loss. Although the advice given is similar to that recommended by many knowledgeable health professionals, the information is meant to complement the advice of your physician, not to replace, countermand, or conflict with it. We strongly recommend that you follow your doctor's advice in dealing with all health issues and problems. Diet, exercise, mental health, and medication decisions should be made between you and your doctor. Accordingly, either you or the professional treating you must take full responsibility for any use made of the information in this book. Information in this book is general and is made with no guarantees by the author or publisher. The author and publisher disclaim all liability in connection with the use of this book.

ABOUT THE AUTHOR

It was one woman's personal experience with the tremendous frustration of diets that led to the important discovery that could change our entire approach to food, eating, health, and fitness. Discouraged by her own battles with excess fat and the futility of diets, Dana Thornock has spent seventeen years studying obesity and experimenting with methods for controlling it. From that study has emerged a revolutionary new key to successful weight control: eating abundantly!

Dana learned that diets actually promote fat gain because the body has an instinctive survival system that works to store fat when it feels threatened by starvation. And dieting signals starvation! So she experimented by gradually increasing her intake of "healthy" calories from 1,000 a day to between 2,000 and 3,500. The result was dramatic. She dropped from size 18 to size 4, where she has remained ever since, even withstanding two pregnancies and extreme stress in her life.

Dana shared her discoveries in the 1988 bestseller Eat and Be Lean and in lectures and classes that have freed thousands of others from the tyranny of fat and diets. She then used her teaching experiences and new discoveries in medical science to refine, simplify, and expand her program. The result is the Dana Thornock LEAN & FREE 2000 PLUS Weight Control System, the most effective and advanced weight control system available.

Unlike diets, the LEAN & FREE 2000 PLUS program doesn't deprive—it provides! Dana has learned through years of experience that keeping *all* foods under 20% fat becomes bland, restrictive, and boring. So Dana has taken foods that are 100 percent fat (like butter), 50 percent fat (like cheese), 20 percent fat, and two percent fat, and fit them deliciously into easy daily menus that have an *overall* fat percentage less than 20 percent! You'll be eating favorite foods like pizza, tacos, and beef stroganoff, and gourmet desserts like cherry cheesecake. Now you can free yourself from the bland restrictions of diets and from the bondage of fat, and maintain that freedom for life—freedom to become and stay lean and healthy eating incredible-tasting foods!

Dana has a Bachelor of Science degree in Child and Family Studies with an emphasis in nutrition. She is a popular lecturer and advisor to many government, corporate, health, and educational institutions. She has been a "low-bounce," "maximum fat loss" aerobics instructor for twelve years. She and her first husband Nyle were married in 1978 and had four sons together. Nyle passed away in 1989 and two years later Dana remarried. She and her current husband, Marty, have eight children together—seven sons and one daughter.

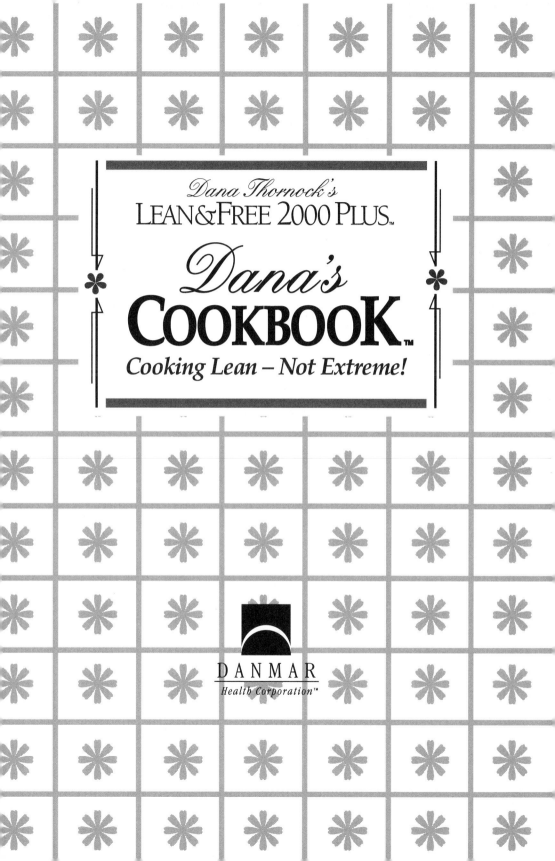

Dana Thornock's
LEAN&FREE 2000 PLUS™

Dana's
COOKBOOK™
Cooking Lean – Not Extreme!

DANMAR
Health Corporation™

Dana's COOKBOOK™
CONTENTS

FOREWORD *By Mary K. Beard, M.D., FACOG*
INTRODUCTION
LEAN & FREE is Not a Diet! —You Must *Read This Carefully.* **1**
COOKING TO BE LEAN *DESIGNER* MENUS
  GRAB 'N' GO MENUS **15**
  BUDGET MENUS. **33**
  DAILY SUCCESS COMPLETE FREEDOM MENUS
    With Detailed Shopping Lists **51**
COOKING TO BE LEAN RECIPES
  Delicious, Normal, and Exceptionally Fast!. **143**

DELICIOUSLY-EASY IDEA LISTS P. 271

Bread, Grain, and Pasta Ideas 272
Bread Spread Ideas
  (*Butter vs. Margarine*) 273
Breakfast Ideas. 274
Cereal Ideas (*Rated A thru F*) 275
Cooking Oil and
  "Real" Food Ideas 279
Dessert and Drink Ideas 281
Dip, Dressing, and Sauce Ideas 283
Food-Storage Ideas 284

Fruit Ideas 285
Legume Ideas
  (*Beans, Peas, and Lentils*) 287
Main Course, Sandwich, and
  Side Dish Ideas 288
Snack Ideas with
  Now and Then Junk-Food Ideas 288
Soup Ideas 290
Vegetable Ideas 291

GROCERY SHOPPING AND LABEL READING. **294**
RECIPE HEALTHIFICATION. **302**

GUIDELINES FOR THOSE WITH SPECIAL NEEDS P. 313

Allergies 316
Amenorrhea 335
Anorexia. 317
Arthritis 319
Back Problems 320
Breast Feeding. 321
Bulimia. 317
Cancer 322
Children 323
Chronic Dieting. 317
Chronic Fatigue. 323
Chronic Sore Throats 324
Constipation 325
Depression 323
Diabetes. 325
Diarrhea 325
Foot Problems 320
Gastrointestinal Distress 337
Hair Problems 333
Headaches. 328
Heart Disease. 329
High Blood Pressure. 328

High Cholesterol 329
High Resistance to Fat Loss. . . . 330
Hypoglycemia 325
Infertility. 335
Knee Problems 320
Leg Problems. 320
Menopause. 330
Morbid Obesity 332
Muscular Disorders 319
Osteoporosis 333
Physical Handicaps. 334
PMS. .334
Pregnancy. 335
Premature Aging 333
Seasonal Affective Disorder . . . 323
Self-Esteem Problems 337
Senior Citizens 336
Skin Problems. 333
Stomach Aches 337
Stomach-Stapling Surgery 317
Stress Control 337
Weight Gain as a Goal 338

FOOD EVALUATION CHARTS AND RECIPE INDEXES P. 339

FAT GRAM/CALORIE EVALUATION CHARTS. 340

RESTAURANT-FOOD EVALUATION CHARTS. 351

FAT-CALORIE PERCENT CHARTS 374

RECIPE TOPICAL INDEX. 376

RECIPE ALPHABETICAL INDEX. 380

ix

*A Personal-Progress Form and LEAN & FREE product order information
are found in the back of this book.*

FOREWORD

Today as never before people have become concerned about being and staying healthy. As a result there has been a bombardment of information about health, diet, exercise, foods and nutrition from magazines, newsletters, television, radio talk shows, etc., making it difficult to evaluate what is valid and what is not. Based on thousands of studies, the relationship between diet and disease has become more and more evident. Of the ten leading causes of death in the United States, five are now seen as being diet-related. Specifically, a diet too high in fats and too low in fruits, vegetables, and grains clearly raises a person's risk of heart disease, some cancers, stroke, adult-onset diabetes and atherosclerosis (hardening of the blood vessels). For many Americans, the link between diet and disease continues at the least to be under appreciated.

The Japanese have the world's highest life expectancy, surpassing Americans in the 1970's and the Swedes in this decade. It is felt that the main reason Japanese live long lives is their healthy diet. Their diet tends to be low in fat and high in fiber, heavy on fish, vegetables and grains, light on beef and dairy products. The Japanese have cholesterol counts that are 20% or more below those found in the United States, and as a result they have one of the lowest levels of heart disease in the world.

Dana has incorporated the sound principles of a nutritionally balanced diet of water, vegetables, grains, proteins, and fruits into a cookbook with recipes and meal plans that will help you develop a new way of life of healthy eating. As the cook and food shopper you have control over what and how your family eats. It can be a fun challenge to prepare nutritious meals or even take your own favorite recipes and make them healthier for your whole family. It is important to follow Dana's enthusiasm and vitality to get you through each day.

Again, remember, this program is not a quick fix. It does not offer caloric or nutrient starvation for your body! It is a way of life that, if followed, should help you to be a healthier, leaner, and much happier person.

Best wishes on becoming a healthier you.

Mary K. Beard, M.D. FACOG
*Private practice in Obstetrics, Gynecology
and Infertility: Associate Clinical Professor
University of Utah, Salt Lake City, Utah.*

INTRODUCTION

Lean & Free is Not a Diet!
You Must Read This Carefully

Welcome to the LEAN & FREE LIFESTYLE and the freedom to eat and be lean for life! Awaiting you is a world of delicious and normal food that will work to keep you healthy and slim! You are embarking on a true adventure—the journey towards a new life filled with energy, confidence, and the long-sought freedom from excess body fat and restrictive diets.

Come with me as I introduce you to easy GRAB 'N' GO MENUS, tight BUDGET MENUS, deliciously-detailed COMPLETE FREEDOM MENUS, and shopping lists so flexible they can be adapted to any lifestyle. Whether you live alone or share your life with a family, you'll find simple ways to adapt the LEAN & FREE 2000 PLUS ULTIMATE WELLNESS/WEIGHT CONTROL LIFESTYLE to your personal needs.

As you study my LEAN & FREE 2000 PLUS book*, audio tapes, "Where Do I Start" video tape, and "Dana, I Need To Know" Video Support Group Series, you'll develop an understanding of exactly how your body stores and burns fat and how it creates energy. And you'll become familiar with the eight powerful steps for attaining optimum health and leanness. We'll briefly review those steps now, so it will be even clearer to you why the principles in this delicious cookbook can pave your way to a much healthier, leaner you.

As you study the time-tested LEAN & FREE program you'll understand:

 1. *Knowledge* of how your body stores and burns fat. You'll discover the twelve avoidable fat-storing "stressors" that can increase

See product information in the back of this book.

excess body fat, reduce your energy level, and promote premature aging and poor health.

As you've already learned, caloric or nutritional starvation (through dieting, skipping meals, and eating mainly junk foods) is the number one fat-storing stressor. It can slow your body's metabolism and cause muscle and water loss, along with resistance to fat loss. It can also make you appear old, lined, and tired. As you gradually begin to increase your high-quality food calories and decrease your junk-food calories, your energy level may markedly increase as your metabolism quickens. You may experience an increase in lean muscle tissue, fat-burning enzymes, and body hydration. You may begin to look and feel vibrant, healthy, and full of vitality.

Always remember: you're not concerned with *calorie numbers*. Instead, simply listen to your body and respond to its needs. These needs may fluctuate. Over the last twelve years, my own daily caloric demands average between 2,000 calories and 3,500 calories each day. Yet, there are days when I'm as high as 4,000 or as low as 1,600. Other people I've observed experience a range of about 1,500 to 2,500. Still others are in a 3,000 to 5,000 calorie range. But for people who start out with a low metabolism and significantly reduced muscle tissue, the range may be as low as 1,200 to 1,500 calories per day, or even lower if they've been chronically anorexic. (See page 317.) This range gradually increases with their lean muscle tissue and their metabolic rates.

Your hunger and energy needs are as individual as you are. They'll be different from those of other people, and they'll vary from day to day. So it's important to follow this simple guideline: eat until you feel comfortably satisfied. (Carefully study the Satisfaction Chart on the next page.) That satisfaction should come from drinking water and eating vegetables, grains, protein, and fruit. The ideal balance of nutrients for health and fat loss is contained in every menu in this book.

How I FEEL
When I'm Experiencing Fat Loss

When you first begin LEAN & FREE, you may not receive signals of hunger and fullness if you've dieted or skipped meals for many years. So simply eat small meals often (3 to 6 or more times each day; see pages 317-319). Soon your body will respond and start "talking" to you again—correct food in—correct feedback out! And you'll finally have the physical and emotional energy to fully enjoy your life! The following chart indicates my satisfaction level and the satisfaction level of my students while experiencing fat loss.

SATISFACTION CHART

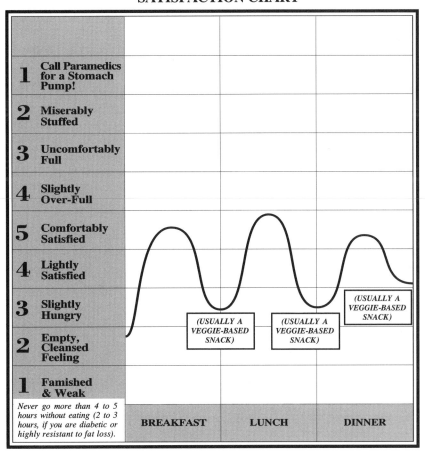

		BREAKFAST	LUNCH	DINNER
1	Call Paramedics for a Stomach Pump!			
2	Miserably Stuffed			
3	Uncomfortably Full			
4	Slightly Over-Full			
5	Comfortably Satisfied			
4	Lightly Satisfied			
3	Slightly Hungry			*(USUALLY A VEGGIE-BASED SNACK)*
2	Empty, Cleansed Feeling	*(USUALLY A VEGGIE-BASED SNACK)*	*(USUALLY A VEGGIE-BASED SNACK)*	
1	Famished & Weak			

Never go more than 4 to 5 hours without eating (2 to 3 hours, if you are diabetic or highly resistant to fat loss).

*Score the **Comfortable Satisfaction** section on your Left-Brain Planner (in the back of the LEAN & FREE 2000 PLUS book) according to this chart. I have difficulty discerning hunger and fullness only when I'm eating too many sweets. I therefore avoid sweets for seven hard days and by the eighth day, it's effortless. I don't crave them at all!*

Be certain to avoid the following:

The Ten Worst Eating Habits

1. Skipping meals or going more than four or five hours in between meals!!! (Two or three hours if you are diabetic, hypoglycemic, or highly resistant to fat loss.)
2. Eating sweets on an empty stomach!
3. Eating the *same* foods over and over again with little variety or eating only fruit by itself.
4. Changing too rapidly from low-fiber foods to high-fiber foods. (Example: white bread and very few vegetables and fruits to 100% whole-wheat bread and lots of "raw" vegetables and fruits—very bad!)
5. Eating *too much* or *too little* fat and protein.
6. Eating too many grains and too few vegetable-based foods like vegetable soup, stew, casserole, stir-fry, etc.
7. Not including water, vegetables, grains, protein, and fruit at each meal! (Exception: breakfast vegetable.)
8. Eating so lightly that you still feel quite hungry.
9. Eating too quickly until you are stuffed and sick to your stomach and want to lie down.
10. Not following the delicious, quick, perfectly balanced LEAN & FREE MENUS and the Recipe Healthification guidelines.

Once again: Eat until you are comfortable on water, vegetables, grain, protein, and fruit. If you omit even one of these elements, you may be *full*, but you won't be *satisfied*. You'll still be craving fats and sweets and hunting for something else to satisfy you (like chocolate cake). Your body will feel nutritionally dissatisfied and will therefore resist fat loss.

It is also very important to keep your fat intake between 10 and 20 percent of your total calories (10 and 15 percent if you're highly resistant to fat loss and 20 to 30 percent from "good" fats if you need to gain weight in a "healthy" manner). Keeping your fat intake below 10 percent on a regular basis can weaken your immune system and promote dry skin, brittle hair, and actual resistance to body fat loss, since you'll be deficient in essential nutrients—omega 3 and omega 6 fatty acids.

4

To adjust your fat grams to between 10 and 20 percent, follow these simple steps:

How Many Fat Grams Should I Eat Each Day?

1. Add up your daily fat grams and calories at least one day a month (ideally once a week) on your Left-Brain Planner found at the back of the LEAN & FREE 2000 PLUS book.

2. Then adjust your fat grams to equal 10 to 20 percent of your total daily calorie intake. Here's an example. Let's say you average 1,600 calories a day. There are nine calories in one gram of fat. (We can round that out to ten because we won't count fat traces). Remove the last 0 from 1,600 and you have the number of calories that equal 10 percent of 1,600: 160. Double 160 to 320 and you have the number of calories that equals 20 percent of 1,600. Now take the 0 off 160 and the 0 off 320 to equal 16 to 32 grams of fat. So 16 to 32 is the ideal number of fat grams to eat a day if you average 1,600 calories. Remember that your fat grams must be proportional to the number of calories you eat. Fat gram numbers alone are completely irrelevant because your body handles fats more efficiently when they are combined with high-fiber foods. Study the simple chart below and remember that every menu in this book already has the ideal-fat and nutrient balance figured into it so that you don't have to worry about it! True freedom to EAT and enjoy!

CALORIES	10% FAT FAT GRAMS		20%FAT FAT GRAMS
1,200	12	to	24
1.400	14	to	28
1,600	16	to	32
1,800	18	to	36
2,000	20	to	40
2,500	25	to	50
3,000	30	to	60
3,500	35	to	70
4,000	40	to	80
4,500	45	to	90
5,000	50	to	100

*Women who are highly resistant to fat loss do well when they keep their fat grams between 10 and 15 percent of their overall calories—usually about **15 to 40** fat grams.*

5

2. Commitment or motivation, and developing a passion to be LEAN & FREE, are critical. We just discussed step 1 of the 8 steps, which is *knowledge*, the knowledge of how our bodies store and burn fat. Commitment naturally follows this exciting understanding. Commitment is directly fueled by maintaining your Physical and Emotional Health Chart and your Body Measurement Chart (on pages 137 and 138 in your LEAN & FREE 2000 PLUS book) *every* week. I used to complete my charts every six weeks, but I've learned that *every* week is a much more effective routine. You'll get so excited about regular, predictable inch loss, that the hot fudge sundae will suddenly lose all its appeal and exercise will become the "candy bar" of your day. During this process, never put any stock in the scales. Ten weeks ago, I tuned my habits up from a "B–" to an "A+". The recorded changes were remarkable. Did I lose 27 overall inches with a 20-pound weight loss? No! A 15-pound loss? No! An eight-pound loss? No! No! No! I lost 27 inches with a four and one-half-pound weight loss! Really. I can't even believe it myself! With changes such as these it suddenly becomes a compliment to be considered *dense*—because that density comes from increases in muscle mass, bone mass, and body hydration. With such changes, you may also find that you're beginning to look much younger. Many people in their 60's tell me they're now often mistaken for being in their early 40's. I think these principles are as close as we'll come to a true fountain of youth. My 22-year-old stepson was recently married—and I, at 35, was mistaken as his "new bride" several times. Now, that's fun. And it creates real COMMITMENT!

Make certain to study my detailed measurement chart on page 154 in your LEAN & FREE 2000 PLUS BOOK. It's amazing—even to me! Also study the FAT-STORING, NEUTRAL, and FAT-BURNING phases in your LEAN & FREE BOOK and the highly motivating success stories. If you are in a state of poor health brought on by years of caloric and nutritional starvation, your body will heal from the inside out. You'll get healthy while you gradually create a fat-burning body. So if you're in a *fat-storing* state right now, it may not yet be time to do your weekly *Measurement Chart.* But start today doing your *Physical and Emotional Health Chart.*

3. Nurturing and loving yourself and your body becomes so much easier when you're feeding your mind and body nourishing, balanced foods—and you'll feel absolutely free of guilt. Finally, you'll be working *with* your body, not against it! And, when the caloric and nutrient starvation are gone, so much of the emotional starvation is gone as well because your brain is a *physical* organ.

4. Nourishment and *5. Motion* are two subjects that involve extensive amounts of breakthrough research and explanation. It's best to simply read your LEAN & FREE 2000 PLUS book, listen to your audio tapes and watch your video tapes—especially do the maximum-fat-loss, very gently exercise tapes. People tell me continually how many new things they learn and absorb each time through the books and tapes. Repetition and practice are the keys to success with these two steps—*Nourishment* and *Motion* can provide you with a beautiful body along with happiness and vitality.

6. Service is the ultimate focus of LEAN & FREE because service to others is the only source of real and lasting happiness. But remember, the "grit your teeth and do it" attitude that applied to dieting DOESN'T WORK here! It has to be service that is reflected in the *face* and comes from the *heart* as well as the hands. Only then does it bring real fulfillment, peace, and joy. When you use your new-found energy and health to help others, you actually *lose* yourself, and in the process, paradoxically, you find yourself. Life has a purpose, a higher purpose, that instills you with even more energy. Steadily, your love for life becomes more and more complete and rewarding—and that is the whole purpose of your new LEAN & FREE LIFESTYLE.

7. Planning is described in detail in the planning chapter of your LEAN & FREE 2000 PLUS book and on the Lecture Series tapes. There are extra *Right-* and *Left-Brain Success Planners* in the back of the LEAN & FREE 2000 PLUS book for your personal use.

7

Remember to complete the Left-Brain Success Planner once a week. It looks rather like an IRS form, but don't let that intimidate you. It takes only about 15 minutes to complete. This planner will give you an invaluable wellness/weight-control education. Your Right-Brain Success Planner takes less than one minute to complete! Fill it out every day without fail (except on the days you complete your Left-Brain Planner) if you genuinely desire optimal health, energy, and permanent leanness.

8. Action is the step in which you really take flight. You learn how to develop the eating and exercise behaviors that will empower your life. And you'll learn to adapt LEAN & FREE to your individual needs and lifestyle. I've included four pages from my LEAN & FREE 2000 PLUS book that will remind you just how to adapt these menus, recipes, and detailed shopping lists to your personal needs and preferences.

So read on. Have fun! Take it one day at a time. Go for it and do it NOW! Keep your eye on that LEAN & FREE beautiful body ahead and on a life free from diets, avoidable health problems, guilt, fatigue, and depression. Best of all, it's a life free from the worry of ever becoming fat again. Happy Day! I'm so glad you're on board.

LEAN & FREE Is Not a Diet!

My definition of a diet is any eating program that directs you to eat less than your own personnal comfortable-satisfaction requirements and reduces your fat, carbohydrate, or protein intake below a healthy level. These unhealthy, fat-storing pseudo-approaches are always tasteless, bland, and boring. LEAN & FREE, on the other hand, offers you and your entire family vast arrays of normal, delicious foods that will keep you healthy and fit, and it's so easy to select and prepare them! Just use the *Five Fingers of Ideal Nutrient Balance*, illustrated on the following page, as your guideline:

THE FIVE FINGERS OF IDEAL NUTRIENT BALANCE

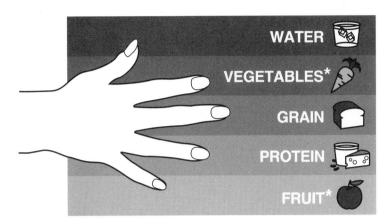

Within **each** of the following delicious, easy menus is a little gold mine of nutrients that will lead you to optimal health and leanness. Each menu contains the *Five Fingers of Ideal Nutrient Balance* and all the essential elements discussed in the *Nourishment* chapter on pages 54 through 81 of your LEAN & FREE 2000 PLUS book. For complete success, these menus and their companion shopping lists must be adapted to your personal needs. Carefully study the sample menu on the next page.

Personalize These Delicious Menus

The following GRAB 'N' GO menu can easily be adapted to meet personal needs such as

1. Time schedule.

2. Budget needs.

3. Special health needs *(allergies, diabetes, etc.)*.

4. Family needs and tastes *(whether you live alone or cook for a family)*.

5. Calorie and fiber needs *(increase fiber and calories very gradually)*.

*Medical science has totally refuted the notion that a fruit and a vegetable eaten at the same meal ferment in your stomach. And NEVER eat only fruit until noon because this will create substantial rises and drops in blood sugar and energy levels, thus encouraging fat storage.

9

LEAN & FREE 2000 PLUS™	GRAB 'N' GO DAILY SUCCESS MENU	

			FG/CAL
Breakfast	Water	12 oz. water	
	Grain	1 1/2 cups Kellogg's Just Right Fruit & Nut Cereal	2/280
	Protein	1 1/2 cups skim milk	t/129
	Fruit	(in cereal)	
Snack	Water	12 oz. water	
	Veggie+	6 baby carrots	0/35
Lunch	Water	8 oz. water	
	Vegetable	(in sandwich)	
	Grain	1/2 foot long Subway Turkey Breast Sandwich with extra veggies and no oil or mayonnaise on a whole-grain bun	
Fast Food Subway	Protein	(turkey and cheese)	10/337
	Fruit	1 lg. orange (bring orange from home or count the tomato as your fruit)	t/62
Snack	Water	12 oz. water	
	Veggie+	1/2 leftover footlong sandwich (if hungry)	10/337
Dinner	Water	8 oz. water	
	Vegetable	1 1/2 cup Quick, Delicious Beef Stew* p. 155	12/453
	Grain	1 slice whole-grain bread with 1 Tb. All Fruit Jam* p. 164	t/158
	Protein	(in beef stew)	
	Fruit	1 apple	t/81
Snack	Water	12 oz.	
	Veggie+	2 cup Shortcut Tossed Salad* p. 266 with 4 Tb. Buttermilk Dressing* p. 210 (or bottled fat free or lowfat dressing)	t/234±

34 fat grams x 9 calories = 306 calories from fat

306 ÷ 2,106 = **15% FAT**

Total: 34/2,106

How to Personalize This Menu for You

1. Time Schedule: If you hate to cook or simply never have time, the *Grab 'n' Go* menu (on the previous page) is adapted to your needs. What could be quicker to prepare than cold cereal, pre-cut (at the grocery store) vegetables and leafy tossed salads, fast-food sandwiches, fruits, and canned stew and vegetables? This menu is deliciously fast and easy the Lean & Free way!

To avoid being overwhelmed by the multitude of delicious Lean & Free choices in this book, simply *choose seven meals* that meet your tastes, budget, and time schedule. Then, when you're in the mood for new variety, pick seven more. I even eat breakfast choices at dinner sometimes, with an added veggie, of course.

2. Budget Needs: Oatmeal or cracked wheat with honey and bananas make very inexpensive breakfasts. A homemade sandwich for lunch and homemade stew for dinner are also very frugal choices. To save additional money (and time) on this menu, make extra stew and freeze it. Remember, it's most economical to buy fruits and vegetables in season. You may also make your own bread or purchase it from a discount bread store in quantity and freeze some of it.

3. Special Health Needs: (allergies, diabetes, etc.) A small amount of diluted non-dairy coffee creamer (that does not contain palm or coconut oil) on cereal will suffice when milk isn't tolerated well, or try soy-milk products if you like them. When preparing your sandwiches, simply omit the cheese. If you're allergic to wheat, try wheat-free breads, cereals, muffins, and pasta. Use corn tortillas for sandwiches.

If you suffer from diabetes, an additional change in this menu would be to select a cold cereal with three grams of sugar or less per serving. Try mixing cornflakes, shredded wheat, and Grape-nuts. Enjoy sliced bananas, strawberries, or peaches for added sweetness. All Fruit Jam (page 164) makes an excellent sweetener for hot cereal.

4. Family Needs and Tastes: Adjust your shopping lists to fit the size of your family. Include a lot of your family's favorites while you

11

gradually introduce new delicious foods. Don't *force* your family members to change. Make certain that changes are *their decision* and *don't talk their ears off* about it!

5. Calorie and Fiber Needs: Never focus on calories or fat gram *numbers*. Focus instead on eating until you are *comfortably* satisfied on *correct balance* and keeping fat grams in the *10 to 20 percent* range as we've already discussed. Eat at least *three* times a day. There's evidence that people who eat *six* times a day may lose body fat *twice* as fast because of thermogenesis (increased heat production and metabolism that occur during digestion) and more even energy and blood- sugar levels. *Start out by eating six little meals* and very gradually increase as your hunger increases. This will happen as your metabolism and muscle tissue increase. (It's normal for hunger to fluctuate from day to day.)

Remember that leftovers from your meal make great snacks, especially those that focus mainly on vegetables like soups, stews, salads, stir-frys, casseroles, and sandwiches with lots of veggies inside. Also, remember to mix and match the breakfasts, lunches, and dinners that best meet your individual needs. Circle your favorites with a yellow highlighter pen.

You'll be excited to know that as you live your new LEAN & FREE LIFESTYLE, your entire body chemistry will change, including your taste buds. Many people who used to absolutely relish junk food and hate veggies, experience a gradual and complete reversal of these preferences.

When starting out, choose more canned and steamed vegetables and fruits rather than fresh vegetables and fruits. These choices are easier on your digestive system. Also, use some *white* and some *whole-wheat* flour until your system has had time to adjust—which may take a year or more for some individuals. The sudden addition of more fiber and greater calories can stress your body and make you sick. It also encourages excess body fat gain. Carefully study the *Fiber-Progression Chart* on the following page.

FIBER PROGRESSION CHART

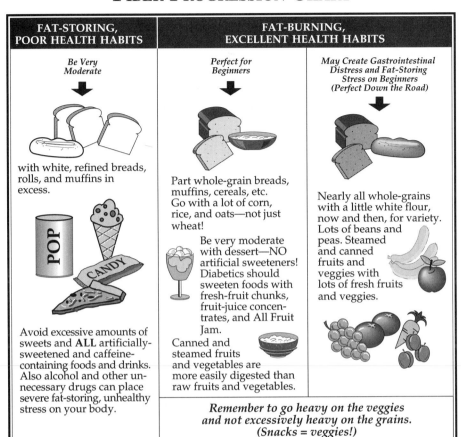

FAT-STORING, POOR HEALTH HABITS	FAT-BURNING, EXCELLENT HEALTH HABITS	
Be Very Moderate	*Perfect for Beginners*	*May Create Gastrointestinal Distress and Fat-Storing Stress on Beginners (Perfect Down the Road)*
with white, refined breads, rolls, and muffins in excess.	Part whole-grain breads, muffins, cereals, etc. Go with a lot of corn, rice, and oats—not just wheat!	Nearly all whole-grains with a little white flour, now and then, for variety. Lots of beans and peas. Steamed and canned fruits and veggies with lots of fresh fruits and veggies.
Avoid excessive amounts of sweets and **ALL** artificially-sweetened and caffeine-containing foods and drinks. Also alcohol and other unnecessary drugs can place severe fat-storing, unhealthy stress on your body.	Be very moderate with dessert—NO artificial sweeteners! Diabetics should sweeten foods with fresh-fruit chunks, fruit-juice concentrates, and All Fruit Jam. Canned and steamed fruits and vegetables are more easily digested than raw fruits and vegetables.	
	Remember to go heavy on the veggies and not excessively heavy on the grains. (Snacks = veggies!)	

*It takes many individuals a year or more to graduate from the middle of this chart to the far-right column. Be gentle and kind to your body and make **very** gradual changes. Your body will pay you back with much more rapid physical and emotional health improvements and more consistent body-fat loss.*

13

At last! Fun, Fast, Incredible-Tasting Menus that are Actually Good for You, too!

Grab 'n' Go Menus

I designed these delicious GRAB 'N' GO Menus specifically to meet the needs of the many people whose schedules are so demanding they can spend only minimal time on meal planning and preparation. I've also included suggestions for meal choices when eating out. The quick in-home meals in this section offer an almost endless array of choices! You can mix and match the GRAB 'N' GO Breakfasts, Lunches, and Dinners into many different meal combinations that reflect personal needs and preferences. Circle your favorites with a highlighter pen.

Amounts and serving sizes are not specified in these GRAB 'N' GO Menus because you should instead respond to your own body's hunger and fullness signals. Until you can "hear" these signals, simply eat small, balanced meals often (see pages 3 and 317-319).

Each menu contains an ideal nutrient balance for fat loss and health. The fat content ranges between 10 and 20 percent of your total calories.

See page 143 for an explanation of "A" and "B" food choices.

SAMPLE GRAB 'N' GO MENU

*The following three GRAB 'N' Go Menus illustrate how to put the 22 GRAB 'N' Go Breakfasts, Lunches, and Dinners together. Mix and match the meals to meet your tastes and lifestyle. Make certain to keep the balance! *Throughout all of the menus, a single asterix indicates that a recipe page number follows.*

BREAKFAST 1

Water

Post Banana Nut Crunch Cereal *(or another low sugar—8 grams or less—lowfat whole-grain cereal* p. 275 —3 grams of sugar or less if you are diabetic)*

Skim or 1% milk *(or a milk substitute if you have a dairy allergy* p. 316)*

Orange *(or another citrus fruit)*

LUNCH 15

Water

Sliced cucumber *(or other green or yellow vegetables with lowfat or nonfat dip)*

Whole-grain toast** with fat free strawberry cream cheese

Potato-Corn Soup* p. 259 *(or another lowfat soup choice)*

Apple *(or another in-season fruit)*

DINNER 13

Water

Tempting Tacos* p. 148 loaded with veggies

Baked tortilla chips*** with chunky salsa and fat free sour cream dip

Red or green grapes *(or another in-season fruit)*

SNACKS

Water

Veggie soup, stew, stir-fry, etc.
If you are not hungry but have time to snack in between meals, snack mainly on vegetable-based foods. If you are hungry, snack on veggies and other nutritious foods.

**Go with part *whole-grain breads or rolls if you are accustomed to eating mainly white bread.*

***My family's favorite "baked" tortilla chips are cool Ranch-flavored Baked Tostitos.*

Sample Grab 'n' Go Menu

BREAKFAST 7

Water

Breakfast Shake* p. 168

Whole-grain toast with fat free cream cheese and
All Fruit Jam* p. 164

LUNCH 22

Water

Blimpie's Veggie & Cheese Pita Pockets without
oil and mayonnaise *(or a Blimpie turkey, tuna, or seafood
sandwich with a whole-grain bun, extra veggies, and no
oil or mayonnaise)* or LEAN & FREE Nachos* p. 145

Pears (or another fruit from home)

DINNER 2

Water

Steamed or raw veggies

Belgian Waffles* p. 166
topped with Yogurt Fruit Delight* p. 219

SNACKS

Water

Veggies, veggie soup, veggie salad, a few whole grains
(if hungry), etc.

Sample Grab 'n' Go Menu

BREAKFAST 12

Water

Whole- or part whole-grain bagels topped with fat free
   strawberry cream cheese

Nonfat fruit yogurt *(Alta Dena nonfat yogurt is sweetened
   with fruit juice.)*

Grapefruit, kiwifruit, strawberries *(or another in-season,
   high-vitamin C fruit)* or Fruit Juice Popsicles

LUNCH 7

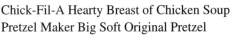

Water

Chick-Fil-A Hearty Breast of Chicken Soup

Pretzel Maker Big Soft Original Pretzel
   (with butter and salt = 4 fat grams; plain = 1 fat gram)

Chick-Fil-A Carrot-Raisin Salad

DINNER 7

Water

Green Beans

Chilighetti *(Serve chicken chili or lowfat beef chili over cooked
   spaghetti or macaroni noodles.)*

Instant Blueberry Ice Cream* p. 194

SNACKS

Water

Assorted raw or steamed veggies, soup, etc.

*If you are still hungry after a **large** "vegetable-based" snack at mid-morning or mid-afternoon, add a grain, a protein, and a fruit to your snack. Example: leftover tuna (canned in water) sandwich on whole- or part whole-grain bread with fat free mayonnaise, stuffed with sprouts, tomatoes, green peppers, onions, leafy lettuce, and /or whatever other vegetables you prefer. (Your desire and taste for more good veggies will gradually increase.) Then throw in a glass of water and an apple, orange, banana, peach, or nectarine and you have a delicious, satisfying "snack" for those extra-hungry times! A simpler snack would be baby carrots, a banana, and a slice of whole-grain bread.)*

GRAB 'N' GO BREAKFASTS

*GRAB 'N' GO Breakfasts should all include **water**, **grain**, **protein**, and **fruit**. Citrus fruits are excellent for breakfast and insure appropriate amounts of vitamin-C intake for the day. Vegetables do not usually fit at breakfast (except with a veggie omelet and hash browns) so they are included in abundance throughout the rest of the day. Many of these breakfasts have a fat percentage ranging between 10 and 20 percent. Some are lower, but your overall day is in this ideal range. Remember to mix and match these menus to meet your personal needs and tastes. These breakfasts may also be used as occasional lunches or dinners as long as plenty of vegetables are added.*

1

Water

Kellogg's Raisin Squares or another "A" or "B" Choice cold cereal* p. 275
Skim or 1% milk *(or a milk substitute if you have a dairy allergy)*
Fruit* p. 285
Special Note: If you are allergic to dairy products, check your local health-food store for healthy, lowfat alternatives and add another protein source from Grab 'N' Go lunches and dinners

---

2

Water

Store-bought, lowfat, whole-grain muffins *(Or better yet, make LEAN & FREE Muffins in bulk and freeze for quick use. Krusteaz has delicious fat free muffin mixes. These are "B+" Choices and not for diabetics because of added sugar. Many large, store-bought muffins have **20** to **30** fat grams **each**, so beware!)*
Skim or 1% milk
Fruit* p. 285

3

Water

1 or 2 packages prepared Quaker Plain Instant Oatmeal mixed with 1 or 2 packages prepared Quaker Flavored Instant Oatmeal *(This will reduce the percentage of sugar per bowl and it tastes great.)*
Skim or 1% milk
Fruit* p. 285

4

Water

Kellogg's Mueslix cereal mixed with nonfat or lowfat fruit yogurt and banana chunks *(Diabetics should use fruit-juice sweetened yogurt—delicious!)*

5

Water

Skippy Reduced Fat LEAN & FREE Peanut Butter & Jam

   Sandwich* p. 251 *("B+" Choice—not for quick fat loss,*
   but much better than no breakfast)

Skim* or 1% milk
Fruit* p. 285

6

Water
Kellogg's Nutrigrain Almond Raisin Cereal mixed with

   Post Grape-nuts Cereal
Skim or 1% milk

Fruit* p. 285 *(Or purchase fruit-juice sweetened jam at the*

   supermarket; use regular jam in moderation.)

7

Water

Breakfast Shake* p. 168

Whole-grain toast with fat-free cream cheese and
   Smucker's Simply Fruit Spread

8

Water
Super-Quick Pancakes* 177
   topped with Smucker's Simply Fruit Spread and nonfat or
   lowfat fruit or vanilla yogurt
Fruit* p. 285

9

Water
Quaker Toasted Oatmeal with banana slices
Skim or 1% milk

10

Water
Veggie Pizza Wheels left over from Day 9 lunch
Fruit* p. 285

*Viva has a new fat free (skim) milk on the market that tastes much richer than ordinary skim milk because it has added milk solids which do not increase the fat content.

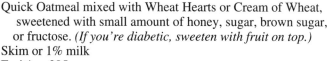

11

Water

Quick Oatmeal mixed with Wheat Hearts or Cream of Wheat,
    sweetened with small amount of honey, sugar, brown sugar,
    or fructose. *(If you're diabetic, sweeten with fruit on top.)*
Skim or 1% milk
Fruit* p. 285

12

Water

Whole- or part whole-grain bagels with fat-free cream cheese
Skim or 1% milk or nonfat fruit yogurt
Fruit Juice Popsicle *(Freeze any type of all-natural fruit juice in
    a popsicle tray = "A–" Choice because it lacks the fiber that
    the "whole" fruit contains.)*

13

Water

Whole-grain toast with fat free cream cheese and All Fruit Jam* p. 165
One Fried Egg* p. 172 *(No more than 2 to 3 whole eggs per
    week is ideal. Use egg whites in cooking.)*
Fruit* p. 285

14

Water

Fast-food big soft pretzels with fat free strawberry
cream cheese (Or make Big Soft Pretzels* p. 158 and freeze
for quick use.)
Nonfat or lowfat fruit yogurt *(Alta Dena nonfat, fruit-juice
    sweetened yogurt is the best yogurt I've ever tasted and it's
    perfect for diabetics and those who are highly resistant to
    fat loss.)*
Fruit* p. 285

15

Water

Whole-grain toast or Kellogg's Nutri Grain Eggo Whole-Grain
    Waffles with fat free cream cheese and/or Smucker's Simply
    Fruit Spread
Fruit* p. 285

21

16

Water

Store-bought, lowfat, whole-grain muffins
    or pre-made LEAN & FREE Muffins* p. 272
Yogurt Fruit Delight* p. 219

GRAB 'N' GO BREAKFASTS

17

Water

Toasted whole-grain English muffins topped with fat free
 cream cheese and Smucker's Simply Fruit Spread

Skim or 1% milk

Fruit* p. 285

18

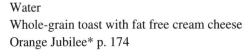

Water

Whole-grain toast with fat free cream cheese

Orange Jubilee* p. 174

19

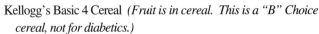

Water

Kellogg's Basic 4 Cereal *(Fruit is in cereal. This is a "B" Choice
 cereal, not for diabetics.)*

Skim or 1% milk

20

Water

Date Bars* p. 191 *(Make extra and freeze for quick use.)*

Nonfat Vanilla Yogurt

21

Water

Leftovers from last night's dinner *(such as Chicken Broccoli
 Casserole* p. 180 or Chicken-Chili stufffed Potatoes*
 p. 245. These choices are excellent for individuals with dairy
 allergies who need an alternative source of protein at breakfast.)*

Whole-grain bread or rolls with fat free cream cheese and All
 Fruit Jam* p. 165 or Smucker's Simply Fruit Spread

Fruit* p. 285

22

Water

Several Quaker Carmel Corn Cakes *(not for diabetics)* or other
 rice or corn cakes *(for diabetics if no sugar added)*

One stick Frigo String Cheese *(6 fat grams)*

Bananas or Apples

*This breakfast is perfect for eating on the run or in the car. Take a large
towel for your lap. Put water in a covered container with a straw.*

Instant Blueberry and Peach Ice Cream accompanied by
Date Bars—No-Sugar Style with Apple Raspberry Filling

Fast-Food Salads and Potatoes

GRAB 'N' GO LUNCHES

*GRAB 'N' GO Lunches should all include at least eight ounces of cool **water**, **veggies**, **grain**, **protein**, and **fruit**. They all have a fat percentage range between approximately 10 and 20 percent. Choose the lunches you like best, and be creative and make up your own. Remember to go heavy on the veggie-based foods, a little lighter on the grains, and be moderate with meats and dairy products, avoiding foods you are allergic to.*

1

Water
Mixed raw veggies with lowfat or nonfat dip* p. 211
Whole-grain toast with fat free cream cheese
Vegetable Beef Soup or another quick, delicious
    soup* p. 290
Fruit* p. 285

2

Water
Arby's Light Roast Chicken, Turkey, or Roast Beef Sandwich
    with extra lettuce, tomatoes, pickles, onions, and light
    mayonnaise or no mayonnaise
Fruit* p. 285

3

Water
Veggies* p. 291
Whole-grain toast with Smucker's Simply Fruit Spread
Spaghetti O's *(or another lowfat canned pasta choice)*
Fruit* p. 285

4

Water
KFC Vegetable Medley Salad
KFC Bread Sticks or Sour Dough Rolls *(omit butter)*
KFC Rotisserie Gold Chicken *(white quarter without skin)*
Apple *(from home)*

23

5

Water

Creamed Tuna on Toast* p. 252 topped with lots of cooked

    peas *(Frozen peas are best.)*
Fruit* p. 285

6

Water

Burger King BK Broilers with extra lettuce,
    tomatoes, pickles, onions, and no sauces or use fat free

    or lowfat sauce from home
Fruit* p. 285

7

Water

Chick-Fil-A Large Hearty Breast of Chicken Soup

Pretzel Maker Big Soft Pretzel (Original with butter
    and salt = 4 fat grams; plain = 1 fat gram.)
Chick-Fil-A Carrot-Raisin Salad

8

Water

Ham 'n Cheese Sandwich with extra veggies* p. 249 or a
    Turkey, fat free Cream Cheese, and Cranberry Sandwich
    with veggies on the side. Delicious!
Fruit* p. 285

9

Water

Mixed veggies* p. 265

Pizza Wheels* p. 152
Fruit* p. 285

10

Water

Bean Burritos *(whole-wheat or corn tortillas filled with lowfat*
    refried beans, lettuce, onions, tomatoes, green pepper

    chunks, and picante sauce; warm in microwave)

Fruit* p. 285

11

Water
Subway Turkey Sandwich with extra veggies and nonfat
   dressing from home *(if desired)*
Fat free French fries *(Check the freezer section of your local
   grocery store.)*
Fruit* p. 285

12

Water
Veggies* p. 291
Quaker Oat Squares or another "A" or "B" Choice cold
   cereal* pgs. 275-277
Skim or 1% milk
Fruit* p. 285

13

Water
Taco Time Veggie Burritos & Soft Chicken Tacos
   *(Omit cheese and sour cream; add fat free sour cream
   from home, if desired.)*
Fruit* p. 285

14

Water
Wendy's Salad Bar
   *(Go extra light on dressings, nuts, seeds, and beans in oil.
   Add extra cottage cheese in place of extra dressing. You
   might even bring nonfat dressing from home. Make certain
   to include some fruit and bread sticks.)*
Wendy's Chili Potato with no cheese or sour cream
   (ask for extra chili and onions)

15

Water
Carrot and celery sticks with lowfat or nonfat dip
Whole-grain toast with fat free strawberry cream cheese and /or
   Quaker Fat Free Carmel Corn Cakes *("A–" Choice)*
Chicken Noodle or Creamy Bean 'n Ham Soup* p. 256
   left over from Day 14 dinner or Potato-Corn Soup* p. 259
Fruit* p. 285

16

Water

Mixed raw veggies

Taco Bell Bean Burritos & Chicken Fajitas *(omit cheese and sour cream)*

Fruit* p. 285

17

Water

Hardee's Ham, Turkey, Roast Beef, or Combo
   Sub Sandwiches with extra lettuce, tomatoes, and onions,
   and a small amount of light mayonnaise

Fruit* p. 285 *(You can count the tomato but it's a stretch.)*

18

Water

Chinese Take-Out
   (Go heavy on the stir-fried vegetables and rice. Avoid deep-fried foods.)

Fruit* p. 285

19

Water

Any sandwich filling* pgs. 249-251 rolled in corn,
   whole-wheat, or regular torillas or stuffed in whole-grain or
   regular pita pockets with lots of veggies

Fruit* p. 285

20

Water

Mixed Veggie Festival* p. 265 left over from
   Day 19 dinner

Store-bought big soft pretzels or lowfat, whole-grain crackers
   (Some crackers say "lowfat", but are not. Read the labels carefully.)

Fruit* p. 285

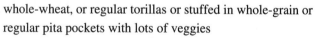

21

Water

Veggies* p. 291

Chef Boy•ar•dee Macaroni Shells in Tomato Sauce

Skim or 1% milk

Fruit* p.285

22

Water

Blimpie's Cheese and Veggie Pockets without oil
   and mayonnaise and/or LEAN & FREE Nachos*
   p. 145 ("B" Choice)

Fruit* p. 285

27

GRAB 'N' GO DINNERS

*GRAB 'N' Go Dinners all include **water**, **veggies**, **grain**, **protein**, and **fruit**. The fat percentage range is 10 to 20 percent. Also enjoy healthifying your own quick recipes. Remember to go heavy on the veggie-based foods, and eat them first so you'll eat more of them.*

1

Water

Quick, Delicious Beef Stew* p. 155 in a bun (Stew in a Bun)
(Purchase large whole-wheat or white soup buns at your bakery and hollow out the centers. Fill with stew and top with bread lid. Call your bakery and order them if they don't regularly make them available.)

Fruit* p. 285

2

Water

Steamed or raw veggies* p. 291

Belgian Waffles* p. 166
  topped with Yogurt Fruit Delight* p. 219 *(Breakfast foods make delicious dinners now and then.)*

3

Water

Short-Cut Tossed Salad* p. 266 with lowfat or nonfat
  dressing* p. 211 and lowfat croutons

Chicken-Chili Stuffed Potato* p. 245 with fat free sour cream
Applesauce with fresh apple chunks and cinnamon

4

Water

Steamed vegetables
Store-bought whole-grain rolls with All-Fruit Jam* p. 165
Chicken Bake* p. 179

Fruit* p. 285

5

Water
Veggies* p. 291
Ralston Almond Raspberry Muesli or another "A" or "B" Choice
    cold cereal* pgs. 275-277
Skim or 1% milk
Fruit* p. 285 *(If not in cereal)*

6

Water
Veggies* p. 291
Whole-grain toast with fat free cream cheese and
    Smucker's Simply Fruit Spread
One Fried Egg* p. 172 *(Two or three whole eggs per week
    is ideal.)*
Fruit* p. 285

7

Water
Veggies* p. 291
Chilighetti
    *(Serve chicken chili or lowfat beef chili over cooked spaghetti
    or macaroni noodles.)*
Instant Blueberry Ice Cream* p. 194

8

Water
Green veggies* p. 291 *(Remember to include a variety of
    colors in your meals to increase both nutritional and
    visual appeal.)*
Creamed corn served over whole-grain toast
Yogurt Fruit Delight* p. 219

9

Water
Raw Veggies with lowfat or nonfat dip* p. 211
One or two Healthy Choice Hotdogs (Pigs in a Blanket)
    *(Serve in a bun, or roll in a crescent-dough triangle and bake
    about 7 to 10 minutes at 350 degrees. Serve with ketchup.)*
Fat free French fries and ketchup *(ask your grocer—should be
    in freezer section)* or Tostito's Ranch-Flavored Baked
    Tortilla Chips
Instant Blueberry, Peach, Strawberry, or Pine-Orange-Banana
    Ice Cream* p. 194

Kids LOVE this meal!

29

10

Water

Veggies* p. 291

Blintzes* p. 167 topped with Yogurt Fruit Delight* p. 219

11

Water

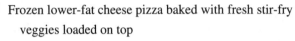
Frozen lower-fat cheese pizza baked with fresh stir-fry
   veggies loaded on top

Fruit* p. 285

12

Water

Easy Chicken 'n Dumplings* p. 183

Fruit* p. 285

13

Water

Tempting Tacos* p. 148 loaded with veggies

Baked tortilla chips (ask grocer) with chunky salsa and
   fat free sour cream dip

Fruit* p. 285

14

Water

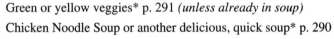
Green or yellow veggies* p. 291 *(unless already in soup)*

Chicken Noodle Soup or another delicious, quick soup* p. 290

Whole-grain toast with fat free cream cheese and All-Fruit
   Jam* p. 290

Fruit* p. 285

15

Water

Tuna Sandwiches* p. 250 loaded with veggies

Fresh mixed melons and berries topped with sherbet *(Delicious*
for summer = "B" Choice with sherbet; "A" Choice without.)

16

Water

Mexicali Salad *(Short-Cut Tossed Salad * p. 266 topped*

with lowfat chili or canned pinto beans and crumbled,
Tostitos Ranch-Flavored, Baked Tortilla Chips)
Fruit* p. 285

17

Water

Green or yellow veggies* p. 291
Baked potato topped with fat free sour cream

and chives *(prick potato several times with a fork*
and cook on high in microwave for about 5 minutes.
Let stand for 10 minutes.)

Whole-grain bread, rolls, or lowfat muffins.

Red Snapper* p. 254
Fruit* p. 285

18

Water

Broccoli Casserole* p. 260 or other vegetables* p. 291

Whole-grain bread, rolls, or lowfat muffins

Lowfat fish sticks or fish fillets with Kraft Fat Free Tartar Sauce

Fruit* p. 285 or Pineapple and Cottage Cheese Salad* p. 215

19

Water
Mixed Veggie Festival* p. 265
Store-bought big soft pretzels
Fruit* p. 285

20

Water
Tossed Salad* p. 267 with homemade lowfat or nonfat
   dressing* p. 241
Savory Meat and Cheese Manicotti* p. 241
   (Make extra and freeze.)
Fruit* p. 285

21

Water
Veggies* p. 291
Chicken and Rice* p. 179
Fruit* p. 285

22

Water
La Choy Chicken Chow Mein with 1/3 cup chow
   mein noodles or plenty of quick, brown or white rice
   (Brown rice is the more nutritious, high-fiber choice, but
   white rice is satisfactory.)
Whole-grain rolls with fat free cream cheese
Dole Tropical Fruit Mix

Budget Menus

I designed these delicious BUDGET MENUS specifically to meet the needs of my many students who have limited food budgets. But these meals are not just remarkably cost-effective; they are time-effective as well. They're quick and economical, yet they offer you a wide variety of choices. The Budget Breakfasts, Lunches, and Dinners can be mixed and matched into many different meal combinations! So use your imagination and indulge in your new FREEDOM TO EAT and enjoy!

Amounts and serving sizes are not specified in these BUDGET MENUS because you should be responding to your own body's hunger and fullness signals. Until you can "hear" those signals, simply eat small, balanced meals often (see pages 3 and 317).

Each menu contains an ideal nutrient balance for fat-loss and health. The fat content ranges between 10 and 20 percent of total calories.

See page 143 for an explanation of "A" and "B" food choices.

SAMPLE BUDGET MENU

The following three Sample Budget Menus illustrate how to put the Budget Breakfasts, Lunches, and Dinners together. To avoid being overwhelmed by the multitude of delicious LEAN & FREE choices, simply choose seven meals that meet your tastes, budget, and time schedule needs and rotate them. Then, when you desire a change, choose seven more. It's that easy!

BREAKFAST 1

 Water

 Oatmeal (*Mix with a small amount of honey, cinnamon, brown sugar, sugar, maple syrup, fructose, apple-juice concentrate, or All-Fruit Jam* p. 165*)

 Skim or 1% milk (*Mix equal parts of regular milk with prepared powdered milk to save money.*)

Grapefruit (*or another in-season or on-special fruit that's high in vitamin C*)

LUNCH 1

 Water

 Tuna Salad Sandwiches* p. 250 loaded with veggies

Apple or applesauce (*or another in-season fresh fruit or canned fruit in extra-light syrup or fruit juice*)

DINNER 12

 Water

 Hawaiian Haystacks* p. 183

Whole-grain lowfat bread, rolls, or muffins* p. 272

 Red grapes (*or another in-season or on-special fruit* p. 285*) (*Bread and grapes are fun extras but are not necessary for the completeness of this meal because veggies, grain, protein, and fruit are all contained in the Haystacks.*)

SNACK

 Water

Veggies, Tuna Sandwiches, leftover Haystacks, etc. (*Snacking mainly on veggie-based food may help accelerate your rate of fat loss.*)

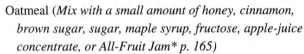

Sample Budget Menu

BREAKFAST 15

Water

Peach Pancakes* p. 177

(Top with Yogurt Fruit Delight p. 219)*

LUNCH 2

Water

Chicken Fajitas* p. 149 loaded with veggies

Orange *(or another in-season or on-special fruit)*

DINNER 5

Water

Minestrone Soup* p. 258

Marvelous Muffins* p. 231

Yogurt Fruit Delight* p. 219

SNACKS

Water

Veggies, leftover Chicken Fajitas (if hungry),

    Minestrone Soup, etc.

(You should feel neither stuffed nor hungry at the end of your meal, and you should get hungry for your next meal.)

BUDGET MENUS

SAMPLE BUDGET MENU

BREAKFAST 8

Water

Breakfast Fruit Compote* p. 168

Skim or 1% milk

LUNCH 14

Water

Celery sticks

Whole-grain bread, rolls, or muffins* p. 272

Fast & Creamy Clam Chowder* p.257

Apple *(or another in-season or on-special fruit)*

DINNER 20

Water

Mixed raw veggies* p. 291 with homemade
   lowfat or nonfat dressing* p. 211

Whole-grain bread *(if desired)*

Savory Meat and Cheese Manicotti* p. 241
   (Make extra and freeze.)

Yogurt Fruit Delight* p. 219

SNACKS

Water

Veggies, leftover Clam Chowder, leftover tossed salad, etc.

Remember to snack just on veggies if you aren't hungry, and veggies plus other nutritious choices if you are hungry. Fruits are best when included with a meal or other more complex foods (vegetables and grains) because of their high natural sugar content. Combining fruits and vegetables does not cause them to ferment in the stomach. This notion has been dismissed by medical professionals as sheer quackery! It is completely false.

BUDGET BREAKFASTS

*Budget Breakfasts all include **water**, **grain**, **protein**, and **fruit**. Vegetables do not usually fit at breakfast (except with a veggie omelet) so they are included in abundance throughout the rest of the day. Many of these breakfasts have a fat percentage ranging between 10 and 20 percent. Some are lower, but your overall day is in this ideal range. Remember to mix and match these menus to meet your personal needs and tastes.*

1

Water
Oatmeal
*(Mix with a small amount of honey, jam,
All-Fruit Jam* p. 165, brown sugar, sugar, maple syrup,
fructose, or apple juice concentrate* p. 274*

Skim or 1% milk
*(Mix equal parts of regular milk with, prepared
powdered milk to save money.)*
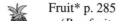
Fruit* p. 285
*(Buy fruits in season or on special, and purchase
cases or half cases if you can use up that much
before spoilage occurs.)*

2

Water
Cracked Wheat, Raisin, and Honey Cereal* p. 169
Make in large quantity to save time and money.

Skim or 1% milk *(Or a milk substitute if you have a dairy
allergy—p. 316.)*

Fruit* p. 285

3

Water
Crunchy Granola* p. 170
Make in large quantity to save time and money.

Skim or 1% milk

Fruit* p. 285

4

Water

Veggie & Cheese Egg Scramble* p. 175
Whole-grain toast

Fruit* p. 285

37

BUDGET BREAKFASTS

5

Water

Belgian Waffles* p. 166 *(topped with applesauce and
nonfat vanilla yogurt)*

6

Water

Cornflakes *(Buy generic brands in bulk.)*

Skim or 1% milk

Fruit* p. 285

7

Water

Cracked Wheat Cereal *(Follow basic recipe on page 169 and
omit raisins. Mix with small amount of honey, brown sugar,
sugar, fructose, jam, or All Fruit Jam* p. 165 .)*

Skim or 1% milk

Fruit* p. 285

8

Water

Breakfast Fruit Compote* p. 168

Skim or 1% milk

9

Water

French Toast* p. 171

*(Top with small amount of bulk maple syrup or use
All Fruit Jam* p. 165 and nonfat fruit or vanilla-
flavored yogurt. Make your own bread for an excellent*

*money saver or buy it in bulk at discount bread stores and
freeze it. Make large quanities to save time and money.)*

Skim or 1% milk

Fruit* p. 165

10

Water

Blender Whole-Wheat Pancakes* p. 177
*(Top with a small amount of bulk maple syrup or
All Fruit Jam* p. 165 and nonfat fruit yogurt.)*

Skim or 1% milk

Fruit* p. 285

11

Water

Whole-grain toast with All Fruit Jam* p. 165

Breakfast Shake* p. 168
*(Use powdered milk and make your own yogurt
to save money.)*

12

Water

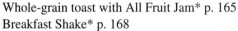
Granola* p. 172
*(Make large quantities and freeze the extra to save time
and money.)*

Skim or 1% milk

Fruit* p. 285

13

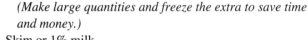
Water

Country Corn Bread* p. 159
*(Make large quantities and freeze the extra to save time
and money.)*

One Fried Egg* p. 172

Fruit* p. 285

14

Water

Cinnamon-Maple Oatmeal* p. 169

Skim or 1% milk

Fruit* p. 285

15

Water

Peach Pancakes* p. 177

Top with Yogurt Fruit Delight* p. 219

16

Water
Three Bear Porridge and Honey* p. 175
Skim or 1% milk
Fruit* p. 285

17

Water
Better Bran Muffins* p. 227
   (Make large quantities and freeze to save time and money.)
Skim or 1% milk
Fruit* p. 285

18

Water
Oatmeal Pancakes* p. 177
Top with Yogurt Fruit Delight* p. 219

19

Water
Big Soft Pretzels* p. 158
Nonfat fruit yogurt
Fruit* p. 285

20

Water
Egg and Cheese Muffins* p. 171
Fruit* p. 285

21

Water
Oatmeal Raisin Muffins* p. 232
Skim or 1% milk
Fruit* p. 285

22

Water
Super Cinnamon Rolls* p. 161
   (Make large quantities and freeze to save time and money.)
Skim or 1% milk
Fruit * p. 285

BUDGET LUNCHES

Budget Lunches all include at least eight ounces of cool **water**, **veggies**, **grain**, **protein**, and **fruit**. Choose the lunches you like best. Also be creative and make up your own. Remember to go heavy on the veggie-based foods, a little lighter on the grains, and be moderate with meats and dairy products, avoiding foods you are allergic to. And remember that leftovers make excellent money savers!

1

Water

Whole-grain Chicken, Club, Corned Beef,
    Ham 'n Cheese, Pastrami, Roast Beef 'n Cheddar, Seafood,
    Tuna Salad, Turkey Club, Turkey 'n Provolone Cheese, or
    Turkey Sandwiches* pgs. 249- 250

Fruit* p. 285

2

Water

Chicken Fajitas* p. 149 left over from Day 1 dinner
Fruit* p. 285

3

Water

Veggies* p. 291

Whole-grain toast or rolls
Beef Stroganoff* p. 150 left over from Day 2 dinner
Fruit* p. 285

4

Water

Green veggies* p. 291

Leftover Chili Skillet* p. 237 left over from Day 3 dinner, stuffed
    in a microwaved, baked potato

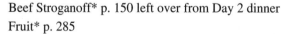
Fruit* p. 285

5

Water

Veggie & Cheese Egg Scramble* p. 175 left over from
Day 4 breakfast

Hash Browns * p. 246
Whole-grain toast

Fruit* p. 285

6

Water

Tossed Salad* p. 267 with lowfat or nonfat dressing* p. 211

Enchilada Casserole* p. 141 left over from Day 4 dinner

Fruit Gelatin* p. 214

7

Water

Chicken Broccoli Casserole* p. 180 left over from
Day 6 dinner

Whole-grain lowfat bread, rolls, or muffins

Fruit * p. 285

8

Water

Veggies* p. 291

Whole-grain rolls
Homemade Macaroni & Cheese* p. 238 left over
from Day 7 dinner

Fruit* p. 238

9

Water

Raw veggies dipped in fat free sour cream mixed
with your favorite dip mix or spices
Breakfast Fruit Compote* p. 168 left over from
Day 8 breakfast

Skim or 1% milk

10

Water

Raw veggies with fat free dip* p. 211

Marvelous Muffins* p. 231

Easy Chicken 'n Dumplings* p. 183 left over from
    Day 9 dinner

Fruit* p. 285

11

Water

Spaghetti Salad* p. 242 left over** from Day 10 dinner

Whole-grain lowfat bread, rolls, or muffins* p. 272 with
    All Fruit Jam* p. 165

Yogurt Fruit Delight* p. 219

12

Water

Veggies* p. 291

Garlic Cheese Toast* p. 159

Luscious Lasagna* p. 239 left over from Day 11 dinner

Fruit* p. 285

13

Water

Hawaiian Haystacks* p. 183 left over from
    Day 12 dinner

Whole-grain lowfat bread, rolls, or muffins* p. 272

Fruit* p. 285

**Leftovers are marvelous money savers. Store them in air-tight containers and refrigerate or freeze them.

14

Water

Veggies* p. 291

Whole-grain lowfat bread, rolls, or muffins* p. 272

Fast & Creamy Clam Chowder* p. 257

Fruit* p. 285

15

Water

Veggies* p. 291

Taco Casserole* p. 157 leftover from Day 14 dinner

Fruit* p. 285

16

Water

Lots of veggies* p. 291 with Ranch Dip* p. 212

Super Cinnamon Rolls* p. 161

Yogurt Fruit Delight* p. 219

17

Water

Veggies* p. 291

Blueberry Muffins* p. 227

Porcupine Meatballs* p. 153 leftover from Day 16 dinner

Fruit* p. 285

18

Water

Celery stuffed with fat free strawberry cream cheese

Better Bran Muffins* p. 227 leftover from Day 17 breakfast

Potato-Corn Soup* p. 259

Lowfat or fat free fruit yogurt *(Fruit-juice sweetened, Alta Dena
Yogurt is ideal for diabetics and those people who are highly
resistant to fat loss. And it's delicious!)*

Fruit* p. 285

19

Water
Green Veggies* p. 291
Chicken-Chili Enchiladas* p. 144 left over from Day 18 dinner
Whole-grain bread *(If desired—tortillas surrounding
   enchiladas will suffice as the grain, but additional
   bread is also a good choice. But remember to go heavy on
   the veggies and eat them first so you'll eat more of them.)*
Fruit* p. 285

20

Water

Vegetable Beef Soup* p. 290 – right column

Big Soft Pretzels* p.158 left over from Day 19 breakfast

Yogurt Fruit Delight* p. 219

21

Water

Tossed Salad* p. 267 with lowfat or nonfat dressing* p. 211

Savory Meat and Cheese Manicotti* p. 241 left over

   from Day 20 dinner

Fruit* p. 285

22

Water

Veggies* p. 291

Chili-Stuffed Potato* p. 245

   (with part-skim mozzarella cheese and fat free sour cream)

Whole-grain lowfat bread, rolls, or muffins* p. 272

Fruit* p. 285

BUDGET DINNERS

*Budget Dinners all include **water**, **vegetable**, **grain**, protein and **fruit**. Relish eating like royalty (healthy, lean royalty, that is) on the tightest of budgets!*

1

Water

Chicken Fajitas* p. 149 loaded with veggies

Fruit* p. 285

2

Water

Veggies* p. 291

Beef Stroganoff* p. 150

(Make a large quantity and freeze extra to save time and money.)

Fruit* p. 285

3

Water

Dark green or yellow veggies* p. 291

Chili Skillet* p. 237

(Make a large quantity and freeze extra to save time and money.)

Fruit* p. 285

4

Water

Tossed Salad* p. 267 with homemade lowfat or nonfat dressing* p. 211

Enchilada Casserole* p. 151

Fruit* p. 285

5

Water

Minestrone Soup* p. 258 *(Make extra and freeze.)*

Marvelous Muffins* p. 231 *(Make extra and freeze.)*

Yogurt Fruit Delight* p. 219

Tempting Tacos and Enchilada Casserole

Tuna Salad Sandwich complemented by
applesauce with added apple chunks

An assortment of LEAN & FREE *Muffins*

Easy Chicken 'n' Dumplings with fresh melon balls

6

Water

Chicken Broccoli Casserole* p. 180

Whole-grain lowfat bread, rolls, or muffins* p. 272

Fruit* p. 285

7

Water

Veggies* p. 29

 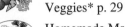
Homemade Macaroni and Cheese* p. 238 or Cheese-Stuffed
   Jumbo Shells* p. 236 *(These are two delicious family favorites!)*

Fruit* p. 285

8

Water

Shepherd's Pie* p. 156 *(Make extra and freeze.)*

Whole-grain lowfat bread, rolls, or muffins* p. 272

Fruit* p. 285

9

Water

Easy Chicken 'n Dumplings* p. 183 *(Make extra and freeze.*
   For a nutritional money saver, use fresh-from-your-garden
   vegetables instead of canned veggies.)

Fruit* p. 285

10

Water

Spaghetti Salad* p. 242

Whole-grain bread, rolls, or muffins* p. 272

Pineapple & Cottage Cheese Salad* p. 215

11

Water

Veggies* p. 291

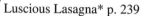

Blueberry Muffins* p. 227

Luscious Lasagna* p. 239

Fruit* p. 285

12

Water

Hawaiian Haystacks* p. 183

Blueberry Muffins* p. 227 left over from Day 11 dinner

Fruit* p. 285

13

Water

Green veggies* p. 291

Perfect Potato Casserole* p. 247

Whole-grain lowfat bread, rolls, or muffins* p. 272

BBQ Chicken* p. 178

Fruit* p. 285

14

Water

Tossed Salad* p. 267 with lowfat or nonfat dressing* p. 211

Taco Casserole* p. 157

(Make extra and freeze.)

Tostitos Baked, Ranch-Flavored Tortilla Chips

with chunky salsa and fat free sour-cream dip

(Mix salsa and fat free sour cream together.)

Fruit* p. 285

15

Water
Mixed steamed veggies
Whole-grain lowfat bread, rolls, or muffins* p. 272
Pineapple-Lime Chicken* p. 184
 (Skin at home to save money.)
Fruit* p. 285

16

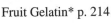

Water
Sliced purple cabbage
Fat free French fries with ketchup *(Cut potatoes in strips and
 bake on a nonstick cooking-sprayed cookie sheet at 375 to
 400 degrees until brown. Moderately salt to taste.)*
Sloppy Joes* p. 156
Fruit* p. 285

17

Water
Tossed Salad* p. 267 with lowfat or nonfat dressing* p. 211
Green beans
Spaghetti with Econo-Sauce* p. 222
Garlic Cheese Toast* p. 159
Fruit Gelatin* p. 214

18

Water
Tossed Salad and lowfat dressing left over from Day 17 dinner
Chicken-Chili Enchiladas* p. 144 *(Make extra and freeze.)*
Fruit* p. 285

19

Water
Zucchini Soup* p. 239
Whole-grain lowfat bread, rolls, or muffins* p. 272
Yogurt Fruit Delight* p. 219

20

Water

Mixed raw veggies* p. 291 with homemade lowfat or nonfat
   dip* p. 211

Savory Meat and Cheese Manicotti* p. 241 *(Make extra
   and freeze.)*

Whole-grain bread *(if desired)*

Yogurt Fruit Delight* p. 219

21

Water

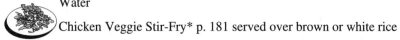Chicken Veggie Stir-Fry* p. 181 served over brown or white rice

   (Purchase whole fryer on sale. Skin and debone to save money.)

Fruit* p. 285

22

Water

Tossed Salad* p. 267 with homemade lowfat or nonfat
   dressing* p. 211

Whole-grain lowfat bread, rolls, or muffins* p. 272

Creamy Bean & Ham Soup* p. 256

Fruit* p. 285

Daily Success Complete Freedom Menus

*I designed these **Daily Success Complete Freedom Menus** specifically to meet the needs of people who find preparation and detail to be tedious! So the work's done for them. The results are both time-saving and delicious. These menus are some of the most nutritious, healthy, and comprehensive menus in the world. They offer a complete eating program for people with all kinds of special needs—people who want to lose excess body fat; people who have high cholesterol or high blood pressure, or even diabetes. They are the perfect solution for people who desire optimal health and energy. And yet each menu is so normal and delicious that you wouldn't even suspect it's actually "good for you." They can also be mixed and matched into a vast array of different menus!*

If you choose to follow the menus exactly day-by-day, you may use their accompanying shopping lists. They will save you invaluable time and effort. They do require an initial investment of time and money, and you'll want to organize some food-storage space at home. Your long-term savings later will be immense.

Once you have the MASTER LIST items in stock (I recommend shopping for in-store specials and case-lot sales), your weekly grocery list will be very short and inexpensive. Then you'll begin to fully enjoy the amazing freedom of your new, healthy LEAN & FREE LIFESTYLE!

These menus and shopping lists took thousands of hours to complete. They are very detailed. If you find them TOO detailed for your needs, enjoy the simplicity built into the Grab 'N' Go and Budget Menus.

*The ideal nutrient balance of complex carbohydrates, proteins, fats, vitamins, and minerals is included in each of these menus. The weekly fat percentage ranges between 10 and 20 percent—usually 10 and 15 percent for individuals who are resistant to fat loss. Others may choose to keep their fat percentage around 20 percent. (A little added cheese, butter, and peanut butter will do that in a flash! Avocados, olives, nuts, and seeds are all very high in "good" cholesterol-fighting fat.) This ideal nutrient balance is essential for optimum health and energy, along with the **permanent** loss of excess body fat.*

See page 143 for an explanation of "A" and "B" food choices. It is also extremely important to review pages 3 and 8 – 13 prior to using these Daily Success Menus!

MENU MUSTS
URGENT—YOU MUST READ THIS!

Before you turn another page, you must read this page. The following COMPLETE FREEDOM MENUS range between 1,600 and 4,000 calories. You *must adjust* these calories to meet your own personal hunger and metabolic needs. If you have a 1,000 calorie metabolism today, you will not have a 2,000 calorie metabolism tomorrow. Your metabolism will increase gradually. So how do you adjust the menus to meet your personal metabolic needs? Start by writing down exactly what you ate today (or on any "average" day) on the DAILY SUCCESS MENU PLANNER on the next page. Then add up your fat grams and calories by referring to the fat gram/calorie charts beginning on page 340.

This is absolutely essential for the prevention of unnecessary body-fat gain because, if you are a dieter* or a meal skipper, you must *increase your calories very gradually* from where you are right now. You should never feel miserably stuffed. You should feel comfortably satisfied. Start by eating six small meals and gradually increase as your metabolism and lean muscle tissue increase.

If you look at a 3,000-calorie menu and you normally eat 1,500 calories, simply cut the portion sizes in half and gradually increase them as your hunger and energy gradually increase.

If you look at a 2,000-calorie menu, and you normally eat 1,000 calories, simply cut each portion size in half. But if you normally eat 4,000 calories, you may want to double each portion size to meet your metabolic needs. And make certain not to exclude one food and double up on another. The balance is essential!

If you do not increase your calories and your high-fiber foods gradually, you may place unnecessary "fat-storing" stress on your body, so please –*listen to your body*!** You should get hungry for your next meal, not be stuffed all day long, and your calorie needs will vary from day to day. Mine range between 2,000 and 3,500 calories on different days. However, there are days when I'm as high as 4,000 or as low as 1,600. I never worry about calories. I simply *listen to my body*. Beginners often range between 1,200 and 1,500 calories.

Also, remember that you can mix and match your meals and the foods at your meals as long as you include water, vegetable, grain, protein, and fruit at each meal. (Exception: breakfast vegetables; refer to the Nourishment chapter in your LEAN & FREE 2000 PLUS book for more information.) You may find it very helpful to go through all of the menus and circle the ones (with a yellow highlighter pen) that best fit your personal tastes, budget, time schedule, and overall lifestyle. And choose just seven meals at a time to rotate.

Relax—at last you can *eat and enjoy real, normal food*! This is truly not a diet. It's a delicious, easy, abundant way of life with enough menus and recipes for an entire lifetime!

Chronic dieters and individuals suffering from eating disorders, see pages 317-319.

** See pages 3 and 317-319 to learn how to "listen to your body".*

LEAN&FREE 2000 PLUS™

DAILY SUCCESS MENU

Date:_____

			FG/CAL
Breakfast	Water		
	Grain		
	Protein		
	Fruit		
Snack	Water		
	Veggie+		
Lunch	Water		
	Vegetable		
	Grain		
	Protein		
	Fruit		
Snack	Water		
	Veggie+		
Dinner	Water		
	Vegetable		
	Grain		
	Protein		
	Fruit		
Snack	Water		
	Veggie+		

DAY'S TOTAL ▶

Calories: _____
Fat Grams: _____
Percent Fat:* _____

53

© Dana Thornock 1994

*To figure fat percentage: Fat Grams____ x 9 = ____ ÷ Calories____ = ____% fat

But I Can't Eat 2000 Calories!

Dieters and meal skippers say this all the time. Examine the following "fat-storing" days and ask yourself if you've ever eaten 2,000 or more calories in a day. Then compare these four low-quantity, high-fat days to the fifty six high-quantity, lowfat, perfect nutrient balanced days that follow them.

EATING OUT

	fg/cal
Breakfast - *Burger King*	
Sausage, Egg, and Cheese Croissan'wich	40/534
Diet Cola	0/0
Lunch - *Jack-In-The-Box*	
Side Salad with Buttermilk Dressing	39/413
Diet Cola	0/0
Dinner - *Taco Bell*	
Taco Salad with Ranch Dressing	86/1141
Diet Cola	0/0
Total: 71% FAT	**165/2088**

HIGH PROTEIN DAY

	fg/cal
Breakfast	
1 cup Roasted Peanuts	73/855
Lunch	
1 Seafood Salad with Ranch Dressing	66/884
Dinner	
Super Nachos	34/657
Snack	
2 oz. Skittles	5/320
Total: 59% FAT	**178/2716**

NIBBLE DAY

	fg/cal
Breakfast	
5 oz. M & M	30/720
Lunch	
9 Ritz & Butter Sandwiches	71/898
Snack	
1 Dairy Queen Chocolate Malt	25/1060
Dinner	
1 Apple Fritter	37/580
Total: 45% FAT	**163/3258**

ON THE RUN DAY

	fg/cal
Breakfast	
2 cups Coffee	0/0
2 Chocolate Donuts	42/648
Snack	
1 Snickers Bar (3.7 oz.)	24/510
Lunch - *Burger King*	
1 Chicken Specialty Sandwich	42/700
1 Large Fry	21/400
Dinner	
one 9" Turkey Pot Pie	42/750
1/2 bag Sour Cream and Onion Potato Chips	80/1280
Total: 53% FAT	**251/4288**

DAILY SUCCESS COMPLETE FREEDOM MENUS

This clock indicates that the meal takes between about 2 and 15 minutes to prepare.
Always look ahead for recipes marked "make ahead to save time."

DAY 1

			fg/cal
		Breakfast	
	Water	8 oz. water	
	Grain	1 cup Kellogg's Strawberry Fruit Wheats	0/180
	Protein	1 cup skim milk	t/86
	Fruit	1 banana, sliced on cereal	0/105
	Water/Snack	12 oz. water/ 1 celery stalk	t/18
		1/2 cup Strawberry Fruit Wheats with	
		1/2 cup skim milk	t/133

		Lunch	
	Water	8 oz. water	
	Vegetable	one half 19 oz. can Campbell's Chunky	
		Bean & Ham Soup (Try Chicken Vegetable	
		Soup if beans disturb your system.)	8/250
	Grain	1 slice whole or cracked-wheat toast with	
		1 Tb. All Fruit Jam* p. 164	1/99
	Protein	(ham; beans and bread combined)	
	Fruit	1/2 cup green grapes	t/54
	Water/Snack	8 oz. water/ 1 cup steamed veggies	t/76±
		other half of 19 oz. can soup	8/250

*Single asterisks come before recipe page numbers.

		Dinner	
	Water	8 oz. water	
	Vegetable	2 Pizza Wheels* p. 152 (1 vegetable	
		and 1 Canadian bacon, pineapple, and	
		mushroom)	14/439
	Grain	(pizza buns)	
	Protein	(pizza meat and cheese)	
	Fruit	1 cup Instant Peach Ice Cream* p. 194	t/117
	Water/Snack	12 oz. water/ 5 baby carrots	0/20

> Total: 31/1827
> 31 fat grams x 9 calories = 279 calories from fat
> $279 \div 1827 = $ **15% FAT**

To avoid fat-storing stress on your body, it is essential that you increase your calories and fiber gradually. Eat each meal and snack until you are comfortably full, not stuffed! If this is too much food for your comfortable satisfaction, decrease the amounts but keep the balance and eat often! If this isn't enough, eat more and keep the balance.

Canned soup is moderately-high in sodium, but your overall day is not. If you suffer from high-blood pressure, make soups from scratch or purchase low-sodium canned soups.

FREEDOM MENUS

DAY 2

			fg/cal
		Breakfast	
	Water	8 oz. water	
	Grain	1 Super Cinnamon Roll* p. 161 (very light frosting—make ahead to save time)	5/218
	Protein	1 cup skim milk	0/86
	Fruit	1 cup cantaloupe chunks	t/57
	Water/Snack	12 oz. water	
		1 cup mixed vegetable chunks	t/50±

Fast Food KFC**		**Lunch**	
	Water	12 oz. water	
	Vegetable	Vegetable Medley Salad	4/126
		BBQ Beans	2/132
		Mashed Potatoes with Gravy	1/70
	Grain	Sourdough Roll	2/128
	Protein	Rotisserie Gold Chicken (white quarter without skin)	6/199
	Fruit	1 banana (from home)	t/105
	Water/Snack	8 oz. water	

Easy		**Dinner**	
	Water	8 oz. water	
	Vegetable	(in salad)	
	Grain	1 large slice Zucchini Pineapple-Nut Bread* p. 163	6/230
	Protein	1 cup Veggie-Tuna Pasta Salad* p. 243	1/215
		one 8 oz. glass skim milk	t/86
	Fruit	3 sliced kiwifruit	t/138
	Water/Snack	8 oz. water/ 1 sliced cucumber	t/39

Total: 27/1879

27 fat grams x 9 calories = 243 calories from fat

243 ÷ 1879 = **13% FAT**

56

If you aren't accustomed to eating whole-grain breads, fruits, and raw vegetables, go with part whole-grains such as cracked-wheat breads and rolls, and eat steamed or canned vegetables and fruits. Adding too much fiber too quickly places fat-storing stress on your body. It may take you a year or more to tolerate lots of raw veggies, raw fruits, and 100 percent whole grains. Some individuals may always need to be moderate with these very complex foods.

**Refer to the Restaurant Food Evaluation Charts beginning on page 351. There are multiple regular and fast-food restaurants to choose from with many good "A" and "B" Choices as well as C, D, and F poor-food choices.

DAY 3

	Breakfast	fg/cal
Water	8 oz. water	
Grain	2 French Toast slices* p. 171 with	
	4 Tb. syrup (All-Fruit Jam* p. 164 and	
	nonfat vanilla yogurt is a better fat-loss choice.)	1/191
Protein	(egg in French Toast), 8 oz. skim milk	t/86
Fruit	1 cup mixed fresh fruit	t/100±
Water/Snack	12 oz. water/ 1 cup steamed veggies	t/76

	Lunch	
Water	12 oz. water	
Vegetable	(lettuce, tomatoes, onions, and taco sauce)	
Grain	(corn taco shells)	
Protein	2 large Tempting Tacos* p. 147	16/578
Fruit	1 cup sliced apples in lemon water	t/81
Water/Snack	8 oz. water/ 1 large. Tempting	
	Taco leftover from lunch	8/289

	Dinner	
Easy	**Dinner**	
Water	12 oz. water	
Vegetable	1 cup Tossed Salad* p. 167 with 2 Tb.	
	lowfat or fat free dressing	1/142±
Grain	1 cup cooked noodles	2/200
Protein	1 cup Beef Stroganoff* p. 150	4/254
Fruit	3/4 cup Fruit Gelatin (cherry)* p. 214	0/75
Water/Snack	8 oz. water/1 1/2 cups leftover Tossed Salad	
	with 2 Tb. lowfat or nonfat dressing	1/192±

Total: 33/2264

33 fat grams x 9 calories = 297 calories from fat

297 ÷ 2264 = **13% FAT**

My kids love this menu. The French Toast is a favorite, along with the Tempting Tacos. They especially love the Beef Stroganoff and Fruit Gelatin.

If you are highly-resistant to fat loss, you may do well to keep your fat intake in the 10 to 15% range which is about 15 to 40 fat grams for most women and 20 to 50 for most men. Coasting or "B" Choice, non-fat-loss days may range between 15 and 25% fat. Highly resistant individuals would also do well to avoid "B" Choice desserts. Main course "B" Choices are fine as long as they fit into a 10 to 15% fat day.

57

FREEDOM MENUS

DAY 4

		Breakfast	fg/cal
	Water	12 oz. water	
	Grain	1 cup Nutri Grain Almond Raisin Cereal	3/210
	Protein	1 cup skim milk	t/86
	Fruit	1/2 large grapefruit**	0/50
	Water/Snack	8 oz. water/ 5 baby carrots	0/20

		Lunch	
	Water	12 oz. water	
	Vegetable	1 cup Short-cut Tossed Salad* p. 266, with 2 Tb. Buttermilk Dressing* p. 210	
	Grain	1 Blueberry Muffin* p. 227 (Make ahead to save time.)	3/151
	Protein	1/2 large Chili-Stuffed Baked Potato (stuff with lowfat chili)	6/357
	Fruit	1 large slice watermelon**	t/50±
	Water/Snack	8 oz. water	
		1 cup mixed, raw or steamed vegetables	t/45

		Dinner	
	Water	8 oz. water	
	Vegetable	3/4 cup Au Gratin Potatoes* p. 244	6/314
		2 cups steamed broccoli	0/48
	Grain	1 slice Perfect Whole-Wheat Bread* p. 160	1/88
	Protein	one 5 oz. Parmesan Halibut Steak* p. 254	8/245
	Fruit	1 cup fresh strawberries**	1/45
	Water/Snack	12 oz. water	

Total: 29/1856

29 fat grams x 9 calories = 261 calories from fat

261 ÷ 1856 = **14% FAT**

**Purchase fruits that are in season and on sale.

Remember, this is not a diet! You do not have to eat everything on this page. Just do a little mixing and matching and make sure you keep your meals balanced. A cheaper breakfast may include oatmeal and honey with bananas and skim or 1% milk. A faster dinner might include a tuna fish or turkey sandwich stuffed with veggies and a bowl of peaches. Simply delicious!

FREEDOM MENUS

SHOPPING LISTS FOR THE COMPLETE FREEDOM MENUS
SHOPPING MADE EASY!

Stock your kitchen and storeroom with the following Master List items. You will use these foods often and will not need to purchase them weekly. A significant amount of time and money spent stocking shelves in the short-run will create marked time and money savings in the long-run. (You may also save a lot on doctor bills!) And remember to watch for in-store specials and case-lot sales.

These lists are ideal for individuals desiring a usable, practical supply of food storage items. If these lists are too detailed to meet your needs, enjoy the simplicity of the GRAB 'N GO and BUDGET MENUS.

MASTER LIST

BAKING

baking powder
baking soda
cocoa powder
cooking spray, nonstick
corn meal
cornstarch
egg whites, powdered, *(optional; food-storage stores often have them)*
flour,
    barley
    white
    whole-wheat
gelatin, unflavored
honey
mapleine
oil, *good*, (see page 279)
sugar,
    brown
    powdered
    white granulated
vanilla
wheat gluten *(optional; check food-storage stores)*
wheat grinder *(an excellent investment; check K-Tec stores)*

CONDIMENTS

cheese, parmesan, grated
gravy, dry mixes, beef, chicken, and
    turkey
jams or jellies, all-fruit *(fruit-juice sweetened)*
juice, lemon
ketchup
mayonnaise, fat free
Miracle Whip, fat free, Kraft
mustard
pickles, dill and/or sweet
salad dressings and dry mixes, fat free
    and lowfat
salsa, chunky
sauce,
    Worcestershire
    taco
seasoning, taco *(dry mix)*
syrup, maple
vinegar, red wine

59

SPICES

allspice
almond extract
barbecue spice
basil leaves
beef bouillon
chicken bouillon
chili powder
chives, chopped
cinnamon
cloves
cream of tartar
curry powder
dill weed
dried parsley flakes
dry mustard
garlic
garlic salt
ginger
Italian seasoning
minced garlic
minced onion
nutmeg
oregano
paprika
parsley flakes
pepper
rosemary
salt
salt, coarse
seasoned salt
soy sauce
tarragon leaves
thyme

60

CANNED AND BOTTLED GOODS

You may choose to purchase the following items in lesser or greater bulk for storage. I stock 1/4 to 2 cases of each of the following:

applesauce, lightly sweetened
   (Sweetened with apple-juice concentrate or unsweetened if you are diabetic.)
apricots in extra-light syrup
bamboo shoots
beans,
   great white northern *(or just white)*
   green, French and regular-cut
   kidney
   navy
   refried, lowfat or nonfat
   sprouts
   white
broth,
   chicken
   beef
chili, chicken or turkey or beef, lowfat
chow mein noodles *(just a few cans)*
corn,
   cream style
   whole kernel
fruit cocktail, chunky in extra-light
   syrup or fruit juice
juice, V-8
milk, evaporated skim
mushrooms, stems and pieces
olives *(high in good, cholesterol-fighting fat)*
oranges, mandarin
peaches in extra-light syrup
pears in extra-light syrup
pineapple,
   chunks in own juice
   crushed in own juice
   rings in own juice
   tidbits in own juice
salmon
sauce, spaghetti and pizza
shrimp *(optional)*
soups, a variety of Chunky Campbell's
   or Progresso *(Look for six or fewer fat grams per serving. If you suffer from high blood pressure, purchase low-sodium soups or make them from scratch.)*

Good soup choices include:
beef barley, black bean, chicken
vegetable, chicken noodle, chunky
bean and ham, lowfat cream of celery,
lowfat cream of chicken, lowfat cream
of mushroom, cream of potato
(Campbell's is lowfat), lentil, split pea,
steak and potato, tomato, vegetable
beef, etc.
soup mix, dry onion *(This is not in cans.)*
stew, beef or chicken *(moderate to lowfat)*
tomato paste
tomato sauce
tomatoes, stewed
tuna, regular in water
tuna, all-white in water *(optional)*
water, bottled *(if your tap water is
not completely pure or good tasting)*
water chestnuts

DRY GOODS

*I stock a moderate to significant amount
of each of the following:*

barley *(just a moderate amount)*
beans, dry *(a variety)*
lentils
milk, powdered *(optional)*
millet *(check food-storage stores)*
oats, rolled
pasta,
whole-wheat, artichoke, and/or
white spaghetti, macaroni, manicotti,
lasagna, jumbo shells, wide egg
noodles, etc.
popcorn, hard yellow and microwave,
light butter
potatoes, instant
rice, brown and/or white *(check
food-storage stores)*
taco shells, jumbo, regular, and/or
mini-size
wheat, white kernels *(Check food-
storage stores. This is a highly-
nutritive, very delicious wheat variety
called "white wheat" that creates less
gastrointestinal distress in most*

*individuals than does red wheat. It
makes light, delicious bread products.)*

FROZEN FOODS

bread, including:
whole-grain rolls, pita pockets,
English muffins *(Buy several loaves
or bags on sale and freeze.)*
butter *(freezes well)*
cheese,
grated part-skim mozzarella and
grated cheddar *(Buy already grated
cheese or purchase large bricks on
sale. Then grate and freeze.)*
grated Parmesan
fruit,
blueberries, peaches, raspberries,
strawberries, etc. *(Buy already frozen,
or buy fresh, on-sale fruit. Spread on
a cookie sheet. Freeze and put into
freezer bags.)*
juice concentrates,
Dole Country Raspberry, Dole
Orchard Peach, Dole Pine-Orange-
Banana, Dole Mountain Cherry, apple,
orange, pineapple *(When finances are
pinched, eliminate these juices and
look for fresh, on-sale fruits only.)*
tortillas,
corn, and whole-wheat
(Purchase several bags and freeze.)
vegetables,
mixed, stir-fry, carrots, peas, hash
brown potatoes *(no fat added)*, etc.

MEAT

*Purchase moderate amounts of the
following meats when they are on sale.*

beef: ground: extra-lean
chicken breasts: skinned and deboned
fish: halibut steaks, orange roughy,
red snapper, etc.
ham: extra-lean, thinly sliced
turkey: white, sliced meat or roast

61

FREEDOM MENUS

SHOPPING LIST / DAYS 1 - 4

SHOPPING MADE EASY
ADJUST TO YOUR NEEDS

*These shopping lists are structured for families of four adults eating approximately 2,000 to 3,000 calories each. Adjust them to your family size or single needs and your own personal taste, budget, time schedule, calorie needs, food allergies, and special health needs. (See pages 314-338.) I generally buy food for seven to ten people. I find that a **four**-day shopping list, adjusted to my family's size, usually lasts us **six** or **seven** days because of leftovers and unplanned eating-out excursions. The first time you shop for unfamiliar food items, it may take longer than you're used to spending. As you become familiar with new food locations in your grocery store, your shopping time will markedly decrease, becoming very fast and easy!*

BREAD / CEREAL / GRAIN

cereal,
    Kellogg's Strawberry Fruit
      Wheats, 1 box
    Kellogg's Nutri Grain Almond
      Raisin, 1 box

FRESH FRUITS
AND VEGETABLES

Or purchase other fruits and vegetables that are in season or on sale.

apples, 4
bananas, 8
cantaloupe, 1
grapefruit, 2
grapes, 1 large bunch
kiwifruit, 6
strawberries, 1 quart
watermelon, 1 half
broccoli, 2 large bunches

carrots, baby, 1 small bag
celery, 1 bunch
cucumbers, 3
lettuce, leafy, 1 bunch
onions, green, 1 bunch
potatoes, baking, 8
potatoes, medium, 12
tomatoes,
    cherry, 10
    slicing, medium, 6
tossed salad, leafy – *(not iceberg)*
    lettuce, 1 bag
zucchini, medium, 2

MEAT AND DAIRY*

bacon, Canadian, 4 oz.
beef, top sirloin, 1/2 lb.

buttermilk, 1 quart
cream cheese, nonfat, 1 package
eggs, 1 dozen *(you'll use mostly whites)*
milk, skim, 2 gallons *(1% will do)*
sour cream, nonfat, 1 pint
yogurt, nonfat vanilla

*Meats and dairy products are used in great moderation. Egg whites, which are fat free, generally replace the whole egg. Small amounts of butter replace margarine and shortening because butter is a highly saturated "natural" fat rather than a man-made, "heat-damaged," partially saturated fat. Be very moderate in its use. (See page 273 for more information.)

*If you choose to buy many of your bread items already made, such as bread, muffins, cinnamon rolls, etc., you will need to purchase fewer eggs and less butter. Be carful with store-bought muffins. The large muffins often contain **20 to 30** fat grams **each**!*

MISC.

Schilling Beef Stroganoff Mix, 1 envelope
walnuts, 1/2 cup

Master List / Check List
Days 1 – 4

Check to be sure that you have the following Master List items already in stock. Baking items, condiments, and spices are not included in this list. They are listed on pages 59-60.

BREAD / CEREAL / GRAIN

Purchase breads, rolls, buns, etc., on sale and freeze.

bread, whole-wheat, 1 loaf
hamburger buns, whole-wheat, 1 dozen
noodles, whole-wheat or white, 12 oz.
taco shells, corn, 12 jumbo

MEAT AND DAIRY

Purchase in moderate quantities on sale and freeze. Grate cheese before freezing.

halibut, 4 steaks

butter, 1/2 lb.
cheese,
    mozzarella, part-skim, grated,
    2 lbs.
    Parmesan, grated, 3 oz.

CANNED GOODS

applesauce, unsweetened or lightly
    sweetened, one 16 oz. can or jar
beans, refried, no-fat added,
    one 16 oz. can
chili, chicken, four 15 oz. cans
fruit cocktail, in extra-light syrup
    or fruit juice, one 16 oz. can
milk, evaporated skim, one 12 oz. can
mushrooms, one 8 oz. can
pineapple,
    tidbits, own juice, one 15 oz. can
sauce, pizza quick, one 15 oz. can
soup, Campbell's Chunky Bean and Ham,
    four 19 oz. cans *(or homemade)*
tuna, white or regular, two 6 1/2 oz. cans

FROZEN / MISC.

blueberries, 1 cup
juice concentrates,
    apple, one 12 oz. can
    Dole Mountain Cherry, one 12 oz. can
    Dole Orchard Peach, one 12 oz. can
peaches, 4 cups
vegetables, mixed (broccoli, pea pods,
    onions, carrots), two 32 oz. bags

dressing, ranch, nonfat, 1 bottle
    (or homemade)

DAY 5

		Breakfast	fg/cal
	Water	16 oz. water	
	Grain	1 1/2 cups General Mills Triples Cereal	2/220
	Protein	1 cup skim milk	t/86
	Fruit	1/2 cup sliced strawberries	1/45
	Water/Snack	12 oz. water	

		Lunch	
	Water	16 oz. water	
	Vegetable	one half 19 oz. can Campbell's Chunky Chicken Vegetable Soup	5/170
	Grain	1 slice whole-wheat toast/1 Tb. All Fruit Jam* p. 164	t/87
	Protein	(chicken in soup)	
	Fruit	1 cup peaches (rinse light syrup)	t/109
	Water/Snack	8 oz. water	

**Fast Food
Pizza Hut**

		Dinner	
	Water	8 oz. water	
	Vegetable	2 medium slices Vegetable Pizza Hut Pan Pizza ("B+" Choice—order cheese pizza with lots of veggies on top.)	18/560
	Grain	(pizza crust)	
	Protein	one 6 oz. nonfat fruit yogurt (fruit-juice sweetened is healthiest choice)	t/150
	Fruit	1 cup mixed-fruit cocktail in fruit juice (or drain and mix with yogurt if desired)	0/180
	Water/Snack	12 oz. water	

> Total: 26/1607
> 26 fat grams x 9 calories = 234 calories from fat
> 234 ÷ 1607 = **15% FAT**

Although fast-food pizza is not usually an "A" Choice, this particular pizza choice is only 29 percent fat and fits easily into an under-20 percent fat day. Some pizza choices are loaded with extra cheese and meat and can be as high as 50 to 70 percent fat. The "made-from-scratch" pizza in this book or the Pizza Wheels would make even better choices— lower in fat, and higher in complex carbohydrates.

*If you order a "B" Choice pizza, make certain to have lowfat food just before, it arrives at your door. I have a big bowl of vegetable beef soup, two slices of whole-grain toast, and an apple. I **ALWAYS** do this. Otherwise, I eat* eight *slices of pizza instead of* two *and any inch-loss is shot for the week!*

DAY 6

		Breakfast	fg/cal
	Water	8 oz. water	
	Grain	1 cup oatmeal with	
		2 Tb. of honey (optional)	2/265
	Protein	1 cup skim milk	t/86
	Fruit	1 large sliced banana, (on cereal)	t/105
	Water/Snack	12 oz. water/ 1 cup mixed	
		vegetables with 2 Tb. lowfat dip	1/90±

		Lunch	
	Water	8 oz. water	
	Vegetable	1 1/2 cups green peas	t/231
	Grain	(1 slice whole-or part whole-grain toast)	t/71
	Protein	1 cup Creamed Tuna on Toast* p. 252	3/164
	Fruit	1 orange, sliced	t/62
	Water/Snack	8 oz. water	

		Dinner	
	Easy		
	Water	8 oz. water	
	Vegetable	2 cups green beans with 1 tsp. butter	4/116
	Grain	1 cup Homemade Macaroni and Cheese*	
		p. 238 ("B" Choice)	11/340
	Protein	(cheese and yogurt)	
	Fruit	1 cup kiwi, strawberry, and pineapple	
		chunks topped with nonfat vanilla yogurt	t/180
	Water/Snack	12 oz. water	

Total: 21/1710

21 fat grams x 9 calories = 189 calories from fat

189 ÷ 1710 = **11% FAT**

This is a fun, easy menu including two family favorites, Creamed Tuna on Toast at 16 percent fat and Homemade Macaroni and Cheese at 29 percent fat. And this entire day contains only 11 percent fat. Remember that fat gram numbers are irrelevant! The important factor is your overall fat percentage for the day and week which should range between 10 and 20 percent—10 and 15 percent if you are highly resistant to fat loss. Your body handles fats much more efficiently when they are combined with more high-fiber, complex-carbohydrate foods.

65

FREEDOM MENUS

DAY 7

		Breakfast	fg/cal
	Water	12 oz. water	
	Grain	4 Banana Pancakes* p. 176	8/384
	Protein	6 oz. strawberry nonfat yogurt (on pancakes)	t/150
	Fruit	4 Tb. All Fruit Jam* p. 164 (on pancakes)	t/64
	Water/Snack	8 oz. water/ 1 sliced cucumber, 2/3 cup Post Great Grains Cereal and 1 cup skim milk	6/346

		Lunch	
	Water	12 oz. water	
	Vegetable	1/2 can Campbell's Old Fashioned Vegetable Beef Soup with 1/2 cup kidney beans	5/280
	Grain	2 slices whole-wheat toast with 2 Tb. All Fruit Jam* p. 164 or fat free cream cheese and jam	1/142
	Protein	(beef in soup)	
	Fruit	1 cup grapes	0/108
	Water/Snack	12 oz.water/ 1 sliced green pepper	t/26

Easy		**Dinner**	
	Water	12 oz. water	
	Vegetable	1 1/2 cups broccoli	t/69
	Grain	1 cup brown rice with	t/180
		1 cup Mushroom Gravy* p. 220	2/108
	Protein	one 6 oz. Baked Chicken Breast* p. 178	6/284
	Fruit	1 1/2 cups chunk watermelon	t/75
	Water/Snack	8 oz. water/ 5 baby carrots	0/20

Total:	28/2236

28 fat grams x 9 calories = 252 calories from fat

252 ÷ 2236 = **11% FAT**

If you are just starting this program and you are too full on this much food, just eat one or two pancakes with less yogurt and jam, one slice of bread at lunch, one-half cup rice at dinner, and half of a chicken breast. Your appetite will gradually increase as your metabolism increases, and it will vary from day to day. Both starving and stuffing create body fat increase, so listen to your body!

DAY 8

			fg/cal
Water	**Breakfast**		
Grain	12 oz. water		
	2 slices whole-wheat toast and 2 Tb.		
	Apple-Raspberry Butter* p. 165		
	(Make in advance to save time.)		1/172
Protein	1 Fried Egg* p. 172		6.5/83
Fruit	1/2 grapefruit		0/50
Water/Snack	8 oz. water/ 6 oz. V–8 Juice		0/35

**Fast Food
Burger King**

	Lunch		
Water	12 oz. water		
Vegetable	(extra lettuce, tomatoes, pickles, and onions)		t/60
Grain	BK Broiler Bun		
Protein	1 Burger King BK Broiler (without sauce)		4/220
Fruit	(tomatoes)		
Water/Snack	8 oz. water/ vegetables/ whole-wheat Super		
	Cinnamon Roll* p. 161 (if hungry—veggies		
	only if not hungry)		5/268
	12 oz. skim milk		t/129

Easy

	Dinner		
Water	8 oz. water		
Vegetable	1 1/2 cups Tossed salad with 4 Tb. Butter-		
	milk Dressing* p. 210		t/234
Grain	1 cup Spaghetti* p. 242 with 1 cup		
	Spaghetti Econo-Sauce* p. 222		1/257
	1 slice Garlic Cheese		
	Toast* p. 159 ("B–" Choice)		5/118
Protein	2 Tb. grated parmesan cheese on spaghetti		3/46
Fruit	1 cup honeydew melon		t/60
Water/Snack	12 oz. water		

Total: 25.5/1732

25.5 fat grams x 9 calories = 229.5 calories from fat

229.5 ÷ 1732 = **13% FAT**

Two to three whole eggs per week is an ideal amount. One yolk is high in cholesterol and contains 6 1/2 grams, mostly from saturated fat. The whites contain no fat or cholesterol. So, in cooking, use two egg whites in place of one whole egg. Powdered egg whites can be found in some health-food stores and offer an economical alternative to throwing yolks down the "cholesterol-filled" drain.

Shopping List / Days 5 – 8

*This **four**-day shopping list may last your family **six** or **seven** day if you eat out often.*

BREADS / CEREALS / GRAINS

cereal, Kellogg's Triples, 1 box
cereal, Post Great Grains, 1 box

FRESH FRUITS
AND VEGETABLES

Or purchase other fruits and vegetables that are in season or on sale.

bananas, 6 large
grapefruit, 2
grapes, 1 large bunch
kiwifruit, 6
melon, honeydew, 1
melon, watermelon, 1/2
oranges, 4
raisins, 1 medium box
strawberries, 1 quart

broccoli, 3 large bunches
carrots, baby, 1 small bag
cucumbers, 4
lettuce, leafy, 1 large bunch
onions, 2
peppers, green, 5
tomatoes, medium, 2

MEAT AND DAIRY

buttermilk, 1 pint *(You may have some left over from Days 1 – 4 shopping list.)*
cream cheese, nonfat, 4 oz.
eggs, 1 dozen *(you'll use mostly whites)*
milk, skim, 1 to 2 gallons
yogurt,
  nonfat, 1 quart
  vanilla, nonfat, 1 quart
  strawberry, nonfat, 24 oz.
  mixed fruit, nonfat, 24 oz.

(Lowfat yogurt will suffice if you can't find nonfat yogurt. Fruit-juice sweetened non-fat Alto Dena yogurt is the perfect choice if you are diabetic or highly resistant to fat loss. Make certain to avoid ALL artificially sweetened yogurts like the plague!)

MASTER LIST – CHECK LIST DAYS 5 – 8

Check to be sure that you have the following Master List items already in stock. Baking items, condiments, and spices are not included in this list. They are listed on pages 59-60.

BREAD / CEREAL / GRAIN

Purchase bread, rolls, buns, etc., on sale and freeze.

bread, whole-wheat, 1 to 2 loaves
brown rice, cooked, 4 cups
macaroni, whole-wheat or white, 12 oz.
spaghetti, whole-wheat or white, 12 oz.

MEAT AND DAIRY

Purchase in moderate quantities, on sale and freeze. Grate cheese before freezing.

chicken, boneless and skinless,
    4 to 8 breasts

butter, 1/2 lb.
cheese,
    American, cheddar, or Swiss,
        grated, 4 oz.
    Parmesan, grated, 4 oz.

CANNED GOODS

applesauce, unsweetened or lightly
    sweetened, 3 cans
beans,
    green, four 16 oz. cans
    kidney, two 15 oz. cans
fruit cocktail, own juice,
    two 16 oz. cans
juice, V-8, four 6 oz. cans
milk, evaporated skim, two
    12 oz. cans
peaches, in own juice or fresh, 1 quart
pineapple, chunks, in own juice,
    one 20 oz. can
sauce, tomato, six 8 oz. cans
soup,
    Campbell's Chunky Chicken
        Vegetable, two 19 oz. cans
    Campbell's Old Fashioned
        Vegetable Beef, two 19 oz. cans
    lowfat cream of mushroom, two
        10 3/4 oz. cans
    lowfat cream of celery, one 10 3/4
        oz. can
tuna, white, water-packed, two 6 1/2
    oz. cans

FROZEN

juice concentrates,
    apple, one 12 oz. can
    Dole Country Raspberry,
        one 12 oz. can
peas, green, two 24 oz. bags

69

DAY 9

			fg/cal
		Breakfast	
	Water	12 oz. water	
	Grain	1 cup Three Bear Porridge* p. 175 with	
		1/4 cup raisins and 2 Tb. honey	t/397
	Protein	1 cup 1% milk	3/102
	Fruit	(raisins)	
	Water/Snack	8 oz. water/ vegetables/ 1 Banana Muffin*	
		p. 226 (make ahead)	3/194±

		Lunch	
Fast Food			
Subway			
	Water	12 oz. water	
	Vegetable	(extra vegetables on sandwich)	
	Grain	(whole-wheat bun)	
	Protein	1 foot-long Turkey Breast Sandwich	
		(with no mayonnaise or oil)	20/674
	Fruit	1 medium orange (from home)	t/62
	Water/Snack	12 oz. water (Perhaps eat 1/2 of sandwich	
		at lunch and 1/2 for your snack if you are	
		hungry for a snack.)	

		Dinner	
	Water	12 oz. water	
	Vegetable	1 1/2 cups mixed steamed vegetables	t/114
	Grain	1 slice whole-wheat toast	t/71
	Protein	one half 15 oz. can Hormel Chicken Chili	
		served over toast	3/200
	Fruit	2 pears—fresh or in light syrup (rinsed)	0/196
	Water/Snack	8 oz. water/ 1 cup Mixed Veggie Festival*	
		p. 265	2/162

Total: 31/2172
31 fat grams x 9 calories = 279 calories from fat
279 ÷ 2172 = **13% FAT**

When you eat sandwiches at fast-food restaurants, always ask for extra tomatoes, pickles, onions, and any other vegetables they have available. Have them leave off the oil and mayonnaise or ranch-style sauces. One-fourth of an avocado contains seven grams of good fat and is 82 percent fat. I have some avocado occasionally. Olives are over 90 percent fat. However, they are full of "good" fat, and eight small olives contain only three fat grams. So don't omit all of the avocados and olives!

FREEDOM MENUS

Veggie Lasagna and Garlic Cheese Toast (bottom);
Cappellino Primavera (top)

Veggie and Cheese Egg Scramble, Hash Browns,
*Perfect Whole-Wheat Bread, **real** butter, and All Fruit Jam*

DAY 10

	Breakfast	fg/cal
Easy		
Water	12 oz. water	
Vegetable	3/4 cup Hash Browns* p. 246	
	(and veggies in Scramble)	6/155
Grain	one 3" square Country Corn Bread* p. 159	5/201
Protein	3/4 cup Veggie and Cheese Egg Scramble*	
	p. 175 ("B+" Choice)	7/217
Fruit	1 cup Orange Jubilee* p. 174	0/157
Water/Snack	8 oz. water	
	1 stalk celery	0/20

	Lunch	
Water	12 oz. water	
Vegetable	(lettuce, tomato, and pickles)	
Grain	(whole-wheat bread)	
Protein	1 Tuna Salad Sandwich* p. 250	2/400
Fruit	1 apple	t/81
Water/Snack	8 oz. water/1/2 sliced sweet potato	
	(raw or cooked)	t/59

	Dinner	
Easy		
Water	12 oz. water	
Vegetable	1 cup green peas	t/122
Grain	1 large slice Luscious Lasagna* p. 239	13/404
Protein	(meat and cheese in Lasagna)	
Fruit	1 cup Instant Blueberry Ice Cream* p. 194	t/149
Water/Snack	12 oz. water/ 3 cups plain popcorn	
	with butter flavor sprinkles	t/50

Total: 33/2015

33 fat grams x 9 calories = 297 calories from fat

297 ÷ 2015 = **15% FAT**

It's so exciting and freeing to be moderate, not extreme, with fats. Many cheeses are 50 to 80 percent fat. Your overall day is 20 percent fat or less, but not every food that goes into your mouth needs to be under 20 percent fat. Veggie and Cheese Egg Scramble and Luscious Lasagna are truly delicious. "Grandma's home Cookin" type foods fit nicely into an under 20 percent fat day but are not under 20 percent fat by themselves.

71

DAY 11

		fg/cal
	Breakfast	
Water	12 oz. water	
Grain	1 cup Kellogg's Nutri Grain Almond Raisin Cereal	3/210
Protein	1 cup skim milk	t/86
Fruit	1 cup fresh raspberries (Place on cereal, or use another "in-season" fruit.)	1/61
Water/Snack	12 oz. water/ 6 oz. V-8 Juice	0/35
	Lunch	
Water	8 oz. water	
Vegetable	1/2 large Veggie-Stuffed Potato* p. 247	3/238
Grain	1 Apple-Cinnamon Muffin* p. 226 (Make ahead and freeze to save time.)	3/149
Protein	(cheese on potato)	
Fruit	2 sliced kiwifruit	t/92
Water/Snack	12 oz. water/ 1/2 leftover Veggie-Stuffed Potato	3/238
	Dinner	
Water	8 oz. water	
Vegetable	3/4 cup Egg Drop Soup* p. 257	2/85
	2 cups Chinese Salad Bar* p. 262	t/250±
Grain	1 cup brown rice	t/180
Protein	1 cup Pork Chow Mein* p. 154	8/302
Fruit	6 apricot halves (fresh or rinsed) on a bed of lettuce topped with 1/2 cup lowfat cottage cheese	2/218
	1 fortune cookie	t/40±
Water/Snack	12 oz. water/ 3/4 cup leftover Egg Drop Soup	2/85

Total: 27/2269

27 fat grams x 9 calories = 243 calories from fat

243 ÷ 2269 = **11% FAT**

If you are allergic to the lactose in milk (milk sugar), you may try adding lactaid drops to your milk. These are found at most pharmacies. Or dilute a non-dairy coffee creamer with water. Use it very sparingly just to wet your cereal. (Make certain that the coffee creamer does not contain palm or coconut oil.)

DAY 12

	Breakfast	fg/cal
Water	12 oz. water	
Grain	1 Super Cinnamon Roll* p. 161	
	(Make ahead and freeze to save time.)	5/218
Protein	1 cup skim milk	t/86
Fruit	1 cup mixed melon chunks	t/55
Water/Snack	8 oz. water/ 1 cup raw vegetables with	
	2 Tb. Delicious Dill Dip* p. 211	

	Lunch	
Water	12 oz. water	
Vegetable	1 cup Quick, Delicious Beef Stew* p. 155	8/302
Grain	1 slice whole-wheat toast with 1 Tb.	
	All Fruit Jam* p. 164	t/87
Protein	(meat in stew)	
Fruit	1/2 cup mandarin oranges (rinsed) mixed	
	with 1/2 cup nonfat vanilla yogurt	t/226
Water/Snack	8 oz. water/ 1/2 cup leftover stew	4/151

	Dinner	
Water	12 oz. water	
Vegetable	1 cup Mashed Potatoes* p. 246	
	1/2 cup peas/1/2 cup carrots/1/2 cup corn	1/297
Grain	1 Apple-Cinnamon Muffin* p. 226	3/149
Protein	one 4 oz. slice Cranberry-Glazed	
	Turkey Breast* p. 182	4/215
	1/2 cup Quick Turkey Gravy* p. 222	
	(on potatoes)	t/47±
Fruit	1/2 cup Pineapple and Cottage Cheese	
	Salad* p. 215	1/101
Water/Snack	8 oz. water/ 11/2 cups mixed peas,	
	carrots, and corn	1/297

Total: 28/2321
28 fat grams x 9 calories = 252 calories from fat
252 ÷ 2321 = **11% FAT**

73

White whole-wheat makes wonderfully delicious, light cinnamon rolls and breads. It can be purchased at most Kitchen-Bosch stores or food-storage stores. Many people digest white wheat more easily than red wheat. It is just as high in nutrients and fiber as red wheat.

SHOPPING LIST / DAYS 9 – 12

*This **four**-day shopping list may last your family **six** or **seven** days if you eat out often.*

BREAD / CEREAL / GRAINS

cereal, Kellogg's Nutri Grain Almond
   Raisin, 1 box

FRESH FRUITS
AND VEGETABLES

Or purchase other fruits and vegetables that are in season or on sale.

apples, 8
bananas, 6
kiwifruit, 8
melons,
   cantaloupe, 1
   honeydew, 1
oranges, 4
raisins, 1 lb.
raspberries, 1 quart

cabbage,
   purple, 1 head
   yellow, 1 head
carrots, 5 lbs.
celery, 2 bunches
lettuce, leafy, 1 large bunch

onions, 2
onions, green, 1 bunch
pea pods, 8 oz.
potatoes,
   sweet *(yams)**, 2
   baking, 4
tomatoes,
   cherry, 1 pint
   slicing, 2 medium

*Jersey sweets are sweet potatoes that are dry and pale yellow; yams are moist and orange. They are cooked the same way. The yams are very tasty raw. The jersey sweets are not.

MEAT AND DAIRY / MISC.

pork, extra-lean, 1/2 lb.

cottage cheese, lowfat, 2 quarts
cream cheese, nonfat, 4 oz.
eggs, 2 - 3 dozen *(unless you have powdered egg whites)*
milk, skim or 1%, 1 to 2 gallons
sour cream, nonfat, 1 pint
yogurt, vanilla, nonfat, 1 pint

cookies, fortune, 1 package ("B" Choice)
Catalina dressing, fat free,
   one 16 oz. bottle

MASTER LIST / CHECK LIST
DAYS 9 – 12

Check to be sure that you have the following Master List items already in stock. Baking items, condiments, and spices are not included in this list. They are listed on pages 59-60.

BREAD / CEREAL / GRAIN

Purchase breads, rolls, buns, etc., on sale and freeze.

bread, whole-wheat, 1 to 2 loaves
    flour, whole-wheat
millet, 1 cup
noodles, lasagna, whole-wheat or white,
    10 oz.
popcorn, kernels, 2 cups
rice, brown or white, 1 cup
wheat, white kernels, 1 cup

MEAT AND DAIRY

Purchase in moderate quantities on sale and freeze. Grate cheese before freezing.

beef, extra-lean ground, 1/2 lb.
turkey, precooked lean roast, 1
pork, lean, 1 lb.

cheese,
    mozzarella, part-skim, 2 lbs.
    Parmesan, 2 oz.

CANNED GOODS

applesauce*, unsweetened or lightly
    sweetened, two 16 oz. cans
apricots, one 16 oz. can
bamboo shoots, two 8 oz. cans
beans*,
    green, one 16 oz. can
    kidney, one 15 oz. can
    sprouts, two 14 oz. cans
    white or, one 16 oz. can

beef stew, Nalley's Big Chunky,
    one 40 oz. can
chili, chicken, two 15 oz. cans
corn,
    cream style, one 17 oz. can
    whole kernel, three 16 oz. cans
juice, V-8, four 6 oz. cans
milk, evaporated skim, one 12 oz. can
mushrooms, stems and pieces,
    one small can
noodles, chow mein, one 5 oz. can
oranges, mandarin, two 11 oz. cans
pears, one 16 oz. can
pickles, 1 medium jar
pineapple,
    chunks, in own juice, one 20 oz. can
    crushed, in own juice, one 151/4 oz. can
soup,
    Campbell's Chunky Beef and
        Vegetable, two 17 oz. cans
    Campbell's Cream of Chicken,
        lowfat, four 103/4 oz. cans
    chicken broth, four 101/2 oz. cans
tomato, paste, three 6 oz. cans
tuna, water pack, two 61/2 oz. cans
water chestnuts, one 8 oz. can

FROZEN

blueberries, 16 oz.
juice, concentrates,
    apple, one 12 oz. can
    orange, one 12 oz. can
    pineapple, one 12 oz. can
peas, 2 lbs.
potatoes, hash browns, 2 lbs.
vegetables, mixed, two 16 oz. bags
vegetables; peas, carrots, and corn,
    one 16 oz. bag

MISCELLANEOUS

potatoes, instant mashed, 8 servings

*See the italics statement at the bottom of page 81.

DAY 13

			fg/cal
	Breakfast		
Water	8 oz. water		
Grain	2/3 cup Crunchy Granola* p. 170		
	(Prepare in advance to save time.)		16/489
Protein	1 cup skim milk		t/86
Fruit	1 cup sliced bananas and strawberries		
	(on granola if you like)		t/75
Water/Snack	8 oz. water/ 6 oz. V-8 juice		0/35
	Lunch		
Water	8 oz. water		
Vegetable	(lettuce, tomatoes, sprouts, onions		
	and peppers on sandwiches)		
Grain	(whole or cracked-grain bread)		
Protein	1 Turkey Breast Sandwich* p. 250		
	(use turkey breast leftover from Day 12)		2/340
Fruit	2 large fresh plums		t/72
Water/Snack	12 oz. water/ 1 leftover Turkey Sandwich		2/340
	1 cup skim milk		t/86
Easy	**Dinner**		
Water	12 oz. water		
Vegetable	(in Easy Chicken 'n' Dumplings)		
Grain	(2 dumplings)		
Protein	2 cups Easy Chicken 'n' Dumplings* p. 183		10/554
Fruit	one 21/2" square Apple Cobbler* p. 187		
	(B+ Choice)		6/316
Water/Snack	8 oz. water		

Total: 36/2393

36 fat grams x 9 calories = 324 calories from fat
324 ÷ 2393 = **14% FAT**

Homemade Crunchy Granola is about 29 percent fat from "good" fat. It's amazing how it fits perfectly into this 14 percent fat day, even with apple cobbler for an evening dessert.

DAY 14

		Breakfast	fg/cal
Water		12 oz. water	
Grain		1 cup Rice-'n'-Honey	
		Pudding with Raisins* p. 198	1/285
Protein		1 cup skim milk	t/86
Fruit		(raisins)	
Water/Snack		8 oz. water/1 cup leftover Rice Pudding/	
		with 1 cup skim milk/ vegetables	1/421

		Lunch	
Water		8 oz. water	
Vegetable		(1 cup sprouts and avocados in pita pockets)	
Grain		(whole-wheat pita pockets)	
Protein		1 Seafood 'n' Avocado Pita Pocket* p. 250	11/450
Fruit		2 fresh nectarines (or another in-season fruit)	2/134
Water/Snack		12 oz. water/ 1 leftover Pita Pocket	11/450

		Dinner	
Easy			
Water		8 oz. water	
Vegetable		(see enchiladas) Relish Tray with Delicious	
		Dill Dip* p. 211	
		(1 cup vegetables and 2 Tb. dip)	1/90
Grain		(tortillas in enchiladas)	
Protein		2 Chicken-Chili Enchiladas* p. 144	11.5/516
Fruit		11/2 cups watermelon, cantaloupe,	
		honeydew, and pineapple chunks	t/103
		2 Date Bars* p. 191	4/232
Water/Snack		12 oz. water/ 1 leftover Chicken-Chili	
		Enchilada	6/258

> Total: 48.5/3025
>
> 48.5 fat grams x 9 calories = 436.5 calories of fat
>
> 436.5 ÷ 3025 = **14% FAT**

*Wow! Look at those calories. You may be at only 1,500 calories for comfortable satisfaction, so follow the menu and **balance** your meal. Just cut the portion sizes in half. Remember, **stuffing** yourself or **starving** yourself both can promote excess fat gain. Listen to your body! And if you do eat 3,000 calories for comfortable (not stuffed satisfaction) notice that you MUST have more good fat grams to stay in the ideal 10 to 20 percent fat range.*

FREEDOM MENUS

DAY 15

		Breakfast	fg/cal
	Water	12 oz. water	
	Grain	2 cups Kellogg's Rice Krispies	0/220
	Protein	1 cup skim milk	t/86
	Fruit	1 sliced banana	t/105
	Water/Snack	12 oz. water	

		Lunch	
	Water	8 oz. water	
	Vegetable	(in soup)	
	Grain	2 slices whole-wheat toast with 2 Tb. strawberry cream cheese	5/202
	Protein	one half 19 oz. can Campbell's Chunky Split Pea and Ham Soup* p. 254	5/210
	Fruit	1 slice Whole-Wheat Angel Food Cake* p. 202 with strawberries (make ahead)	t/165
	Water/Snack	12 oz. water/ 1 cup sweet potato and zucchini slices	t/68
		1 cup skim milk	t/86

		Dinner	
Easy			
	Water	8 oz. water	
	Vegetable	1/2 cup Cauliflower 'n' Cheddar* p. 261 ("B+" Choice) or 2 cups steamed cauliflower without cheese	8/184
	Grain	2 Zucchini Muffins* p. 234	6/286
	Protein	6 oz. Red Snapper* p. 254	3/217
	Fruit	1 cup grapes, strawberries, and pineapple rings	t/100±
	Water/Snack	8 oz. water	

Total: 27/1929

27 fat grams x 9 calories = 243 calories from fat

243 ÷ 1929 = **13% FAT**

*Many canned soups are relatively high in sodium, but your overall day is moderate in sodium and you are drinking plenty of water to balance out any excess salt intake. However, if you already suffer from high blood pressure or a **very** tight budget, it is best to make your soups from scratch. You may also consider purchasing lower in sodium, canned soups. (Watch for case-lot sales.)*

DAY 16

			fg/cal
		Breakfast	
	Water	8 oz. water	
	Grain	2 Date Bars—No-Sugar Style* p. 192	
		or regular Date Bars left over from Day 14	4/226
	Protein	1 cup skim milk	t/86
	Fruit	2 fresh peaches	t/74
	Water/Snack	12 oz. water	

Restaurant		**Lunch**	
Big Boy's (JB's)			
	Water	8 oz. water	
	Vegetable	Chicken 'n' Vegetable Stir-Fry	14/562
	Grain	Whole-grain Dinner Roll (if available)	t/45
	Protein	(chicken in stir-fry)	
	Fruit	1 orange *(from home; or ask for fresh fruit)*	t/62
	Water/Snack	12 oz. water (If you are comfortably satisfied at lunch and you have leftovers, eat them for your snack.)	

Easy		**Dinner**	
	Water	8 oz. water	
	Vegetable	1 1/2 cups Tossed Salad* p. 267 with 4 Tb. Easy Lowfat Dressing* p. 211	2/234±
	Grain	2 helpings Mexican Lasagna* p. 146	6/371
	Protein	(in lasagna)	
	Fruit	1 cup low-sugar applesauce with fresh apple chunks and cinnamon	t/106
	Water/Snack	12 oz. water/ 1 serving leftover Mexican Lasagna	3/186

Total: 29/1952

29 fat grams x 9 calories = 261 calories from fat

261 ÷ 1952 = **13% FAT**

My family loves the Mexican Lasagna. Notice how the snacks always include a vegetable and many times include foods left over from the previous meal. Mexican Lasagna is full of delicious vegetables.

FREEDOM MENUS

SHOPPING LIST / DAYS 13 – 16

*This **four**-day shopping list may last your family **six** or **seven** days if you eat out often.*

BREAD / CEREAL / GRAINS

Bisquick, 1 box
cereal,
   bran, 1 box
   Kellogg's Rice Krispies, 1 box

FRESH FRUITS
AND VEGETABLES

Or purchase other fruits and vegetables that are in season or on sale.

apples, 8
avocados, 1
bananas, 8
dates, 2 lbs.
grapes, red or green seedless, 2 cups
lemon, 1
melons,
   cantaloupe, 1
   honeydew, 1
   watermelon, 1/2 to 1 whole
nectarines, 8
oranges, 4
peaches, 8
plums, 8
raisins, 1/2 lb.
strawberries, 1 quart

carrots, baby, 1 small bag
cauliflower, 1 head
celery, 1 bunch
lettuce, leafy, 1 large bunch
onions, 2
onions, green, 1 bunch
peppers, green, 6
potatoes, sweet (yams), 2
radishes, 1 bunch
sprouts, 1 package
tomatoes,
   cherry, 1 pint
   medium, 4
zucchini, 3

MEAT AND DAIRY

crab, imitation, 1 lb.

cottage cheese, lowfat, 1 pint
cream cheese, nonfat, 2 oz.
cream cheese, nonfat strawberry, 2 oz.
eggs, 1 to 2 dozen *(you'll use mostly whites; or use powdered egg whites)*
milk, skim or 1%, 1 to 2 gallons
sour cream, nonfat, 2 pints

CANNED GOODS / MISC.

chilies, green, diced, one 4 oz. can
onions, whole, one 16 oz. can

almonds, slivered, 1 oz.
coconut, 2 oz.

MASTER LIST / CHECK LIST
DAYS 13 – 16

Check to be sure that you have the following Master List items already in stock. Baking items, condiments, and spices are not included in this list. They are listed on pages 59 and 60.

BREAD / CEREAL / GRAIN

Purchase breads, rolls, buns, etc., on sale and freeze.

bread, whole-wheat, 1 to 2 loaves
pita pockets, whole-wheat, 1 dozen
rice, brown or white 2 cups
tortillas, whole-wheat, 2 dozen

MEAT AND DAIRY

Purchase in moderate quantities on sale and freeze. Grate cheese before freezing.

chicken, pieces, 1 lb.
fish, red snapper, four 6 oz. fillets
turkey, breast, 1 lb. *(if no leftovers)*

butter, 1/2 lb.
cheese,
    cheddar, grated, 6 oz.
    mozzarella, part-skim, 1 lb.
    (grated if desired)

CANNED GOODS

applesauce*, unsweetened or lightly
    sweetened, two 16 oz. cans
beans*,
    green, two 16 oz. cans
    refried, no fat added, two 16 oz. cans
    white, one 16 oz can
broth, chicken, two 10 1/2 oz. cans
carrots, sliced, one 16 oz. can *(or frozen is more nutritious)*
chili, chicken, two 15 oz. cans
corn, whole kernel, one 17 oz. can
juice, V-8, four 6 oz. cans
milk, evaporated skim, two 12 oz. cans
picante sauce, hot, medium, or mild,
    two 16 oz. jars
pineapple,
    chunks, in own juice, one 20 oz. can
    rings, in own juice, one 20 oz. can
soup, Campbell's Split Pea,
    two 19 oz. cans
spaghetti sauce, one 28 oz. jar or can
tomatoes, chopped, one 14 1/2 oz. can

FROZEN

apple-juice concentrate, one 12 oz. can
pineapple-juice concentrate, one 12 oz. can
(if you make the "Date Bars—No-Sugar Style")

You may choose to save leftover applesauce and leftover puréed beans in 1/2 cup containers and freeze for future use in muffin, cake, and cookie recipes.

81

FREEDOM MENUS

DAY 17

			fg/cal
	Breakfast		
Water	12 oz. water		
Grain	four 5" Blender Whole-Wheat Pancakes* p. 176		8/344
Protein	1 1/2 cups nonfat vanilla yogurt		0/270
Fruit	1 cup mixed fresh or frozen (thawed) blueberries, raspberries, and boysenberries (or other in-season fruit)		t/80*
Water/Snack	8 oz. water/ 1 cup mixed raw vegetables		t/50*

	Lunch		
Water	12 oz. water		
Vegetable	1 cup sliced purple cabbage		t/20
Grain	2 slices whole-grain toast with 2 Tb. fat free cream cheese and 2 Tb. Smuckers Simply Fruit Spread		1/268
Protein	one 19 oz. can Progresso Split Pea and Ham Soup		6/320
Fruit	1 cup pineapple chunks in vanilla yogurt		t/180
Water/Snack	8 oz. water/ 1 cup celery sticks		t/18

	Dinner		
Easy			
Water	8 oz. water		
Vegetable	large baked potato with 1/2 cup lowfat cottage cheese and 2 Tb. Buttermilk Dressing* p. 210		3/362
	1 1/2 cups broccoli		t/69
Grain	2 Marvelous Muffins* p. 231		6/296
Protein	5 oz. Orange Roughy with Tartar Sauce* p. 253		8/254
Fruit	one 2" slice Strawberry Pie* p. 199 ("B" Choice)		7/180
Water/Snack	12 oz. water/ 1 cup cauliflower chunks		t/24

82

Total: 38/2467

38 fat grams x 9 calories = 342 calories from fat

342 ÷ 2467 = **14% FAT**

If your body is already under 20 percent fat and you'd like to be lower, you may find that a 10 to 15 percent fat range in your menus is ideal for body fat loss for you. But remember that children and those not interested in fat loss may choose to keep their "good" fat percentage in the 20 to 30 percent range.

DAY 18

		Breakfast	fg/cal
	Water	8 oz. water	
	Grain	11/2 cups Kellogg's Just Right Cereal	2/280
	Protein	11/2 cups skim milk	t/129
	Fruit	(in cereal)	
	Water/Snack	12 oz. water	

		Lunch	
	Water	8 oz. water	
	Vegetable	one 19 oz. can Campbell's Chunky Steak and Potato Soup and 1 stalk celery or baby carrots	8/340±
	Grain	2 slices whole-wheat toast	1/142
	Protein	(meat in soup)	
	Fruit	1 cup chunky mixed fruit cocktail in fruit juice	t/112
	Water/Snack	8 oz. water/ 3 cups Light Butter Popcorn* p. 225	3/80±

		Dinner	
	Water	8 oz. water	
	Vegetable	11/2 cups mixed steamed vegetables with 1 tsp. butter	4/150
	Grain	13/4 cups Cappelino Primavera* p. 235	6/383
	Protein	one 8 oz. glass skim milk	t/86
	Fruit	1 piece Apple Cobbler* p. 187 ("B+" Choice)	6/316
	Water/Snack	12 oz. water	
		1 cup steamed veggies	t/76

Total: 30/2094

30 fat grams x 9 calories = 270 calories from fat

270 ÷ 2094 = **13% FAT**

*This "A" day includes a delicious "B+"Choice dessert. Some people have very resistant bodies and see more optimal fat loss with no desserts. Others see excellent results with desserts that are moderate in fat **after** full satisfaction on water, veggie, grain, protein, and fruit. Adjust to your individual needs and enjoy!*

83

FREEDOM MENUS

DAY 19

		Breakfast	fg/cal
	Water	8 oz. water	
	Grain	1 cup Breakfast Fruit Compote* p. 168	
		(Prepare large quantities of brown rice	
		and then freeze it, (on Compote) as a big	
		time saver.)	t/264
	Protein	1 cup skim milk (on Compote)	t/86
	Fruit	(in compote)	
	Water/Snack	8 oz. water/ 1 cup Breakfast Fruit Compote,	t/264
		1 cup skim milk	t/86
		1 sliced turnip	t/36

		Lunch	
	Water	8 oz. water	
	Vegetable	(lettuce and tomato on sandwich)	
	Grain	1 Ham 'n Cheese Sandwich* p. 249	13/406
	Protein	(ham and cheese)	
	Fruit	2 cups honeydew melon chunks	
		(or canned fruit in light syrup)	t/120
	Water/Snack	12 oz. water/ 1 cup raw, mixed vegetables	
		(or steamed)	t/50*

		Dinner	
Easy			
	Water	8 oz. water	
	Vegetable	2 cups Tossed Salad with 8 Tb. Easy	
		Lowfat Dressing* p. 211	2/390*
	Grain	one 3" square Veggie Lasagna* p. 243	10/350
	Protein	(cheese)	
	Fruit	3/4 cup Fruit Gelatin* p. 214	0/75
	Water/Snack	8 oz. water	

Total: 25/2127

25 fat grams x 9 calories = 225 calories from fat

$225 \div 2127 = $ **11% FAT**

The LEAN & FREE Ham 'n Cheese Sandwich is 29 percent fat. The Lasagna is 26 percent fat. Notice how nicely these two choices fit into an overall day of only 11 percent fat because the days focus is on vegetables, grains, and fruits with moderate amounts of lowfat dairy products and lean meats.

DAY 20

		Breakfast	fg/cal
	Water	12 oz. water	
	Grain	three 5" Super Quick Pancakes* p. 177	6/309
		with 8 Tb. maple syrup (For fat loss, enjoy	
		All Fruit Jam and nonfat fruit yogurt.)	0/440
	Protein	(milk in Jubilee; and yogurt)	
	Fruit	1 cup Orange Jubilee* p. 174	0/157
	Water/Snack	8 oz. water	

		Lunch	
Fast Food			
Dairy Queen			
	Water	8 oz. water	
	Vegetable	(in sandwich)	
	Grain	1 Grilled Chicken Sandwich with	
		extra lettuce, tomato, pickle, and onion	
		(omit mayonnaise)	8/300
	Protein	(chicken in sandwich)	
	Fruit	1 large Chocolate-Banana Blueberry or	
		Strawberry (etc.) Yogurt Breeze	
		("B" Choice this is not for diabetics or	
		those resistant to fat loss.)	1/300±
	Water/Snack	12 oz. water	
		1 cup sliced purple cabbage	t/20

		Dinner	
Easy			
	Water	8 oz. water	
	Vegetable	1 1/2 cups steamed carrots and 1 tsp. butter	4/141
	Grain	1 cup brown rice	t/180
	Protein	1 cup Chicken Divan* p. 181	5/245
	Fruit	3/4 cup Fruit Gelatin left over from Day 19	0/75
	Water/Snack	12 oz. water	

Total: 24/2167

24 fat grams x 9 calories = 216 calories from fat

216 ÷ 2167 = **10% FAT**

When I'm in the mood for an extra large, double thick chocolate malt (one of my favorite desserts equaling about 30 fat grams), I get a chocolate-banana or a chocolate-malt Yogurt Breeze at Dairy Queen. This is a delicious "B" Choice with virtually no fat in it at all, depending on the flavorings used. But I don't have this when I'm really intent on seeing fat loss.

FREEDOM MENUS

*This **four**-day shopping list may last your family **six** or **seven** days if you eat out often.*

BREAD / CEREAL / GRAIN

bread crumbs, 1 to 2 cups
cereal, Kellogg's Just Right, 1 box
crackers, graham or gingersnaps, 1 box
    ("B" Choice)
pancake mix, whole-wheat, 1 medium-
    size bag
pasta, angel hair, 1 lb.

FRESH FRUITS
AND VEGETABLES

Or purchase other fruits and vegetables that are in season or on sale.

apples,
    green, 8
    red, 2
melon, honeydew, 1 large
strawberries, 2 quarts

broccoli, 5 bunches
cabbage, purple, 1 large head
carrots,
    regular, 4 lbs.
    baby, 1 small bag
cauliflower, 1 head
celery, 1 bunch
cucumbers, 3
lettuce, leafy, 2 large bunches
mushrooms, 1 cup
onions, yellow, 2
parsley, 1 bunch
peppers, green, 2
potatoes, baking, 4
tomatoes, medium, 5
turnips, 4
zucchini, 2

MEAT AND DAIRY

buttermilk, 1 pint
cottage cheese, lowfat, two 16 oz.
    cartons
cream cheese, nonfat, 4 oz.
cream, whipped, lowfat, 8 oz.
eggs, 1 dozen *(you'll use mostly whites)*
milk, skim or 1%, 1 to 2 gallons
ricotta cheese, fat free, 4 oz.
yogurt,
    fruit, nonfat, 32 oz.
    vanilla, nonfat, one to two 32 oz.
        containers

FROZEN

boysenberries, 8 oz.

MASTER LIST / CHECK LIST
DAYS 17 – 20

Check to be sure that you have the following Master List items already in stock. Baking items, condiments, and spices are not included in this list. They are listed on pages 59-60.

BREAD / CEREAL / GRAIN

Purchase breads, rolls, buns, etc., on sale and freeze.

bread, whole-wheat, 1 to 2 loaves
lasagna, whole-grain or white, 1 lb.
popcorn, microwave light,
    one 4-count package
rice, brown or white, 2 cups

MEAT AND DAIRY

Purchase in moderate quantities on sale and freeze. Grate cheese before freezing.

chicken, breasts, boneless and skinless, 2
ham, extra-lean, thinly sliced, 4 oz.
fish, orange roughy, 4 fillets

butter, 1 lb.
cheese,
    cheddar, grated, 2 oz.
    mozzarella, part-skim, grated, 10 oz.
    Parmesan, grated, fresh or canned, 6 oz.

CANNED GOODS

applesauce*, unsweetened or lightly
    sweetened, one 16 oz. can
beans*, white, one 15 oz. can
fruit cocktail, in own juice,
    two 16 oz. cans
pineapple, chunks, in own juice,
    one 20 oz. can
soup,
    Campbell's Chunky Steak and Potato,
        four 19 oz. cans
    lowfat cream of chicken,
        one 103/4 oz. can
    Progresso Split Pea and Ham,
        four 19 oz. cans
tomato paste, three 6 oz. cans

FROZEN

blueberries, one 8 oz. bag
juice concentrates,
    apple, two 12 oz. cans
    Dole Mountain Cherry, one 12 oz. can
    orange, one 12 oz. can
raspberries, 8 oz.
vegetables, mixed, two 16 oz. bags

*See the statement at the bottom of page 81

FREEDOM MENUS

DAY 21

		fg/cal
	Breakfast	
Water	8 oz. water	
Grain	2 cups Post Raisin Nut Bran	8/400
Protein	1 1/2 cups skim milk	t/129
Fruit	(in cereal)	
Water/Snack	12 oz. water/ 1 cup Raisin Nut Bran	4/200
	3/4 cup skim milk	t/64
	1/2 fresh cup broccoli chunks (or steamed)	t/12

	Lunch	
Water	8 oz. water	
Vegetable	2 cups Tossed Salad* p. 267 with	
	8 Tb. Easy Lowfat Dressing* p. 211	2/390±
Grain	3 slices whole or part whole-grain toast with	
	3 Tb. Simply Fruit Spread	1/357
Protein	1 1/2 cups Campbell's Barbecue Beans	6/375
Fruit	2 nectarines	2/134
Water/Snack	12 oz. water/ 6 cups Lite Butter Popcorn*	
	p. 225	6/160±

	Dinner	
Water	8 oz. water	
Vegetable	1 1/2 cups Mashed Potatoes* p.246 with	
	1 cup Quick Turkey Gravy* p. 222	t/287
	1 1/2 cups Great Green Beans* p. 265	4.5/144
Grain	2 Pumpkin-Carrot Muffins* p. 233	2/240
Protein	4 oz. Cranberry-Glazed Turkey Breast*	
	p. 182	4/388±
Fruit	1 1/2 cups fresh green grapes, pineapple	
	rings, and strawberries	t/150±
	one 2" slice Pumpkin Pie* p. 197 with 1 cup	
	ice milk ("B–" Choice)	12/387
Water/Snack	12 oz. water / 1 cup raw mixed vegetables	
	(or steamed)	t/50±

Total: 51.5**/3867

51.5 fat grams x 9 calories = 463.5 calories from fat

463.5 ÷ 3867 = **12% FAT**

This day represents the way I ate for fat loss when I was nursing a baby. If I was down around 3,000 calories and I forgot to snack on veggies, I saw zero fat loss. When I ate like this, I dropped from my post-pregnancy size 10 to a size 4 in two months. Other nursing mothers may need more or less. They must learn to listen to their bodies.

**Remember that fat gram numbers are irrelevant. It's your overall daily and weekly fat percentage that counts. This day has 51.5 fat grams, yet is only 12 percent fat because of its high calorie number. Your body handles fat differently when it is combined with more good, high-fiber food. Some fat may actually attach to the fiber and be wasted from your body.

DAY 22

			fg/cal
	Breakfast		
	Water	8 oz. water	
	Grain	2 Cranberry-Orange Muffins* p. 230 (Make ahead in quantity and freeze to save time and money.)	t/270
	Protein	(yogurt)	
	Fruit	1 cup Yogurt Fruit Delight* p. 219 (Double this recipe if you'd like some left over for dinner.)	0/146
	Water/Snack	8 oz. water/ 5 baby carrots	0/20
	Lunch		
	Water	8 oz. water	
	Vegetable	(lettuce, pickles, tomatoes, and onions on sandwich)	
	Grain	1 Corned Beef Sandwich* p. 249 with mustard, 1 tsp. nonfat salad dressing, and 1 tsp. nonfat mayonnaise	3/293
	Protein	(1 slice corned beef)	
	Fruit	1 apple	t/81
	Water/Snack	12 oz. water/ 1 Corned Beef Sandwich left over from lunch	3/293
		1 cup honeydew melon chunks	t/60
Easy	**Dinner**		
	Water	8 oz. water	
	Vegetable	1 cup sliced purple cabbage	t/26
	Grain	2 Corn Muffins* p. 229 (or Cranberry-Orange Muffins left over from breakfast)	6/286
	Protein	1 cup Chili Skillet* p. 237	7/369
	Fruit	1 cup Yogurt Fruit Delight left over from breakfast	0/146
	Water/Snack	12 oz. water/ 1/2 cup leftover cabbage	t/13
		1 Corn Muffin left over from dinner	3/143
		8 oz. skim milk	t/86

Total: 22/2232

22 fat grams x 9 calories = 198 calories from fat

198 ÷ 2232 = **9% FAT****

*We love Yogurt Fruit Delight at our house. We make it with nonfat or lowfat fruit yogurt and fresh or canned (in light syrup) fruit.

**This particular day is a little low in fat, but your overall week averages out nicely to between 10 and 20 percent fat; and if you add in the "traces" of fat, this becomes a 10% fat day.

DAY 23

			fg/cal
		Breakfast	
	Water	12 oz. water	
	Grain	2 slices whole- or cracked-grain toast	1/142
		with 2 Tb. All Fruit Jam* p. 164	t/32
	Protein	1 cup Veggie and Cheese Egg	
		Scramble* p. 175	9/289
	Fruit	1 cup Orange Jubilee* p. 174	0/157
	Water/Snack	8 oz. water/ 1 sliced zucchini with	
		2 Tb. Ranch Dip left over from Day 23	t/53

Fast Food		**Lunch**	
Arby's			
	Water	16 oz. water	
	Vegetable	(extra tomatoes, pickles, and	
		onions in sandwiches)	
	Grain	1 Light Roast Chicken and 1 Light Roast	
		Turkey Deluxe Sandwiches (sparing with	
		light mayonnaise)	13/536
	Protein	(chicken and turkey in sandwiches)	
	Fruit	(tomato in sandwiches)	
	Water/Snack	8 oz. water	
		(Save one sandwich for a snack if you're	
		comfortably satisfied eating *one* at your meal.)	

Easy		**Dinner**	
	Water	8 oz. water	
	Vegetable	1 cup corn/ 1 cup green beans	2/220
	Grain	2 cups Spaghetti* p. 242 with 1 cup Quick	
		Spaghetti Sauce* p. 221	4/478
		1 slice Garlic-Cheese Toast* p. 159	
		("B–" Choice)	5/118
	Protein	1/4 cup grated Parmesan cheese	6/92
	Fruit	1 cup green grapes	t/108
		one 2" square Texas Brownie* p. 200	
		("B–" Choice – not for fat loss or for diabetics)	4/138
	Water/Snack	12 oz. water	

90

> Total: 44/2363
> 44 fat grams x 9 calories = 396 calories from fat
> 396 ÷ 2363 = **17% FAT**

*Texas Brownies rate a "B–", whereas most higher-fat, higher-sugar brownies rate a "C" or "D." Individuals who are **not** highly resistant to fat loss may see fat loss while including "B–" desserts **after** a balanced meal.*

FREEDOM MENUS

TIME SAVER

DAY 24

		Breakfast	fg/cal
	Water	8 oz. water	
	Grain	2 cups General Mills Multi Grain Cheerios	2/200
	Protein	11/2 cups skim milk	t/129
	Fruit	1/2 cup blueberries (on cereal, fresh or frozen and slightly thawed)	t/41
	Water/Snack	12 oz. water/ 1 cup sliced cucumbers	t/39

		Lunch	
	Water	8 oz. water	
	Vegetable	1 sliced zucchini with 2 Tb. Delicious Dill Dip* p. 211 1 sliced tomato	1/88
	Grain	(2 slices whole- or part whole-grain toast)	1/142
	Protein	11/2 cups Creamed Tuna on Toast* p. 252	4.5/246
	Fruit	3 plums	t/108
	Water/Snack	12 oz. water/ 11/2 cups Mixed Veggie Festival* p. 265	3/243

Easy		Dinner	
	Water	8 oz. water	
	Vegetable	1 cup mixed raw vegetables with 4 Tb. Ranch Dip* p. 212	t/120±
	Grain	2 whole-grain rolls	t/90
		with 2 Tb. All Fruit Jam* p. 164	t/32
	Protein	11/3 cups Fast and Creamy Clam Chowder* p. 257	2/138
	Fruit	1 cup Yogurt Fruit Delight* p. 219 or plain fresh or canned fruit	0/146
	Water/Snack	12 oz. water	

Total: 13.5/1762

13.5 fat grams x 9 calories =121.5 calories from fat

$121.5 \div 1762 = \textbf{7\% FAT**}$

*Snacking on complex carbohydrates is essential for optimal body-fat loss because of the increased heat production of the body during the digestion process. This process is called thermogenesis.

**Seven percent fat is low for one day, but your overall week averages to between 10 and 20 percent fat.

SHOPPING LIST / DAYS 21 – 24

*This four-day shopping list may last your
family six or seven days if you eat out often.*

BREAD / CEREAL / GRAINS

cereal,
General Mills Multi Grain Cheerios,
1 box
Post Raisin Nut Bran, 1 box
crackers, graham or gingersnaps,
1 box *("B" Choice)*

FRESH FRUITS
AND VEGETABLES

*Or purchase other fruits and vegetables
that are in season or on sale.*

apples, 4
cranberries, 8 oz.
grapes, 6 lbs.
melon, honeydew, 1
nectarines, 8
orange, 1
plums, 12
raisins, 1 lb.
strawberries, 1 quart

broccoli, 3 bunches
cabbage, purple, 1 head
carrots, 5 lbs.
carrots, baby, 1 small bag
cucumbers, 8
lettuce, leafy, 2 large bunches
onions,
yellow, 3
green, 2 bunches

peppers, green, 3
potatoes, baking, 11
tomatoes, medium, 7
zucchini, 8

MEAT AND DAIRY

corned beef, extra-lean, sliced, 8 oz.

buttermilk, 1 quart
cottage cheese, lowfat, 8 oz.
cream cheese, lowfat, 4 oz.
eggs, 1 to 2 dozen *(You'll use
mostly whites.)*
milk, skim or 1%, 1 to 2 gallons
sour cream, nonfat, 16 oz.
yogurt, nonfat, vanilla, 32 oz.
yogurt, nonfat fruit-flavored, 32 oz.

CANNED GOODS

beans, Campbell's BBQ, six 16 oz. cans
clams, minced, 2 small cans
cranberry sauce, one 16 oz. can
pumpkin, two 16 oz. cans

FROZEN / MISC.

ice milk, 1 quart ("B" Choice: not
for fat loss)

chocolate chips, 6 oz. *("B–" Choice:
not for fat loss)*
corn syrup, 4 oz. *("B" Choice: not for
fat loss)*

MASTER LIST / CHECK LIST
DAYS 21 - 24

Check to be sure that you have the following Master List items already in stock. Baking items, condiments, and spices are not included in this list. They are listed on pages 59 - 60.

BREAD / CEREAL / GRAIN

Purchase breads, rolls, buns, etc., on sale and freeze.

bread, whole-wheat, 1 to 2 loaves
macaroni, whole-wheat or white, 8 oz.
popcorn, microwave light,
    one 4-count package
rolls, whole-grain, 8
spaghetti, whole-wheat or white, 16 oz.

MEAT AND DAIRY

Purchase in moderate quantities on sale and freeze. Grate cheese before freezing.

beef, extra-lean ground, 1/2 lb.
turkey, precooked extra-lean roast, 1

butter, 1 lb.
cheese,
    mozzarella, part-skim, grated 8 oz.
    Parmesan, grated fresh or canned,
        8 oz.

CANNED GOODS

applesauce, unsweetened or lightly
    sweetened, one 16 oz. can
beans,
    green, three 16 oz. cans
    white, one 15 oz. can *(Or use
    frozen-thawed leftovers from the last
        time you made muffins.)*
corn, whole-kernel, three 17 oz. cans
fruit cocktail, chunky, unsweetened or
    lightly sweetened, six 16 oz. cans
oranges, mandarin, one 11 oz. can
pineapple,
    chunks, in own juice, one 20 oz. can
    rings, in own juice, one 20 oz. can
soup,
    lowfat cream of celery,
        one 10 3/4 oz. can
    Campbell's Cream of Potato,
        one 10 3/4 oz. can
spaghetti sauce, lowfat, 1 jar or can
tomatoes, stewed, 1 quart
tuna, water-pack, two 6 1/2 oz. cans

FROZEN

blueberries, one 16 oz. bag
juice concentrates, orange,
    two 12 oz. cans
vegetables, mixed, five 16 oz. bags

MISCELLANEOUS

gravy mix, turkey, 4 packages
salad dressing, Hidden Valley Lite
    Ranch Dressing, 1 package
nuts, 1/3 cup, *(optional)*

FREEDOM MENUS

93

DAY 25

			fg/cal
		Breakfast	
	Water	12 oz. water	
	Grain	three 5" Peach	
		Pancakes* p. 177	6/276
	Protein	1 cup nonfat vanilla yogurt	0/180
	Fruit	11/2 cups peach slices,	
		fresh or canned in extra-light syrup (Serve	
		peaches and yogurt on top of pancakes.)	t/164
	Water/Snack	8 oz. water/ 1 cup corn and green beans	
		left over from Day 24	1/100
Easy		**Lunch**	
	Water	12 oz. water	
	Vegetable	1 cup mixed raw	
		vegetables with 4 Tb. Creamy Onion	
		Dip* p. 210	2/130
	Grain	2 slices whole-grain toast with 2 Tb.	
		Simply Fruit Spread	1/238
	Protein	11/2 cups homemade Creamy	
		Bean and Ham Soup* p. 256 (or Campbell's)	1/365
	Fruit	1 sliced apple	t/81
	Water/Snack	8 oz. water/ 1 sliced green pepper	t/26
Easy		**Dinner**	
	Water	8 oz. water	
	Vegetable	1 cup sliced purple cabbage	t/26
	Grain	2 cups LEAN & FREE Nachos* p. 145	
		("B" Choice)	10/271
	Protein	1 cup Chili Skillet* p. 237	7/369
	Fruit	11/2 cups Fresh-fruit Combination Trays*	
		p. 213 with 1/2 cup Sour Cream Fruit	
		Dip* p. 212	t/310
	Water/Snack	12 oz. water/ 1 cup leftover cabbage	t/26

Total: 28/2562
28 fat grams x 9 calories = 252 calories from fat
252 ÷ 2562 = **10% FAT**

Leftovers make great snacks and excellent "GRAB 'N' GO" meals. Remember, if you're on the run, mix and match the Quick & Easy and Fast-Food meals. Even if all you eat are veggies, fruits, whole-grain cereals, canned soups, and fast food "LEAN & FREE STYLE" sandwiches, you'll most likely be eating better than 95 percent of the population!

A variety of LEAN & FREE *Pancakes topped with cherry
and peach Fruit Syrup*

Creamy Bean and Ham Soup and Short-Cut Tossed Salad

Pizza Wheels and Yogurt Fruit Delight

Lean & Free Peanut Butter and Jelly Sandwiches, purple cabbage slices with Delicious Dill Dip, and pears for dessert

DAY 26

			fg/cal
		Breakfast	
	Water	16 oz. water	
	Grain	1 cup Cracked Wheat, Raisin, and Honey Cereal* p. 169 with 2 Tb. honey	1/450±
	Protein	1 cup skim milk	t/86
	Fruit	1 cup sliced strawberries (or another in-season fruit)	1/45
	Water/Snack	8 oz. water/ vegetables/ 1 1/4 cups Cheerios with 1 cup skim milk	2/246±

		Lunch	
	Water	8 oz. water	
	Vegetable	1 1/2 cups sliced cucumbers and tomatoes in vinegar and water	t/50±
	Grain	(whole-wheat bread)	
	Protein	1 LEAN & FREE Peanut Butter and Jam Sandwich* p. 251 ("B+" Choice)	12/400
	Fruit	2 pears (fresh or rinsed)	0/196
	Water/Snack	12 oz. water/ 1 cup cucumbers and tomatoes	t/35±

		Dinner	
	Easy		
	Water	12 oz. water	
	Vegetable	3/4 cup Veggie and Cheese Egg Scramble* p. 175 ("B+" choice)	7/217
		3/4 cup Hash Browns p. 246	6/155
	Grain	two 4" Belgian Waffles p. 166 with 4 Tb. Fruit Syrup* p. 214	4/200
	Protein	(egg and cheese in Scramble)	
	Fruit	1 sliced orange	t/62
	Water/Snack	8 oz. water/ 1 cup cauliflower chunks	t/24

Total: 33/2166

33 fat grams x 9 calories = 297 calories from fat

297 ÷ 2166 = **14% FAT**

Even a peanut-butter sandwich fits well into this 14 percent fat day. Skippy Reduced Fat Peanut Butter has six grams of fat per tablespoon and is 27 percent fat. It contains good fat, but be moderate with it if you are trying to lose excess body fat.

DAY 27

		fg/cal
Easy	**Breakfast**	
Water	8 oz. water	
Grain	2 Cheese Muffins* p. 228	12/370
Protein	1 cup skim milk	t/86
Fruit	2 cups honeydew melon chunks	t/120
Water/Snack	12 oz. water	
	1 cup cucumbers and tomatoes left over from Day 26 (or other veggies if you don't have leftovers)	t/35±
	Lunch	
Water	8 oz. water	
Vegetable	1 cup Lentil and Barley Soup* p. 258 (prepared earlier and warmed up to save time)	1/238
Grain	1 Club Sandwich* p. 249	4/410
Protein	(meat in sandwich) and 1 cup skim milk	t/86
Fruit	1 sliced orange	t/62
Water/Snack	8 oz. water	
Easy	**Dinner**	
Water	8 oz. water	
Vegetable	2 cups steamed broccoli with 1 tsp. butter	4/128
Grain	1 cup Homemade Noodles* p. 242 with 1/2 cup Mushroom Gravy* p. 220	5/294
Protein	one 5 oz. Parmesan Halibut Steak* p. 254	8/245
Fruit	one 4" slice Whole-Wheat Angel Food Cake* p. 202 ("B+" Choice) with 1 cup strawberries	1/285
Water/Snack	12 oz. water	

Total: 35/2359

35 fat grams x 9 calories = 315 calories from fat

315 ÷ 2359 = **13% FAT**

Scratch muffins are quick and easy to prepare. Double or triple the recipe and freeze some for later. Or faster yet, purchase lowfat, low-sugar, whole-grain muffins or muffin mixes at your grocery store. Or simply use regular whole-wheat or cracked-wheat breads and rolls instead.

Make certain you know the fat content of store-bought muffins. Some of the jumbo bakery muffins contain 20 to 30 fat grams each and some are also very high in sugar. If your bakery can't provide you with nutrition facts about their muffins, don't eat them. Your local bakery might even make "your" lowfat, high-fiber recipes. Ask if you can special-order large quantities. Then freeze them in freezer bags for future use.

FREEDOM MENUS

DAY 28

		Breakfast	fg/cal
	Water	12 oz. water	
	Grain	2 slices whole-grain toast with 2 Tb. Smucker's Simply Fruit Spread	t/238
	Protein	1 Fried Egg* p. 172	6.5/83
	Fruit	2 cups cantaloupe chunks	1/114
	Water/Snack	8 oz. water/ 1 1/2 cups corn flakes, 1 cup skim milk, and 1 sliced banana	t/341
		6 oz. V-8 juice	0/35

		Lunch	
Fast Food			
Chick-Fil-A			
	Water	8 oz. water	
	Vegetable	1 large bowl Breast of Chicken Soup	9/432
	Grain	2 Better Bran Muffins* p. 227 (from home or big, soft Pretzelmaker pretzels are a good "A–" Choice—delicious too!)	4/184
	Protein	(in soup)	
	Fruit	1 large serving Chick-Fil-A Carrot-Raisin Salad	5/116
	Water/Snack	12 oz. water/ 1 Better Bran Muffin* p. 227	2/92
		1 cup chunk raw veggies	t/50±
		1 cup skim milk	t /86

		Dinner	
	Water	8 oz. water	
	Vegetable	2 cups Chinese Salad Bar* p. 262	t/250±
	Grain	(Chinese Noodles)	
	Protein	1 cup Pork Chow Mein* p.154 and 3/4 cup Egg Drop Soup* p.257	10/387
	Fruit	1 1/2 cups Tropical Fruit Ice* p. 218	1/228
		1 fortune cookie	t/30
	Water/Snack	12 oz. water/ 1 cup leftover Chinese Salad Bar	t/125

Total: 38.5/2791

38.5 fat grams x 9 calories = 346.5 calories from fat

346.5 ÷ 2791 = **12% FAT**

Chinese food can be one of your best or one of your worst eating-out choices. Go for rice and lots of veggies. Avoid deep-fried dishes completely, especially if you suffer from high cholesterol or are highly resistant to fat loss.

FREEDOM MENUS

SHOPPING LIST / DAY 25 – 28

*This **four**-day shopping list may last your family **six** or **seven** days if you eat out often.*

BREAD / CEREAL / GRAINS

cereal,
General Mills Cheerios, 1 box
cornflakes, 1 box
Post Raisin Bran, 1 box
pancake mix, whole-wheat, 1 small bag

FRESH FRUITS AND VEGETABLES

Or purchase other fruits and vegetables that are in season or on sale.

apples, 6
bananas, 8
grapes, 1 lb.
kiwifruit, 4
melons,
cantaloupes, 2
honeydew, 1
oranges, 12
peaches, 6
raisins, 8 oz.
strawberries, 3 quarts

broccoli, 4 bunches
cabbage,
green, 1 head
purple, 1 head
carrots, 5 lbs.
cauliflower, 1 head
celery, 2 bunches
cucumbers, 5

garlic, 1
lettuce, leafy, 2 large bunches
onions,
green, 2 bunches
yellow, 4
pea pods, 8 oz.
peppers, green, 6
tomatoes,
cherry, 1 pint
slicing, medium, 5

MEAT AND DAIRY

beef, extra-lean, sliced, 8 oz.
ham, extra-lean, 8 oz.
pork, extra-lean, 8 oz.

buttermilk, 1 quart
cottage cheese, lowfat, 8 oz.
cream cheese, nonfat, 4 oz.
eggs, 1 dozen *(you'll use mostly whites)*
milk, skim or 1%, 2 gallons
sour cream, nonfat, 16 oz.
yogurt, vanilla, nonfat, 1 quart

CANNED GOODS / MISC.

cookies, fortune, 1 bag *("B" Choice)*
peanut butter, Skippy Reduced Fat,
1 jar *("B+" Choice)*
salad dressing, Catalina fat free, 1 bottle
tortilla chips, baked, 1 bag

MASTER LIST / CHECK LIST
Days 25 - 28

Check to be sure that you have the following Master List items already in stock. Baking items, condiments, and spices are not included in this list. They are listed on pages 59 - 60.

BREAD / CEREAL / GRAIN

Purchase breads, rolls, buns, etc., on sale and freeze.

barley, 8 oz.
barley flour, 4 oz.
bread, whole-wheat, 1 to 2 loaves
macaroni, whole-wheat or white, 8 oz.
wheat, whole-kernel, 21/2 cups

MEAT AND DAIRY

Purchase in moderate quantities on sale and freeze. Grate cheese before freezing.

beef, extra-lean, ground, 1 lb.
fish, halibut steaks, 4
ham, sliced, extra-lean, 8 oz.
turkey, sliced, lean, 8 oz.

butter, 1/2 lb.
cheese,
    cheddar, grated, 8 oz.
    mozzarella, part-skim, grated 8 oz.
    parmesan, fresh or canned, 6 oz.
eggs, 1 dozen *(You'll use mostly whites.)*

CANNED GOODS

applesauce*, unsweetened or lightly
    sweetened, one 16 oz. can
bamboo shoots, two 8 oz. cans
bean,
    navy, two 15 oz. cans

refried, lowfat or nonfat,
    one 16 oz. can
sprouts, two 14 oz. cans
white*, one 16 oz. can
broth, chicken or beef,
    six 101/2 oz. cans or 3 large cans
carrots, two 16 oz. cans
corn, whole-kernel, one 17 oz. can
juice, V-8, four 6 oz. cans
milk, evaporated skim, one 12 oz. can
mushrooms, one 4 oz. can
noodles, chow-mein, one 5 oz. can
olives, 1 small can
oranges, mandarin, three 11 oz. cans
pears, in own juice, one 16 oz. can
pineapple, chunks, in own juice,
    one 20 oz. can
salsa, 1 medium-size jar
soup,
    lowfat cream of mushroom,
        two 103/4 oz. cans
    dry onion, 1 package
tomato sauce, one 8 oz. can
tomatoes, stewed, two 28 oz. cans
    or 2 quarts
tomatoes, one 16 oz. can
water chestnuts, one 8 oz. can

FROZEN

juice concentrates,
    apple, one 12 oz. can
    pineapple, one 12 oz. can
potatoes, hash browns, two 16 oz. bags
vegetables, mixed, one 16 oz. bag
vegetables; peas, carrots, and corn,
    one 16 oz. bag

MISCELLANEOUS

lentils, 8 oz.
potatoes, instant mashed, 8 servings

See the italics statement at the bottom of page 81.

99

DAY 29

		Breakfast	fg/cal
	Water	8 oz. water	
	Grain	1 cup Kellogg's Basic 4	4/220
	Protein	1 cup skim milk	t/86
	Fruit	(in cereal)	
	Water/Snack	12 oz. water	
		1 cup raw or steamed veggies	t/50±

		Lunch	
	Water	8 oz. water	
	Vegetable	11/2 cups Chinese Salad Bar left over from Day 28 (Make more if you don't have enough leftovers.)	t/187±
	Grain	1 slice Roman Meal Honey Wheat Berry toast with 1 Tb. All Fruit Jam* p. 164	1/82
	Protein	5 oz. Van de Kamp's Today's Catch Fish Fillets	4/100
	Fruit	1/2 cup Pineapple-Marshmallow Coleslaw* p. 216	t/56
		1 cup Dole Mountain Cherry Juice mixed with 1/2 cup 7-Up ("B" Choice - not for fat loss)	t/90
	Water/Snack	12 oz. water/ 1 cup chunk raw veggies	t/50±

		Dinner	
Easy			
	Water	8 oz. water	
	Vegetable	(in Fajitas)	
	Grain	2 Beef Fajitas p. 149	12/550
	Protein	(beef in fajitas) and 1 cup skim milk	t/86
	Fruit	11/2 cups honeydew melon chunks	t/90
	Water/Snack	8 oz. water	

Total: 21/1647

21 fat grams x 9 calories = 189 calories from fat

189 ÷ 1647 = **11% FAT**

If you follow this menu and are still hungry, make certain to increase the veggies, grains, and fruits. Increase proteins (meats and dairy products) moderately. If you're too full, decrease the portion sizes, but keep the balance!

FREEDOM MENUS

DAY 30

		Breakfast	fg/cal
	Water	12 oz. water	
	Grain	1 cup Cinnamon-Maple Oatmeal* p. 169	2/278
	Protein	1 cup skim milk	t/86
	Fruit	1/2 grapefruit (Eat before oatmeal or it will taste too sour.)	0/50
	Water/Snack	8 oz. water/ 1 cup steamed vegetables	t/75±

		Lunch	
	Water	12 oz. water	
	Vegetable	(pickles, tomato, sprouts, lettuce in sandwiches)	
	Grain	(whole-wheat or part whole-wheat bread)	
	Protein	1 Tuna Salad Sandwich* p. 250 (tuna mixed with fat free mayonnaise and fat free salad dressing)	2/400
		1 cup skim milk	t/86
	Fruit	1 large slice honeydew left over from Day 29	t/60
	Water/Snack	8 oz. water	

		Dinner	
Easy			
	Water	12 oz. water	
	Vegetable	1 cup Chicken Veggie Stir-Fry* p. 181	8/367
	Grain	1 cup Brown Rice* p. 223 (use white rice while you gradually adjust to more fiber)	t/180
	Protein	(chicken)	
	Fruit	2 peaches (fresh or light syrup, rinsed)	t/74
	Water/Snack	8 oz. water/ 6 oz. V-8 Juice	0/35

Total: 12/1691
12 fat grams x 9 calories = 108 calories from fat
108 ÷ 1691 = **6% FAT****

*We're hearing a lot about the merits of oat bran. Oat bran is a good choice. However, the whole oat (oatmeal) is much more nutritious than the sum of its parts after they have been separated. So eat the whole oat!

**Six percent fat is low for one day, but your overall week averages to 12.5 percent fat— an ideal fat percentage for individuals who are highly resistant to fat loss (10 to 15 percent). You can easily increase your fat percentage to approximately 20 percent if you are not resistant to fat loss or struggling with high blood cholesterol.

DAY 31

		fg/cal
	Breakfast	
Water	12 oz. water	
Grain	1 cup Cracked Wheat, Raisin, and Honey Cereal* p. 169	1/450
Protein	1 cup skim milk	t/86
Fruit	1 sliced orange	t/62
Water/Snack	8 oz. water	

Easy	**Lunch**	
Water	8 oz. water	
Vegetable	(in salad)	
Grain	1 cup Salmon Pasta Salad* p. 240 ("A–" to "B+" Choice)	14/358
	stuffed in a homemade or store-bought whole-wheat pita pocket	2/150
Protein	(salmon in salad) and 1 cup skim milk	t/86
Fruit	1 fresh pear	0/98
Water/Snack	12 oz. water	

Easy	**Dinner**	
Water	12 oz. water	
Vegetable	2 cups steamed cauliflower, broccoli, and carrots	t/150±
Grain	2/3 cup Brown Rice left over from Day 30 with 2/3 cup Mushroom Gravy* p. 220	2/192
Protein	3 Porcupine Meatballs* p. 153 ("B" Choice)	12/249
Fruit	one 3" square Apple Cake p. 186 ("B" Choice)	7/283
Water/Snack	8 oz. water	

Total: 38/2164

38 fat grams x 9 calories = 342 calories from fat

342 ÷ 2164 = **16% FAT**

If you are highly resistant to fat loss, you may be fine with a small amount of "B" Choice main courses (such as the Porcupine Meatballs) because your day's overall fat percentage is well under 20 percent. However, you may choose to avoid the "B" Choice desserts such as the Apple Cake because of its sugar content that can affect your blood sugar level and insulin level, encouraging your body to resist excess fat loss. Other individuals may have no problem with nutritious desserts after full satisfaction. Listen to your body!

DAY 32

		fg/cal
Easy	**Breakfast**	
Water	8 oz. water	
Grain	2 slices whole-grain toast	1/142
Protein	1 large piece Omelet Supreme* p. 174	
	("B+" Choice)	10/254
Fruit	1 grapefruit	0/100
Water/Snack	16 oz. water/ 1 cup raw or steamed veggies	t/50±

Fast Food	**Lunch**	
Domino's Pizza		
Water	8 oz. water	
Vegetable	(onions, green peppers, and mushrooms on pizza)	
Grain	2 large slices Veggie Fest Pizza ("B+" Choice)	13/390
Protein	(cheese on pizza)	
Fruit	12 oz. Sparkling Apple Juice ("B+" Choice)	0/180
Water/Snack	12 oz. water/ 1 cup chunk raw veggies	t/50±

Easy	**Dinner**	
Water	8 oz. water	
Vegetable	11/2 cups Chicken Broccoli Casserole* p. 180 (Double this recipe if you would like leftovers for tomorrow.)	7/393
Grain	(rice in casserole left over from Day 30)	
Protein	(chicken and cheese in casserole)	
Fruit	3 peach halves on lettuce topped with 1/2 cup lowfat cottage cheese	2/162
Water/Snack	8 oz. water/ 5 baby carrots	0/20

> Total: 33/1741
> 33 fat grams x 9 calories = 297 calories from fat
> 297 ÷ 1741 = **17% FAT**

*Occasionally, sparkling apple juice is a good choice when you want something carbonated. However, for optimal fat loss and good health, be very moderate with carbonated beverages and **avoid diet pop** like the plague!*

Clean, clear water is the ideal beverage for beautiful skin and optimal fat loss.

FREEDOM MENUS

FREEDOM MENUS

SHOPPING LIST / DAYS 29 – 32

*This **four**-day shopping list may last your family **six** or **seven** days if you eat out often.*

BREAD / CEREAL / GRAINS

cereal, Kellogg's Basic 4, 1 box

FRESH FRUITS AND VEGETABLES

Or purchase other fruits and vegetables that are in season or on sale.

apples, 4
grapefruit, 8
melon, honeydew, 2
oranges, 4
pears, 8
raisins, 8 oz.

broccoli, 3 bunches
cabbage, green, 1 head
carrots,
    baby, 1 large bag
    regular, 5 lbs.
cauliflower, 1 head
celery, 2 bunches
lettuce, leafy, 1 large bunch

onions,
    green, 1 bunch
    yellow, medium, 3
peppers,
    green, 8
    red, 4
raisins, 1/2 lb.
sprouts, 1 package
tomatoes, medium, 4

MEAT AND DAIRY

fish, Van de Kamp's Today's Catch
    fillets, 1 box
round steak, extra-lean, 12 oz.

cottage cheese, lowfat, 8 oz.
eggs, 1 dozen *(you'll use mostly whites)*
sour cream, nonfat, 1 pint

CANNED GOODS / MISC.

oriental-style sauce, 1 jar

7-Up, 1 liter *("B" Choice)*
almonds, slivered, 2 oz.
marshmallows, miniature, 1 small bag
    ("B" Choice)
sparkling apple juice *("B+" Choice)*,
    48 oz. *(Or purchase sparkling apple
    juice at fast-food restaurants,
    if available; or simply choose
    "A+" water!)*

MASTER LIST / CHECK LIST
DAYS 29 - 32

Check to be sure that you have the following Master List items already in stock. Baking items, condiments, and spices are not included in this list. They are listed on pages 59 - 60.

BREAD / CEREAL / GRAIN

Purchase breads, rolls, buns, etc., on sale and freeze.

bread, Roman Meal Honey Wheat Berry,
   1 to 2 loaves
oatmeal, 3 cups
pasta, whole-wheat or white, 10 oz. *(dry)*
pita pockets, whole-wheat, 4
rice, brown or white, 2 - 3 cups
tortillas, whole-wheat, or white 1 dozen
wheat, white kernels, 1 - 2 cups

MEAT AND DAIRY

Purchase in moderate quantities on sale and freeze. Grate cheese before freezing.

beef, extra-lean, ground, 1 lb.
chicken, boneless and skinless, 1/2 lb.
chicken breasts, pre-cooked regular or
   mesquite-flavored, 6

butter, 1/2 lb.
cheese,
   mozzarella, part-skim, grated, 8 oz.
   Parmesan, fresh or canned, grated,
    4 oz.
milk, skim or 1%, 1 to 2 gallons

CANNED GOODS

fish,
   salmon, one 14 oz. can
   tuna, water-packed, two 61/2 oz. cans
juice, V-8, four 6 oz. cans
milk, evaporated skim, one 12 oz. can
olives, sliced, one 2 oz. can
peaches, in own juice or light syrup,
   four 16 oz. cans
pineapple, chunks, in own juice,
   one 81/4 oz. can
soup,
   lowfat cream of chicken,
    one 103/4 oz. can
   lowfat cream of mushroom,
    two 103/4 oz. cans
tomato paste, one 6 oz. can

FROZEN

juice concentrate, Dole Mountain Cherry,
   one 12 oz. can
vegetables,
   mandarin blend, three 16 oz. bags
   mixed, one 32 oz. bag

FREEDOM MENUS

105

FREEDOM MENUS

DAY 33

		Breakfast	fg/cal
	Water	12 oz. water	
	Grain	1 cup Corn Chex Cereal	0/110
	Protein	1 cup skim milk	t/86
	Fruit	1/2 cup sliced peaches (on cereal)	t/55
	Water/Snack	8 oz. water/ 1 cup Chicken Broccoli Casserole left over from Day 32	4.5/262

		Lunch	
	Water	8 oz. water	
	Vegetable	(extra lettuce, tomatoes, sprouts, pickles, and onions on sandwich)	
	Grain	1 Oscar Mayer Pastrami Sandwich* p. 249	t/306
	Protein	(pastrami) and 1 cup nonfat vanilla yogurt	0/180
	Fruit	1/2 grapefruit	0/50
	Water/Snack	12 oz. water	

		Dinner	
	Water	8 oz. water	
	Vegetable	(in stew)	
	Grain	1 Cheese Muffin* p. 228 (Make ahead to save time, or simply have whole-grain bread instead.)	6/185
	Protein	1 cup Quick Delicious Beef Stew* p. 155	8/302
	Fruit	2 large plums	t/72
	Water/Snack	12 oz. water	

Total: 18.5/1608

18.5 fat grams x 9 calories = 166.5 calories from fat

166.5 ÷ 1608 = **10% FAT**

I never order pastrami because of its high fat content, so I was amazed as I put these menus together and found that some pastrami choices contained only a trace of fat. Others are very high in fat, so read the labels carefully!

DAY 34

		Breakfast	fg/cal
	Water	12 oz. water	
	Grain	1 cup Three Bear Porridge* p. 175	t/272
	Protein	1 cup evaporated skim milk (on Porridge)	t/200
	Fruit	1/4 cup raisins (in porridge)	0/125
	Water/Snack	8 oz. water/ 1 Big Soft Pretzel* p. 158	1/52
		(make ahead and freeze)	
		1/2 cup chunk raw veggies	t/25±

		Lunch	
	Water	8 oz. water	
	Vegetable	(sprouts, lettuce, tomatoes, onions, and	
		pickles in sandwich)	
	Grain	1 Turkey 'n' Provolone Cheese Pita	
		Sandwich* p. 250	7/462
	Protein	(turkey and cheese in sandwich)	
	Fruit	6 oz. Dole Pine-Orange-Banana Juice	
		(Be moderate in the use of this "B+" Choice.)	t/90
	Water/Snack	8 oz. water/ 1 Turkey Sandwich	
		left over from lunch (no cheese)	1/362

		Dinner	
Easy			
	Water	8 oz. water	
	Vegetable	1 cup Great Green Beans* p. 265 (Double	
		recipe if you desire leftovers.)	3/96
		1 cup creamed corn	0/160
	Grain	2 Blueberry Muffins* p. 227 (Make a	
		double batch if you desire leftovers.)	6/302
	Protein	1 1/2 cups Savory Meat and Cheese	
		Manicotti* p. 241	7.5/365
	Fruit	1 cup mixed fresh fruit chunks	t/100
		one 2 1/2" slice Minute Cherry Cheesecake*	
		p. 195 ("B–" Choice—not for fat loss)	9.5/300
	Water/Snack	12 oz. water/ 1 sliced cucumber	t/39

> Total: 35/2950
> 35 fat grams x 9 calories =315 calories from fat
> 315 ÷2950 = **11% FAT**

When I was a litle girl, my grandpa used to fix Three Bear Porridge for me—I love it. I also love Savory Manicotti, a very easy, absolutely delicious main course.

FREEDOM MENUS

DAY 35

			fg/cal
	Breakfast		
Water	12 oz. water		
Grain	1 cup Cracked Wheat, Raisin, and Honey Cereal* p. 169		1/450
Protein	1 cup skim milk		t/86
Fruit	1 sliced orange		t/62
Water/Snack	8 oz. water/ 1 cup crisp green cabbage		t/16
	Lunch		
Water	12 oz. water		
Vegetable	1 1/2 cups Potato-Corn Soup* p. 259		4.5/192
Grain	2 Blueberry Muffins left over from Day 34		6/302
Protein	(yogurt in fruit)		
Fruit	1 cup Yogurt Fruit Delight* p. 219 (Double this recipe if you would like leftovers for tomorrow.)		0/146
Water/Snack	8 oz. water/ 1 cup Great Green Beans left over from Day 34		3/96
Easy	**Dinner**		
Water	12 oz. water		
Vegetable	three 2 1/2" slices Vegetable Pizza* p. 268 (Make two pizzas.)		6/447
Grain	(pizza crust)		
Protein	(cream cheese on pizza and frozen dairy dessert)		
Fruit	2 cups watermelon chunks		t/100
	8 oz. Mint Chocolate Chip Healthy Choice Frozen Dessert ("B'Choice—not for fat loss)		4/280
Water/Snack	12 oz. water/ one 2 1/2" slice leftover Vegetable Pizza		2/149

> Total: 26.5/2326
> 26.5 fat grams x 9 calories = 238.5 calories from fat
> 238.5 ÷ 2326 = **10% FAT**

It's so fun to mix and match foods and experiment with new ideas. Potato-Corn Soup is one of my experiments—extremely fast and very delicious! Have fun! Experiment a little. Add any steamed veggies you happen to have leftover in your refrigerator to your Potato-Corn Soup. You now have delicious, quick, cream of vegetable soup!

DAY 36

		Breakfast	fg/cal
	Water	8 oz. water	
	Grain	2 cups Kix Cereal	1/147
	Protein	1 cup skim milk	t/86
	Fruit	1 cup mixed fresh fruit (or canned in light syrup)	t/100±
	Water/Snack	12 oz. water	

		Lunch	
	Water	12 oz. water	
	Vegetable	one half 19 oz. can Campbell's Chunky Split Pea Soup	5/210
	Grain	1 hot Ham 'n' Cheese Sandwich* p. 249	13/406
	Protein	(meat and cheese in sandwich)	
	Fruit	1 orange	t/62
	Water/Snack	8 oz. water	

		Dinner	
	Water	8 oz. water	
	Vegetable	(tomatoes, lettuce, and onions in tacos)	
	Grain	2 jumbo Tempting Tacos* p. 148	16/578
	Protein	(meat or beans and cheese in tacos and yogurt in Yogurt Fruit Delight)	
	Fruit	1 cup Yogurt Fruit Delight left over from Day 35	0/146
	Water/Snack	12 oz. water/ 1 cup celery sticks	t/18

> Total: 35/1753
>
> 35 fat grams x 9 calories =315 calories from fat
>
> 315 ÷1753 = **18% FAT**

My boys love Tempting Tacos in three sizes: mini, medium, and jumbo. These tacos make a fun, easy meal, sometimes topped off with lowfat ice-cream cones or homemade shakes with ice milk, skim milk, fat free fudge sauce and malt, which I have only a taste of if I'm really intent on seeing fat loss. I don't crave anything unless I start eating lots of sweets or I don't balance my meals with water, veggies, grains, protein, and fruit. If I'm coasting and not intent on seeing fat loss, I have a lowfat shake occasionally.

SHOPPING LIST / DAYS 33 -36

*This **four**-day shopping list may last your family **six** or **seven** days if you eat out often.*

BREAD / CEREAL / GRAINS

bread, seasoned dry crumbs, 1/4 cup
cereal,
    General Mills Kix, 1 box
    Ralston Corn Chex, 1 box

FRESH FRUITS
AND VEGETABLES

Or purchase other fruits and vegetables that are in season or on sale.

bananas, 6
grapefruit, 2
melon, watermelon, 1
oranges, 10
peaches, 6
plums, 10
raisins, 1/2 lb.

broccoli, 1 bunch
cabbage, green, 1 head
carrots, 5 lb.
cauliflower, 1 head
celery, 1 bunch
cucumbers, 4
lettuce, leafy, 2 bunches
onions,
    green, 1 bunch
    yellow, medium, 2

peppers,
    green, 2
    red, 1
radishes, 1 bunch
sprouts, 1 package
tomatoes, medium, 7
zucchini, 4

MEAT AND DAIRY

bacon, extra-lean, 2 strip
pastrami, Oscar Mayer lowfat, 1 package

cheese,
    provolone, 8 oz.
    ricotta, fat free or lowfat, 8 oz.
cream cheese, lowfat, 24 oz.
eggs, 1 dozen *(you'll use mostly whites)*
milk, skim or 1%, 1 to 2 gallon
sour cream, nonfat, 1 pint
yogurt,
    fruit flavored, nonfat, 16 oz.
    vanilla, nonfat, 48 oz.

CANNED GOODS

milk, sweetened condensed, one 14 oz. can
pie filling, light, apple, cherry, or
    blueberry, one 21 oz. can

FROZEN / MISC.

Healthy Choice Chocolate Mint
    Frozen Dessert, 1/2 gallon
    ("B" Choice—not for fat loss)
graham cracker crust, ready baked, 1
    ("B" Choice—not for fat loss)

MASTER LIST / CHECK LIST DAYS 33-36

Check to be sure that you have the following Master List items already in stock. Baking items, condiments, and spices are not included in this list. They are listed on pages 59-60.

BREAD / CEREAL GRAIN

Purchase breads, rolls, buns, etc., on sale and freeze.

bread, whole-wheat, 2 loaves
manicotti, 1 box
millet, 4 oz.
pitas, whole-wheat, 1 dozen
rice, brown or white, 1 cup
taco shells, corn, 8 jumbo and 24 mini
wheat, whole-kernels, 2 - 3 cups

MEAT AND DAIRY

Purchase in moderate quantities on sale and freeze. Grate cheese before freezing.

beef, extra-lean ground, 1/2 lb.
ham, sliced, extra-lean, 8 oz.
turkey, sliced, extra-lean,
  (white, skinless) 8 oz.

butter, 1/4 lb.
cheese,
  cheddar, grated, 12 oz.
  mozzarella, part-skim, grated, 8 oz.
  parmesan, fresh or canned, grated,
    2 oz.

CANNED GOODS

applesauce*, unsweetened or lightly
  sweetened, one 16 oz. can
beans,
  green, three 16 oz. cans
  kidney, one 15 oz. can
  refried, lowfat or nonfat
    two 16 oz. cans
  white*, one 15 oz. can
beef stew, Nalley's Big Chunk,
  one 40 oz. can
corn, whole kernel, one 17 oz. can
corn, cream style, three 16 oz. cans
fruit cocktail, in own juice,
  three 16 oz. cans
milk, evaporated skim, two 12 oz. cans
pineapple, tidbits, in own juice,
  one 20 oz. can
salsa, one 161/2 oz. far
soup,
  Campbell's Chunky Beef and
    Vegetable, two 17 oz. cans
  Campbell's Chunky Split Pea,
    two 19 oz. cans
  Campbell's Cream of Potato,
    two 103/4 cans
spaghetti sauce, lowfat, one 28 oz.
  jar or can

FROZEN

blueberries, one 8 oz. bag
juice concentrate, Dole Pineapple-
  Orange-Banana, one 12 oz. can

*See italics statement at the bottom of page 81.

111

DAY 37

		fg/cal
	Breakfast	
Water	12 oz. water	
Grain	2 Granola Bars* p. 173 (make ahead)	4/130
Protein	1 cup skim milk	t/86
	1 sliced orange	t/62
Water/Snack	8 oz. water/ 1 cup raw veggies	t/50±
	Lunch	
Water	8 oz. water	
Vegetable	1 1/2 cups La Choy Shrimp Chow Mein	2/90
Grain	1/2 cup Chow Mein Noodles	5/228
Protein	1 1/2 cups La Choy Sweet and Sour Oriental with Chicken	4/480
Fruit	2 sliced kiwifruit	t/92
Water/Snack	12 oz. water	
	Dinner	
Water	8 oz. water	
Vegetable	1/2 cup Perfect Potato Casserole* p. 247	8/288
Grain	1 slice Perfect Whole-Wheat Bread* p. 160 with 2 Tb. All Fruit Jam* p. 164	1/120
Protein	5 oz. Orange Roughy* p. 253	8/254
	with 2 Tb. Tartar Sauce* p. 253	t/14
	one 8 oz. glass skim milk	t/86
Fruit	1 cup Pineapple-Marshmallow Coleslaw* p. 216 (Triple this recipe if you would like leftovers.)	t/112
Water/Snack	12 oz. water/ 1 cup Pineapple-Marshmallow Coleslaw left over from dinner	t/112

(Time Saver icon shown beside Lunch)

Total: 32/2204

32 fat grams x 9 calories = 288 calories from fat

288 ÷ 2204 = **13% FAT**

Perfect potato casserole is one of my mom's best dishes. I just lowered the fat significantly by decreasing the amount of butter by half and using fat free sour cream and lowfat cream of mushroom soup. This recipe is a real crowd-pleaser! It's great with chicken, turkey, fish, or beef.

FREEDOM

DAY 38

			fg/cal
	Breakfast		
Water	12 oz. water		
Grain	two 4" Belgian Waffles* p. 166		4/180
Protein	1 1/2 cups nonfat vanilla or fruit yogurt (on waffles)		0/270
Fruit	1 sliced banana (on waffles)		t/105
Water/Snack	8 oz. water/ 1 cup mixed raw vegetables with 3 Tb. nonfat dressing		t/110±

Fast Food Hardee's	**Lunch**		
Water	8 oz.		
Vegetable	(Request extra tomatoes, pickles, and onions on sandwiches along with no bacon or mayonnaise.)		
Grain	2 Turkey Club Sandwiches (on whole-grain buns, if available)		12/520
Protein	(turkey in sandwiches)		
Fruit	1 orange (from home)		t/62
Water/Snack	12 oz. water		
	1 cup coleslaw left over from Day 37		t/112

Easy	**Dinner**		
Water	12 oz. water		
Vegetable	(in omelet)/ 3/4 cup Hash Browns* p. 246		6/155
Grain	2 slices whole-grain toast		1/142
Protein	one 5" x 6" serving Omelet Supreme* p. 174 (Double this recipe if you would like leftovers for tomorrow.)		10/254
Fruit	1 cup Fresh Fruit Combination Tray* p. 213 (Use peaches, pears, and plums, or other on-sale fruits.)		t/100±
	1/4 cup Sour Cream Fruit Dip* p. 212		0/80
Water/Snack	12 oz. water/ 1 cup vegetable soup		2/90

Total: 35/2180

35 fat grams x 9 calories = 315 calories from fat

315 ÷ 2180 = **14% FAT**

We eat breakfast foods for brunch and breakfast foods for dinner. Even a bowl of cereal or, on occasion, "graham crackers and milk" make a real hit at our house! ("Graham crackers and milk" is not a fat-loss choice.)

FREEDOM MENUS

DAY 39

		Breakfast	fg/cal
	Water	12 oz. water	
	Grain	11/2 cups Kellogg's Oatmeal Raisin Crisp	
		("B" Choice)	4/260
	Protein	11/2 cups skim milk	t/129
	Fruit	(raisins in cereal)	
	Water/Snack	8 oz. water/ 1 serving Omelet Supreme	
		left over from Day 38	10/254

		Lunch	
	Water	8 oz. water	
	Vegetable	2 cups Zucchini Soup* p. 259 (make ahead)	2/152
	Grain	1 Bacon, Lettuce, and Tomato Sandwich*	
		p. 248 ("B" Choice)	8/244
	Protein	1 cup nonfat fruit yogurt	0/200
	Fruit	1 grapefruit	0/100
	Water/Snack	12 oz. water/ 1 cup Zucchini Soup	
		left over from lunch	1/76

		Dinner	
Easy			
	Water	8 oz. water	
	Vegetable	(included in Spaghetti Salad)	
	Grain	2 cups Spaghetti Salad* p. 242	2/490
		1 slice Garlic Cheese Toast* p. 159	
		("B" Choice)	5/118
	Protein	one 8 oz. glass skim milk	t/86
	Fruit	1 cup green grapes	t/72
	Water/Snack	12 oz. water/ 1 cup mixed fresh vegetables	
		with 4 Tb. Ranch Dip* p. 212	t/120

Total: 32/2301

32 fat grams x 9 calories =288 calories from fat

288 ÷ 2301 = **13% FAT**

114

Oatmeal Raisin Crisp Cereal rates a "B" because of the grams of sugar. However, it is a better choice than a "B" rated dessert because I'm harder on main courses than I am on desserts. Main courses should be very nutritious and very moderate in sugar. The Bacon, Lettuce, and Tomato Sandwich is 30 percent fat; and the Garlic Cheese Toast is 38 percent fat. Isn't it nice to have all of this already figured for you into a day that has an overall fat content of 13 percent?! Put away your calculator and enjoy your freedom to eat!

DAY 40

			fg/cal
	Water	**Breakfast** 8 oz. water	
	Grain	4 Blueberry Pancakes* p. 177	8/376
		6 Tb. maple syrup (not a fat loss choice)	0/330
	Protein	1 cup skim milk	t/86
	Fruit	(in blueberry pancakes)	
	Water/Snack	12 oz. water/ 2 Zucchini Muffins* p. 234	6/286
		1 sliced orange	t/62

		Lunch	
Fast Food			
Skipper's			
	Water	12 oz. water	
	Vegetable	Green Salad (Use fat free dressing from home. A baked potato would also make a good choice here.)	0/24
	Grain	Whole-grain roll (if available, or see snack)	t/45
	Protein	Baked Fish	3/147
	Fruit	1 banana (from home)	t/105
	Water/Snack	8 oz. water/ 2 Zucchini Muffins left over from breakfast	6/286
		1 cup skim milk	t/86

		Dinner	
	Water	8 oz. water	
	Vegetable	1 cup Glazed Carrots, Cauliflower, and Broccoli* p. 264 ("B" Choice)	7/126
	Grain	2 slices whole-wheat toast with 2 Tb. All Fruit Jam* p. 164	t/174
	Protein	1 breast Pineapple-Lime Chicken* p. 184	6/344
	Fruit	1 cup Pineapple-Orange-Banana Gelatin* p. 217	0/233
	Water/Snack	12 oz. water	

> Total: 36/2710
> 36 fat grams x 9 calories = 324 calories from fat
> 324 ÷ 2710 = **12% FAT**

115

Try the Pineapple-Lime Chicken. It's a real taste-treat for company or family. And it's so easy to prepare!

Remember, you may eat only half of what is on this page to achieve comfortable satisfaction. Both starvers and stuffers see body fat increase, so listen to your body! When I'm really intent on fat loss, I only eat vegetable-based snacks, especially in the evening. (Examples: veggie soups, stews, stir-fries, veggie-stuffed pitas, steamed veggies, raw veggies, tossed salad, etc.)

Shopping List / Days 37 - 40

*This **four**-day shopping list may last your family **six** or **seven** days if you eat out often.*

BREAD / CEREAL / GRAINS

cereal,
    cornflakes, 1 box
    General Mills Triples, 1 box
    Kellogg's Oatmeal Raisin Crisp, 1 box
pancake mix, whole-wheat, 1 bag

FRESH FRUITS
AND VEGETABLES

Or purchase other fruits and vegetables that are in season or on sale.

bananas, 12
grapefruit, 4
grapes, 2 lbs.
kiwifruit, 8
lemon, 1
lime juice, 1 small bottle
oranges, 12
peaches, 4
pears, 4
plums, 4
raisins, 1/2 lb.

broccoli, 4 bunches
cabbage, green, 1 head
carrots,
    baby, 2 small bags
    regular, 5 lbs.
cauliflower, 1 head
cucumbers, 4
lettuce, leafy, 1 large bunch

onions,
    red, 1
    yellow, medium, 3
parsley, fresh, 1 bunch
tomatoes, large, 4
zucchini, 6

MEAT AND DAIRY

bacon, extra-lean, 1/2 lb.

cottage cheese, lowfat, 16 oz.
eggs, 1 to 2 dozen *(you'll use mostly whites)*
milk, skim or 1%, 1 to 2 gallons
sour cream, nonfat, 1 pint
yogurt,
    fruit, nonfat, 32 oz.
    vanilla, nonfat, 32 oz.

CANNED GOODS

LaChoy Sweet and Sour Chicken,
    two 43 1/2 oz. cans
LaChoy Shrimp Chow Mein,
    two 42 oz. cans
pimento, one small jar

MISCELLANEOUS

almonds, sliced, 2 oz.
    chocolate chips or dried fruit, 6 oz.
    (chocolate chips = "B–" Choice)
coconut, 4 oz.
marshmallows, miniature,
    1 small bag = *("B" Choice)*
salad dressing, fat free Italian,
    one 16 oz. bottle

MASTER LIST / CHECK LIST
DAYS 37 - 40

Check to be sure that you have the following Master List items already in stock. Baking items, condiments, and spices are not included in this list. They are listed on pages 59 - 60.

BREAD / CEREAL / GRAIN

Purchase breads, rolls, buns, etc., on sale and freeze.

bread, whole-wheat, 1 to 2 loaves
oats, rolled, 6 cups
spaghetti, whole-wheat or white, *(dry)*
    16 oz.
wheat, whole-kernel, 1 cup

MEAT AND DAIRY

Purchase in moderate quantities on sale and freeze. Grate cheese before freezing.

chicken, breasts, boneless and skinless, 4
fish, orange roughy, 4 fillets
ham, extra-lean, 4 oz.

butter, 1 lb.
cheese,
    mozzarella, part-skim, grated, 12 oz.
    Parmesan, fresh or canned, grated,
        4 oz.

CANNED GOODS

applesauce*, unsweetened or lightly
    sweetened, one 16 oz. can
beans*, white, one 15 oz. can
noodles, chow mein, one 9 oz. can
oranges, mandarin, one 11 oz. can
pineapple,
    chunks, in own juice, three 81/4 oz. cans
    crushed, in own juice, one 20 oz. can
    tidbits, in own juice, one 20 oz. can
soup,
    chicken broth, one 103/4 oz. can
    lowfat cream of chicken,
        two 103/4 oz. cans
    vegetable, two 103/4 oz. cans

FROZEN / MISC.

blueberries, 4 oz.
juice concentrate, Dole Pine-Orange-
    Banana, one 12 oz. can
potatoes, hash browns, unseasoned, 4 lbs.

salad dressing, Hidden Valley Lite Ranch
    Dressing, 1 package

*See italics statement at the bottom of page 81.

DAY 41

		fg/cal
Easy	**Breakfast**	
Water	12 oz. water	
Grain	2 Big Soft Pretzels* p. 158 (Make extra if you would like leftovers.)	2/104
Protein	1 cup skim milk	t/86
Fruit	1 1/2 cups Super Citrus Salad* p. 218 (make ahead)	0/190
Water/Snack	8 oz./ 1 Big Soft Pretzel 1 cup mixed vegetables with 4 Tb. Creamy Onion Dip* p. 210	3/182±

	Lunch	
Water	8 oz. water	
Vegetable	1 stalk celery	t/6
	one 19 oz. can Progresso Hearty Black Bean Soup	4/280
Grain	2 slices whole-grain toast with 2 Tb. Smucker's Simply Fruit Spread	t/238
Protein	1 cup nonfat vanilla yogurt	0/180
Fruit	1 orange	t/62
Water/Snack	12 oz. water/ 1 stalk celery	t/6
	one 19 oz. can Campbell's Chunky Vegetable Beef Soup and	10/340
	2 Big Soft Pretzels left over from breakfast (if you're hungry)	2/104

	Dinner	
Water	8 oz. water	
Vegetable	2 cups Tossed Salad* p. 267 with	t/200±
	6 Tb. Easy Lowfat Dressing* p. 211	3/120±
Grain	2 Banana Muffins* p. 226 (Make ahead to save time.) (Noodles are also a grain.)	6/288
Protein	1 1/2 cups Company Casserole* p. 252 over 1 1/2 cups hot noodles	4.5/522
Fruit	1 1/2 cups sliced, canned peaches (in extra-light syrup or own juice)	t/164
	2 Chocolate Chip Cookies* p. 205 ("B" Choice)	5/172
Water/Snack	12 oz. water/ 1 Pretzel, 1 cup veggies, and 4 Tb. dip (left over from morning snack)	3/182±

Total: 42.5/3426
42.5 fat grams x 9 calories = 382.5 calories from fat
382.5 ÷ 3426 = **11% FAT**

When I'm shopping at the mall with my kids and we've already eaten a good meal, my kids love to get treats. Often, they get fat free or lowfat frozen yogurt or jumbo cinnamon pretzels with only four fat grams per pretzel. (Plain are nearly fat free.) I usually order two original pretzels with butter and salt. They have four fat grams each and no sugar. They are delicious!

*This day's menu may feature a lot more food than is comfortable for you. Remember, neither STARVE nor STUFF! Listen to **your** body.*

FREEDOM MENUS

*Pineapple-Orange-Banana Gelatin, Super Citrus Salad,
and Fruit Gelatin*

Light Butter Popcorn and Big Soft Pretzels

DAY 42

		Breakfast	fg/cal
	Water	12 oz. water	
	Grain	(1 whole-grain English muffin)	
	Protein	1 Egg and Cheese Muffin* p. 171	5.5/305
		1 cup skim milk	t/86
	Fruit	1 grapefruit	0/100
	Water/Snack	8 oz. water	
		6 cups Light Microwave Butter Popcorn*	
		p. 225**	6/160
		1 sliced zucchini	t/28

		Lunch	
Fast Food			
McDonald's			
	Water	12 oz. water	
	Vegetable	1 Side Salad with Lite Vinaigrette Dressing	3/80
	Grain	1 McGrilled Chicken Sandwich (Request	
		extra veggies and no sauce.)	6/300
	Protein	(chicken in sandwich)	
	Fruit	1 apple (from home—or count the tomato)	t/81
	Water/Snack	8 oz. water	

		Dinner	
	Water	8 oz. water	
	Vegetable	2 cups green beans	0/80
	Grain	(noodles)	
	Protein	1/2 Crock Pot Chicken Breast* p. 182 with	
		1/2 cup sauce over 1 cup hot, cooked	
		noodles (Prepare this in the morning.)	6/393
	Fruit	1 cup Yogurt Fruit Delight* p. 219	0/146
	Water/Snack	12 oz. water	

Total: 26.5/1759

26.5 fat grams x 9 calories =238.5 calories from fat

238.5 ÷ 1759 = **14% FAT**

FREEDOM MENUS

**Light, microwave butter-flavor popcorn makes a delicious, anytime snack. Sometimes I eat an entire bag full of Act II lite microwave butter popcorn—my favorite, equaling 10 cups and 10 fat grams. My children love this popcorn, too.*

DAY 43

		Breakfast	fg/cal
	Water	12 oz. water	
	Grain	2 cups Quaker Oat Squares	4/400
	Protein	1 1/2 cups skim milk	t/129
	Fruit	1 1/2 cups honeydew chunks	t/90
	Water/Snack	8 oz. water/ 6 oz. V-8 juice	0/35

		Lunch	
	Water	8 oz. water	
	Vegetable	1 cup fresh mixed vegetables/ 4 Tb. Ranch Dip* p. 212	t/120±
	Grain	7.5 oz. Chef Boy·ar·dee Cheese Ravioli in Beef and Tomato Sauce	3/200
	Protein	(meat and cheese)	
	Fruit	2 large fresh plums	t/72
	Water/Snack	12 oz. water	
		1/2 cup mixed vegetables	t/50±

		Dinner	
	Water	8 oz. water	
	Vegetable	2 cups Shrimp Salad* p. 255 (Double this recipe if you would like leftovers.)	2/218
	Grain	1 slice Perfect Whole-Wheat Bread* p. 160 with 1 Tb. All Fruit Jam* p. 164	1/104
	Protein	1 cup Pork Chow Mein p. 154	8/302
	Fruit	1 cup Tropical Fruit Ice* p. 218	t/152
	Water/Snack	12 oz. water/ 1 cup Shrimp Salad left over from dinner	1/109
		1/2 cup lowfat cottage cheese	2/100

Total: 21/2081

21 fat grams x 9 calories = 189 calories from fat

189 ÷ 2081 = **9% FAT****

**This 9 percent fat day would become 10 percent if we added in the fat traces.
Perfect Whole-Wheat Bread is soft, moist, and delicious. But if you're not into bread making, trade off with different brands of 100% whole-wheat bread, part whole-wheat bread, and just a little white French bread or sour-dough bread for variety. Buy extra loaves on sale and freeze some. Also, check discount bread stores for savings.

DAY 44

	Breakfast	fg/cal
Water	12 oz. water	
Grain	2 slices French Toast* p. 171	1/191
	6 Tb. maple syrup (not a fat-loss choice—	0/330
	All Fruit Jam with nonfat vanilla yogurt	
	on top is a fat-loss choice**)	
Protein	1 cup nonfat vanilla yogurt	0/180
Fruit	1 cup Dole Pineapple-Orange-Banana	
	Juice ("B+" Choice)	t/120
Water/Snack	8 oz. water/ 2 cups Shrimp Salad left over	
	from Day 43	2/218

	Lunch	
Restaurant		
Shoney's		
Water	12 oz. water	
Vegetable	Green Salad with lowfat Dressing and	
	1 Baked Potato	1/327
Grain	1 slice Grecian Bread	2/80
Protein	Charbroiled Shrimp	3/138
Fruit	1 apple (from home)	t/81
Water/Snack	8 oz. water	
	(If you are comfortably satisfied at your	
	meal and you have leftovers, eat them	
	for your snack.)	

	Dinner	
Easy		
Water	8 oz. water	
Vegetable	2 cups green beans	0/80
Grain	1 cup Homemade Macaroni and Cheese*	
	p. 238 ("B" Choice)	11/340
Protein	(cheese) and one 8 oz. glass skim milk	t/86
Fruit	1 cup red grapes	t/72
Water/Snack	12 oz. water	

Total: 20/2243

20 fat grams x 9 calories = 180 calories from fat

$180 \div 2243 = $ **8% FAT***

**If you are diabetic, try All Fruit Jam by itself or mixed into plain nonfat yogurt with perhaps a little fruit-juice concentrate on pancakes, French toast, and waffles. Apple-Raspberry Butter is also very tasty.*

***Eight percent fat is low for one day. However, your overall week averages to between 10 and 20 percent fat—the ideal range for health, energy, and excess fat loss.*

SHOPPING LIST / DAYS 41 - 44

*This **four**-day shopping list may last your family **six** or **seven** days if you eat out often.*

BREAD / CEREAL / GRAIN

cereal, Quaker Oat Squares, 1 box

FRESH FRUITS AND VEGETABLES

Or purchase other fruits and vegetables that are in season or on sale.

apples, 4
bananas, 8
grapefruit, 4
grapes, red, 1 large bunch
melon, honeydew, 1
oranges, 4
plums, 8
strawberries, 1 quart *(or frozen)*

cabbage, purple, 1 head
carrots,
 baby, 2 small bags
 regular, 5 lbs.
celery, 2 bunches
cucumbers, 4
lettuce, leafy, 2 large bunches

onions,
 green, 1 bunch
 yellow, 4
parsley, 1 small bunch
peppers, green, 4
tomatoes, medium, 2
 (for mixed vegetable snacks)
zucchini, 5

MEAT AND DAIRY

pork, extra-lean*, 8 oz.

cheese, American, 8 oz.
cottage cheese, lowfat, 16 oz.
cream cheese, nonfat, 4 oz.
eggs, 2 dozen *(you'll use mostly whites)*
milk, skim or 1%, 1 to 2 gallons
sour cream, nonfat, 8 oz.
yogurt, vanilla, nonfat, 32 oz.

CANNED GOODS / MISC.

Chef Boy·ar·dee Cheese Raviolis in
 Beef & Tomato Sauce,
 two 15 oz. cans

chocolate chips, 6 oz. *("B–" Choice)*

*Notice the small amounts of meat that are used in these menus. Yet they are not void of meat. Moderation, (not extremes) is the key to permanent leanness and optimum health, as well as food that tastes great!

MASTER LIST / CHECK LIST
DAYS 41 - 44

Check to be sure that you have the following Master List items already in stock. Baking items, condiments, and spices are not included in this list. They are listed on pages 59 - 60.

BREAD / CEREAL / GRAIN

Purchase breads, rolls, buns, etc., on sale and freeze.

bread, whole-wheat, 1 to 2 loaves
macaroni, whole-wheat or white, 8 oz.
muffins, English, whole-wheat, 1 dozen
noodles, whole-wheat or white, 32 oz.
oats, rolled, 3/4 cup
popcorn, microwave, light butter,
    6-count package

MEAT AND DAIRY

Purchase in moderate quantities on sale and freeze. Grate cheese before freezing.

chicken breasts, boneless and skinless, 4

butter, 1/2 lb.
cheese,
    mozzarella, part-skim, grated, 10 oz.
    Parmesan, fresh or canned, grated,
      4 oz.

CANNED GOODS

applesauce, unsweetened or lightly
    sweetened, one 16 oz. can
bamboo shoots, two 8 oz. cans

beans,
    green, eight 16 oz can
    sprouts, one 14 oz. can
    white*, 15 oz. can
fish, tuna, water-pack, two 61/2 oz. cans
juice, V-8, four 6 oz. cans
milk, evaporated skim, one 12 oz. can
mushrooms, one 4 oz. can
noodles, chow-mein, one 5 oz. can
oranges, mandarin, three large cans
peaches, in own juice, two 29 oz. cans
pineapple, tidbits or chunks, in own juice,
    one 20 oz. can
salad shrimp, two 41/2 oz. cans
soup,
    Campbell's Chunky Vegetable Beef,
      four 19 oz. cans
    Chicken broth, one 103/4 oz. can
    lowfat cream of mushroom,
      five 103/4 oz. cans
    onion, dry mix, 1 envelope
    Progresso Hearty Black Bean,
      four 19 oz. cans
water chestnuts, one 8 oz. can

FROZEN / MISC.

juice concentrates,
    apple, one 12 oz. can
    Dole Mandarin-Tangerine,
      one 12 oz. can
    Dole Pine-Orange-Banana,
      one 12 oz. can
    pineapple, one 12 oz. can
peas, petite, three 16 oz. bags
vegetables, mixed, one 16 oz. bag

salad dressing, Hidden Valley Lite,
    (any flavor) 2 packages

*See the italics statement at the bottom of page 81.

FREEDOM MENUS

DAY 45

		fg/cal
	Breakfast	
Water	12 oz. water	
Grain	2 Blueberry Muffins* p. 227 (make ahead and freeze)	6/302
Protein	1 cup Breakfast Shake* p. 168	0/244
Fruit	(in shake)	
Water/Snack	8 oz. water	

	Lunch	
Water	12 oz. water	
Vegetable	2 cups Minestrone Soup* p. 258 (homemade or Campbell's)	10/432
Grain	1 slice whole-wheat toast with	t/71
	1 Tb. Apple-Raspberry Butter* p. 165 (make ahead)	0/15
Protein	1 cup skim milk	t/86
Fruit	2 nectarines	t/134
Water/Snack	12 oz. water/ 1 sliced zucchini	t/27

	Dinner	
Easy		
Water	8 oz. water	
Vegetable	1 1/2 cups Tossed Salad* p. 167 with 6 Tb. Buttermilk Dressing* p. 210	3/276±
Grain	2 Blueberry Muffins left over from breakfast	6/302
Protein	1 cup Shepherd's Pie* p. 156	6/358
Fruit	1 cup Instant Blueberry Ice Cream* p. 194	t/244
Water/Snack	12 oz. water	

	Total:	31/2491

31 fat grams x 9 calories = 279 calories from fat

279 ÷ 2491 = **11% FAT**

Instant Ice Cream is one of my favorite taste treats. For extra richness, use evaporated skim milk instead of regular skim milk. If you have a dairy allergy, use ice water. This dessert is both fat- and sugar-free, and kids and company have no idea it's good for them. They absolutely love it!

DAY 46

		Breakfast	fg/cal
	Water	12 oz. water	
	Grain	1 1/3 cups Nutri Grain	
		Almond Raisin Cereal	4/280
	Protein	1 cup skim milk	t/86
	Fruit	1 sliced banana	t/105
	Water/Snack	8 oz. water/ 1 cup Minestrone Soup	
		left over from Day 45	5/216

		Lunch	
Fast Food			
Jack-In-The-Box			
	Water	12 oz. water (Request a medium	
		or large water.)	
	Vegetable	1 Fajita Pita and	7/278
		1 Chicken Fajita Pita	8/292
	Grain	(pita bread)	
	Protein	(meat in pitas)	
	Fruit	1 sliced orange (from home)	t/62
	Water/Snack	8 oz. water	

		Dinner	
Easy			
	Water	8 oz. water	
	Vegetable	1 cup Broccoli Casserole* p. 160	4/200
	Grain	2 Apple-Cinnamon Muffins* p. 226	
		(make ahead)	6/298
	Protein	1 piece Teriyaki Chicken* p. 185	3/156
	Fruit	1 cup Pineapple and Cottage Cheese Salad*	
		p. 215	2/202
	Water/Snack	12 oz. water	

Total: 39/2175

39 fat grams x 9 calories = 351 calories from fat

351 ÷ 2175 = **16% FAT**

Be sure to adjust these menus to fit into your personal budget and time schedule. A cheaper breakfast might include oatmeal and honey. A faster dinner could spotlight baked potatoes (pricked several times with a fork and microwaved for five minutes each) stuffed with chicken chili. Green grapes, whole-grain bread, and sliced purple cabbage would make your "colorful" evening meal complete.

DAY 47

			fg/cal
Easy	**Breakfast**		
Water	8 oz. water		
Grain	Two 2" pieces Blueberry Streusel Coffee Cake* p. 189 ("B" Choice—make ahead as a time saver.)		8/360
Protein	1 cup nonfat vanilla yogurt (on fruit)		0/180
Fruit	1 cup mixed fresh fruit chunks		t/100±
Water/Snack	8 oz. water/ 1 cup V-8 juice		0/47

	Lunch		
Water	8 oz. water		
Vegetable	(green pepper, onion, lettuce, and tomato in pita pocket)		
Grain	1 Tuna Salad Pita Pocket* p. 250		2/400
Protein	(tuna) and one 8 oz. glass milk		t/86
Fruit	1/2 cup Mandarin oranges		0/60
Water/Snack	12 oz. water		

Easy	**Dinner**		
Water	8 oz. water		
Vegetable	1 1/2 cups Homestyle Salad Bar* p. 267 with 6 Tb. lowfat dressing (or Short-Cut Tossed Salad* p. 266)		3/276±
Grain	2 Sweet Potato Muffins* p. 234 (make ahead)		4/198
Protein	1/2 cup Campbell's Barbeque Beans (Beans and grain together make a complete protein.)		2/125
Fruit	1/2 cup applesauce with cinnamon (lightly sweetened or no sugar added)		t/53
Water/Snack	8 oz. water		

Total: 19/1885

19 fat grams x 9 calories = 171 calories from fat

171 ÷ 1885 = **9% FAT****

Become creative with your salad bars. Try fresh and canned beans and vegetables that you may have never thought to try before, such as crunchy, sweet jicama—my family's favorite raw vegetable. But you may have to tell the grocery store clerk what jicama (pronounced hickumu) actually is. Clerks sometimes don't recognize it.

**If you added up the fat traces, this 9 percent fat day would become 10 percent and fall into the ideal range of 10 to 20 percent fat.

DAY 48

		fg/cal
Easy	**Breakfast**	
Water	12 oz. water	
Grain	Two 2" pieces Blueberry Streusel Coffee Cake left over from Day 47 ("B" Choice)	8/360
Protein	1 Fried Egg* p. 172 (Two to three whole eggs per week is the ideal amount.)	6.5/83
Fruit	2 cups cantaloupe, honeydew, and watermelon chunks with 6 Tb. Sour Cream Fruit Dip* p. 212	t/240
Water/Snack	8 oz. water/ 1 cup mixed vegetable chunks	t/50±

Restaurant	**Lunch**	
Red Lobster		
Water	8 oz. water	
Vegetable	1 large baked potato with 1/2 cup lowfat cottage cheese melted on top; and green vegetables (Ask for extra vegetables.)	2/420±
Grain	2 whole-grain rolls with 2 Tb. jam (if available)	2/208±
Protein	1 Rock Lobster Tail	5/250
Fruit	1 orange (from home)	t/62
Water/Snack	12 oz. water/ 3 baby carrots and 1 sliced zucchini	0/40

Easy	**Dinner**	
Water	12 oz. water	
Vegetable	11/2 cups Zucchini Au Gratin* p. 270 (You may choose to double this recipe and use leftovers for snacks.)	7.5/363
Grain	2 whole-wheat rolls	t/90
Protein	(cheese in casserole)	
Fruit	3/4 cup Fruit Gelatin* p. 214	0/75
Water/Snack	8 oz. water/ 1 sliced green pepper	t/26

Total: 31/2267

31 fat grams x 9 calories = 279 calories from fat

279 ÷ 2267 = **12% FAT**

We eat leftovers at our house all the time. A great job for boys (and we have five at home) is cleaning out the refrigerator. Then you don't end up with all kinds of "new growths" in the back of the fridge.

If I leave the boys to do it on their own, it doesn't work. When I work with them, it actually becomes quite fun. And cooking is so much more enjoyable when the kitchen cupboards, drawers, and refrigerator are clean and orderly. When mine are a mess, I'd much rather eat out.

SHOPPING LIST / DAYS 45 - 48

This four-day shopping list may last your family six or seven days if you eat out often.

BREAD / CEREAL / GRAIN

cereal, Kellogg's Nutri Grain Almond
    Raisin, 1 box

FRESH FRUITS
AND VEGETABLES

Or purchase other fruits and vegetables that are in season or on sale.

apples, 6
bananas, 6
grapes, green, 2 lbs.
melons,
    cantaloupe, 2
    honeydew, 1
    watermelon, 1
nectarines, 8
oranges, 8
raisins, 4 oz.

broccoli, 2 bunches
cabbage, green, 1 head
carrots,
    carrots, baby, 1 medium bag
    regular, 5 lbs.

celery, 1 bunch
lettuce, leafy, 1 large bunch
onions,
    green, 1 bunch
    yellow, medium, 7
peppers, green, 5
potatoes,
    baking, 5
    sweet *(yams)*, 1
tomatoes, medium, 4
zucchini, medium, 14

MEAT AND DAIRY

chicken, whole fryer, 1

buttermilk, 1 pint
cottage cheese, lowfat, 16 oz.
eggs, 1 to 2 dozen
    (you'll use mostly whites),
milk, skim or 1%, 1 to 2 gallons
sour cream, nonfat, 1 pint
yogurt,
    fruit, nonfat, 8 oz.
    plain, nonfat, 24 oz.
    vanilla, nonfat, 32 oz.

CANNED GOODS / MISC.

beans,
    Campbell's BBQ, two 16 oz. cans
    garbanzo, one 15 oz. can

walnuts, 6 oz.

MASTER LIST / CHECK LIST
DAYS 45 - 48

Check to be sure that you have the following Master List items already in stock. Baking items, condiments, and spices are not included in this list. They are listed on pages 59 - 60.

BREAD / CEREAL / GRAIN

Purchase breads, rolls, buns, etc., on sale and freeze.

barley, 2 oz.
bread, whole-wheat, 1 to 2 loaves
   (I purchase an occasional loaf of fresh French bread.)
macaroni, whole-wheat or white, 8 oz.
oats, rolled, 1 1/2 cups
pitas, whole-wheat, 1 dozen
rolls, whole-grain, 1 dozen

MEAT AND DAIRY

Purchase in moderate quantities on sale and freeze. Grate cheese before freezing.

beef, extra-lean, ground, 1/2 lb.

cheese, mozzarella, part-skim, grated, 16 oz.

CANNED GOODS

applesauce*, unsweetened or lightly
   sweetened, two 16 oz. cans
beans*,
   green, two 16 oz. cans
   kidney, one 15 oz. can
   white*, one 16 oz. can
corn, whole kernel, one 17 oz. can
fish, tuna, water-pack, two 61/2 oz. cans
fruit cocktail, in own juice,
   one 16 oz. can
juice, V-8, four 6 oz. cans
milk, evaporated skim, one 12 oz. can
oranges, mandarin, two 11 oz. cans
pineapple, crushed, in own juice,
   one 20 oz. can
soup,
   lowfat cream of chicken,
      one 13/4 oz. can
   tomato, one 103/4 oz. can
tomato sauce, one 8 oz. can
tomatoes, diced, one 16 oz. can

FROZEN

blueberries, three 16 oz. bags
juice concentrates,
   apple, one 12 oz. can
   Dole Country Raspberry,
      one 12 oz. can
   Dole Mountain Cherry,
      one 12 oz. can
   orange, one 12 oz. can
   pineapple, one 12 oz. can
peas, petite, one 16 oz. bag
vegetables, mixed, one 16 oz. bag

*See the italics statement at the bottom of page 81.

DAY 49

			fg/cal
		Breakfast	
	Water	12 oz. water	
	Grain	Three 5" round Banana Pancakes* p. 176	6/288
	Protein	1 1/2 cups nonfat vanilla yogurt	0/270
	Fruit	6 Tb. All Fruit Jam* p. 164 (on pancakes— bananas in the pancakes also add to the fruit category here)	t/96
	Water/Snack	8 oz. water	

		Lunch	
	Water	8 oz. water	
	Vegetable	1 cup Mixed Veggie Festival* p. 265	2/162
	Grain	(whole-grain bread for sandwich)	
	Protein	1 Ham 'n' Cheese Sandwich* p. 249	13/406
	Fruit	1/2 cup green grapes	t/36
		8 oz. orange juice (or one whole orange for more fiber and less concentrated natural sugar)	0/120
	Water/Snack	8 oz. water/ 1 cup cauliflower chunks	t/24

		Dinner	
Easy			
	Water	8 oz. water	
	Vegetable	2 cups Homestyle Salad Bar* p. 267 with 8 Tb. Buttermilk Dressing* p. 210	4/368±
	Grain	One 3" square Country Corn Bread* p. 159 (make ahead)	5/201
	Protein	1 1/3 cups Fast and Creamy Clam Chowder* p. 157	2/138
	Fruit	1 cup Instant Peach Ice Cream* p. 194	t/117
	Water/Snack	12 oz. water	

Total 32/2226
32 fat grams x 9 calories =288 calories from fat
288 ÷ 2226 = **13% FAT**

130

Many grocery stores now offer bags of pre-cut, fresh mixed vegetables—a nice convenience item. Lowfat plain or garlic breadsticks make another handy convenience item. (They bake in about five minutes.) Let me know if you find whole-wheat breadsticks. We have white ones now and then.

DAY 50

			fg/cal
	Water	**Breakfast** 12 oz. water	
	Grain	2 cups Kellogg's Raspberry Fruit Wheats	0/360
	Protein	11/2 cups skim milk	t/129
	Fruit	1 orange	t/62
	Water/Snack	8 oz. water/ 1 cup celery sticks	t/18

Fast Food		**Lunch**	
Taco Time			
	Water	12 oz. water	
	Vegetable	1 Veggie Burrito (no cheese or sour cream; add fat free sour cream from home)	8/427
	Grain	(tortillas)	
	Protein	1 Chicken Soft Taco (no cheese or sour cream)	5/327
	Fruit	1 apple (from home)	t/81
	Water/Snack	8 oz. water	

	Water	**Dinner** 8 oz. water	
	Vegetable	3/4 cup Au Gratin Potatoes* p. 244	9/418
		2 ears corn on the cob	1/118
		with 1 Tb. butter	11/100
		(Omit butter to delete 11 fat grams and make this an 11 percent fat day.)	
		1 cup green beans with butter-flavored sprinkles	0/40
	Grain	2 whole-grain rolls with	t/90
		2 Tb. All Fruit Jam* p. 164	t/32
	Protein	6 oz. Red Snapper* p.254 with	3/217
		1/4 cup Tartar Sauce* p. 253	t/28
	Fruit	1 cup Yogurt Fruit Delight* p. 219	0/146
	Water/Snack	12 oz. water/ 1 cup cauliflower chunks	t/24

Total: 37/2617

37 fat grams x 9 calories = 333 calories from fat

333 ÷ 2617 = **13% FAT**

131

Fish is an excellent choice when you're trying to reduce your cholesterol level. It contains Omega 3 fatty acids that help to increase good cholesterol (HDL) and decrease triglycerides, arterial blockage, and bad cholesterol (LDL).

When eating at Taco Bell, I often order two bean burritos without cheese. They are inexpensive, nutritious, and low in fat.

FREEDOM MENUS

DAY 51

	Breakfast	fg/cal
Water	12 oz. water	
Grain	1 cup Breakfast Fruit Compote* p. 168	t/264
	(make ahead)	
Protein	1 cup skim milk (or evaporated skim milk)	t/86
Fruit	(in compote)	
Water/Snack	12 oz. water	

	Lunch	
Water	8 oz. water	
Vegetable	one 19 oz. can Campbell's Chunky Chicken	
	Vegetable Soup	12/340
Grain	1 slice whole-grain toast with 1 Tb.	
	All Fruit Jam* p. 164	t/87
Protein	(chicken in soup)	
Fruit	1 sliced orange	t/62
Water/Snack	8 oz. water/ 1 cup mixed vegetables	
	with 4 Tb. lowfat dip	2/130±

Easy	Dinner	
Water	8 oz. water	
Vegetable	1 cup steamed broccoli**	t/46
Grain	2 Zucchini Muffins** p. 234 (make ahead)	6/286
Protein	1 tortilla roll of Enchilada Casserole* p. 151	6/287
Fruit	3 pear halves on lettuce with red grapes,	
	1/2 cup lowfat cottage cheese, and paprika	2/272
Water/Snack	12 oz. water/ 1 cup celery sticks	t/6

Total: 28/1866

28 fat grams x 9 calories = 252 calories from fat

252 ÷ 1866 = **14% FAT**

Notice how you never leave out the meats and the dairy products, but they don't take over your day. Your focus is on veggies, grains, and fruits. But proteins also play an essential role for growth and repair of muscle tissue. However, excess protein can actually lead to water and muscle loss. Moderation is the key.

**Double or triple broccoli and muffin recipe if you would like these as leftovers tomorrow.

DAY 52

	Breakfast	fg/cal
Water	12 oz. water	
Grain	2 Zucchini Muffins left over from Day 51	6/286
Protein	1 cup Veggie and Cheese Egg	
	Scramble* p. 175	9/289
	1 cup nonfat fruit yogurt	0/200
Fruit	1 grapefruit	0/100
Water/Snack	8 oz. water	
	2 cups steamed broccoli left over	
	from Day 51 with butter flavor sprinkles	t/92

	Lunch	
Fast Food		
Wendy's		
Water	12 oz. water	
Vegetable	Broccoli Potato without cheese	
	(By requesting no cheese you delete	
	10 fat grams.)	4/370
Grain	1 leftover Zucchini Muffin	3/143
Protein	one 8 oz. order chili	6/190
Fruit	1 apple (from home)	t/81
Water/Snack	12 oz. water	
	baby carrots and celery sticks	t/40±

	Dinner	
Easy		
Water	12 oz. water	
Vegetable	2 cups Hawaiian Haystacks* p.183	6/468
Grain	(brown rice in Haystacks)	
Protein	(chicken in haystacks) and one 8 oz. glass	
	skim milk	t/86
Fruit	1 cup Fresh Fruit Combination Trays* p. 213	t/100±
	with 4 Tbs. Sour Cream Fruit Dip* p. 212	0/80
Water/Snack	8 oz. water	

> Total: 34/2525
> 34 fat grams x 9 calories = 306 calories from fat
> 306 ÷ 2525 = **12% FAT**

One-half cup loosely packed grated cheddar cheese equals two ounces and contains eighteen fat grams. It is 74 percent fat. If you choose to leave the cheese on your Wendy's Broccoli Potato, your overall daily totals will be 42 fat grams and 2203 calories, with 17 percent of your calories coming from fat. Seventeen percent is not too high unless you're highly resistant to fat loss. If you are highly resistant, go lower by omitting the cheese.

FREEDOM MENUS

SHOPPING LIST / DAYS 49 - 52

*This **four**-day shopping list may last your family **six** or **seven** days if you eat out often.*

BREAD / CEREAL / GRAIN

cereal,
   cornflakes, 1 box
   Kellogg's Raspberry Fruit Wheats,
     1 box

FRESH FRUITS
AND VEGETABLES

Or purchase other fruits and vegetables that are in season or on sale.

apples, 10
bananas, 4
grapefruit, 4
grapes,
   green, 2 lbs.
   red, 2 lbs.
lemon, 1
nectarines, 4
oranges, 8

broccoli, 5 bunches
carrots,
   baby, 1 small bag
   regular, 5 lbs.

cauliflower, 2 heads
celery, 1 bunch
corn, on the cob, 8
lettuce, leafy, 1 large bunch
mushrooms, 1 cup
onions,
   green, 1 bunch
   yellow, medium, 2
peppers, green, 3
potatoes, baking, 12
tomatoes, medium, 4
zucchini, 2

MEAT AND DAIRY

buttermilk, 1 pint
cottage cheese, lowfat, 32 oz.
cream cheese, nonfat, one 8 oz. tub
eggs, 1 to 2 dozen *(you'll use mostly whites)*
milk, skim or 1%, 1 to 2 gallons
sour cream, nonfat, 16 oz.
yogurt,
   fruit, nonfat, 32 oz.
   vanilla, nonfat, 32 oz.
   (If you are diabetic, purchase plain nonfat yogurt and sweeten it with All Fruit Jam and / or fruit-juice concentrate.)

CANNED GOODS

chicken, cooked chunk, one 4 oz. can
clams, two 6 1/2 oz. cans
pimentos, 1 small can or jar
sauce, enchilada, one 14 oz. can

MASTER LIST /CHECK LIST
DAYS 49 - 52

Check to be sure that you have the following Master List items already in stock. Baking items, condiments, and spices are not included in this list. They are listed on pages 59 - 60.

BREAD / CEREAL / GRAIN

Purchase breads, rolls, buns, etc., on sale and freeze.

bread, whole-wheat, 1 to 2 loaves
oats, rolled, 1 cup
rice, brown or white, 3 cups
rolls, whole-grain, 1 dozen
tortillas, whole-wheat, 1 dozen
wheat, whole-kernels, 3/4 cup

MEAT AND DAIRY

Purchase in moderate quantities on sale and freeze. Grate cheese before freezing.

beef, extra-lean ground, 1/2 lb.
fish, red snapper, four 6 oz. fillets
ham, sliced, extra-lean, 8 oz.

butter, 1/2 lb.
cheese,
    cheddar, lowfat or regular, grated, 8 oz.
    mozzarella, part-skim, grated, 16 oz.
eggs, 1 dozen *(You'll use mostly whites.)*

CANNED GOODS

applesauce*, unsweetened or lightly sweetened, one 16 oz. can
beans,
    green, two 16 oz. cans
    refried, nonfat or lowfat, one 16 oz. can
    white*, one 15 oz. can
corn, cream style, one 16 oz. can
milk, evaporated skim, one 12 oz. can
noodles, chow mein, one 5 oz. can
olives, sliced, one 2 oz. can
oranges, mandarin, one 11 oz. can
pears, one 29 oz. can
pineapple,
    chunks, in own juice, two 20 oz. cans
    crushed, in own juice, one 20 oz. can
soup,
    Campbell's Chunky Chicken Vegetable, four 19 oz. cans
    Campbell's Cream of Potato, one 103/4 oz. can
    dry mix, onion, 1 envelope *(This is not in a can.)*
    lowfat cream of chicken, one 103/4 oz. can
tomato sauce, one 8 oz. can

FROZEN

blueberries, one 16 oz. bag
juice concentrates,
    apple, one 12 oz. can
    Dole Orchard Peach, one 12 oz. can
peaches, one 16 oz. bag
peas, petite, one 16 oz. bag
vegetables, mixed, three 16 oz. bags

*See the italics statement at the bottom of page 81.

135

FREEDOM MENUS

DAY 53

		Breakfast	fg/cal
	Water	12 oz. water	
	Grain	1 cup Cinnamon-Maple Oatmeal* p. 169	3/278
	Protein	1 cup skim milk	t/86
	Fruit	1 large sliced orange	t/62
	Water/Snack	8 oz. water	
		1 cup purple cabbage slices	t/20

		Lunch	
	Water	8 oz. water	
	Vegetable	one half 19 oz. can Campbell's	
		Old Fashioned Vegetable Beef Soup	5/160
	Grain	2 Marvelous Muffins* p. 231 (Make extra	
		if you would like leftovers for tomorrow.)	6/296
	Protein	1 cup nonfat fruit yogurt	0/200
	Fruit	1 cup honeydew melon chunks	t/60
	Water/Snack	12 oz. water/ 8 baby carrots	0/35

		Dinner	
Easy			
	Water	8 oz. water	
	Vegetable	2 cups Easy Cabbage Dinner* p. 263	9/620
	Grain	1 Marvelous Muffin left over from lunch	3/148
	Protein	(beef in cabbage dinner)	
	Fruit	One 21/2" by 2" square Peach Cobbler*	
		p. 196 ("B+" Choice)	6/316
	Water/Snack	12 oz. water	

Total: 32/2281

32 fat grams x 9 calories = 288 calories from fat

288 ÷ 2281 = **13% FAT**

This is what I call a "cabbage day". Even people who formerly didn't like cabbage love this Easy Cabbage Dinner.

DAY 54

			fg/cal
Easy	**Breakfast**		
Water	12 oz. water		
Grain	2 slices Zucchini-Pineapple-Nut Bread*		
	p. 163 (Make ahead and this meal is		
	a time saver!)		6/230
Protein	1 cup nonfat fruit yogurt		0/200
Fruit	(pineapple in bread)		
Water/Snack	8 oz. water/ 1 cup mixed fresh vegetables		
	with 4 Tb. lowfat dip of your choice		1/120±

Restaurant	**Lunch**		
Village Inn*			
Water	12 oz. water		
Vegetable	Fresh Veggie Omelet		18/701
Grain	Fruit and Nut Pancakes (Ask for a side		
	order = three 4" round pancakes instead		
	of toast. Be extremely moderate with syrup.)		9.5/468
Protein	(eggs and cheese in omelet)		
Fruit	side order of fresh mixed fruit chunks		
Water/Snack	8 oz. water		

Easy	**Dinner**		
Water	8 oz.water		
Vegetable	1 1/4 cups Saucy Green Beans and		
	Almonds* p. 266		7/139
	1/2 large baked potato with 3 Tb. lowfat		
	dip left over from snack		1/163
Grain	1 Marvelous Muffin left over		
	from Day 53		3/148
Protein	1 breast BBQ Chicken* p. 178		6/236
	one 8 oz. glass skim milk		t/86
Fruit	1 cup sliced kiwi fruit, strawberries,		
	and bananas		t/110
Water/Snack	12 oz. water/ 1 sliced cucumber		t/39

Total: 51.5/2640
51.5 fat grams x 9 calories = 463.5 calories from fat
463.5 ÷ 2640 = **18% FAT**

Village Inn has some of my favorite healthy choices. (See the Restaurant Food Evaluation Charts *on page 351.) I love their Fresh Veggie Omelet and their Fruit and Nut Pancakes served with a side of fruit. Other restaurants, such as Denny's, will make me an omelet with two egg whites and one whole egg, and* all *veggies in the center. This is not on their menu, but they are very good with special requests. A "two egg white"—"one whole egg" omelet is even better than a "low-cholesterol egg substitute" omelet because it is completely natural and is much lower in grams of fat.*

FREEDOM MENUS

DAY 55

		Breakfast	fg/cal
	Water	12 oz. water	
	Grain	1 1/2 cups corn flakes mixed with 1/2 cup	
		Post grape-nuts	0/385
	Protein	1 1/2 cups 1% milk	4.5/153
	Fruit	1 sliced banana (on cereal)	t/105
	Water/Snack	8 oz. water/ 1 1/2 cups Total cereal/ 1 cup	
		1% milk	4.5/252
		8 baby carrots	0/35

		Lunch	
	Water	12 oz. water	
	Vegetable	11 oz. LaChoy Fresh and Lite Beef Broccoli	7/290
	Grain	1/2 cup Chow Mein Noodles	5/228
	Protein	1 1/2 cups LaChoy	
		Sweet and Sour Oriental with Chicken	4/480
	Fruit	1 1/2 cups Tropical Fruit Ice* p. 218	1/228
	Water/Snack	8 oz. water/ 2 slices Zucchini-Pineapple-Nut	
		Bread left over from Day 54	6/230

		Dinner	
Easy			
	Water	8 oz. water	
	Vegetable	1 1/2 cups Tossed Salad* p. 267 with 6 Tb.	
		Buttermilk Dressing* p. 210	3/276±
	Grain	(whole-grain hamburger buns)	
	Protein	2 Sloppy Joes* p. 156 ("A–" to "B+" Choice)	26/824
	Fruit	1 cup green grapes	t/72
		Dessert: 1 1/2 cups root-beer float (1 cup	
		root beer with 1/2 cup vanilla	
		ice milk = "B" Choice—not for fat loss)	2/270
	Water/Snack	12 oz. water/ 1 cup leftover	
		Tossed Salad with 4 Tb. lowfat dressing	2/184±

Total: 65/4012

65 fat grams x 9 calories = 585 calories from fat

585 ÷ 4012 = **15% FAT**

My teenage boys sometimes eat more than this menu illustrates. I sometimes eat this much if I'm exercising a lot (hiking, etc.) or nursing a baby. Less than half this much may fill you up, so make certain to adjust this menu to your individual needs. Success is a feeling, not a number! If you're a stuffer, lighten up your meals a little. Go heavier on the veggies and lighter on the grains. Enjoy the freedom to feel energized, not miserable after a meal. And, snack only on veggies, (unless you're really hungry) especially in the evening. Also, remember to eat slowly and enjoy your food to avoid gastrointestinal distress.

DAY 56

		Breakfast	fg/cal
	Water	12 oz. water	
	Grain	One 3" square Country Corn Bread* p. 159	5/201
		with 1 Tb. honey butter	
		("B–" Choice—not for fat loss.	
		Make ahead as a time-saver.)	6/80
	Protein	1 1/2 cups Breakfast Shake* p. 168	
	Water/Snack	12 oz. water/ 1 sliced zucchini	t/18

		Lunch	
	Water	8 oz. water	
	Vegetable	1 cup fresh carrot and celery sticks with	
		4 Tb. lowfat dip of your choice	2/145±
	Grain	15 oz. Franco-American PizzO's	
		("B+" Choice)	4/340
	Protein	(in PizzO's and cottage cheese)	
	Fruit	1 cup Pineapple and Cottage Cheese	
		Salad* p. 215	2/202
	Water/Snack	12 oz. water/ 1 sliced cucumber	t/39

		Dinner	
Easy			
	Water	8 oz. water	
	Vegetable	2 cups Zucchini Casserole* p. 270	12/366
	Grain	(stuffing in casserole)	
	Protein	(yogurt in casserole and cottage cheese)	
	Fruit	1 cup Pineapple and Cottage Cheese Salad	
		left over from lunch	2/202
	Water/Snack	12 oz. water/ 1 cup Kellogg's Crispix Cereal**	0/110
		with 3/4 cup 1% milk	2/76
		1 sliced green pepper	t/26

Total: 35/2049

35 fat grams x 9 calories = 315 calories from fat

315 ÷ 2049= **15% FAT**

*This menu contains **35** fat grams and is 15 percent fat. Day 55 contains **65** fat grams and is 15 percent fat. How could this be? Day 55 contains 4012 calories and Day 56 has 2,049 calories, so it takes about twice as many fat grams to give the first day the same fat percentage as the second day. Your hunger and energy needs may easily vary 500 calories or more on any given day. I average between about 2,000 and 3,500 calories a day. In hot weather hunger lessens; with more activity hunger increases. LISTEN to your body!*

**Snack ONLY on veggie-based foods in the evening if you are highly resistant to fat loss.

Shopping List / Days 53 - 56

*This **four**-day shopping list may last your family **six** or **seven** days if you eat out often.*

BREAD / CEREAL / GRAIN

cereal,
   cornflakes, 1 box
   General Mills Total, 1 box
   Kellogg's Crispix, 1 box
   Post grape-nuts, 1 box

FRESH FRUITS AND VEGETABLES

Or purchase other fruits and vegetables that are in season or on sale.

apples, 4
bananas, 9
grapefruit, 4
grapes, 2 lbs.
melon, honeydew, 1
oranges, 4
peaches, 10
pineapple, 1
strawberries, 1 quart *(or frozen)*

cabbage,
   green, 1 head
   purple, 1 head
carrots,
   baby, 1 large bag
   regular, 5 lbs
celery, 1 bunch
cucumbers, 8
lettuce, leafy, 2 large bunches
onions, medium, 4
peppers, green, 5
potatoes, baking, 9
tomatoes, medium, 3 - 4
zucchini, 14

MEAT AND DAIRY

buttermilk, 1 pint
cottage cheese, lowfat, 32 to 48 oz.*
eggs, 1 dozen *(you'll use mostly whites)*
milk, skim or 1%, 1 to 2 gallons
sour cream, nonfat, 16 oz.
yogurt,
   fruit-flavored, nonfat, 32 oz.
   plain, nonfat, 16 oz.
   vanilla, nonfat, 32 oz.

CANNED GOODS

Franco American PizzO's,
   four 15 oz. cans
LaChoy Fresh and Lite Beef and
   Broccoli, one 431/2 oz. can
LaChoy Sweet and Sour Oriental
   with Chicken, two 431/2 oz. cans

MISCELLANEOUS

almonds, slivered, 4 oz.
ice milk, vanilla, 1/2 gallon *("B" Choice)*
root beer, 1 liter *("B" Choice)*
stuffing mix, lowfat, 1 medium package
walnuts, 2 oz.

*See the first italics statement at the bottom of the next page.

MASTER LIST / CHECK LIST
Days 53 - 56

Check to be sure that you have the following Master List items already in stock. Baking items, condiments, and spices are not included in this list. They are listed on pages 59 - 60.

BREAD / CEREAL / GRAIN

Purchase breads, rolls, buns, etc., on sale and freeze.

buns, hamburger, whole-grain or white,
    one 8-count package
oats, rolled, 5 cups

MEAT AND DAIRY

Purchase in moderate quantities on sale and freeze. Grate cheese before freezing.

beef, extra-lean ground, 1 1/2 lbs.
chicken, breasts, boneless and skinless, 8

butter, 1/2 lb.
cheese, cheddar, grated, 4 oz.

CANNED GOODS

applesauce**, unsweetened or lightly
    sweetened, two 16 oz. cans
beans,
    green, French-cut, two 16 oz. cans
    white*, one 15 oz. can

corn,
    cream style, one 16 oz. can
    whole kernel, one 17 oz. can
milk, evaporated skim, one 12 oz. can
noodles, chow-mein, one 5 oz. can
oranges, mandarin, two 11 oz. cans
pineapple, crushed, in own juice,
    three 20 oz. cans
soup,
    Campbell's Old Fashioned
        Vegetable Beef, two 19 oz. cans
    lowfat cream of chicken,
        one 103/4 oz. can
    lowfat cream of mushroom,
        one 103/4 oz. can
    tomato, two 103/4 oz. cans
tomato sauce, one 8 oz. can

FROZEN

fruit, *(any type),* one 16 oz. bag
juice, concentrate,
    apple, one 12 oz. can
    Dole Country Raspberry,
        one 12 oz. can
    Dole Orchard Peach, one 12 oz. can
    orange, one 12 oz. can
    pineapple, one 12 oz. can

MISCELLANEOUS

salad dressing, mix, Hidden Valley Lite
Ranch**, 2 envelopes

Purchase an additional 16 ounces of cottage cheese and this salad dressing mix if the "lowfat dip of your choice," on menus 54 and 56, is the "Ranch Dip" on page 212.

**See the italics statement at the bottom of page 81.*

FREEDOM MENUS

*When I stopped dieting
to be thin and started eating
to be healthy, the weight
came off and stayed off!*

Fresh apples, Potato Corn Soup, whole-wheat bread with fat free cream cheese and All Fruit Jam, and fresh vegetables with Ranch Dip

Sloppy Joes, corn on the cob, Apple Cobbler, and vanilla ice milk

Chinese Salad Bar

Veggie-Stuffed Potato, Pineapple-Lime Chicken, Cranberry-Orange Muffins and Minute Cherry Cheesecake

Recipes

Normal! Delicious! Exceptionally Fast!

"A" Choices = *Excellent, nutritional fat-loss choices when combined with other good foods. The balance of water, veggie, grain, protein, and fruit is essential!*

"B" Choices = *Good coasting or maintenance choices. Some people see optimal fat loss with a few "B" Choices added into their "A" days. Others have much more resistant bodies and see more success with ALL "A" Choices. Main course items are judged more strictly than dessert items because their nutritional value should be the highest. In other words, a "B" Choice main course is nutritionally superior to a "B" Choice dessert. Listen to your body and adjust to your needs.*

Ratings are based on fat, sugar, sodium, and fiber content, and the overall nutrient value of the food. Some foods with a fat percentage over 20 percent still recieve an "A" rating because of the excellent nutrition they provide. These foods are placed into menus with overall fat percentages ranging between 10 and 20 percent—the ideal range for optimum health and excess fat loss.

If you are diabetic, hypoglycemic, or highly resistant to excess fat loss, choose "A" and "B" Choice main courses with an emphasis on the "A" Choices; and choose ONLY "A" Choice desserts.

FREEDOM RECIPES

BEANS / LEGUMES

Chicken-Chili Enchiladas ("A" Choice)

12	tortillas, whole-wheat
1	large can (31 oz.) refried beans, lowfat
2	cans (15 oz. each) chicken chili, lowfat
2	cups picante sauce; mild, medium, or hot
2	cups spaghetti sauce, canned, lowfat
1	cup green peppers, diced, optional
1	cup onion, diced, optional
1	cup tomato, diced, optional
11/2	cups mozzarella cheese, part-skim, grated

Chicken-Chili Enchiladas	
Calories per serving:	516
Fat grams per serving:	11 1/2
Fat percentage:	20%
Number of servings:	6
Serving size:	2 enchiladas

Combine refried beans and chicken chili in a large bowl. Set aside. Mix together picante sauce and spaghetti sauce in separate bowl. Blend 1/2 cup sauce into bean mixture. Place about 1/3 cup of bean mixture in center of each tortilla from end to end. Sprinkle with diced green pepper, onion, and tomato, if desired, and roll up. Place side by side in a 9 x 13 baking dish that has been thoroughly sprayed with nonstick cooking spray.

Top with 2 to 21/2 cups remaining sauce, cheese, green peppers, onions, and tomatoes. Place 3 green-pepper rings in the center.

Bake in a 375 degree oven for 25-35 minutes. Serve with a fresh-fruit platter.

LEAN & FREE Nachos ("B" Choice*)

2	cups tortilla chips, baked**
1	cup refried beans (no fat added)
1	cup salsa, chunky
1/4	cup cheddar cheese, sharp, grated
1/4	cup olives, sliced
1/4	cup avocado, diced
1/3	cup green onion, diced
1/2	cup green or yellow peppers, diced
1/2	cup tomato, fresh, diced

LEAN & FREE Nachos	
Calories per serving:	271
Fat grams per serving:	9.5
Fat percentage:	32%*
Number of servings:	2
Serving size: approximately 3 cups	

In microwave or two separate saucepans warm refried beans and salsa separately. Place chips on a dinner plate or a heavy paper plate. Top with beans, salsa, cheese, and all other ingredients.

Serve with fruit and water for a kid-pleasing Water, Veggie, Grain, Protein, and Fruit complete meal!

*These 32 percent-fat "B" Choice nachos are a much healthier choice than your average "D" Choice—50 to 80 percent-fat nachos. They fit nicely into a day that has an **overall** fat percentage of less than 20 percent.

**Ask your grocer if he already stocks, or can order in baked tortilla chips. Guiltless Gourmet and Tostitos are excellent brands. My family prefers the Cool Ranch-flavored Baked Tostitos.

FREEDOM RECIPES

145

Mexican Lasagna ("A" Choice)

1	bottle (16 oz.) picante sauce (as hot as you like it)
1	14 1/2 oz. can tomatoes, chopped
12	flour tortillas, whole-wheat or corn tortillas
1	large can refried beans, no fat added
1	large onion, chopped
2	large green peppers, chopped
1	small can green chilies, diced
1/2	cup mozzarella cheese, part-skim, grated (loosely packed)
2	fresh tomatoes, chopped lettuce sour cream, fat free

Mexican Lasagna	
Calories per serving:	371
Fat grams per serving:	6
Fat percentage:	15%
Number of servings:	6
Serving size:	2 tortilla roll-ups

This recipe is a time-saver if the onion and green peppers are chopped in advance. Place in sealed plastic bags or air-tight containers and refrigerate until ready to use.

In a medium saucepan combine picante sauce and chopped tomatoes; heat well.

Spread onto each tortilla 2 tablespoons of beans. Sprinkle with onions, peppers, and chilies (also a very small amount of cheese is good here). Roll tortillas and place in a 9 x 13 baking dish that has been sprayed with nonstick cooking spray. Continue rolling until all tortillas are done. (To make rolling easier, microwave 3 or 4 tortillas at a time for 30 seconds.) Pour sauce mixture over the tortillas. The sauce should cover very well. Sprinkle with remaining onions, peppers, chilies, and cheese. Bake at 350 degrees for 20 to 25 minutes or until heated through and bubbling. Garnish with fresh chopped tomatoes, lettuce, and fat free sour cream, if desired. Serves 6.

Taco Salad with Taco Dressing ("B+" Choice)

1/2   pound ground beef, extra-lean
1/2   cup onion, diced
1/2   envelope of taco seasoning
1/3   to 1/2 cup water
     Guiltless Gourmet or Tostitos Baked No Oil Tortilla Chips
1   can kidney beans
1   onion, purple, sliced
2   cups tomatoes, diced
6   cups lettuce or packaged salad mix
1   cup taco-flavored cheese, shredded

Taco Salad with Taco Dressing	
Calories per serving:	247
Fat grams per serving:	10
Fat percentage:	36%
Number of servings:	6
Serving size:	1 1/2 cup

This recipe is a time-saver if the onions and tomatoes are chopped in advance.

Brown ground beef and onion in skillet. Sprinkle taco seasoning over meat. Add a small amount of water to the meat—about 1/3 to 1/2 cup. This will help the seasonings dissolve. Let simmer about 5 minutes. Remove from heat. Crumble a handful of corn chips on a plate. Add about 1/4 cup meat. Then follow with kidney beans, onions, tomatoes, lettuce, and cheese. Top salad with taco dressing.

Taco Dressing ("A" Choice)

1/2   cup Kraft Miracle Whip Dressing

1/2   cup mayonnaise, fat free

1/2   envelope taco seasoning (the other half of the envelope used above)
     skim milk

Combine all ingredients and thin with skim milk to the desired thickness. Add more seasoning if you like a stronger taco taste.

147

Tempting Tacos ("A" Choice)

8   jumbo corn taco shells
       (regular will do) or
24   mini taco shells
       taco seasoning mix (dry)
2   30 oz. large cans, refried
       beans, no fat added
1   cup cheddar cheese, or
       taco-flavored cheese,
       shredded
1   cup lettuce, shredded
1   cup tomatoes, diced
1   cup onions, diced
1   cup taco salsa or picante
       sauce
1   cup sour cream, fat free

Tempting Tacos	
Calories per serving;	
1 jumbo taco:	289
3 mini tacos:	265
Fat grams per serving;	
1 jumbo taco:	8
3 mini tacos:	7
Fat percentage;	
1 jumbo taco:	25%
3 mini tacos:	24%
Number of servings:	8
Serving size:	1 jumbo or
	3 mini tacos

This recipe is a time-saver if the onions and tomatoes are chopped in advance.

Heat all taco shells in a 250-degree oven while heating refried beans in a saucepan. After beans are thoroughly heated, season to taste with taco seasoning mix. Fill each taco shell about 1/4 to 1/3 full of beans. Then add 2 tablespoons cheese to large tacos and 2 teaspoons cheese to small tacos. Finish with lettuce, tomato, onion, salsa or picante sauce, and fat free sour cream. Both kids and adults love these.

Special Note: You may also decide to use extra- lean ground beef or extra-lean ground turkey in place of the beans. Or, you may choose to mix the beans with equal parts of extra-lean ground meat and season to taste. I prefer the taste of all beans. I like extra fat grams from the cheese, not the meat. Choose what *you* like best.

BEEF / PORK*

Beef Fajitas ("A" Choice)
or turkey or chicken

3 oz. round steak*, extra-lean,
    or skinless turkey or
    chicken breast, thinly sliced
1/2 cup water
1/2 envelope taco mix
1/2 clove garlic, diced
1   onion
2   green peppers
1   red pepper
2   flour tortillas, whole-wheat
    (or white)
1   cup lettuce, shredded
1   cup tomato, diced
2   tablespoons mozzarella
    cheese, part-skim, grated

Beef Fajitas	
Calories per serving:	275
Fat grams per serving:	6
Fat percentage:	20%
Number of servings:	2
Serving size:	1 fajita

This recipe is a time-saver if vegetables are sliced in advance.

Pan-fry the meat until brown. Then add 1/2 cup water and steam for a few minutes. While steaming, add diced garlic and taco mix for flavor.

Slice vegetables into 1/2-inch wedges. When meat is done, add vegetables and stir-fry until tender.

Roll mixture inside soft whole-wheat tortillas and garnish with shredded lettuce, tomato, and a tablespoon of grated cheese.

*Beef and pork are not excluded from LEAN & FREE menus. These meats contain essential nutrients and protein. They make an excellent condiment or complement to a meal but they should never be the center of the meal. Use them in great moderation.

149

D'Ann's Delicious 15 Minute Beef Stroganoff ("A" Choice)

1/2	pound top sirloin cut into very small pieces (fat trimmed)
1/2	cup water
1	envelope Schilling Beef Stroganoff mix
2	cups water
2	tablespoons dry cooking-sherry
2	teaspoons beef bouillon granules
2	cans (4 ounces each) mushroom stems and pieces, drained
1	8 oz. tub cream cheese, fat free
4 - 6	cups noodles, hot, cooked

Beef Stroganoff	
Calories per serving:	254
Fat grams per serving:	4
Fat percentage:	14%
Number of servings:	4
Serving size:	1 cup
	(without noodles)

Simmer meat and 1/2 cup water in covered skillet for 5 minutes. Combine seasoning mix, water, cooking sherry, and beef granules in a separate bowl. Stir into beef. Add mushrooms; simmer 10 minutes. Remove from heat. Add cream cheese; stir and serve over hot, cooked noodles. Delicious!

Recipe Variation: Mushroom Stroganoff. Follow key recipe, except delete top sirloin. This brings the fat grams down to just a trace.

FREEDOM RECIPES

Enchilada Casserole ("A" Choice)

1/2	pound ground beef, extra-lean
1	chopped onion
1	can enchilada sauce
1	small can tomato sauce
1	cup water
1	small can olives, sliced
12	flour tortillas, whole-wheat (or white)
1	small can refried beans, no fat
11/2	cups sour cream, fat free
1	cup mozzarella cheese, shredded, part-skim

Enchilada Casserole	
Calories per serving:	573
Fat grams per serving:	12
Fat percentage:	19%
Number of servings:	6
Serving size:	2 tortilla rolls

Cook ground beef and onion. Add enchilada sauce, tomato sauce, water, and olives and mix well. On flour tortilla, spread 2 tablespoons refried beans, a tablespoon of sour cream, and a spoonful of meat mix. Roll up tortilla and place in a nonstick cooking-sprayed 9 x 13 baking dish. Continue with remaining tortillas. Pour remaining meat mix over all. Top with shredded cheese. Bake at 350 degrees for 20 minutes. Cool slightly. Serves 4 to 6.

FREEDOM RECIPES

151

FREEDOM RECIPES

Pizza Wheels ("A" & "B" Choices)

8   hamburger buns, whole-wheat (16 halves), home-made or grocery-store variety. Sometimes you can't find 100% whole wheat, so get as close as possible. (Whole-grain, lowfat English muffins will also work well.)

2   15 1/2 oz. bottles pizza sauce

1   cup fresh, mixed, broccoli pea pods, onions, and carrot slivers

4   3-inch round Canadian bacon, thin-sliced

1/2   cup pineapple tidbits, in own juice

1/2   cup mushrooms, sliced, fresh

12   1 1/2 inch round pepperonis, thin sliced

3   cups mozzarella cheese, part-skim, grated

Pizza Wheels	
Calories per serving;	
Canadian Bacon, etc:	239
Cheese Only:	185
Pepperoni:	301
Vegetable:	200
Fat grams per serving;	
Canadian Bacon, etc:	8
Cheese Only:	6
Pepperoni:	12
Vegetable:	6
Fat percentage;	
Canadian Bacon, etc:	30%
Cheese only:	29%
Pepperoni:	36%
Vegetable:	27%
Number of servings:	16
Serving size:	1 round

Place pizza rounds on two cookie sheets sprayed lightly with nonstick cooking spray. Bake each sheet for 7 to 10 minutes at 375 degrees.

Pizza Variations

Canadian Bacon, Pineapple, and Mushroom Pizza Rounds: Spread 3 tablespoons pizza sauce on each of 4 bun halves. Place one slice Canadian bacon, 2 tablespoons pineapple tidbits, 2 tablespoons sliced mushrooms, and 3 tablespoons cheese on top of each half.

Cheese Only Pizza Rounds: Spread 3 tablespoons pizza sauce on each of 4 bun halves. Sprinkle with 3 tablespoons cheese.

Pepperoni Pizza Rounds: Spread 3 tablespoons pizza sauce on each of 4 bun halves. Place 3 pepperoni slices and 3 tablespoons cheese on top of each half.

Veggie Pizza Rounds: Spread 3 tablespoons pizza sauce on each of 4 bun halves. Place 1/4 cup mixed vegetables and 3 tablespoons cheese on top of each half. (Check the vegetable section of your grocery store for fresh, pre-cut, stir-fry vegetables in bags.)

Special Note: Children love to help make these. Set up an ingredient assembly line and let them create. Olive eyes, pineapple noses, and green-pepper mouths make "kid-pleasing" Pizza Wheel faces. Encourage creativity and have fun!

A fresh-fruit plate with nonfat vanilla yogurt on the side goes perfectly with this delicious, novel meal.

Porcupine Meatballs ("B–" Choice)

1	lb. pound ground beef, extra-lean
1/2	cup brown rice, cooked
1/2	cup green pepper, chopped
1/2	cup onion, chopped
2	egg whites
1/2	teaspoon salt
1/2	teaspoon pepper
3/4	cup water
6	oz. tomato paste
1	teaspoon Worcestershire sauce

Porcupine Meatballs	
Calories per serving:	249
Fat grams per serving:	12*
Fat percentage:	43%
Number of servings:	6
Serving size:	3 meatballs

This recipe is a time-saver if the rice is prepared in advance and the green peppers and onions are chopped in advance.

Mix all ingredients except water, tomato paste, and Worcestershire sauce. Shape into 18 meatballs. Place in 9 x 9 baking dish. Bake at 375 degrees for 30 minutes. Mix tomato paste, Worcestershire sauce, and water. Pour this mixture over meatballs and bake 30 minutes more. Serve with tossed salad, fruit, and muffins.

*Remember to be very moderate with red meat. This recipe receives a "B–" only because you'll be eating small amounts of it along with generous helpings of vegetables, fruits, and whole grains so that your overall meal will be under 20 percent fat.

153

Pork Chow Mein ("A" Choice)

2	tablespoons "good" oil (see page 280)
1	cup pork, extra-lean, cubed
1	cup onion, chopped
1	cup celery, slant cut
3/4	cup bamboo shoots
1	small can mushrooms
1	can bean sprouts
11/3	cups chicken soup stock
1/2	teaspoon sugar
2	tablespoons soy sauce
2	tablespoons cornstarch chow mein noodles

Pork Chow Mein	
Calories per serving:	302
Fat grams per serving:	8
Fat percentage:	24%
Number of servings:	8
Serving size:	1 cup

This recipe is a time-saver if pork, onions, and celery are cut in advance.

Stir-fry pork in 1 tablespoon vegetable oil in wok or frying pan until brown and tender. Remove pork from pan. Add remaining tablespoon of oil and stir-fry all vegetables for 5 minutes or until vegetables are tender-crisp. Add meat to vegetables and mix well.

Heat soup, sugar, and soy sauce in saucepan. In separate bowl mix 3 tablespoons cold water and cornstarch. Stir into soup mixture and heat until thickened, stirring constantly. Pour over vegetable mixture. Let flavors blend before serving. Sprinkle 1/2 cup chow-mein noodles over each serving.

FREEDOM RECIPES

Quick, Delicious Beef Stew ("A" Choice)

1   can (40 oz.) Nalley's Big Chunk Beef Stew (or another brand with moderate fat content)

2   cans (17 oz. each) Campbell's Chunky Beef and Vegetable Soup

1   can (15 oz.) kidney or pinto beans, drained

1   can (17 oz.) corn, drained

1   can (17 oz.) green beans, drained

Beef Stew	
Calories per serving:	302
Fat grams per serving:	8
Fat percentage:	24%
Number of servings:	8
Serving size:	1 cup

Mix all ingredients together in a large pot or kettle. Heat on medium heat, stirring frequently and scraping bottom, until stew is hot. Serve with whole-grain toast and fruit.

Roast Beef* ("B" Choice)

1   roast, medium size, lean cut. Trim off all visible fat.

Roast Beef	
Calories per serving:	216
Fat grams per serving:	13
Fat percentage:	54%
Number of servings:	16
Serving size:	3 oz.

Brown roast in frying pan. Sprinkle salt, pepper, and garlic salt on all sides. Turn heat down to low. Add 2 to 3 cups water. Let cook slowly for 3 to 6 hours until fork goes in easily.

Fresh vegetables can be added the last 45 minutes of cooking. This roast can be cooked on weekends, then used all week long in soups, stews, casseroles, and sandwiches stuffed full of veggies.

*Beef is high in vitamin B_{12} and other essential nutrients that are not easily found in many foods. Beef also has a substantial amount of saturated fat and cholesterol, so be very moderate with its use.

FREEDOM RECIPES

155

Shepherd's Pie ("A" Choice)

1/2	pound extra-lean ground beef
1	medium onion, chopped
1	can tomato soup
1	can green beans, drained
1	can corn, whole-kernel, drained
5	medium potatoes, cooked, mashed, or 6 servings instant potatoes
1/2	cup mozzarella cheese, part-skim, shredded

Shepherd's Pie	
Calories per serving:	385
Fat grams per serving:	8
Fat percentage:	18%
Number of servings:	6
Serving size:	1 cup

This recipe is a time-saver if you use instant or leftover mashed potatoes.

Brown meat and onions. Drain well. Add soup to meat mixture. Layer meat and vegetables in a 2-quart casserole dish. Put mashed potatoes in mounds along the edge of the mixture, leaving a hole in the center to sprinkle the cheese on top. Bake at 350 degrees for 30 minutes.

Sloppy Joes ("A–" to "B+' Choice*)

1	pound extra-lean ground beef
11/2	cups celery, chopped
11/2	cups onion, chopped
1	can (8 oz.) tomato sauce
1	can tomato soup
1	teaspoon salt
1/4	teaspoon chili powder few drops Tabasco
6	whole-wheat hamburger buns (White will do if you can't find wheat.)

Sloppy Joes	
Calories per serving:	412
Fat grams per serving:	13
Fat percentage:	28%
Number of servings:	6
Serving size: 1/2 cup plus 1 bun	

This recipe is a time-saver if the celery and onions are chopped in advance.

Brown meat in large skillet. Drain meat well. Add celery and onion; cook until tender. Add remaining ingredients. Simmer uncovered 20 minutes. For best flavor, cool and reheat before serving on whole-wheat hamburger buns.

*This rating is dependent upon the fat contents of the ground beef.

156

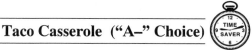

Taco Casserole ("A–" Choice)

1/2	pound ground beef, extra-lean
1	medium onion, chopped
1	can (12 oz.) corn, drained
1/4	teaspoon rosemary
1/4	teaspoon oregano
1/4	teaspoon marjoram
1	teaspoon salt
1/2	teaspoon pepper
2	8 oz. cans tomato sauce
2	10 oz. cans enchilada sauce
1	cup mozzarella cheese, part-skim, shredded
1	package flour (whole-wheat or white) or corn tortillas (small, cut in 1 inch strips)

Taco Casserole

Calories per serving:	332
Fat grams per serving:	10 1/2
Fat percentage:	28%
Number of servings:	6
Serving size: approximately 1 cup	

This recipe is very easy to prepare. It may take slightly longer than 15 minutes.

Brown ground beef and onion. Add corn and spices. Combine tomato sauce and enchilada sauce. Pour half of sauce over meat mixture and simmer 5 minutes. Arrange in a nonstick cooking-sprayed casserole dish—tortilla strips, meat, and shredded cheese; then add tortillas, cheese, and remaining sauce. Bake 15 to 20 minutes at 325 degrees.

FREEDOM RECIPES

157

BREADS

Big Soft Pretzels ("A" Choice) *EASY!*

1	cup flour, whole-wheat
1/2	cup flour, unbleached
2	teaspoons baking powder
1	teaspoon sugar
1/2	teaspoon salt
2/3	cup milk, skim
2	tablespoons butter, soft
1	egg white
	coarse salt

Big Soft Pretzels	
Calories per serving:	52
Fat grams per serving:	1
Fat percentage:	17%
Number of servings:	16
Serving size:	1 pretzel

Mix flours, baking powder, sugar, and salt in bowl. Add milk and soft butter. Mix with fork to make a soft dough. Knead 10 times. Divide dough in half. Roll half of dough into rectangle 12" x 8". Cut lengthwise into eight 1-inch strips. Fold each strip in half lengthwise and pinch edges to seal. Twist each strip into a pretzel shape. Place seam-side down on non-stick cooking sprayed baking sheet. Repeat with remaining half of dough. Beat egg white in small bowl with fork. Brush pretzels with egg and sprinkle lightly with coarse salt. Bake at 400 degrees 16-20 minutes or until golden brown. Makes 16 large pretzels. Remove with wide pancake turner and place on rack to cool.

Country Corn Bread ("A" Choice)

1/2   cup flour, whole-wheat
1/2   cup flour, white
1   cup cornmeal
1/2   teaspoon salt
4   teaspoons baking powder
4   egg whites
2   whole eggs
1/4   cup dairy sour cream,
        fat free
1   can (16 oz.) corn, cream
        style (blended well)
2   tablespoons "good" oil
        (see page 280)

Country Corn Bread	
Calories per serving:	201
Fat grams per serving:	5
Fat percentage:	22%
Number of servings:	9
Serving size:	3" square

Sift dry ingredients and set aside. Beat whole eggs and egg whites until frothy and light. Add sour cream, corn, and oil. Gradually stir in dry ingredients and beat well. Pour into a 9 x 9 pan that has been thoroughly sprayed with nonstick cooking spray. Bake at 400 degrees for 30 minutes. (This recipe can be made into muffins—bake 15-20 minutes at 400 degrees.) *This corn bread is incredible!*

Garlic Cheese Toast ("B–" Choice)

1   slice toast, whole-grain
1   teaspoon butter
        (be very moderate)
1/4   teaspoon garlic salt
1   tablespoon Parmesan
        cheese, grated

Garlic Cheese Toast	
Calories per serving:	118
Fat grams per serving:	5
Fat percentage:	38%
Number of servings:	1
Serving size:	1 slice

Lightly butter whole-grain toast. Sparingly sprinkle with garlic salt and Parmesan cheese. Broil in preheated oven for 3 to 6 minutes, watching closely to avoid burning. Serve with pasta.

This "B–" Choice fits nicely into an "A" day. However, three or four slices are not recommended if you are highly resistant to fat loss.

FREEDOM RECIPES

159

Perfect Whole-Wheat Bread ("A" Choice)

10-12 cups flour, whole-wheat
2   tablespoons dry yeast
1/2 cup wheat gluten
4   cups warm water
     (120-130 degrees)
1/3 cup "good" oil
     (see page 280)
1/3 cup honey
1   tablespoon salt

Perfect Whole-Wheat Bread	
Calories per serving:	88
Fat grams per serving:	1
Fat percentage:	10%
Number of servings:	
	approximately 16 slices
Serving size:	1 slice

Place 6 cups flour into mixer bowl with kneading arm. Add dry yeast and gluten; mix well. Add water and mix for 1 minute. Cover and let dough sit for 10 minutes. This makes the bread lighter. Add oil, honey, and salt. Turn on mixer and quickly add remaining flour, 1 cup at a time, until dough forms a ball and cleans the sides of the bowl. Knead 7 to 10 minutes; by hand 12 to 15 minutes. Dough should be smooth and elastic.

Preheat oven to 150 degrees. Lightly oil hands. Divide dough into four equal portions. Shape and place in nonstick cooking-sprayed bread pans. Place into warm oven and let rise about 15 to 20 minutes. When it is almost double in size, turn oven to 350 degrees and bake about 25 minutes or until golden brown. Turn out of pans onto a wire cooling rack immediately. When it is cool, store bread in plastic bags in the freezer. Makes four 1-pound loaves.

Sourdough Starter

1   tablespoon salt
1   tablespoon sugar
1   tablespoon flour
1   cup potato, raw, grated
1   quart water
1   package dry yeast

Sourdough Starter	
Calories per serving:	206
Fat grams per serving:	trace
Fat percentage:	trace

Combine all ingredients except yeast in a saucepan and bring to a boil. Cook until the mixture becomes clear, taking care not to burn it. When cool, stir in the yeast until thoroughly dissolved. Cover and let stand at room temperature for at least 24 hours before using.

This starter should be used at least once a week. Reserve any leftovers in the fridge. This starter will last longer than a week, but it should not be used if it turns orange. Sometimes liquid will rise to the top, but just mix it in before using. Use it to make pancakes, waffles, and bread. Use approximately 1/2 cup sourdough starter per loaf of bread.

FREEDOM RECIPES

Super Cinnamon Rolls ("A–" Choice)

1	12 oz. can evaporated milk, nonfat
1 1/2	cups water, warm
1 1/2	tablespoons yeast
1/2	cup "good" oil (see p. 280)
1	tablespoon lemon juice, freshly squeezed
3/4	cup honey*
1	egg white
1	teaspoon salt
1 1/2	teaspoons baking powder
8	cups flour, white-wheat

Super Cinnamon Rolls	
Calories per serving:	218
Fat grams per serving:	5
Fat percentage:	21%
Number of servings:	24
Serving size:	1 large roll

2-3	tablespoons butter, melted
1	tablespoon cinnamon
4	tablespoons brown sugar*
1 1/2	cups raisins (optional)

Warm the milk and add warm water. Dissolve the yeast in the liquid mixture. Mix the remaining ingredients into the liquid and add just enough flour to make a soft dough. (If you want light rolls, make sure the dough is soft and not stiff. The flour is the ingredient that determines the dough texture.) Knead the dough for 10 minutes and let it relax for 15 minutes. Take half of the dough and roll it out with a rolling pin to 1/4 to 1/2 inch thickness. Brush the surface lightly with melted butter and sprinkle with cinnamon and a thin amount of brown sugar. Sprinkle with raisins, if desired, and press them lightly into dough. Roll up the dough like a jelly roll and cut into 1" slices. Put them on nonstick cooking-sprayed cookie sheets and allow them to rise until they are double in bulk. Bake at 350 degrees for 20 minutes or until lightly brown. Remove and eat as is, or frost *lightly* with powdered sugar and water or skim milk mixed.

Finely ground "white wheat" flour (a new variety of whole wheat) makes delectable cinnamon rolls.

For faster raising, place in oven set at 150 degrees for 15 minutes; then bake.

These cinnamon rolls are excellent with diced apples in the filling.

If you are diabetic, replace 3/4 cup honey with 1/3 cup apple-juice concentrate and a heaping 1/3 cup pineapple-juice concentrate; and avoid the brown sugar and the frosting.

FREEDOM RECIPES

Whole-Wheat Pita Bread
("A" Choice)

5 to 6 cups flour, whole-wheat
1   package dry yeast
1   teaspoon salt
2   cups warm water
     (120 to 130 degrees)

Whole-Wheat Pita Bread	
Calories per serving:	201
Fat grams per serving:	trace
Fat percentage:	trace
Number of servings:	12
Serving size:	1 pita

Stir 2 cups of flour, yeast, and salt in a large bowl. Stir in water gradually; beat until smooth. Add 3/4 cup more flour; beat again. Stir in enough flour to make a soft dough. Beat well. Turn out onto a floured board; knead until smooth and elastic. Let rise 1 hour; should be doubled. Punch down; let rise 30 more minutes. Divide into 12 equal pieces and shape into balls. Roll out into 5- to 6-inch circle. Bake on a nonstick cooking-sprayed cookie sheet on the bottom rack at 450 degrees for about 2 1/2 to 3 minutes on each side until pitas puff and both sides are brown.

Whole-Wheat Tortillas
("A" Choice)

4   cups flour, whole-wheat
1/4   teaspoon baking powder
1/4   cup "good" oil
     (see p. 280)
1   cup warm water
11/2   teaspoons salt

Whole-Wheat Tortillas	
Calories per serving:	163
Fat grams per serving:	3
Fat percentage:	17%
Number of servings:	12
Serving size:	1 tortilla

Rolling time may go slightly over 15 minutes.

Combine all ingredients. Knead 5 minutes (may need more water). Dough should be stiff. Shape into 12 balls. Roll thin. Cook on hot nonstick grill 2 to 3 minutes on each side.

Zucchini-Pineapple-Nut Bread
("B+" Choice)

6   egg whites
1/2 cup "good" oil (see p. 280)
2   cups sugar*
2   cups zucchini, grated
1   cup pineapple, crushed,
     well-drained
1/2 cup walnuts or pecans,
     chopped (optional)
3   teaspoons vanilla
3   cups flour, whole-wheat
1/2 teaspoon salt
3   teaspoons cinnamon
11/2 teaspoons baking powder
11/2 teaspoons baking soda

Zucchini-Pineapple Bread
(without optional nuts)

Calories per serving:	115
Fat grams per serving:	3
Fat percentage:	23%
Number of servings:	34
Serving size:	1/2" slice or 1" slice mini loaf

One serving *with* nuts = 126 calories;
  4 fat grams; 28% fat

Mix together egg whites, oil, and sugar. Add zucchini, pineapple, nuts, and vanilla, and stir into the mixture. In a separate bowl, sift together flour, salt, cinnamon, baking powder, and baking soda; blend well. Stir dry mixture into wet mixture. Blend well.

Pour into small, nonstick cooking-sprayed pans. Bake for 60 minutes at 325 degrees. (This bread freezes well.) For cupcakes, bake 30 minutes at 325 degrees.

This is not a diabetic recipe. This bread is excellent with a meal. If you have it for a snack, have a vegetable choice with it.

Bread Spreads

All Fruit Jam* ("A" Choice)

2   envelopes, gelatin, unflavored
1/2 cup apple-juice, frozen
       concentrate**,
       unsweetened, thawed
1/2 cup Dole Mountain
       Cherry juice frozen
       concentrate**, thawed
11/2 quarts strawberries,
       fresh, washed, hulled,
       and mashed
1   tablespoon lemon juice

All Fruit Jam	
Calories per serving:	32
Fat grams per serving:	trace
Fat percentage:	trace
Number of servings:	48
Serving size:	2 tablespoons

Sprinkle gelatin over 1/2 cup apple-juice concentrate and set aside. Combine 1/2 cup cherry juice concentrate, strawberries, and lemon juice in heavy saucepan. Cook over medium-low heat for 10 to 15 minutes, stirring constantly.

Remove from heat and add softened gelatin mixture, stirring constantly until gelatin is completely dissolved. Cool at room temperature. Store in refrigerator. Makes approximately 6 cups.

This is an excellent sweetener for diabetics and individuals who are highly resistant to fat loss to use in hot cereals and on toast, pancakes, waffles, etc. Apple-Raspberry Butter is also excellent.

Jam Variations
- Dole Orchard Peach juice frozen concentrate with pureéd peaches.
- Dole Country Raspberry juice frozen concentrate with mashed raspberries
- Dole Pine-Orange-Banana juice frozen concentrate with mashed or pureéd pineapple, oranges, and ripe bananas.
- white-grape juice frozen concentrate with mashed boysenberries or blackberries
- pineapple- and apple-juice frozen concentrates (equal parts of each) with mashed blueberries and whole small blueberries

**Special Note: Make certain that all of the frozen juice concentrates are free of sugar and artificial sweeteners.

FREEDOM RECIPES

Apple-Raspberry Butter
("A" Choice)

3   cups applesauce, unsweetened
1   cup frozen apple-juice concentrate, unsweetened, thawed
1/2 cup Dole Country Raspberry-juice frozen concentrate, thawed
2   teaspoons ground cinnamon
2   teaspoons ground ginger
1   teaspoon cloves

Apple-Raspberry Butter	
Calories per serving:	30
Fat grams per serving:	0
Fat percentage:	0%
Number of servings:	32
Serving size:	2 tablespoons

Combine all ingredients in a heavy saucepan. Simmer, stirring occasionally for about 2 hours or until thick. Makes approximately 4 cups.

Cranberry Sandwich Spread
("A–") Choice

1/4 cup Miracle Whip Salad Dressing, fat free
1/4 cup mayonnaise, fat free
1/2 cup cranberry sauce, canned

Cranberry Sandwich Spread	
Calories per serving:	35
Fat grams per serving:	0
Fat percentage:	0%
Number of servings:	8
Serving size:	2 tablespoons

Mix all ingredients together. Great on turkey sandwiches. Makes 1 cup.

Honey Butter ("B–" Choice)
Not a Fat-Loss or a Diabetic Choice!

1/2 cup butter, softened
1   egg yolk
1/4 teaspoon vanilla
1/2 cup honey

Honey Butter	
Calories per serving:	80
Fat grams per serving:	6
Fat percentage:	68%
Number of servings:	16
Serving size:	1 tablespoon

165

Beat softened butter until light and fluffy. Soft fry egg yolk then beat in yolk and vanilla. Gradually add honey while whipping. This tastes wonderful! Use it *very* sparingly. It rates a "B–" instead of a "C–" because you'll be using it very moderately on *whole-grain* breads and muffins, and eating abundant amounts of vegetables and fruits.

Store Variety Jams, Jellies, Syrups ("A," "B," and "D"* Choices)

If you are diabetic or highly resistant to excess fat loss, avoid sugar-sweetened jams, jellies, and syrups and stay with naturally fruit-juice sweetened varieties—the "A" Choices. Completely avoid artificially sweetened products because of negative fat-storing stress and health risks they may place on your body.

If you have *no* intolerance towards sugar, some good "B" Choices include the low-sugar varieties of jams and jellies or small amounts the regular varieties. Rather than purchasing "lite maple syrup," I use the regular kind. Its flavor is much more satisfying. I spread it on pancakes with a knife rather than dumping it on top. I use enough that the pancakes (or French toast or waffles) taste great and are lightly sweet, yet aren't drowning in syrup. (Mrs. Butterworth's is my favorite.)

When I desire fat loss, I use All Fruit Jam and fruit-juice sweetened, nonfat yogurt on my pancakes, waffles, and French toast.

"D" Choices have artificial sweeteners.

BREAKFAST FOODS

Belgian Waffles ("A" Choice)

Follow pancake batter recipe or directions on whole-wheat pancake mix. Spray Belgian waffle iron or regular waffle iron thoroughly (between each waffle removal) with nonstick cooking spray. Pour enough batter in center of preheated iron to spread over two-thirds of the iron. Close and let cook to desired doneness. Open and remove with the help of a fork. Respray and repeat. Top lightly with real maple syrup, fruit sauce, or fresh fruit and vanilla yogurt.

Belgian Waffles	
Calories per serving:	90
Fat grams per serving:	2
Fat percentage:	20%
Number of servings:	16
Serving size:	one 4" waffle

*Cracked Wheat, Raisin, and Honey Cereal; and Cinnamon Maple
Oatmeal sweetened with All Fruit Jam or honey*

Super Cinnamon Rolls with Raspberry and Strawberry
Breakfast Shakes

Blintzes (light, fluffy pancakes) ("A" Choice)

3	egg whites
1	whole egg
1	cup cottage cheese, lowfat
1/3	cup skim milk
1/4	cup flour, whole-wheat
1	teaspoon vanilla

Blintzes	
Calories per serving:	57
Fat grams per serving:	1
Fat percentage:	16%
Number of servings:	8
Serving size:	1 blintze

In a medium bowl, beat egg whites until stiff. In a blender, beat cottage cheese and yolk until smooth. Add milk, flour, and vanilla and blend well. Pour into a separate bowl. Fold in egg whites. Cook on a nonstick cooking-sprayed pan until top is bubbly. Turn and cook until lightly browned. Serve with fruit rolled inside and Fruit Syrup or All Fruit Jam on top. Nonfat, fruit-juice-sweetened yogurt is also delicious on the fruit inside the Blintzes.

Breakfast Burrito ("A–" Choice)

9	egg whites
3	whole eggs*
2/3	cup skim milk
1 1/2	teaspoons salt
1/2	teaspoon pepper
1	cup mozzarella cheese, part-skim, shredded
2	cups mixed vegetables, steamed in microwave

Breakfast Burrito	
Calories per serving:	289
Fat grams per serving:	9
Fat percentage:	28%
Number of servings:	4
Serving size:	approximately 1 cup

4	flour tortillas, whole-wheat or white

Whip eggs, milk, salt, pepper, and cheese together in a separate bowl. Heat frying pan to medium high until water droplets scatter. Spray thoroughly with nonstick cooking spray. Pour whipped mixture onto medium hot frying pan and stir constantly to scramble. When eggs are almost firm, add vegetables (if desired) and blend into egg mixture.

Roll egg mixture in a whole-wheat or white soft flour tortilla. Serve with your favorite salsa and fat free sour cream. Deliciously fast for breakfast, lunch, or dinner!

Remember to eat only two to three "whole" eggs per week. You eat less than one whole egg with this recipe.

FREEDOM RECIPES

FREEDOM RECIPES

Breakfast Fruit Compote ("A" Choice)

2	cups (cold) cooked brown rice or brown rice and bulgur wheat combination, cooked and cooled
1	cup pineapple, crushed, drained
1	cup apples, chopped (peels add more fiber, if desired)
1/2	cup apple-juice frozen concentrate, thawed
1/4	cup honey (leave out if diabetic)

Breakfast Fruit Compote	
Calories per serving:	264
Fat grams per serving:	trace
Fat percentage:	trace
Number of servings:	4
Serving size:	1 cup

This recipe is a time-saver if the brown rice is made ahead of time. White rice will suffice if brown rice creates gastrointestinal distress for you.

Combine ingredients. Chill. Delicious for breakfast and snacks. Kids love this!

Breakfast Shake ("A" Choice)

3/4	cup skim milk
1/2	cup yogurt, nonfat any flavor
1	banana, ripe, peeled and frozen
1/4	cup fruit, sliced, frozen (any type of fruit you would like)
1/4	cup orange juice

Breakfast Shake	
Calories per serving:	244
Fat grams per serving:	0
Fat percentage:	0%
Number of servings:	2
Serving size:	1 cup

Blend ingredients together in blender. Delicious! Be creative and try a variety of fruits combined with juices.

To freeze bananas: remove peel, cut in half, wrap each piece in plastic, and freeze. Never throw away over-ripe bananas. Always freeze them for breakfast shakes. Over-ripe bananas are very sweet.

Cinnamon-Maple Oatmeal ("A" Choice)

regular oatmeal
cinnamon
maple syrup*

Cinnamon-Maple Oatmeal	
Calories per serving:	417
Fat grams per serving:	3
Fat percentage:	6%
Serving size:	1 1/2 cups

Prepare oatmeal according to package directions. Add cinnamon and maple syrup to taste. (Go for lightly sweet, not heavily sweetened cereal.)

If you are diabetic, omit syrup and use All Fruit Jam and fruit-juice sweetnened, nonfat yogurt.

Cracked Wheat, Raisin, and Honey Cereal ("A" Choice)

11/2	cups wheat, cracked (cracked in blender)
6	cups water, boiling
1/2	teaspoon salt
1/4	cup raisins
1/4	to 1/2 cup honey*

Cracked Wheat Raisin and Honey Cereal	
Calories per serving:	450±
Fat grams per serving:	1
Fat percentage:	2%
Number of servings:	5 to 6
Serving size: approximately 1 cup	

Add salt to boiling water. Stir in wheat and cook on warm for 10 to 25 minutes, covered. (Cooking time depends on how crunchy you like your cereal.) Stir in raisins and honey. Serve with skim, 1%, or evaporated skim milk.

If you are diabetic, sweeten with All Fruit Jam.

FREEDOM RECIPES

Crunchy Granola ("B" Choice)

1   cup oats, quick-cooking
1/2   cup bran cereal
1/2   cup flour, whole-wheat
1/4   cup coconut, flaked
1   tablespoon almonds,
        chopped
3   tablespoons safflower oil
        (or another "good" oil
        (see p. 280)
2/3   cup honey*
1   teaspoon vanilla
1/2   teaspoon maple flavoring
        or Mapleine
1/4   cup raisins

Crunchy Granola	
Calories per serving:	489
Fat grams per serving:	16
Fat percentage:	29%
Number of servings:	4
Serving size:	approximately
	2/3 cup

This recipe may take slightly longer than 15 minutes to prepare.

Heat oven to 300 degrees. Mix oats, bran cereal, flour, coconut, and almonds in a mixing bowl. Spread mixture evenly in the bottom of a 9 x 13 x 2 pan sprayed thoroughly with nonstick cooking spray. Heat oil and honey in a one-quart saucepan over medium heat, stirring constantly until bubbly; stir in vanilla and Mapleine. Pour honey mixture over oat mixture and mix thoroughly. Bake until light brown, 30 to 35 minutes. Stir in raisins and cool 15 minutes. (This recipe is high in "good," cholesterol-fighting fat.)

If you are diabetic, replace 2/3 cup honey with 1/3 cup apple-juice frozen concentrate and 1/3 cup pineapple-juice frozen concentrate—use more or less to taste.

FREEDOM RECIPES

Egg and Cheese Muffins ("A" Choice)

Use recipe for Veggie and Cheese Egg Scramble found on page 175. Purchase Oro-Wheat Health Nut English muffins (part whole wheat). Toast English muffin halves and place 1/2 cup egg mixture on one half of muffin. Place the other muffin half on top of egg mixture.

Egg and Cheese Muffins	
Calories per serving:	305
Fat grams per serving:	5 1/2
Fat percentage:	16%
Number of servings:	6
Serving size:	1 muffin

Fat free mayonnaise mixed with an equal amount of fat free salad dressing makes this sandwich very moist and tasty.

French Toast ("A" Choice)

6   slices bread, whole-grain
4   egg whites, lightly beaten
1/4 teaspoon salt
1/2 cup skim milk
1/4 teaspoon vanilla
1/8 teaspoon ground
     cinnamon

French Toast	
Calories per serving:	191
Fat grams per serving:	1
Fat percentage:	5%
Number of servings:	3
Serving size:	2 slices

In a shallow bowl, beat together egg whites, salt, milk, vanilla, and cinnamon. Dip bread into egg mixture, coating both sides. Do not drench.

Heat skillet on medium heat until water droplets scatter. Spray with nonstick cooking spray, or grease with a very small amount of butter or oil. Cook bread on both sides until golden brown. Serve with syrup, fruit sauces, or fresh fruit and vanilla yogurt.

171

Fried Eggs ("B" Choice)

In heavy skillet, heat 1/2 teaspoon butter (for each egg) until just hot enough to sizzle water droplets. Crack each egg onto buttered surface. Immediately reduce heat to low.

When whites are firm, serve sunny-side up or gently turn over for medium to well-done eggs. Salt and pepper to taste. Butter-flavored sprinkles are excellent on top.

Note: Nonstick cooking sprays work well in place of butter. However, they do not enhance the flavor as completely as butter. Remember to eat only 2 to 3 whole eggs per week. Use mainly egg whites; they are completely fat and cholesterol free.

This 71 percent fat choice rates a "B" because it will be included in a day that has an overall fat content of less than 20 percent, and because it has a high nutrient value.

Fried Eggs	
Calories per serving:	83
Fat grams per serving:	6 1/2
Fat percentage:	71%
Number of servings:	1
Serving size:	1 egg

Granola ("A–" Choice)

8   cups rolled oats
1   cup wheat germ
1/2   cup almonds, chopped
1/2   cup coconut
11/2   cups brown sugar*
1/3   cup "good" oil
      (see p. 280)
1/3   cup water
1/3   cup apple-juice frozen
      concentrate, thawed
1   teaspoon vanilla

Granola	
Calories per serving:	544
Fat grams per serving:	12
Fat percentage:	20%
Number of servings:	11
Serving size:	1 cup

Combine rolled oats, wheat germ, almonds, and coconut in a large bowl. Mix brown sugar, oil, water, apple-juice concentrate, and vanilla together. Pour over dry ingredients and mix well. Spread onto a large sheetcake pan. Bake in oven for about 30 to 60 minutes at 300 degrees. Granola should be a nice golden brown when done. Store in an airtight container.

This recipe is not a good diabetic choice.

Granola Bars ("B+" Choice)

3   cups Rice Krispies or
      Triples cereal
5   cups rolled oats
11/2 cups flour, whole-wheat
2   tablespoons cinnamon
1/4 cup almonds, chopped
1   cup raisins
1   cup coconut (unsweetened)
3/4 cup mini chocolate chips*
      (optional) or 3/4 cup
      dried, chopped fruit
11/4 cups honey*
2   tablespoons Mapleine
      flavoring

1/2 teaspoon almond flavoring
11/2 teaspoons salt
2   tablespoons vanilla

Granola Bars	
Calories per serving:	65
Fat grams per serving:	2
Fat percentage:	28%
Number of servings:	80
Serving size:	1 bar

Mix cereal, oats, flour, cinnamon, almonds, raisins, coconut, and chocolate chips or dried fruit together until well blended.

In a 2-cup measure, mix together honey, Mapleine, and almond flavoring, salt, and vanilla.

Add enough water to bring liquid mixture to the 1 3/4 to 2 cups mark (about 1/2 to 3/4 cup). Mix well and pour over dry ingredients until covered well. Put 1/2 of granola on a large, bakery-size cookie sheet and 1/2 on another. Place wax paper on top of each sheet of mixture to prevent rolling pin from sticking to the mixture. Roll out mixture on cookie sheets until each is completely covered. Remove wax paper. Cut each sheet of granola into 40 bars. Bake at 400 degrees 7 to 10 minutes.

This recipe is not a good diabetic choice.

Omelet Supreme ("B+" Choice)

9 egg whites
3 whole eggs
2/3 cup skim milk
3/4 teaspoon salt
1/2 teaspoon pepper
2 cups carrots, cauliflower, and broccoli, glazed (see glaze recipe for glazed carrots, etc., p. 264) Cooked, diced red potatoes are also delicious.
1 cup part-skim mozzarella cheese

butter and sour-cream flavored sprinkles (optional)

Omelet Supreme	
Calories per serving:	254
Fat grams per serving:	10
Fat percentage:	35%
Number of servings:	4
Serving size:	one 5" x 6" omelet

Whip together eggs, milk, salt, and pepper. Heat large frying pan to medium high until water droplets scatter. Spray thoroughly with nonstick cooking spray. Pour egg mixture into pan, completely covering pan bottom. Cover and let cook for 7 to 10 minutes or until eggs are completely soft set.

Place 2 cups glazed vegetables evenly across center of eggs from end to end. Sprinkle about 1/3 cup cheese over vegetables. Slide 2 pancake turner spatulas carefully under one side of the eggs and gently flip over the top of the veggies. Repeat procedure with other side. When omelet is folded, sprinkle remaining cheese and butter, or sour-cream flavored sprinkles over the top. Serve with toast and fruit.

Orange Jubilee* ("A–" Choice)

1/2 cup skim milk
1/4 cup orange-juice frozen concentrate
1 teaspoon vanilla
1/4 cup sugar* (optional)

Orange Jubilee	
Calories per serving:	157
Fat grams per serving:	0
Fat percentage:	0%
Number of servings:	1
Serving size:	1 cup

Place all ingredients in blender. Blend on medium to high speed until well mixed and frothy. Serve with whole-grain toast or muffins.

This delicious drink should be enjoyed with a full meal, not on an empty stomach. Diabetics, hypoglycemics, and individuals who are highly resistant to fat loss should avoid the added sugar. I prefer it without.

Three Bear Porridge and Honey ("A" Choice)

1/2 cup millet, cracked
1/2 cup brown rice
1/2 cup wheat, whole-kernel, cracked
1/2 teaspoon salt
4 cups water
    bananas, sliced (optional)
2 tablespoons honey* (per serving)

Three Bear Porridge and Honey	
Calories per serving:	272
Fat grams per serving:	trace
Fat percentage:	trace
Number of servings:	2
Serving size:	1 cup porridge with 2 Tbsp. honey
(Sweeten to taste with honey—1 to 2 Tbsp.)	

Bring salted water to near boiling. Gradually stir in freshly cracked grains (cracked in blender), stirring constantly. Add more wheat for thicker cereal. Serve with bananas and honey.

If you are diabetic, replace honey with All Fruit Jam.

Veggie and Cheese Egg Scramble or Cheese Egg Scramble ("A–" and "B" Choices)

9 egg whites
3 whole eggs
2/3 cup skim milk
11/2 teaspoons salt
1/2 teaspoon pepper
1 cup mozzarella cheese, part-skim, shredded
2 cups steamed mixed vegetables (optional)

Veggie & Cheese or Cheese Egg Scramble		
Calories per serving:	289	/ 214
Fat grams per serving:	9	/ 9
Fat percentage:	28%	/ 38%
Number of servings:	4	/ 4
Serving size:	1 cup	/ 2/3 cup

Whip eggs, milk, salt, pepper, and cheese together in a separate bowl. Heat frying pan to medium high until water droplets scatter. Spray thoroughly with nonstick cooking spray. Pour whipped mixture onto medium-hot frying pan and stir constantly to scramble. When eggs are almost firm, add vegetables (if desired) and blend into egg mixture.

Serve with toast or pancakes and fruit. Delicious!

175

FREEDOM RECIPES

Lean & Free Pancakes

 Blender Whole-Wheat Pancake
("A" Choice)

1 cup skim milk
11/3 cups wheat, whole-kernel
3 egg whites
1 tablespoon sugar
1/4 teaspoon salt
2 tablespoons olive oil or
another "good" oil
(see p. 280)
1 teaspoon baking soda
2 teaspoons baking powder

Whole-Wheat Pancakes	
Calories per serving:	86
Fat grams per serving:	2
Fat percentage:	21%
Number of servings:	10
Serving size: one 5" round pancake	

Pour milk and wheat into blender. Liquefy for 4 minutes. While still mixing, add egg whites, sugar, salt, oil, and baking soda. Add baking powder last. Stop blender as soon as ingredients are thoroughly mixed. Bake on hot griddle sprayed with nonstick cooking spray after each batch. Serve hot.

Banana Pancakes ("A" Choice)

Make key recipe. Cut 1 banana into quarter-inch pieces. Stir banana pieces and 1/4 teaspoon ground nutmeg into batter.

Banana Pancakes	
Calories per serving:	96
Fat grams per serving:	2
Fat percentage:	19%
Number of servings:	10
Serving size: one 5" round pancake	

Blueberry Pancakes ("A" Choice)

Make key recipe. Gently stir 1/2 cup fresh or frozen blueberries (thawed and well drained) into batter.

Blueberry Pancakes	
Calories per serving:	94
Fat grams per serving:	2
Fat percentage:	19%
Number of servings:	10
Serving size: one 5" round pancake	

Oatmeal Pancakes ("A" Choice)

In key recipe reduce whole-kernel wheat to 1 1/8 cup and add 1/2 cup quick-cooking oats after wheat has blended for 4 minutes. Replace white sugar with 2 tablespoons brown sugar.

Oatmeal Pancakes	
Calories per serving:	94
Fat grams per serving:	2
Fat percentage:	19%
Number of servings:	10
Serving size: one 5" round pancake	

Peach Pancakes ("A" Choice)

Make key recipe. Beat in 1/4 teaspoon ground cinnamon. Stir in 1 medium peach, peeled and cut into small pieces.

Peach Pancakes	
Calories per serving:	92
Fat grams per serving:	2
Fat percentage:	20%
Number of servings:	10
Serving size: one 5" round pancake	

Super Quick Pancakes ("A" Choice)

Purchase a whole-wheat pancake mix and follow the instructions on the package. I do this all the time! I just add milk or water—so easy!

Super Quick Pancakes	
Calories per serving:	103
Fat grams per serving:	2
Fat percentage:	17%
Number of servings:	10
Serving size: one 5" round pancake	

177

CHICKEN / TURKEY

Baked Chicken Breasts ("A" Choice)

Purchase precooked, boneless, skinless chicken breasts and follow heating instructions. Serve with tossed salad, fresh fruit, and toast or muffins. (To save money, buy whole fryers on special. Then skin and debone at home.)

Baked Chicken Breasts	
Calories per serving:	284
Fat grams per serving:	6
Fat percentage:	19%
Number of servings:	1
Serving size:	1 breast (6 oz.)

BBQ Chicken ("A" Choice)

1	medium onion, chopped
2	tablespoons butter
2	tablespoons vinegar
2	tablespoons brown sugar
1	cup ketchup
3	tablespoons Worcestershire sauce
1	teaspoon mustard
1	cup water
11/2	teaspoons chili powder salt and pepper to taste
8	chicken breasts, skinless, boneless

BBQ Chicken	
Calories per serving:	236
Fat grams per serving:	6
Fat percentage:	23%
Number of servings:	8
Serving size:	1 piece

This recipe may take slighthy longer than 15 minutes to prepare.

In a medium saucepan saute onion in butter. Then stir in vinegar, brown sugar, ketchup, Worcestershire sauce, mustard, water, chili powder, salt, and pepper. Cook for 10 to 15 minutes. Then pour sauce over chicken breasts.

Bake for 1 hour and 15 minutes at 350 degrees. These are also delicious when cooked on the grill. Serve on whole-grain hamburger buns (or white if you can't find whole-wheat). Add all the lowfat trimmings and enjoy!

FREEDOM RECIPES

Chicken and Rice ("A" Choice)

11/2 cups brown rice, uncooked
3/4 cup cheese, shredded
 salt (sparingly)
3 cups water, hot
1 chicken*, skinless, cut up
1 package dry onion soup mix
2 cans cream of chicken soup,
 lowfat

Chicken and Rice	
Calories per serving:	298
Fat grams per serving:	6
Fat percentage:	18%
Number of servings:	6
Serving size:	1 breast with 1/2 cup rice

Spread rice and cheese evenly over the bottom of a nonstick cooking-sprayed 9" x 13" baking pan.   Sprinkle lightly with salt. Pour hot water over mixture. Place chicken pieces over rice. Cream together cream of chicken soup and dry onion soup mix and spread evenly over chicken and rice. Cover and bake 2 hours at 350 degrees. (If you choose "quick" cooking brown rice, decrease baking time to 1 hour.)

A whole fryer chicken that you skin and cut up yourself is general-ly the most economical choice here. Pre-skinned chicken breasts are the fastest and lowest-in-fat choice here.

Chicken Bake ("A" Choice)

21/2 pounds skinless, boneless
 chicken breasts
1 can (103/4 oz.) condensed
 lowfat cream of
 mushroom soup
1/2 envelope onion soup mix

Chicken Bake	
Calories per serving:	225
Fat grams per serving:	5
Fat percentage:	20%
Number of servings:	10
Serving size:	one 4 to 5 oz. chicken breast

Heat oven to 375°. Arrange chicken in baking pan sprayed with nonstick cooking spray. Mix mushroom soup and dry onion soup mix. Spread evenly over chicken. Cover tightly with foil and bake for 30 minutes. Uncover and bake 45 minutes longer or until done.

Chicken Broccoli Casserole ("A" Choice)

2   cups brown rice, cooked
1   cup chicken, white, cooked
     (skin before cooking)
2   cups broccoli, cooked
1   cup evaporated skim milk
1   can cream of chicken soup,
     lowfat
    parmesan cheese

Chicken Broccoli Casserole	
Calories per serving:	262
Fat grams per serving:	4 1/2
Fat percentage:	15%
Number of servings:	4
Serving size:	1 cup

This recipe is a time-saver if you prepare the rice and broccoli in advance.

Layer rice, chicken, and broccoli in a 9 x 13 baking pan. Mix evaporated skim milk and cream of chicken soup and pour evenly over other ingredients. Top with a light sprinkle of Parmesan cheese. Bake at 350 degrees for 20 minutes or until heated through.

Chicken Casserole ("A" Choice)

3   tablespoons cornstarch
1   cup skim milk
2   cups chicken broth
1/4 teaspoon turmeric or curry
1/4 teaspoon paprika
1/4 teaspoon oregano
4   chicken breasts, skinless,
      boneless
2   cups brown rice, cooked
1/2 onion, chopped
1/2 cup mozzarella cheese,
      part-skim, grated

Chicken Casserole	
Calories per serving:	291
Fat grams per serving:	5
Fat percentage:	15%
Number of servings:	4
Serving size:	1 breast with
	1/2 cup rice

This recipe is a time-saver if you cook the rice in advance.

Combine cornstarch, milk, and chicken broth. Add spices and cook over medium heat until thick. Arrange chicken breasts in casserole dish with the rice and onion. Cover with the heated liquid and top with cheese. Bake at 350 degrees for 30 minutes.

FREEDOM RECIPES

Chicken Divan ("A" Choice)

2	chicken breasts, skinless, boneless
2	cups broccoli florets
1	can cream of chicken soup, lowfat
1/2	cup mayonnaise, nonfat
1/2	cup ricotta cheese, fat free
1/2	teaspoon lemon juice
1/4	teaspoon curry powder
1-2	cups bread crumbs, whole-wheat

Chicken Divan	
Calories per serving:	245
Fat grams per serving:	5
Fat percentage:	18%
Number of servings:	4
Serving size:	1 heaping cup

2	teaspoons butter, melted
1/2	teaspoon salt
1/4	teaspoon pepper

Cook chicken without skin in microwave until tender, about 4 to 6 minutes on high, covered with wax paper. Cut into pieces. Steam broccoli in a small amount of water until crispy-tender. Mix soup, mayonnaise, ricotta cheese, lemon, and curry in saucepan and warm over medium heat. In a frying pan pour melted butter, salt, and pepper over crumbs. Cook until crunchy. Layer broccoli on the bottom of a nonstick cooking-sprayed casserole dish; then add chicken and soup mix.

Top with bread crumbs. (One half cup grated part-skim mozzarella cheese is excellent sprinkled over the top of the crumbs.) Bake at 350 degrees for 30 minutes.

Chicken Veggie Stir-Fry ("B" Choice)

2	tablespoons "good" oil (see p. 280)
6	chicken breasts, precooked, cut in chunks
1	cup Oriental-Style Sauce (purchase already prepared or see Oriental-Style Sauce recipe on p. 221)
3	packages (14 to 16 oz. each) Oriental-style vegetables, frozen

Chicken Veggie Stir-Fry	
Calories per serving:	734
Fat grams per serving:	16
Fat percentage:	20%
Number of servings:	6
Serving size:	Approximately 2 cups

1/2	cup slivered almonds
5	cups cooked brown rice

Heat wok or frying pan on medium-high heat until water droplets scatter. Add 2 tablespoons "good" oil. Then add chicken chunks and cook thoroughly, pouring in 1/2 cup Oriental Sauce after 2 or 3 minutes.

Add vegetables, almonds, and 1/2 cup remaining sauce. Continue cooking with lid on, stirring every 2 or 3 minutes until vegetables are crispy-tender.

Serve over brown rice. Add additional (heated) Oriental-Style Sauce to taste. A small amount of mesquite flavoring adds a delicious flair to the sauce.

181

Cranberry-Glazed Turkey Breasts ("A–" Choice)

1   can (7 oz.) cranberry sauce, jellied
1/4   cup corn syrup*
1   teaspoon lemon peel, grated
1   teaspoon lemon juice
2   tablespoons orange-juice frozen concentrate, thawed
4   4 oz. turkey breast slices, skinless, extra-lean

Cranberry-Glazed Turkey Breasts	
Calories per serving:	388± (173 in glaze)
Fat grams per serving:	4± (trace in glaze)
Fat percentage:	9%
Number of servings:	4
Serving size:	one 4 oz. slice turkey breast with 1/3 cup glaze

Heat first five ingredients over low heat, stirring frequently until blended. Spread turkey slices out on a cookie sheet sprayed with nonstick cooking spray. Spread cranberry mixture over slices. Bake in a 350-degree oven for 10 to 15 minutes.

If you are diabetic, replace 1/4 cup corn syrup with 1/4 cup apple-juice concentrate.

Crock-Pot Chicken ("A" Choice)

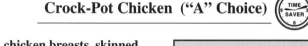

4   chicken breasts, skinned and deboned
2   cans cream of mushroom soup, lowfat
1   onion, chopped
3   stalks celery, chopped
1/2   soup can skim milk
1   tablespoon parsley, chopped
8   cups noodles*, cooked

Crock-Pot Chicken	
Calories per serving:	393
Fat grams per serving:	6
Fat percentage:	14%
Number of servings:	8
Serving size:	1/2 breast and 1/2 cup sauce over 1 cup noodles

Combine chicken, soup, onion, celery, milk, and parsley in crock pot. Cook on high 5 to 6 hours. Serve over hot cooked noodles or brown rice.

Whole-wheat noodles contain the highest fiber content, but white noodles are very acceptable.

FREEDOM RECIPES

Thanksgiving or Christmas Dinner features Mashed Potatoes with Quick Turkey Gravy, Cranberry-Glazed Turkey Breast, Saucy Green Beans and Almonds, Fresh Cranberry Relish, Pumpkin Carrot Muffins, and (Chiffon) Pumpkin Pie

*Fresh-Fruit Combination Tray, Tropical Fruit Ice,
and Orange Jubilee*

Beef Fajitas and Pineapple Marshmallow Coleslaw

*Chicken Veggie Stir-Fry, Teriyaki Chicken,
and Sweet and Sour Chicken*

Easy Chicken 'n' Dumplings ("A" Choice)

2	cups chicken or turkey, white, skinless, cooked and cubed
1	can (16 oz.) onions, whole, with liquid
1	can (16 oz.) carrots, with liquid, sliced
1	can (16 oz.) green beans, with liquid, cut-up
1	can (16 oz.) corn, with liquid (optional)
2	cups chicken broth, canned
11/2	teaspoons barbecue spice or seasoning packet
1/2	teaspoon salt
1/4	teaspoon thyme
	dumpling dough (Bisquick enough for 12 dumplings)

Easy Chicken 'n'Dumplings

Calories per serving:	277
Fat grams per serving:	5
Fat percentage:	16%
Number of servings:	6
Serving size:	1 1/2 cups chicken mixture with 2 dumplings

This recipe is a time-saver if the chicken is prepared in advance.

In a large pot combine chicken, onions, carrots, green beans, corn, chicken broth, barbecue spice, salt, and thyme. Heat to boiling, stirring occasionally.

Mix dumpling dough according to Bisquick package directions. Drop dough by tablespoonfuls onto hot vegetables and chicken.* Cook uncovered for 10 minutes. Then cover and cook 10 more minutes. Liquid should gently bubble.

Serve in soup bowls. A bowl of peaches or cut-up melons goes nicely with this dish.

*You can opt to cook the dumplings as biscuits on a pancake grill in a very small amount of butter.

Hawaiian Haystacks ("A" Choice)

2	cups brown rice, cooked
1/2	cup skim milk
1	can chicken, cooked chunk
1	can cream of chicken soup, lowfat
	green peppers, diced
	tomatoes, diced
	mushrooms, sliced
	pineapple chunks
	green onions, diced
	green peas, cooked
	chow mein noodles

Hawaiian Haystacks

Calories per serving:	234±
Fat grams per serving:	3±
Fat percentage:	12%±
Number of servings:	4
Serving size:	approximately 1 cup

Heat milk, chicken, and soup. Let each person make his or her own haystack. Layer rice, chicken mix, and a variety of vegetables. Sprinkle some oriental noodles on top (just a few).

FREEDOM RECIPES

Pineapple-Lime Chicken ("A" Choice)

8	chicken breasts, skinless
1/2	cup honey*
4	tablespoons soy sauce
1/2	cup lime juice
4	teaspoons cornstarch
1-2	cans pineapple tidbits

Pineapple-Lime Chicken	
Calories per serving:	344
Fat grams per serving:	6
Fat percentage:	16%
Number of servings:	8
Serving size:	1 breast

Brown chicken breasts in pan with nonstick cooking spray. While cooking, drain juice from one can of pineapple tidbits and add pineapple to honey, soy sauce, lime juice, and cornstarch. Pour over chicken. Continue to simmer until sauce is thickened. Serve with pineapple tidbits over the top. Delightful for company!

If you are diabetic, you may choose to replace the honey with 1/2 cup pineapple-juice frozen concentrate. But, perhaps the very small amount of honey you'll be eating (1/2 cup divided by 8 servings) will not create a blood-sugar problem for you. Listen to your body!

Sweet and Sour Chicken ("A" Choice)

2	chicken breasts, boneless, skinless, cubed
1	clove garlic, finely diced
1/2	teaspoon salt
1	cup green-pepper strips
1/2	cup onion, diced
1	cup carrot strips
11/4	cups chicken broth
1/4	cup soy sauce
1/4	cup vinegar
2	tablespoons brown sugar
1/2	teaspoon ginger
1	cup pineapple chunks, with juice

Sweet and Sour Chicken	
Calories per serving:	329
Fat grams per serving:	3
Fat percentage:	8%
Number of servings:	4
Serving size: approximately 1 1/2 cups chicken mixture over 1/2 cup rice	

| 2 | Tablespoons cornstarch |
| 1/4 | cup water |

Cook chicken in microwave until tender, about 5 minutes. Remove chicken and pour liquid into a medium saucepan. Add garlic, salt, green pepper, onion, and carrots to the liquid. Cook until tender-crisp. Add chicken back in with broth, soy sauce, vinegar, brown sugar, ginger, and pineapple with juice. Bring to full a boil. Thicken with cornstarch mixed with water. Serve over hot brown or white rice. (Brown rice is highest in fiber and nutrition but white rice is acceptable.) This recipe can also be cooked in a wok. *(Diabetics should use this recipe in moderation.)*

Teriyaki Chicken ("A" Choice)

1	fryer*, skinless, cut up
1/2	cup green onions, chopped
1	tablespoon vinegar
2	teaspoons orange peel, grated
1/4	teaspoon ground ginger
1/4	teaspoon red pepper
1/4	teaspoon garlic powder
1/3	cup soy sauce
1	tablespoon soy sauce
1	tablespoon brown sugar

Teriyaki Chicken	
Calories per serving:	156
Fat grams per serving:	3
Fat percentage:	17%
Number of servings:	8
Serving size:	1 piece

This recipe is a time saver, not including cooking time.

Reserve 1 tablespoon green onion for garnish. Combine onion, vinegar, orange peel, ginger, red pepper, garlic powder, and 1/3 cup soy sauce; stir well. Place chicken pieces in a nonstick cooking-sprayed broiling pan. Brush pieces with soy sauce mixture. Broil at 450 degrees for 25 minutes about 7 to 9 inches from heat. Turn chicken and brush with sauce. Broil 20 minutes longer, brushing with sauce often during the last 10 minutes of broiling time. In a small cup, mix soy sauce and brown sugar. Brush chicken with this sauce and broil 30 seconds longer to glaze. Garnish chicken with reserved green onion to serve.

The white skinless meat is the lowest in fat.

FREEDOM RECIPES

DESSERTS / COOKIES

Apple Cake ("B" Choice) *EASY!*

1/2 to 2/3 cup honey or
      brown sugar*
1/2 teaspoon salt
1/4 cup butter, softened
1 egg
2/3 cup skim milk
11/2 cups flour, whole-wheat
1 teaspoon cinnamon
      dash nutmeg
1 teaspoon baking soda
2 cups apples, chopped

Apple Cake	
Calories per serving:	283
Fat grams per serving:	7
Fat percentage:	22%
Number of servings:	9
Serving size:	3" square

Topping Ingredients:
1/3 cup brown sugar*
1 teaspoon cinnamon
2/3 cup rolled oats

Mix together honey or brown sugar, salt, butter, egg, and milk. Stir in flour, cinnamon, nutmeg, soda, and apples. Spread mixture evenly in a 9 x 9 baking pan sprayed with nonstick cooking spray.

In a medium bowl, mix together brown sugar, cinnamon, and oatmeal. Sprinkle on top of cake mixture. Bake at 350 degrees for 45 minutes or until a toothpick inserted in center of cake comes out clean.

*If you are diabetic, you could replace the brown sugar or honey with apple-juice concentrate and slightly increase the flour in the cake and the rolled oats in the topping to balance out the solids and liquids.

Apple Cobbler
("B+" Choice)

Apple Filling:

6	cups apples, sliced, peeled
1/3	cup sugar*
3	tablespoons apple-juice, frozen, concentrate, thawed
1	tablespoon lemon juice
2	tablespoons water, cold
1	tablespoon cornstarch

Apple Cobbler	
Calories per serving:	316
Fat grams per serving:	6
Fat percentage:	17%
Number of servings:	6
Serving size: one 4" x 2 2/3" piece	

Cook and stir 6 cups sliced apples with the sugar, thawed apple-juice concentrate, and lemon juice. Stir until boiling; reduce heat. Cover and simmer for 5 minutes, stirring occasionally until fruit is almost tender. Combine 2 tablespoons cold water and 1 tablespoon cornstarch. Add to filling, cooking and stirring until thick and bubbly. Keep hot.

For topping:

1	cup flour, whole-wheat	3	tablespoons butter
1/4	cup sugar*	2	egg whites, beaten
1	teaspoon baking powder	3	tablespoons skim milk
1/2	teaspoon ground cinnamon		

Mix flour, sugar, baking powder, and cinnamon. Cut in butter until mixture looks like coarse crumbs. Combine egg and milk. Add to flour mixture. Stir just until moist.

Pour apple filling into an 8 x 8 x 2 baking dish. Drop topping into 6 equally-spaced mounds on top of the filling. Bake at 400 degrees for 20 to 25 minutes or until toothpick comes out clean. Top with vanilla ice milk, if desired.

*Diabetics may choose to omit the sugar and slightly increase the apple-juice concentrate in the filling and topping. Also slightly increase the flour in the topping to balance out the solids and liquids. Omit the ice milk.

187

FREEDOM RECIPES

Apple-Raspberry Bars* ("A–" Choice)

Apple-Raspberry Filling:
11/2 cups raspberries, frozen
1/4   cup Dole Country
        Raspberry juice
        frozen concentrate
11/2 to 2 cups apples, chopped
1   tablespoon sugar

Apple-Raspberry Bars	
Calories per serving:	116
Fat grams per serving:	2
Fat percentage:	16%
Number of servings:	32
Serving size: one 11/2" x 2" piece	

Follow directions for Date Bars and Date Filling on pages 191 and 192 using Apple-Raspberry Filling ingredients in place of the Date Filling ingredients.

*If you are diabetic, omit the sugar from this filling and follow the Date Bars—No-Sugar Style *recipe and* Date Filling *recipe on page 192.*

Blueberry Streusel Coffee Cake
("B" Choice) *Wonderful!*

Topping:
- 1/2   cup brown sugar*
- 2   teaspoons cinnamon
- 3/4   cup pecans or walnuts, chopped
- 3   tablespoons flour, whole-wheat
- 1   tablespoon butter, melted

Blueberry Streusel Coffee Cake	
Calories per serving:	180
Fat grams per serving:	4
Fat percentage:	20%
Number of servings:	24
Serving size:	one 2" by 2" square

Batter:
- 1   cup sugar*
- 1   cup brown sugar*
- 2   teaspoons lemon juice
- 8   egg whites (powdered are most economical)
- 2   teaspoons baking powder
- 1   teaspoon baking soda
- 1   teaspoon salt
- 4   cups flour, whole-wheat
- 3   cups yogurt, plain, non-fat
- 1   cup blueberries, fresh or frozen

Mix together topping ingredients until crumbly and set aside. Mix sugars, lemon juice, and egg whites until foamy. Stir in baking powder, soda, and salt. Alternate flour and yogurt. Mix well. Pour into a 9 x 13 pan sprayed with nonstick cooking spray. Sprinkle top with blueberries and 2/3 of the topping. With a spatula, fold the batter to produce a marbling effect. Sprinkle with remaining topping. Bake at 350 degrees for 30 to 35 minutes.

*This is not a diabetic recipe.

It's so wonderful to understand how to be "the worst you can be" and still be okay and not develop a "fat-storing" body. These desserts are not fat-loss choices for many people. They are delicious, healthy, coasting choices and rank worlds above typical junk-food sweets. And the cravings are gone because you're eating the ideal "Five Fingers of Nutrient Balance" throughout the day. Sweet, sweet freedom!

FREEDOM RECIPES

Cake-Mix Sweet Rolls ("B" Choice) *EASY*

Merry Christmas! Here is a fast, yummy recipe for your holiday cooking. There are virtually no fat grams, but it is moderately high in refined carbohydrates. Keep eating plenty of good food and be very moderate with desserts, especially if you are highly resistant to fat loss.

1	spice cake mix*
5	cups flour, whole-wheat
2	tablespoons yeast
23/4	cups water, warm (120–130 degrees)
1/4	cup sugar*
1	small package instant butterscotch pudding*

Cake-Mix Sweet Rolls	
Calories per serving:	127
Fat grams per serving:	trace
Fat percentage:	trace
Number of servings:	36
Serving size:	1 roll

Mix together cake mix, 2 cups flour, yeast, and water. Let stand for 5 minutes. Stir in about 3 additional cups of flour. (Keep the dough quite soft and moist.) Let rise 5 minutes. Roll out and moisten dough with a little water. Sprinkle with instant pudding and sugar. Roll up and cut into 36 sweet rolls. Bake at 350° for 15 to 20 minutes.

Make a fun glaze by using a little powdered sugar and frozen-juice concentrate. Mix to desired consistency.

These are not diabetic recipes.

Variations:

Lemon cake mix—use instant lemon pudding and 1/3 cup sugar.
Banana cake mix—use instant banana pudding and 1/4 cup sugar.

FREEDOM RECIPES

Chocolate Frosting* ("B–" Choice)
Not For Fat Loss or Diabetics

2	cups powdered sugar	1	tablespoon skim milk
2	tablespoons cocoa	2	tablespoons butter,
1	teaspoon vanilla		softened

Mix together with electric blender. Add more milk or powdered sugar to create desired consistency. Spread a thin layer of this frosting over lowfat brownies or over my Grandma's Marvelous Chocolate Velvet Cake found on page 193.

Fat gram/calorie information for this recipe is added into the information for Grandma's Marvelous Chocolate Velvet Cake.

Date Bars ("A–" Choice)
Great for Breakfast!

1	cup and 2 tablespoons brown sugar, packed
1/2	cup butter, softened
1/2	cup applesauce, lightly sweetened
2	cups and 2 tablespoons flour, whole-wheat
11/2	teaspoons salt
3/4	teaspoon baking soda
21/4	cups oats, quick-cooking

Date Bars	
Calories per serving:	116
Fat grams per serving:	2
Fat percentage:	16%
Number of servings:	32
Serving size: one 11/2" x 2" piece	

Prepare date filling on the following page. Mix brown sugar and butter. Blend in applesauce. Mix in remaining ingredients. Press half of the mixture into a 13 x 9 x 2 baking pan thoroughly coated with nonstick cooking spray. Spread with date filling. Top with remaining mixture; press lightly.

Bake until light brown, 25 to 30 minutes in preheated 400 degree

FREEDOM RECIPES

Date Filling:

3   cups dates, cut up

11/2 cups water

1/4   cup apple-juice frozen
**   concentrate**

1   tablespoon sugar

Heat dates, water, juice, and sugar over low heat, stirring constantly until thick—about 10 minutes. Cool.

Other Variations:

Date Bars—*"No-Sugar" Style—next recipe.*
Apple-Raspberry Bars—*page188.*

Date Bars – "No-Sugar Style" ("A" Choice)
This is an Excellent Diabetic Dessert!

Replace brown sugar in Date Bars recipe with 2/3 cup thawed apple-juice concentrate and 1/3 cup thawed pineapple-juice concentrate. Heat juices in saucepan until lukewarm. Add butter and stir until melted. Stir in unsweetened applesauce and increase flour to 2 cups. Omit sugar from filling recipe above. These date bars offer a fun change for breakfast.

Date Bars—"No-Sugar Style"	
Calories per serving:	113
Fat grams per serving:	2
Fat percentage:	16%
Number of servings:	32
Serving size:	one 11/2" x 2" piece

Grandma's Marvelous Chocolate Velvet Cake ("B" Choice)

3   cups flour, unbleached
       white* (sift if desired)
1   cup sugar*
4   tablespoons cocoa
1/4   teaspoon salt
1 1/2 teaspoons baking soda
       mixed into 1/4 cup
       water
1   teaspoon vanilla
1/4   cup butter, softened
1/2   cup pureéd beans**, cooked
1 1/2 cups skim milk
2   tablespoons vinegar

Grandma's Marvelous Chocolate Velvet Cake	
Calories per serving:	193
Fat grams per serving:	3 1/2
Fat percentage:	16%
Number of servings:	20
Serving size:	one 11/2" square

This recipe is a time-saver if you pureé the beans in advance. You can freeze the left-over pureéd beans for future use.

In blender, mix well all ingredients, except vinegar, until creamy. Then blend in vinegar.

Spread mixture evenly in a nonstick cooking-sprayed 9 x 13 cake pan. Bake at 350 degrees for 30 to 35 minutes, until a toothpick comes out clean after being inserted in cake center. Top with your favorite lowfat chocolate frosting and vanilla ice milk. (See frosting recipe on page 191.)

My Grandmother Althera has made this delicious cake since I was a little girl. It's the best chocolate cake I've ever tasted! At age 89, she still makes at least two of these a month.

*This is not a diabetic recipe or a fat-loss recipe for those who are highly resistant to fat loss. It is a much better choice than typical chocolate cake which may range from 30 to 50 percent fat!

**Purchase canned white beans and pureé them in your blender. Their consistency should be similar to that of thick wall-paper paste or creamed shortening and sugar. If too thick, add liquid from beans or water (1 to 3 tablespoons).

Grandma's original recipe called for 1/2 cup of butter. When one cup of pureéd beans replaced the butter completely, it took on the texture of dense sponge cake. However, with 1/4 cup butter and 1/2 cup beans, it tastes exactly like the original recipe and the texture is wonderful with 31/2 fat grams per serving instead of 6 fat grams per serving. This brings the overall fat percentage of the cake from 31 percent down to 16 percent—amazing!

193

FREEDOM RECIPES

FREEDOM RECIPES

 Instant Blueberry Ice Cream ("A" Choice)

1	cup skim milk or
	evaporated skim milk
2	cups blueberries, frozen
1/4	cup pineapple-juice
	frozen concentrate
1/4	cup apple slices, frozen

Instant Blueberry Ice Cream	
Calories per serving:	224±
Fat grams per serving:	trace
Fat percentage:	trace
Number of servings:	2
Serving size:	1 1/2 cups

Blend all ingredients in blender until smooth. Serve in parfait glasses. Simply wonderful! You'll never believe this is actually good for you. (Adjust the amount of milk and juice concentrate you add depending on your personal tastes and the consistency you desire.)

Variations:

Try any combination of frozen fruit and fruit-juice concentrate mixed with skim or 1% milk. Be sure to break the fruit into little chunks to aid in the blending process.

You can also use water in place of milk if you have dairy-product intolerance or if you prefer a fruit "ice" instead of a fruit "ice cream."

Instant Peach Ice Cream ("A" Choice)

1	cup skim milk (or 1%)
2	cups peaches, frozen
	(broken apart)
1/2	cup Dole Orchard Peach
	frozen juice concentrate,
	sweeten to taste

Instant Peach Ice Cream	
Calories per serving:	176±
Fat grams per serving:	trace
Fat percentage:	trace
Number of servings:	2
Serving size:	1 1/2 cups

194

Blend all ingredients in blender until smooth. Serve in parfait glasses. You can use canned peaches. Drain and spread on cookie sheet in separate pieces. Freeze and then use. You can also use fresh-frozen peaches or purchase your fruit already frozen for you in bags at your grocery store.

Minute Cherry Cheesecake ("B–" Choice)

1   regular package (8 oz.) cream cheese, lowfat (Do not use spreadable cream cheese.)
1   can sweetened condensed milk*
1/3   cup lemon juice
1   teaspoon vanilla
1   ready graham-cracker pie crust*, baked
1   can (20 oz.) cherry pie filling*, light

Minute Cherry Cheesecake	
Calories per serving:	300
Fat grams per serving:	9 1/2
Fat percentage:	29%
Number of servings:	10
Serving size:	one 2 1/2" slice

Blend cream cheese in mixer until smooth. Continue blending and add milk gradually. Blend in lemon juice and vanilla until smooth. Pour into pie crust. Refrigerate for 3 hours. Serve with light cherry pie filling drizzled over the top. Light blueberry or apple toppings are also delicious.

Save this delicious "B–" dessert for special occasions.

This is not a diabetic recipe and will not encourage highly resistant individuals to see excess fat loss.

195

Peach Cobbler ("B+" Choice) *EASY!*

Peach Filling:

6	cups peaches, sliced
1/3	cup sugar*
3	tablespoons Dole Orchard Peach-juice frozen concentrate, thawed
1	tablespoon lemon juice
2	tablespoons water, cold
1	tablespoon cornstarch

Peach Cobbler

Calories per serving:	316
Fat grams per serving:	6
Fat percentage:	17%
Number of servings:	6
Serving size:	one 4" x 2 2/3" piece

Cook and stir peaches with sugar, juice concentrate, and lemon juice. Stir until boiling; reduce heat. Cover and simmer for 5 minutes, stirring occasionally until fruit is almost tender. Combine cold water and cornstarch; add to filling, cooking and stirring until thick and bubbly. Keep hot.

For topping:

1	cup flour, whole-wheat
1/4	cup sugar*
1	teaspoon baking powder
1/2	teaspoon ground cinnamon

3	tablespoons butter
2	egg whites, beaten
3	tablespoons skim milk

Mix flour, sugar, baking powder, and cinnamon. Cut in butter until mixture looks like course crumbs. Combine egg whites and milk. Add to flour mixture. Stir just until moist.

Pour peach filling into an 8 x 8 x 2 baking dish coated with nonstick cooking spray. Drop topping into 6 equally spaced mounds on top of the filling. Bake at 400 degrees for 20 to 25 minutes or until toothpick comes out clean. Top with vanilla ice milk.

*If you are diabetic, omit sugar in filling and replace it with 1/3 cup peach-juice concentrate plus the 3 tablespoons already called for. Omit the sugar and the milk in the topping and add 1/4 cup peach-juice concentrate as a delicious replacement. Follow remaining directions as outlined.

196

(Chiffon) Pumpkin Pie ("B–" Choice)
A Thanksgiving Tradition!

Crust:

2	tablespoons butter,* melted
11/4	cups gingersnap crumbs**, finely crushed (18 cookies)

Filling:

1	envelope gelatin, unflavored
1/4	cup water, cold
2/3	cup brown sugar**, packed
1/2	teaspoon salt
1/4	teaspoon cloves
2	teaspoons cinnamon
1/2	teaspoon ginger
1/2	teaspoon allspice
13/4	cups pumpkin, mashed, cooked, fresh or canned
3	large egg yolks*
1/2	cup cold skim milk

Pumpkin Pie	
Calories per serving:	207
Fat grams per serving:	8
Fat percentage:	35%
Number of servings:	10
Serving size:	1/10 of pie

Ginger Snap Pie Crust only: (852 cal. / 40 fat grams / 42% fat)
Graham Cracker Pie Crust only: (804 cal. / 42 fat grams / 47% fat)

Meringue:

3	large egg whites
1/4	teaspoon cream of tartar
6	tablespoons sugar**

Mix melted butter with gingersnap crumbs. Pat and press into a 9" pie pan and bake at 325 degrees for 10 minutes. Cool.

Prepare filling: Blend cold water and gelatin together; set aside. Mix remaining ingredients together in a saucepan. Cook over low heat, stirring constantly until mixture boils for 1 minute; then remove from heat. Stir in softened gelatin; cool. When it is partially set, beat until smooth. Set aside.

To make meringue, beat egg whites and cream of tartar until foamy. Beat in sugar, 1 tablespoon at a time; continue beating until stiff and glossy. Do not underbeat.

Carefully fold meringue into pumpkin mixture. Spoon into gingersnap crust. Chill at least 2 hours until set. Top with light whipping cream or vanilla ice milk and gingersnap crumbs.

**This is not a diabetic recipe or a recipe that will encourage excess fat loss in individuals who are highly resistant to fat loss.

Rice 'n' Honey Pudding with Raisins ("A–" Choice)

1 1/2   cups brown rice, cooked
        (hot or cold)
1/2   teaspoon cinnamon
3   tablespoons honey
     to taste*
3   tablespoons raisins,
     optional
1/2   cup evaporated skim milk

Rice 'n' Honey Pudding with Raisins	
Calories per serving:	95
Fat grams per serving:	trace
Fat percentage:	trace
Number of servings:	2
Serving size: approximately 1 cup	

This recipe is a time-saver if the brown rice is prepared in advance.

Mix rice with cinnamon, honey, and raisins. Add milk and stir.

This recipe is tasty for breakfast as well as making a delicious dessert. It is high in fiber and nutrition. It also makes a filling healthy snack, as it is not high in sugar. Remember to include veggies with ALL of your snacks to help increase your metabolism if you are highly resistant to fat loss.

Most desserts DO NOT make the best snacks because of their higher sugar content. This recipe is an exception.

*If you are diabetic, you may try a very small amount of fructose to replace the honey. Or try All Fruit Jam (page 165) an excellent choice.

FREEDOM RECIPES

A LEAN & FREE Cookie assortment featuring: Applesauce, Applesauce Oatmeal Raisin, Chocolate Chip, Oatmeal Raisin, Raisin Chippers, and Zucchini Nut

Whole-Wheat Angel Food Cake with fresh strawberries

Strawberry Pie ("B" Choice)

11/2   quarts strawberries, fresh
1/2   cup sugar*
3   tablespoons cornstarch
2   tablespoons lemon juice
1   gingersnap pie crust**
    (or graham-cracker
    pie crust)
1   scoop vanilla ice milk*,
    or a small amount of
    light whipped cream***

Strawberry Pie	
Calories per serving:	180
Fat grams per serving:	7
Fat percentage:	29%
Number of servings:	10
Serving size:	one 2" slice

Wash berries and remove tops. Reserve half the berries (the nicest ones). Mash the rest and place in medium sauce pan. Mix together cornstarch and sugar; add to the mashed berries. Cook over medium heat until smooth and thick, stirring constantly. Stir in lemon juice. Cool; carefully blend remaining strawberries into mixture.

Pour into gingersnap pie crust or over the top of whole-wheat or regular angel food cake. Top with vanilla ice milk or light whipped cream. When served over angel food cake, one serving contains just one fat gram and becomes a "B+" Choice.

*Omit sugar and replace it with 1/4 cup apple-juice concentrate and 1/4 cup pineapple-juice concentrate if you are diabetic or are highly resistant to fat loss. Serve in a parfait dish, eliminating the pie crust and the ice milk or whipped cream. Fruit-juice sweetened nonfat yogurt is delicious on top!

**Follow the Gingersnap Pie Crust recipe on page 197, or use an already prepared, graham cracker pie crust to save time.

***Whenever I'm in the mood for whipped cream, I choose light, "real" whipped cream. Non-dairy whipped cream contains palm and/ or coconut oils that are even more highly saturated that lard!

Texas Brownies ("B" Choice) *EASY!*

11/2   cups chocolate chips*
1   cup sugar*
1/2   cup applesauce, lightly
       sweetened*
2   tablespoons cream cheese,
       fat free
3   egg whites
1/4   teaspoon baking soda
1/4   teaspoon salt
1   teaspoon vanilla
11/2   cups oat flour
       (blend dry oats
       in blender)
1/3   cup chopped nuts, optional

Texas Brownies	
Calories per serving:	138
Fat grams per serving:	3
Fat percentage:	20%
Number of servings:	20
Serving size:	one 2" x 21/2" square

Heat oven to 350 degrees. In a large saucepan, over low heat, melt together 1 cup chocolate chips, sugar, applesauce, and cream cheese. Remove from heat.

Stir in egg whites, baking soda, salt, and vanilla. Blend well. Mix in remaining chocolate chips and the flour. (If nuts are added, they increase the fat grams by 1 and the calories by 12 per brownie. They are still only 24 percent fat.)

Pour mixture into a nonstick cooking-sprayed 13 x 9 pan. Bake 16 to 20 minutes or until just set. Cool completely before cutting. Cut into 20 squares and serve with vanilla ice milk!

These brownies are not a fat-loss choice but are a delicious "coasting" choice, much healthier and lower in fat than other brownies.

This is not a diabetic recipe.

FREEDOM RECIPES

Tropical Fruit Ice ("A" Choice)

2	bananas, chunked and frozen on cookie sheet
2	large cans mandarin oranges, frozen, on cookie sheet
1	quart strawberries, topped, halved, and frozen on cookie sheet
1/3	cup pineapple-juice frozen concentrate
1/3	cup apple-juice frozen concentrate

Tropical Fruit Ice	
Calories per serving:	228[±]
Fat grams per serving:	1
Fat percentage:	4%
Number of servings:	4
Serving size:	1 1/2 cups

| 1 | cup evaporated skim milk or regular skim milk* |
| 1 | cup vanilla yogurt, nonfat |

Blend all ingredients except yogurt in blender, adding more or less milk to achieve desired consistency and more or less juice concentrate to achieve desired sweetness. Top with 1/4 cup nonfat vanilla yogurt and a tiny oriental umbrella.

Water can replace milk for a more "icy" treat or in the case of a dairy allergy.

Special Dessert Notice

Some people lose body fat very comfortably while including "B" Choice desserts in their daily menus. Others have more resistant bodies and see more success with NO desserts. Remember to work with your body and your individual needs. The "no-sugar" fruit-juice sweetened desserts are excellent for diabetics and for individuals who are highly resistant to fat loss. When the sugar is replaced by fruit-juice concentrates, the "B" Choice desserts become "A" and "A–" Choices.

FREEDOM RECIPES

Whole-Wheat Angel Food Cake*
("A–" Choice)

1   cup flour, whole-wheat
1/2   cup barley flour
3/4   cup sugar**
13/4   cups egg whites at room
         temperature
1/2   teaspoon salt
11/2   teaspoons cream of tartar
1/4   cup sugar**
1   teaspoon almond extract

Whole-Wheat Angel Food Cake	
Calories per serving:	120
Fat grams per serving:	trace
Fat percentage:	trace
Number of servings:	12
Serving size:	one 2" slice

In a small mixing bowl, sift together wheat flour, barley flour, and 3/4 cup sugar. Sift 2 to 3 times. Combine egg whites and salt in mixing bowl. Whip until frothy. Add cream of tartar. Beat until stiff peaks form. Add remaining sugar and almond extract. Whip until glossy. Spoon flour mixture into egg whites 1/3 at a time. Fold in gently. Pour into an ungreased tube pan and bake on bottom rack in oven at 325 degrees for 60 minutes.

*For birthdays, I take two rectangular store-bought or homemade angel food cakes, cut one in half and place each half next to the sides of the other to form an X shape. Then I top it with fresh strawberries and bananas mixed into a small amount of store-bought strawberry sauce. (Marie Calendar's sauce is excellent). Then I line the edges with kiwifruit slices This makes a beautifully delicious "A–" to "B+" Choice birthday cake.

**This is not a diabetic recipe and may not encourage excess fat loss inindividuals who are highly resistant to fat loss.

LEAN & FREE COOKIES

Applesauce Cookies ("B+" and "B–" Choices)

2   cups flour, whole-wheat
1/2 teaspoon salt
1/2 teaspoon cinnamon
1/2 teaspoon cloves
1/4 teaspoon nutmeg
1/2 cup nuts, chopped
       (optional)
1   cup raisins or 1 cup
       chocolate chips*
1   cup beans, puréed
       (see * at bottom of p. 204.)
1   cup sugar*
2   egg whites, beaten
1   cup applesauce,
       unsweetened* or lightly
       sweetened
1   teaspoon soda

Applesauce (Raisin) Cookies ("B+" Choice)	
Calories per serving:	53
Fat grams per serving:	trace
Fat percentage:	trace
Number of servings:	41/2 dozen
Serving size:	1 cookie

Applesauce (Chocolate Chip) Cookies ("B–" Choice)	
Calories per serving:	59
Fat grams per serving:	2
Fat percentage:	31%
Number of servings:	41/2 dozen
Serving size:	1 cookie

Sift flour and measure. Place flour in mixing bowl. Add salt, spices, nuts, and raisins or chocolate chips. In a separate bowl, mix puréed beans and sugar together, stirring very well. Stir soda into applesauce. Combine beaten egg whites, applesauce, and creamed mixture. Add dry ingredients and mix well. Drop by teaspoons onto a cookie sheet sprayed with nonstick cooking spray. Bake at 375 degrees for 12 to 15 minutes. Do not over-bake! Makes 41/2 dozen.

*If you are diabetic, you may choose to replace the sugar with apple-juice concentrate and increase the flour to balance out the solids and liquids. Use raisins instead of chocolate chips and decrease the amount to 2/3 cup. Also use unsweetened applesauce.

FREEDOM RECIPES

Applesauce Oatmeal Raisin Cookies ("B+" Choice)

1	cup pureéd beans*
1	cup sugar**
2	egg whites
4	cups flour, whole-wheat
1	teaspoon baking powder
2	teaspoons baking soda
1	teaspoon salt
2	teaspoons cinnamon
1/2	teaspoon cloves
1/2	teaspoon nutmeg
4	cups applesauce, lightly sweetened**
2	cups rolled oats
1	cup raisins
1/2	cup chocolate chips**

Applesauce Oatmeal Raisin Cookies	
Calories per serving:	66
Fat grams per serving:	trace
Fat percentage:	trace
Number of servings:	60
Serving size:	1 cookie

This recipe is a tim-saver if the beans are prepared in advance and you make these cookies into "bar" cookies.

Cream together pureéd beans, sugar, and egg whites. In a separate bowl mix the flour, baking powder, baking soda and the spices. Add the flour mixture alternately with the applesauce. Beat mixture well after each addition. Add rolled oats and mix well. Add raisins and chocolate chips, and drop by teaspoons on baking sheet sprayed with nonstick cooking spray. Bake at 375 degrees for 12 to 15 minutes. You may also bake them as a bar cookie. To do this, spread the dough evenly on a nonstick cooking-sprayed baking sheet. Follow baking instructions. Bake at 375 degrees for 25 to 30 minutes. Cool and cut into squares. Delicious!

*Purchase canned white beans or finely pureé them in your blender. Their consistency should be like thick wallpaper paste or creamed shortening and sugar. If too thick, add liquid from beans or water (1 to 3 tablespoons). If a cookie recipe calls for 1/2 cup butter, use 1 cup pureéd beans instead. The beans improve texture, increase fiber and nutrition, and greatly decrease fat. They do not affect the flavor of the cookies in the least. A wonderful new idea!

**See italics statements at the bottom of page 206.

Chocolate Chip Cookies ("B" Choice)

2/3   cup applesauce, lightly sweetened or unsweetened*
2/3   cup pureéd beans (See * at bottom of p. 204.)
2/3   cup sugar*
2/3   cup brown sugar*
4   egg whites
2   teaspoons vanilla
3   cups flour, whole-wheat
1   teaspoon soda
1   teaspoon salt
1   cup chocolate chips*

Chocolate Chip Cookies	
Calories per serving:	71
Fat grams per serving:	1
Fat percentage:	13%
Number of servings:	48
Serving size:	1 cookie

Prepare beans in advance. This recipe may take slightly longer than 15 minutes to prepare.

Heat oven to 375 degrees. Mix applesauce, pureéd beans, sugars, egg whites, and vanilla. Stir in remaining ingredients. Drop dough by rounded teaspoons 2 inches apart onto a baking sheet coated with nonstick cooking spray. Bake 8 to 10 minutes or until light brown. Cool slightly before removing from baking sheet.

If you are diabetic use unsweetened applesauce and replace the sugars with 2/3 cup apple-juice concentrate and 2/3 cup pineapple-juice concentrate. Then increase the flour by 1 to 1 1/3 cups to balance out the solids and liquids. Replace the chocolate chips with 2/3 cup raisins.

Remember to have fun experimenting with recipes. Feel free to make moderate changes so that the recipes better fit your individual tastes and needs.

FREEDOM RECIPES

205

FREEDOM RECIPES

Oatmeal Raisin Cookies ("B+" Choice) or
Oatmeal Chocolate Chip Cookies ("B–" Choice)

1 cup brown sugar*, packed
1/2 cup safflower oil (or
 another "good" oil—
 see p. 280)
1 cup skim milk
1 teaspoon vanilla
41/2 cups oats, quick-cooking
2 cups flour, whole-wheat
1 teaspoon baking soda
3/4 teaspoon salt
1 cup raisins or semi-sweet
 chocolate chips*

Oatmeal Raisin Cookies	
Calories per serving:	90
Fat grams per serving:	2
Fat percentage:	20%
Number of servings:	84
Serving size:	1 cookie

Oatmeal Chocolate Chip Cookies	
Calories per serving:	98
Fat grams per serving:	3 1/2
Fat percentage:	32%
Number of servings:	84
Serving size:	1 cookie

This recipe is a time-saver if you make the "Pan-Cookie variation".

Mix brown sugar, oil, milk, and vanilla. Stir in remaining ingredients, adding raisins or chocolate chips after other ingredients are thoroughly mixed.

Shape dough into 1-inch balls. Place about 3 inches apart on a cookie sheet coated with nonstick cooking spray. Flatten cookies with the bottom of a glass dipped in water. Bake in a 375 degree oven until golden brown, about 8 to 10 minutes. Then immediately remove from cookie sheet. Makes about 7 dozen cookies.

Pan-Cookie Variation:

Spread dough evenly on cookie sheet. Bake for 10 to 15 minutes. Cool and cut into squares.

*This recipe is not for diabetics or for those who are highly resistant to fat loss.

Be sure to include desserts in moderation ONLY AFTER a complete water, veggie, grain, protein, fruit meal.

Pumpkin Cake Cookies ("B+" Choice)

1 cup pureéd beans (See * at bottom of p. 204.)
11/2 cups sugar (use part brown sugar or molasses if desired)*
6 egg whites
11/2 cups pumpkin
21/2 cups flour**, whole-wheat
1 teaspoon baking powder
1 teaspoon baking soda
1 teaspoon salt
11/2 teaspoons cinnamon
1/2 teaspoon nutmeg
1/4 teaspoon ginger
1 cup raisins, optional (Soak raisins before adding.)

Pumpkin Cake Cookies	
Calories per serving:	60
Fat grams per serving:	trace
Fat percentage:	trace
Number of servings:	48
Serving size:	1 cookie

This recipe may take slightly longer than 15 minutes to prepare. Prepare the beans in advance.

Beat pureéd beans, sugar, and egg whites until fluffy. Add remaining ingredients and mix until well blended. Drop by teaspoonfuls onto a nonstick cooking-sprayed cookie sheet and bake at 350 degrees for 15 minutes. Chocolate chips and nuts are also delicious in these cookies. They add substantial fat grams, making these cookies a "B–" Choice.

This is not a recipe for diabetics or for those who are highly resistant to fat loss.

**The sugar in this recipe may absorb more slowly into your system because it is combined with high-fiber, whole-wheat flour instead of low-fiber, refined, white flour.*

FREEDOM RECIPES

Raisin Chippers ("B+" Choice) *EASY!*

3/4   cup pureéd beans, cooked
      (See * at bottom of
      p. 204.)
13/4 cups flour, whole-wheat
1/2   cup brown sugar*, packed
1/4   cup honey*
1   teaspoon baking powder
1   teaspoon vanilla
1/4   teaspoon baking soda
4   egg whites, slightly beaten
2   cups rolled oats
1/2   cup semi-sweet
      chocolate chips*
1/2   cup raisins

Raisin Chippers	
Calories per serving:	79
Fat grams per serving:	trace
Fat percentage:	trace
Number of servings:	36
Serving size:	1 cookie

In a mixing bowl, beat pureéd beans, half of the flour, and all of the brown sugar, honey, baking powder, vanilla, and baking soda on medium-high speed until well blended. Add egg whites; beat until completely combined. Beat in remaining flour. Stir in oats, chocolate chips, and raisins.

Drop by rounded teaspoons two inches apart onto a cookie sheet sprayed with nonstick cooking spray. Bake at 375 degrees for 10 to 12 minutes. Cool on a wire rack. Makes approximately 36 cookies.

This is not a recipe for diabetics or for those who are highly resistant to fat loss.

Zucchini-Nut Cookies ("B+" Choice)

1   cup puréed beans, cooked, (see * at bottom of p. 204.)
1/2   cup sugar*
1/2   cup brown sugar*
2   egg whites, beaten until fluffy
1   cup zucchini, grated
2   cups flour, whole-wheat
1   teaspoon baking soda
1/4   teaspoon salt
1/2   teaspoon nutmeg
1   teaspoon cinnamon
1/2   teaspoon ground cloves
1/2   cup nuts, chopped
1   cup raisins

Zucchini-Nut Cookies	
Calories per serving:	39
Fat grams per serving:	trace
Fat percentage:	trace
Number of servings:	6 dozen
Serving size:	1 cookie

This recipe is a time-saver if the beans and the zucchini are prepared in advance.

Cream together puréed beans and sugars. Beat in egg whites and zucchini. Add dry ingredients. Stir in nuts and raisins. Bake 8 to 10 minutes at 350 degrees on a cookie sheet sprayed with a nonstick cooking spray.

*Diabetics and those who are highly resistant to fat loss may replace sugars with 1/2 cup apple-juice concentrate and 1/2 cup pineapple juice concentrate. If cookie dough looks too thin, add more flour (about 1/2 to 1 cup) until dough consistency looks like that of regular cookie dough.

FREEDOM RECIPES

DIPS / DRESSINGS

Bottled Dressings ("A" & "B" Choices)

Try small bottles of lowfat and nonfat dressings to see what you like. I dislike many of the nonfat dressings but thoroughly enjoy many lowfat ones. Mixing a regular dressing half and half with a nonfat dressing often creates a very tasty result.

Bottom line—don't eat it if you don't like it, but be open to trying new foods.

Buttermilk Dressing ("A" Choice) *This is delicious!*

1/2 cup mayonnaise, nonfat
1/4 cup salad dressing, nonfat
1/2 cup buttermilk
1 teaspoon parsley flakes, dried
1/2 teaspoon instant minced onion
1/2 to 1 clove garlic, crushed
1/2 teaspoon salt
dash of pepper

Buttermilk Dressing	
Calories per serving:	42
Fat grams per serving:	trace
Fat percentage:	trace
Number of servings:	8
Serving size:	2 tablespoons

Shake all ingredients together in a covered container and refrigerate 2 to 3 hours. Shake and serve. If dressing is too thick, use additional buttermilk to thin to desired consistency.

Creamy Onion Dip

Prepare Delicious Dill Dip (page 211), except omit onion, dill weed, and seasoned salt. Stir 2 tablespoons regular onion soup mix into beaten cream-cheese mixture. Chill for 24 hours. Makes 2 cups.

Creamy Onion Dip	
Calories per serving:	40
Fat grams per serving:	trace
Fat percentage:	trace
Number of servings:	16
Serving size:	2 tablespoons

FREEDOM RECIPES

Delicious Dill Dip ("A" Choice)

4 oz. cream cheese, fat free
1/2 cup cottage cheese, lowfat
1   8 oz. carton dairy sour cream, fat free
2   tablespoons green onion, finely chopped
2   teaspoons dill weed, dried
1/2 teaspoon seasoned salt

Delicious Dill Dip	
Calories per serving:	35
Fat grams per serving:	trace
Fat percentage:	trace
Number of servings:	16
Serving size:	2 tablespoons

Blend all ingredients on medium speed in blender until fluffy. Chill for 24 hours. If dip becomes too thick, stir in 1 to 2 tablespoons of milk. Serve with vegetables or lowfat crackers. Makes 2 cups.

Easy Lowfat Dressings and Dips ("A" Choice)

Combine any lowfat dressing mix that calls for mayonnaise or salad dressing with equal parts of nonfat mayonnaise and nonfat salad dressing.

For dips, combine fat free sour cream with any lowfat dip or dressing mix.

Easy Lowfat Dressings and Dips	
Calories per serving:	35[±]
Fat grams per serving:	trace[+]
Fat percentage:	trace[+]
Number of servings:	16[±]
Serving size:	2 tablespoons

FREEDOM RECIPES

Ranch Dip ("A" Choice)

1/4 cup skim milk
1 16 oz. carton cottage
   cheese, lowfat
1 envelope Hidden Valley
   Lite Ranch Dressing

Ranch Dip	
Calories per serving:	35
Fat grams per serving:	trace
Fat percentage:	trace
Number of servings:	16
Serving size:	2 tablespoons

Blend all ingredients in blender until smooth. Great for vegetables and lowfat crackers!

Sour Cream Fruit Dip ("A–" Choice)

1/2 cup vanilla yogurt*, nonfat
1/2 cup sour cream, fat free
1/4 cup All Fruit Jam (p. 165)
1/8 teaspoon ground cinnamon

Sour Cream Fruit Dip	
Calories per serving:	40
Fat grams per serving:	0
Fat percentage:	0%
Number of servings:	8
Serving size:	2 tablespoons

Stir together all ingredients. Chill for 12 to 24 hours.

*If you are diabetic, use nonfat, "fruit-juice-sweetened" vanilla yogurt and this "A–" Choice becomes an "A" Choice.

Spinach and Vegetable Dip ("A" Choice)

1 cup cottage cheese, lowfat
1 cup mayonnaise, nonfat
1 cup plain yogurt, nonfat
1 package Knorrs Vegetable
   Soup Mix
1 10 oz. package spinach,
   frozen, chopped, thawed
2 teaspoons dill weed

Spinach and Vegetable Dip	
Calories per serving:	87
Fat grams per serving:	trace
Fat percentage:	trace
Number of servings:	8
Serving size:	1/2 cup

Blend cottage cheese in blender until smooth. Ad all ingredients to the cottage cheese and blend well. (Squeeze all moisture out of spinach before adding to dip mixture.)

FRUIT

Fresh-Fruit Combination Trays ("A" Choices)

By varying the colors and flavors, taste and visual appeal are greatly enhanced along with the nutritional value. Try the following combinations or create your own.

1. Pineapple rings, green grapes, and strawberries.
2. Purple grapes, orange slices, and kiwi slices.
3. Watermelon, cantaloupe, and honeydew chunks.
4. Plum, peach, and pear slices.
5. Mandarin oranges, raspberries, and green grapes.
6. Banana slices, blueberries, and nectarines.

Any one of the previous fruits makes a good meal complement along with:

7. Lightly sweetened or no-sugar-added applesauce with apple chunks mixed in.
8. Apple slices in lemon water.
9. Any canned or bottled fruit in light syrup (rinsed) such as peaches, apricots, pears, fruit cocktail, pineapple, etc.

> **Fresh-Fruit Combination Trays**
> All fruits except coconuts are very low in fat or have no fat at all. Calories range from 35 to 110 calories per one-cup serving. Enjoy a variety and have fun!

Fruit Canning ("A" Choices)

I add 1/8 to 1/3 cup sugar to each quart of fruit, depending on the initial sweetness of the fruit. (I rinse the fruit with water before serving it.) One-fourth to 1/2 cup apple- or pineapple-juice concentrate can substitute for sugar if you are diabetic. This is more expensive, but it's worth it and it tastes great. You can mix the pineapple- and apple-juice concentrate for a more balanced flavor. (Dole Orchard Peach juice concentrate is great for peaches.)

213

Fruit Gelatin* ("A" Choice)

2   envelopes gelatin,
     unflavored
11/2   cups water, boiling
1   cup apple-juice frozen
     concentrate, thawed
1   cup Dole Mountain Cherry
     juice frozen concentrate
     thawed
1   can fruit cocktail, packed in
     fruit juice
1   red apple, diced

Fruit Gelatin	
Calories per serving:	75
Fat grams per serving:	0
Fat percentage:	0%
Number of servings:	6
Serving size:	3/4 cup

In a large bowl pour boiling water over gelatin and let sit about 2 to 3 minutes. Stir until dissolved completely. Add fruit-juice concentrates. Refrigerate until mixture is half-set. Add fruit; mix in well. Refrigerate until firm.

Fruit Syrup* ("A" Choice)
Mountain Cherry, Orchard Peach, etc.

1/2   can (6 oz.) Dole Mountain
     Cherry juice concentrate,
     frozen, thawed
1/2   can (6 oz.) water
1/2   tablespoon cornstarch

Fruit Syrup	
Calories per serving:	10
Fat grams per serving:	0
Fat percentage:	0%
Number of servings:	12
Serving size:	2 tablespoons

Mix cornstarch and water until cornstarch is completely dissolved. Whisk mixture into cold cherry-juice concentrate. Heat over medium heat until boiling, stirring constantly. Serve over warm pancakes, French toast, or waffles.

Variations: Try these same two recipes substituting Dole Orchard Peach, Dole Country Raspberry, Dole Pine-Orange-Banana, Dole Pine-Passion-Banana, apple, or pineapple juice concentrate, etc. Change the fruit in the Fruit Gelatin to complement the different juice-concentrate flavors. (See italics statement at bottom of next page.)

Juice* ("A–" Choices)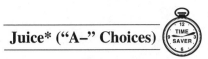

Juice is a far superior choice to soft drinks. However, it takes 3 whole oranges to make 1 glass of orange juice, and it is high in natural fruit sugar (fructose).

What's missing? Most of the fiber—an essential element for optimal health and fat loss.

The solution is to usually eat the *whole* fruit or the *whole* vegetable and drink juice once or twice a week as a fun refresher. If you have an extremely sensitive system that does not tolerate fiber well, you may wisely opt to drink juice more often. For a fun taste treat, mix 1 cup of fresh fruit juice with 1/3 cup of Sprite or 7-Up. (This is not for diabetics or for those who are highly resistant to fat loss = "B+" Choice.)

Variation: **Juice Popsicle**—Freeze all-natural fruit juice in popsicle or ice cube trays. A summer sensation!

Pineapple and Cottage Cheese Salad ("A" Choice)

1 **20 oz. can pineapple, crushed, in its own juice, drained**
2 **cups cottage cheese, lowfat**
1 **teaspoon cinnamon**

Pineapple and Cottage Cheese Salad	
Calories per serving:	202
Fat grams per serving:	2
Fat percentage:	9%
Number of servings:	4
Serving size:	1 cup

Mix together all ingredients. Chill. Serve on a crisp lettuce leaf. Top with a maraschino cherry, if desired. This salad is delicious served with chicken or fish, a variety of vegetables, and whole-grain rolls.

"Juice" receives an "A–" rating, "juice with 7-Up or Sprite" receives a "B+", and "Fruit Gelatin" and "Fruit Syrup" (on the previous page) receive "A"s. In the case of syrup and gelatin, fruit-juice-sweetened varieties are by far the most nutritious choices available and therefore receive "A"s. They should be eaten in moderation **with a meal, **never** on an empty stomach.*

*In the case of juice, it receives an "A–" because it **does** have a superior choice—the WHOLE fruit!*

215

Pineapple-Marshmallow Coleslaw ("A–" Choice)

1/4 cup dairy sour cream, fat free

1 tablespoon mayonnaise, fat free

1 tablespoon salad dressing, fat free

1/4 teaspoon salt

1/4 teaspoon dry mustard dash of pepper

1/4 medium head green cabbage, shredded* (about 2 cups)

1 20 oz. can pineapple chunks, drained

1/2 cup miniature marshmallows**

11/2 teaspoons lemon juice paprika

Pineapple-Marshmallow Coleslaw	
Calories per serving:	112
Fat grams per serving:	trace
Fat percentage:	trace
Number of servings:	4
Serving size:	1 cup

This recipe may take slightly longer than 15 minutes to prepare.

Mix sour cream, mayonnaise, salad dressing, salt, mustard, and pepper. Toss with cabbage. Then blend in pineapple, marshmallows, and lemon juice. Top with paprika. This delicious coleslaw may serve as both a fruit and a vegetable choice at a meal. A sandwich with whole-grain bread and lean meat (protein), along with a cool glass of water would complete this quick, delicious meal.

*Shredding Note: Place chopped cabbage in blender. Cover with water. Then cover with lid and blend on high; drain completely. Or purchase cabbage that is already shredded as a time saver.

**If you are diabetic, hypoglycemic, or highly resistant to fat loss, you may choose to leave out the marshmallows.

FREEDOM RECIPES

Pineapple-Orange-Banana Gelatin ("A" Choice)

2   envelopes gelatin,
      unflavored
11/2 cups water, boiling
2   cups Dole Pineapple-
      Orange-Banana juice
      frozen concentrate,
      unsweetened, thawed
3/4 cup water
11/2 tablespoons lemon juice
1   cup pineapple,
      unsweetened, crushed,
      drained
1   11 oz. can mandarin
      oranges, in light syrup,
      drained and rinsed
1   cup bananas, sliced

Pineapple-Orange-Banana Gelatin	
Calories per serving:	186
Fat grams per serving:	0
Fat percentage	0%
Number of servings:	6
Serving size: approximately 3/4 cup	

Dissolve gelatin in 11/2 cups boiling water and let sit for 5 minutes. In a separate saucepan, bring juice concentrate and 3/4 cup water to a boil. Stir juice concentrate into softened gelatin until dissolved.

Stir in lemon juice and crushed pineapple. Refrigerate until the mixture is about half-set to a thick liquid consistency. Fold in oranges and bananas. Pour into glass cake dish or individual dessert dishes. Refrigerate until completely set. Refreshingly light! This recipe makes a marvelous dessert for everyone, including those with diabetes and a high resistance to fat loss. Eat it **for dessert**, never on an empty stomach.

Variations: Try this recipe with any complementary combination of fruits and fruit-juice concentrates.

Super Citrus Salad ("A" Choice)

1/2   cup water, cold
2   envelopes gelatin, unflavored
11/4   cups water, boiling
1   12 oz. can Dole Mandarin
       Tangerine juice, frozen
       concentrate, or Dole
       Pineapple-Orange juice
       frozen concentrate, thawed
1   15 oz. can pineapple tidbits
       or chunks, packed
       in own juice
1   can mandarin oranges,
       packed in own juice

Super Citrus Salad	
Calories per serving:	95
Fat grams per serving:	0
Fat percentage:	0%
Number of servings:	6
Serving size:	3/4 cup

Drain canned fruit well, reserving the juice. In large bowl dissolve gelatin in cold water. Pour boiling water over gelatin mixture. Stir until completely dissolved. Allow to sit for 2 or 3 minutes. Add fruit juices and juice concentrate. Refrigerate until half set. Add pineapple and oranges. Mix well. Refrigerate until firm.

Special Note: *Fruit makes a fun, refreshing dessert any time of the day. It's clean, delicious taste comes in so many varieties and can serve as a beautiful enhancement to any meal. And remember to always eat fruit with a meal or for dessert—never on an empty stomach. Fruit is high in natural sugar and is the least complex of the complex carbohydrates. It may therefore encourage direct rises in blood-sugar levels when introduced on an empty stomach. Insulin (the "fat-hormone") is then released by your pancreas to drive the high-sugar food into your fat cells. By combining fruit with more complex foods such as grains and veggies, the sugar combines with the fiber. This may keep blood-sugar and energy levels stable. The result may be a significant increase in energy and an accelerated loss of excess body fat.*

Yogurt Fruit Delight ("A–" Choice)

This is an "A" Choice if you use Fruit-Juice-Sweetened
Yogurt or All Fruit Jam-Sweetened Yogurt

2   cups mixed fruit chunks,
     fresh, frozen and slightly
     thawed, or canned (in
     own juice or extra-light
     syrup and rinsed)
3/4 cup yogurt*, nonfat vanilla
     or fruit-flavored

Yogurt Fruit Delight	
Calories per serving:	146
Fat grams per serving:	0
Fat percentage:	0%
Number of servings:	2
Serving size:	1 heaping cup

Mix, chill, and serve.

Be creative and colorful. This simple treat is a real hit at any party. Use fruits in season. Delicious combinations include:

1. Pineapple chunks, mandarin oranges, and bananas mixed with vanilla, orange, or pineapple yogurt.
2. Watermelon, cantaloupe, honeydew, and pineapple chunks mixed with lemon or vanilla yogurt.
3. Blueberries, raspberries, boysenberries, strawberries, fresh peach, pineapple, and plum chunks gently blended with mixed berry yogurt.
4. Canned chunky fruit cocktail, mandarin oranges, pineapple chunks, and bananas mixed with vanilla yogurt and topped with sliced strawberries and kiwi.

*If you are diabetic or highly resistant to fat loss, use plain, nonfat yogurt mixed with All Fruit Jam—a delicious "A" Choice. If you suffer from a lactose (milk sugar) intolerance, try adding "lactaid drops" (found at most pharmacies) to your milk or yogurt; or purchase Alta Dena nonfat, fruit-juice-sweetened yogurt which may solve both problems (diabetes and dairy allergies unless you're allergic to the "protein" in the milk). Not only is Alta Dena nonfat yogurt fruit-juice-sweetened, it also contains acidophilus and active yogurt cultures which adds "good" bacteria to your system.

It is also very helpful to eat this yogurt when you are taking antibiotics which can destroy "good" bacteria along with "bad" bacteria.

GRAVY / SAUCE

Chicken Gravy ("A" Choice)

2	tablespoons flour, whole-wheat
1 1/2	tablespoons chicken bouillon
1/8	teaspoon pepper
1 2/3	cups skim milk

Chicken Gravy	
Calories per serving:	35
Fat grams per serving:	trace
Fat percentage:	trace
Number of servings:	6
Serving size: approximately 1/3 cup	

Mix all ingredients well. Cook and stir over medium heat until thick and bubbly. Continue cooking and stirring for 1 more minute. Makes approximately 2 cups.

Meat Marinade ("A" Choice)
For Chicken or Turkey

1/2	cup soy sauce
1/2	cup 7-Up
1	teaspoon lemon juice
1/2	teaspoon garlic powder

Meat Marinade	
Calories per serving:	130
Fat grams per serving:	trace
Fat percentage:	trace
Number of servings:	4
Serving size: approximately 1/3 cup	

This recipe makes enough marinade for at - least 4 pieces of chicken or turkey.

Combine ingredients. Place meat in marinade and refrigerate several hours. Grill, stir-fry, or broil your meat. Serve with a lot of vegetables, fruit, and some whole-grain breads. Delicious!

Mushroom Gravy ("A" Choice)

| 1 | 10 3/4 oz. can Campbell's Healthy Request Cream of Mushroom Soup |
| 1/2 | can skim milk |

Mushroom Gravy	
Calories per serving:	54
Fat grams per serving:	1
Fat percentage:	17%
Number of servings:	4
Serving size: approximately 1/2 cup	

Blend well. Microwave or heat in saucepan until warm. Serve over brown rice and chicken, hot noodles, potatoes, etc.

FREEDOM RECIPES

Oriental-Style Sauce ("A" Choice)

2   tablespoons cornstarch
1/2 cup water, cold
1/4 cup orange-juice
      frozen concentrate,
      thawed
1/2 cup soy sauce
4   teaspoons sugar
      dash pepper

Oriental-Style Sauce	
Calories per serving:	180
Fat grams per serving:	0
Fat percentage:	0%
Number of servings:	4
Serving size:	1/4 cup

Combine cornstarch and cold water. Stir in orange-juice concentrate, soy sauce, sugar, and pepper. Bring to a boil and let thicken. Pour over oriental stir-fry.

Quick Chicken Gravy ("A" Choice)

1   103/4 oz. can Campbell's
      Healthy Request Cream
      of Chicken Soup
1/2 can skim milk

Quick Chicken Gravy	
Calories per serving:	59
Fat grams per serving:	1
Fat percentage:	15%
Number of servings:	4
Serving size:	1/2 cup

Blend well. Microwave or heat in saucepan until warm.

Quick Spaghetti Sauce ("A" Choice)

I always purchase different varieties of canned or bottled spaghetti sauce. Check the labels and compare the numbers of fat grams in each brand. "Lowest" doesn't necessarily mean "best." Find varieties that you thoroughly enjoy that are moderate to low in fat.

You can also purchase envelopes of dry spaghetti sauce. Mix and prepare them according to their package instructions, or make the delicious, money-saving sauce *Spaghetti Econo-Sauce* on the next page.

221

FREEDOM RECIPES

Quick Turkey Gravy ("A" Choice)

Follow the directions on a turkey gravy packet mix or buy bottled turkey gravy. Lowfat cream of mushroom or cream of chicken soup also makes an excellent gravy. (Do not add milk or water to the soup. Simply heat the condensed soup.

Quick Turkey Gravy	
Calories per serving:	35±
Fat grams per serving:	trace
Fat percentage:	trace
Number of servings:	6
Serving size:	1/3 cup

Then serve over meat, noodles, potatoes, steamed vegetables, etc.)

Spaghetti Econo-Sauce ("A" Choice)

6	8 oz. cans tomato sauce
2	teaspoons oregano
1	teaspoon basil leaves
3	teaspoons brown sugar
1/4	teaspoon marjoram
1	teaspoon garlic salt
2	tablespoons dried parsley flakes

Spaghetti Econo-Sauce	
Calories per serving:	62
Fat grams per serving:	trace
Fat percentage:	trace
Number of servings:	6
Serving size:	3/4 cup
	(without ground beef)

Mix all ingredients together in a saucepan and heat slowly over medium heat. (Add chopped onions, mushrooms, and green pepper if desired.) Warm thoroughly and serve over hot, cooked pasta.

Variation: Add 1/2 pound cooked, extra-lean ground beef to this sauce and create **Spaghetti Econo-Meat Sauce**.

Stir-Fry Sauce ("A" Choice)

2	tablespoons cornstarch
2	tablespoons soy sauce (low-sodium, if desired)
2	cups water
1/2	teaspoon ginger (optional)

Stir-Fry Sauce	
Calories per serving:	18
Fat grams per serving:	0
Fat percentage:	0%
Number of servings:	4
Serving size:	1/2 cup

Combine ingredients in saucepan. Heat on medium heat until thick. Blend into stir-fry veggies and serve over rice.

Spaghetti and other Pasta Varieties accompanied by Spaghetti Econo-Sauce

*Quick Delicious Beef Stew served
in a hollowed-out whole-wheat bread bowl*

LEAN & FREE Homemade Sandwiches (open-face style)

Salmon Pasta Salad and Spaghetti Salad

MISCELLANEOUS

Brown Rice Cooking Hints
("A" Choice)

2   cups brown rice
5   cups water
1   teaspoon salt

Heat rice, water, and salt to boiling, stirring twice; reduce heat. Cover and simmer for 45 to 60 minutes. After 45 minutes, remove lid and fluff with a fork and taste to see if it's done. The rice should have a slightly firm texture and be nutty in taste. If it is hard to chew, it is underdone and should be cooked 5 to 15 minutes longer. If it falls apart and has a mushy texture, it is overdone.

- High quality brown rice is essential for a delicious product. Low quality brown rice will be a disappointment every time.
- Rice cookers are an excellent investment and help to insure perfectly-cooked rice.
- Cook large quantities and then freeze in bags for quick, future use.
- Brown rice is very tasty cooked in chicken broth.

Buying Pizza Out ("B" Choice)

If you can find whole-wheat crust, great—or make your own pizza. Otherwise, choose pizza crusts that have been baked, not fried. Be very moderate with cheese and meat or greasy crusts. Focus on toppings such as onions, mushrooms, green peppers, tomatoes, pineapple, and just a few olives. Ham, pineapple, and mushroom is a much better choice than ham, pepperoni, and sausage. I order tomatoes and pineapple to be put on after the pizza is cooked.

Plain cheese is a reasonably good choice. Eat a big tossed salad first and fruit on the side. Canadian bacon, mushroom, and pineapple comes next followed by pepperoni. The double meat and double cheese pizzas are very high in fat and should be avoided.

I first eat a big tossed salad and a big bowl of vegetable soup with a piece of toast topped with All-Fruit Jam. Then I have 1 piece of vegetable pizza, and 1 piece of Canadian bacon, pineapple, and mushroom pizza that the pizza-delivery man delivers. If I don't eat "A" Choice food first, I end up eating eight pieces of "B" Choice pizza which totally halts my fat loss for the week. Pizza is my childrens' favorite Friday-night food, so I've learned how much of it to eat.

223

FREEDOM RECIPES

Chinese Take-Out
("A" & "B" Choices)

My favorite chinese dishes include chicken cashew (lots of veggies with a little chicken and a few cashews) over rice, and any of the other Chinese dishes that focus mainly on stir-fried vegetables, using meat as the condiment and avoiding deep frying.

If you bring the food home to eat, you can use your own brown rice that you cook and freeze in quantity. You can also use low-sodium soy sauce. Otherwise, a little white rice now and then is not a bad choice. Be moderate with the soy sauce.

If you are sensitive to MSG (monosodium glutamate), which is actually a drug, not a spice, ask the restaurant to please leave MSG out of your order—that is, if they usually put it in.

Also, if you have an intolerance toward MSG, you may need an extra B vitamin supplement in your diet. Some studies suggest an increased tolerance toward MSG when a vitamin B supplement is taken.

Fresh Cranberry Relish
("A–" Choice)

1	package fresh cranberries
2	large sweet apples, chopped
2	oranges, peeled, and chopped
1/4	cup honey, melted

Fresh Cranberry Relish	
Calories per serving:	55
Fat grams per serving:	0
Fat percentage:	0%
Number of servings:	8
Serving size:	1/2 cup

This recipe is a time-saver if the apples and oranges are chopped in advance.

Mash cranberries, apples, and oranges together in the same bowl. (Blend coarsely in the blender if you prefer a finer-textured relish.) Add melted honey to taste and blend well. Let stand in fridge for at least 1 hour. Delicious with turkey for Thanksgiving.

If you are diabetic or highly resistant to fat loss, replace honey with 1/3 cup apple-juice or orange-juice frozen concentrate.

Light Butter Popcorn ("A" & "B" Choices)

Idea #1 = "B+": Purchase microwavable light, butter-flavor popcorn and enjoy. Each brand of popcorn will have a different number of fat grams. Check the label and choose brands with fewer fat grams.

Idea #2 = "B": Air pop your popcorn and drizzle a small amount of melted butter over it. (One teaspoon, added to each cup, will add about 31/2 fat grams per cup. Be careful because it's very easy to eat ten cups and 30 fat grams!)

Idea #3 = "A": Air pop your popcorn. Then spray it very lightly with a fine mist of water from a spray bottle. Sprinkle with Molly McButter, Butter Buds, or butter-flavored salt. (The butter-flavored sprinkles will adhere to the popcorn rather than falling to the bottom of the bowl.) Delicious!

Microwaved Brown Rice ("A" Choice)

2	cups hot water
1	cup brown rice
1/2	teaspoon salt

Brown Rice	
Calories per serving:	115
Fat grams per serving:	0
Fat percentage:	0%
Number of servings:	6
Serving size:	1/2 cup

Combine all ingredients in a large 3-quart casserole dish. Cover and microwave on high for 5 minutes. Reduce power to half and cook for 40 minutes. Let sit for 5 minutes. This brown rice is delicious and fluffy.

FREEDOM RECIPES

FREEDOM RECIPES

MUFFINS

Apple-Cinnamon Muffins ("A" Choice)

Prepare as in key recipe (Marvelous Muffins on page 231), except stir 1 teaspoon ground cinnamon into flour mixture. Then fold 3/4 cup diced apples into completed muffin batter.

These muffins may take 15 to 20 minutes to make if the beans are prepared in advance.

Apple-Cinnamon Muffins	
Calories per serving:	149
Fat grams per serving:	3
Fat percentage:	18%
Number of servings:	12*
Serving size:	1 muffin

Banana Muffins ("A" Choice)

Prepare as in key recipe (Marvelous Muffins on page 231), except reduce milk to 1/4 cup and add 3/4 cup ripe, mashed bananas to the flour and egg mixture. Do not use paper baking cups. Spray muffin tin generously with nonstick cooking spray.

These muffins may take 15 to 20 minutes to make if the beans are prepared in advance.

Banana Muffins	
Calories per serving:	144
Fat grams per serving:	3
Fat percentage:	19%
Number of servings:	12*
Serving size:	1 muffin

*I usually triple or quadruple these recipes and then freeze the extra in freezer bags for quick future use.

Better Bran Muffins ("A–" Choice)

5 cups flour, whole-wheat
5 teaspoons baking soda
2 teaspoons salt
1 20 oz. package raisin bran
   cereal
1 cup honey*
1/2 cup "good" oil
   (see p. 280)
8 egg whites, beaten
1 quart buttermilk

Better Bran Muffins	
Calories per serving:	92
Fat grams per serving:	2
Fat percentage:	20%
Number of servings:	72
Serving size:	1 muffin

Mix dry ingredients first; then drizzle the honey over the top to coat. Mix oil, egg whites, and buttermilk into the dry ingredients. Blend well. Bake in paper muffin cup lined muffin tins, or use a nonstick cooking spray on the muffin tins. Fill cups 1/2 to 3/4 full of batter. Bake at 400 degrees for 15 minutes. These bake more nicely if batter is at room temperature. Recipe makes approximately 6 dozen muffins. Batter will keep 6 weeks in the refrigerator. Muffins freeze very well. (These muffins are an "A–" Choice unless you overdo it and forget the veggie snacks.)

If you are diabetic or highly resistant to fat loss, replace the honey with 1/2 cup pineapple-juice concentrate and 1/2 cup apple-juice concentrate = "A" Choice.

Blueberry Muffins ("A" Choice)

Prepare as in key recipe (Marvelous Muffins on page 231) and gently fold 3/4 cup fresh or frozen blueberries into muffin batter before filling paper baking cups.

These muffins may take 15 to 20 minutes to make if the beans are prepared in advance.

Blueberry Muffins	
Calories per serving:	151
Fat grams per serving:	3
Fat percentage:	18%
Number of servings:	12
Serving size:	1 muffin

227

FREEDOM RECIPES

Carrot Muffins ("A" Choice)

11/3 cups buttermilk
1 tablespoon "good" oil
(see page 280)
4 egg whites
2–4 tablespoons honey* (to taste)
1 cup rolled oats
1/2 cup whole wheat flour
1/2 cup cornmeal
2 teaspoons baking powder
1/4 teaspoon salt
1 teaspoon cinnamon
1 cup shredded carrots

Carrot Muffins	
Calories per serving:	120
Fat grams per serving:	1
Fat percentage:	7.5%
Number of servings:	12
Serving size:	1 muffin

This recipe may take slightly longer than 15 minutes to prepare. Shred the carrots in advance to save time.

Beat buttermilk, oil, egg whites, and honey. Add oats, flour, cornmeal, baking powder, salt, and cinnamon. Fold in carrots. Fill nonstick cooking-sprayed muffin tins 1/2 to 3/4 full. Bake at 400 degrees for 15 to 20 minutes.

*Diabetics may choose to delete the honey.

Cheese Muffins ("B+" Choice)

Prepare as in key recipe (Marvelous Muffins on page 231), except stir 1/2 cup shredded cheddar cheese into flour mixture.

This recipe may take 15 to 20 minutes to make if the beans are prepared in advance.

Cheese Muffins	
Calories per serving:	185
Fat grams per serving:	6
Fat percentage:	29%
Number of servings:	12
Serving size:	1 muffin

FREEDOM RECIPES

Corn Muffins ("A" Choice)

Prepare as in key recipe (Marvelous Muffins on page 231), except delete the oatmeal and reduce the whole-wheat flour to 1 cup. Add 3/4 cup cornmeal to flour mixture. Do not use paper baking cups. Generously spray muffin tins with nonstick cooking spray.

This recipe may take 15 to 20 minutes to make if the beans are prepared in advance.

Corn Muffins	
Calories per serving:	143
Fat grams per serving:	3
Fat percentage:	19%
Number of servings:	12
Serving size:	1 muffin

Cranberry Muffins ("A" Choice)

Prepare as in key recipe (Marvelous Muffins on page 231), except combine 1 cup coarsely-chopped cranberries and 2 tablespoons sugar*; fold into muffin batter.

This recipe may take 15 to 20 minutes to make if the beans are prepared in advance.

Cranberry Muffins	
Calories per serving:	158
Fat grams per serving:	3
Fat percentage:	17%
Number of servings:	12
Serving size:	1 muffin

Diabetics may choose to delete the sugar.

FREEDOM RECIPES

229

Cranberry-Orange Muffins ("A–" Choice)

1   cup cranberries, fresh, chopped in a food processor or blender
1   tablespoon orange peel, grated
1/2 cup honey*
1½   teaspoons baking soda
1/2 cup pineapple or orange-juice frozen concentrate
1   egg white
2   cups flour, whole-wheat

Cranberry-Orange Muffins	
Calories per serving:	135
Fat grams per serving:	trace
Fat percentage:	trace
Number of servings:	12
Serving size:	1 muffin

This recipe may take slightly longer than 15 minutes to prepare.

Mix cranberries, orange peel, honey, soda, juice concentrate, and egg white thoroughly. Gradually add flour and mix well. Fill nonstick cooking-sprayed muffin tin cups 1/2 to 3/4 full of batter. Bake at 375 degrees approximately 18 minutes or until lightly brown.

*Diabetics may choose to delete the honey and replace it with more pineapple or orange-juice concentrate.

Date Muffins ("A–"Choice)

Prepare as in key recipe (Marvelous Muffins on page 231), except fold 2/3 cup chopped dates into muffin batter.

This recipe may take 15 to 20 minutes to make if the beans are prepared in advance.

Date Muffins	
Calories per serving:	179
Fat grams per serving:	3
Fat percentage:	15%
Number of servings:	12
Serving size:	1 muffin

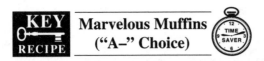

KEY RECIPE Marvelous Muffins ("A–" Choice)

11/2	cups flour, whole-wheat (white wheat—see page 61)
3/4	cup rolled oats
1	teaspoon baking soda
1	teaspoon baking powder
1/2	teaspoon salt
2	egg whites, slightly beaten
1/2	cup skim milk
2	tablespoons "good" oil (see page 280)
1/2	cup honey* or 2/3 cup sugar*
1/2	cup applesauce, lightly sweetened*
1/2	cup pureéd beans**

Marvelous Muffins	
Calories per serving:	148
Fat grams per serving:	3
Fat percentage:	18%
Number of servings:	12***
Serving size:	1 muffin

These muffins may take 15 to 20 minutes to make if the beans are prepared in advance.

In a mixing bowl combine flour, oats, soda, baking powder, and salt. Make a well in the center. In a separate bowl combine egg whites, milk, oil, honey, applesauce, and pureéd beans. Add all at once to flour mixture. Stir just until moist, allowing batter to be lumpy. Line muffin tin with paper baking cups. Fill 2/3 full. Bake at 375 degrees for 15 to 20 minutes or until lightly browned. Remove from pans and serve warm. Makes 12 muffins.

*If you are diabetic, suffer from a sugar allergy, or are highly resistant to fat loss, replace the honey or sugar with 1/4 cup frozen concentrated apple juice and 1/4 cup frozen concentrated pineapple juice. (Add 2 to 4 tablespoons of additional flour if batter looks too thin.) Use unsweetened applesauce. You now have an "A" Choice.

**Purchase canned white beans and finely pureé them in your blender. The consistency should be like thick wall-paper paste or creamed shortening and sugar. If the consistency is too thick, add 1 to 3 tablespoons of water or liquid left over from the beans.

****I always make extra muffins and freeze them in freezer bags for quick future use. And remember, do not **SNACK** on grains first. Snack on veggie-based foods first to accelerate excess fat loss! Then, if you're still hungry, add in the grains, proteins, and fruits.*

231

FREEDOM RECIPES

Minute Muffins ("A" & "B" Choices)

Purchase either store variety lowfat, whole-grain muffins or muffin mixes, or make your own. You could also ask your local bakery or kitchen-center store if they will bake large quantities of your own recipe. I always triple or quadruple amounts so I have plenty to freeze.

Beware of the bakery muffins many stores offer. It is not uncommon for them to contain 20 to 30 fat grams each. Do not purchase them unless you have their fat gram-calorie information, their sugar content, and their nutrient and fiber information. Ask your baker or grocer for this information.

Fruit-juice-sweetened lowfat or nonfat, whole-grain muffins are the only choices that rate a solid "A".

Oatmeal Raisin Muffins ("A–" Choice)

3	cups flour, whole-wheat
2	cups oatmeal
1	teaspoon cinnamon
2	teaspoons baking powder
2	teaspoons baking soda
1	teaspoon salt
2	cups applesauce*
2	cups skim milk
1/3	cup yogurt, nonfat, vanilla*,
1/2	cup honey*
1	cup raisins

Oatmeal Raisin Muffins	
Calories per serving:	258
Fat grams per serving:	2
Fat percentage:	7%
Number of servings:	24
Serving size:	1 muffin

This recipe may take 15 to 20 minutes to make.

Combine dry ingredients. In a separate bowl, combine wet ingredients. Mix together until moist. Mix raisins into batter last. Spray muffin tins with nonstick cooking spray. Fill about 2/3 full. Bake at 400 degrees about 20 minutes.

*Diabetics may choose to delete the honey and use "unsweetened" applesauce and 1/2 cup apple-juice concentrate; and choose fruit-juice-sweetened, nonfat vanilla yogurt = "A" Choice.

FREEDOM RECIPES

Pumpkin-Carrot Muffins ("A–" Choice)

1/2	cup pumpkin, canned
1/3	cup honey or 2/3 cup brown sugar*
4	egg whites, slightly beaten
1/2	cup buttermilk
2	teaspoons baking soda
2	teaspoons cinnamon
1/2	teaspoon salt
3	teaspoons baking powder
1	cup carrots, raw, grated
1	cup raisins, optional
1	to 1 1/4 cups flour, whole-wheat

Pumpkin-Carrot Muffins	
Calories per serving:	120
Fat grams per serving:	1
Fat percentage:	8%
Number of servings:	12
Serving size:	1 muffin

This recipe is a time-saver if the carrots are grated in advance.

Mix all ingredients except flour. Stir in flour just until moistened. Spoon into muffin tins coated with nonstick cooking spray. Bake at 375 degrees for about 15 minutes.

*If you are diabetic, hypoglycemic, or highly resistant to fat loss, replace honey or brown sugar with 1/3 cup pineapple-juice concentrate and 1/3 cup apple-juice concentrate. Increase the flour by 1/3 to 1/2 cup. These muffins are now a delicious "A" Choice.

Pumpkin Muffins ("A–" Choice)

Prepare as in key recipe (Marvelous Muffins on page 231, except add 1 teaspoon ground cinnamon, 1/8 teaspoon ground nutmeg, and 1/8 teaspoon ground cloves to flour mixture. Then add 1/2 cup canned pumpkin to egg mixture. Do not use paper baking cups. Generously spray muffin tins with nonstick cooking spray.

These muffins may take 15 to 20 minutes to make if the beans are prepared in advance.

Pumpkin Muffins	
Calories per serving:	152
Fat grams per serving:	3
Fat percentage:	18%
Number of servings:	12
Serving size:	1 muffin

233

FREEDOM RECIPES

FREEDOM RECIPES

Sweet Potato Muffins ("A–" Choice)

1/3 cup brown sugar*
2 tablespoons "good" oil
   (see page 280)
2 egg whites, beaten
1/2 cup sweet-potato
   pureé, cooked
1/2 cup carrots, raw, grated
3/4 cup flour, whole-wheat
1 teaspoon baking powder
1/2 teaspoon baking soda
1/2 teaspoon cinnamon
1/4 teaspoon salt
1/3 cup raisins, optional

Sweet Potato Muffins	
Calories per serving:	99
Fat grams per serving:	2
Fat percentage:	18%
Number of servings:	15
Serving size:	1 muffin

Beat together brown sugar, oil, egg whites, and sweet-potato pureé. Stir in grated carrots. In a separate bowl combine flour, baking powder, baking soda, cinnamon, and salt; stir into the sweet-potato mixture. Add raisins; lightly blend. Spoon batter into muffin tins thoroughly sprayed with nonstick cooking spray. Bake at 375 degrees for 10 minutes. A southern delight!

If you are diabetic, hypoglycemic, or highly resistant to fat loss, replace the brown sugar with 1/4 cup pineapple-juice concentrate and 1/4 cup apple-juice concentrate. Increase the flour by 1/2 to 3/4 cup. This is now an "A" Choice.

Zucchini Muffins ("A–" Choice)

Prepare as in key recipe (Marvelous Muffins on page 231), except add 1 teaspoon ground cinnamon, 1/2 teaspoon ground nutmeg, and 1/8 teaspoon ground cloves to flour mixture. Then fold 3/4 cup finely-chopped zucchini pieces into finished batter.

234

These muffins may take 15 to 20 minutes to make if the beans are prepared in advance.

Zucchini Muffins	
Calories per serving:	143
Fat grams per serving:	3
Fat percentage:	19%
Number of servings:	12
Serving size:	1 muffin

PASTA

Cappellino Primavera ("A" Choice)

2	tablespoons butter
11/2	cups onion, chopped
3/4	cup carrots, julienne
5	cups broccoli florets
11/4	cups yellow squash, thinly sliced
2	cups tomatoes, chopped
11/2	tablespoon beef bouillon granules
1/2	tablespoon fresh parsley, finely chopped
1/2	teaspoon oregano leaves
1/4	teaspoon ground rosemary
1/8	teaspoon crushed red pepper
8	cups cooked angel-hair pasta
1/2	cup Parmesan cheese

Cappellino Primavera

Calories per serving: 383
Fat grams per serving: 6
Fat percentage: 14%
Number of servings: 8
Serving size: 3/4 cup veggie mixture over 1 cup pasta

Melt butter in heavy pan. Sauté the onions, carrots, and broccoli in butter for 8 minutes. Add rest of vegetables and sauté for 2 minutes longer. Add remaining ingredients. Stir well and bring to a boil. Simmer for 12 minutes or until vegetables are tender. Serve over cooked angel-hair pasta and sprinkle lightly with Parmesan cheese.

Cheese-Stuffed Jumbo Shells ("A" Choice)
An *Easy* Family Favorite!

4   quarts water, boiling
1   teaspoon salt
12 oz. jumbo pasta shells,
      uncooked (American
      Beauty is an excellent
      brand.)
4   cups (2 pounds) ricotta
      cheese, fat free
1   cup cottage cheese, lowfat
2   cups mozzarella cheese,
      shredded, part-skim
      loosely packed
3/4 cup Parmesan cheese, grated
6   egg whites
1   tablespoon parsley, chopped
3/4 teaspoon oregano
1/2 teaspoon salt

Cheese-Stuffed Jumbo Shells	
Calories per serving:	194
Fat grams per serving:	4
Fat percentage:	19%
Number of servings:	18
Serving size:	2 jumbo shells
	with sauce and cheese

1/4 teaspoon pepper
6 - 8 cups (two 32 oz. jars)
      spaghetti sauce, lowfat
      (LEAN & FREE Spaghetti
      Econo-Sauce is excellent.)

Add jumbo shells, 3 or 4 at a time, to boiling, salted water. Boil uncovered for 10 minutes, stirring occasionally. Avoid overcooking. Drain. Cool in a single layer on wax paper or aluminum foil to keep jumbo shells from sticking together.

While shells are cooling, mix together ricotta cheese, cottage cheese, 11/4 cups mozzarella cheese, 1/2 cup Parmesan cheese, egg whites, parsley, oregano, salt, and pepper. Fill each shell with about 2 to 3 tablespoons of cheese mixture. Spread a thin layer of spaghetti sauce on bottom of 13 x 9 x 2 inch baking pan or glass baking dish. (You may need two or three pans. Cover well with plastic wrap and foil and freeze one or two for later use. Always put a note on the cover explaining the name of the item, the cooking time, and the date it was made.) Place the shells, open side down, in a single layer in the pan; cover with the remaining sauce. Sprinkle with remaining mozzarella and Parmesan cheese. Cover with aluminum foil. Bake at 350 degrees for about 35 minutes or until hot and bubbly. Fills about 36 shells.

Chili Skillet ("A" Choice)

1/2	pound ground beef, extra-lean
1/2	cup onion, chopped
1	green pepper, chopped
1	quart stewed tomatoes, cut up
2	teaspoons chili powder
1 1/2	teaspoons salt
1/3	teaspoon black pepper
1	cup macaroni whole-wheat or white macaroni
1	16 oz. can corn, drained

Chili Skillet	
Calories per serving:	369
Fat grams per serving: (if using extra-lean beef)	7
Fat percentage:	17%
Number of servings:	6
Serving size:	1 cup

This recipe is a time-saver if you do not include "simmering" time.

Brown meat with onion. Put in strainer and rinse under hot water to remove excess fat. Return meat to pan. Add green pepper, tomatoes with liquid, chili powder, salt, and pepper. Bring to a boil and stir in macaroni. Simmer 25 minutes or until macaroni is soft. Stir in corn; warm through. Deliciously economical!

It's nice to know that some of the healthiest recipes can also be very fast and economical. My husband, Marty (age 53) has a missing enzyme in his blood that causes his cholesterol and triglycerides to be extremely high. During our three and one half year marriage, both his triglycerides and his cholesterol have decreased substantially because he eats like I eat. Our goal is to get his numbers as low as mine—cholesterol—140 with a high good-cholesterol (HDL) number and a low bad-cholesterol (HDL)) number, with an ideal triglyceride number. We're getting there!

FREEDOM RECIPES

Homemade Macaroni and Cheese
("A–" Choice) *EASY!*

2   cups elbow macaroni, whole-wheat, artichoke, or white (See top of page 242.)

6   cups boiling water

3   teaspoons salt

2   tablespoons butter*

1   medium onion, chopped

1/2 teaspoon salt

1/4 teaspoon pepper

1/4 cup flour, whole-wheat

13/4 cups skim milk or evaporated skim milk

3/4 cup American or Swiss cheese* cut into 1/2-inch cubes

Homemade Macaroni and Cheese	
Calories per serving:	340
Fat grams per serving:	11
Fat percentage:	29%*
Number of servings:	4
Serving size:	1 cup

1   medium tomato, sliced (optional)

1   medium green pepper, sliced (optional)

Pour macaroni into rapidly boiling salted water. Heat to rapid boil. Cook, stirring constantly for 3 minutes. Cover tightly; remove from heat and let stand for 10 minutes. Drain and rinse in cold water. Set aside.

Heat butter, onion, salt, and pepper over medium heat until onion is slightly tender. Blend in flour. Cook over low heat, stirring constantly until mixture is smooth and bubbly. Remove from heat and stir in milk. Heat to boiling, stirring constantly. Boil and stir for 1 minute. Remove from heat and stir in cheese until completely melted.

Place macaroni mixture in 11/2 quart casserole dish. Stir cheese sauce into macaroni. Bake uncovered in a 350-degree oven for 25 to 30 minutes. During the last 5 minutes, arrange tomato and green-pepper slices on top, if desired. Let stand for 10 minutes before serving.

Butter and cheese are high in "naturally" saturated fat. However, this 29% fat choice fits nicely into an "A" day that contains an overall fat percentage of under 20 percent.

Homemade Noodles ("A" Choice) *EASY!*

2	whole eggs
1	egg white
2	teaspoons salt
2	cups flour, whole-wheat
1/4	to 1/2 cup water, cold
3	quarts chicken broth

Homemade Noodles	
Calories per serving:	240
Fat grams per serving:	4
Fat percentage:	15%
Number of servings:	4
Serving size:	2 cups

Beat eggs; add salt; stir in flour. Mix in 1/4 to 1/2 cup cold water, 2 teaspoons at a time. Knead until stiff and smooth. Roll out on floured surface. Roll up like a jelly roll and slice. Separate and dry. Add to boiling, skimmed broth, stirring with a fork to prevent sticking. Cook for 15 minutes or more on low heat, stirring very often.

Luscious Lasagna ("A–" Choice) *Delectable!*

10oz.	lasagna noodles, whole-wheat or white
1/2	pound ground beef, extra-lean
1/2	cup onions, chopped
1/2	cup celery, chopped
1/2	cup carrots, chopped
3	cans (6 oz.) tomato paste
3/4	to 1 cup water
1	teaspoon oregano
1	teaspoon salt
1/2	teaspoon pepper
2	egg whites, beaten

Luscious Lasagna	
Calories per serving:	404
Fat grams per serving:	13
Fat percentage:	29%*
Number of servings:	8
Serving size:	3" square

2	cups cottage cheese, lowfat
1/4	cup Parmesan cheese, grated
10oz.	mozzarella cheese, part-skim, grated

In a large skillet, cook ground beef, onion, celery, and carrots until meat is slightly brown and vegetables are tender. Be sure to drain off the fat and rinse well. Stir in tomato paste, water, oregano, salt, and 1/4 teaspoon pepper. Simmer uncovered for 20 minutes, stirring occasionally. Meanwhile, cook lasagna noodles according to package directions. Drain well. Combine egg whites, cottage cheese, Parmesan cheese, and 1/4 teaspoon pepper in a separate bowl. Arrange half of the lasagna noodles in a 9 x 13 x 2 inch baking dish coated with nonstick cooking spray. Spread with half of the cheese filling. Add half of the meat sauce and mozzarella cheese. Repeat layers. Bake uncovered at 375 degrees for 40 minutes. Let stand for 10 to 15 minutes before serving.

239

FREEDOM RECIPES

Packaged Macaroni and Cheese ("B+" Choice)

If these products are served occasionally with abundant fresh fruits, vegetables, and whole-grain breads or muffins, they are a reasonably good choice. Delete the butter that the directions call for and replace it with the same amount of fat free cream cheese. This tremendously decreases the fat and adds to the meal's healthfulness. It also tastes great!

Kraft Shells and Cheese or Noodle Roni Shells and White Cheddar, or Parmesan Linguini, make tasty, quick meals served with a bowl of tossed salad, purple grapes, and whole-wheat bread with All Fruit Jam. Noodle Roni's Shells and White Cheddar's fat grams go from 16 per cup down to 6 per cup when you replace the 2 tablespoons of butter with 2 tablespoons of fat free cream cheese. And the end result is creamy, rich, and delicious! My family can't tell the difference.

SpaghettiO's and other similar products are also good "B+" Choices. They are low in fat but not extremely high in fiber, so add fiber with lots of vegetables, fruits, and whole-grain breads or rolls.

Remember, the point is not *fanaticism*; it's lifetime liveability!

Salmon Pasta Salad ("A–" to "B+" Choice)

11/2	cups pink salmon (143/4 oz. can) remove skin and bones
5	cups pasta, cooked
1/2	cup carrots, thinly sliced
1/2	cup celery, sliced
1/4	cup olives, thinly sliced, ripe
1/4	cup green onions, chopped
1/4	cup red or green peppers, sliced
2	tablespoons Parmesan cheese, grated
1/2	cup red wine vinegar
4	teaspoons olive oil
1	teaspoon sugar
1	teaspoon oregano
1	teaspoon salt
1/4	teaspoon pepper

Salmon Pasta Salad	
Calories per serving:	358
Fat grams per serving:	14
Fat percentage:	35%*
Number of servings:	8
Serving size:	1 cup

Break salmon into large pieces. In medium bowl combine salmon, pasta, vegetables, and cheese. Combine in small bowl vinegar, oil, sugar, oregano, salt, and pepper. Pour over salmon mixture. Toss carefully to coat. Cover and chill or serve immediately.

This Salmon Pasta salad is moderately high in fat, but the salmon and olive oil contain "good", cholesterol-fighting fatty acids. That's why I sit on the fence with the "A–" to "B+" rating.

Savory Meat and Cheese Manicotti ("A" Choice)

1	box American Beauty Manicotti, uncooked
1/2	pound ground beef, extra-lean
11/2	cups mozzarella cheese, part-skim, grated
1	cup ricotta cheese, fat free
1/4	cup Parmesan cheese, grated
3/4	cup onion, finely chopped
13/4	cups zucchini, diced
8	egg whites, slightly beaten
1/4	cup dry bread crumbs, seasoned
3/4	teaspoon oregano leaves

Savory Meat and Cheese Manicotti	
Calories per serving:	243
Fat grams per serving:	5
Fat percentage:	19%
Number of servings:	8
Serving size: approximately 1 cup	

1/2	teaspoon salt
1/8	teaspoon black pepper
1	jar (14 oz.) spaghetti sauce

Cook pasta according to package directions; drain. Cool in single layer on foil. Heat oven to 350 degrees. In large skillet, brown meat; drain off fat. Stir together meat, 1 cup mozzarella cheese, and all other ingredients except sauce. Spread thin layer of sauce on bottom of a nonstick cooking-sprayed 9 x 13 x 2 glass baking dish. Fill each cooled pasta tube with about 1/4 cup meat filling and place in prepared baking dish; cover with remaining sauce. Sprinkle with remaining mozzarella cheese and a small amount of Parmesan cheese, if desired. Cover with foil. Bake 45 minutes or until hot and bubbly. This is an excellent crowd-pleaser!

Spaghetti and Pasta Varieties
("A" & "B" Choices) *Spaghetti, Macaroni, Fettucini, Lasagna, Wide Egg Noodles, etc.*

The most healthful, high-fiber, nutritious forms of pasta include whole-wheat, corn, mixed-vegetable, and artichoke pasta. However, white pasta is also fine because the rest of your meal should be high in fiber.

Both artichoke and corn pasta make ideal choices for individuals suffering from wheat allergies. These specialty pastas are usually found in the health-food section of your regular grocery store, in health-food stores, and in stores featuring whole-grain products.

Spaghetti Salad ("A" Choice)

1	pound spaghetti or veggie noodles, broken, cooked	
2	tomatoes, chopped	
2	cucumbers, chopped	
2	red onions, chopped	
1/2	to one 16 oz. bottle Italian dressing, fat free	

Spaghetti Salad	
Calories per serving:	490
Fat grams per serving:	2
Fat percentage:	4%
Number of servings:	4
Serving size:	2 cups

Mix together all ingredients. Other veggies can be added to this salad: broccoli florets, cauliflower, carrots, celery, and mushrooms. Refrigerate: serve cool or cold. Try something differently delicious and great for summer!

Veggie Lasagna ("A–" Choice)

Use the Luscious Lasagna recipe on page 239 and make the following changes; instead of using ground beef, replace it with 1 cup sliced mushrooms, 1 cup sliced celery, and 1 cup very thinly sliced zucchini squash. Add these items to the sauce.

You can also add a 10-ounce package of spinach that has been cooked and very well drained to the egg and cheese mixture. This makes the dish very colorful and delicious!

Marvelous!

Veggie Lasagna	
Calories per serving:	350
Fat grams per serving:	10
Fat percentage:	26%
Number of servings:	8
Serving size:	one 3" square

Veggie-Tuna Pasta Salad ("A" Choice)

13/4 cups corkscrew pasta, vegetable, whole-wheat, corn, artichoke, or white
1 cup (8 oz.) cream cheese, fat free
1 cup ranch dressing, nonfat
1 cup skim milk
1 teaspoon dried dill weed
2 cans (61/2 oz.) solid white tuna, drained (Regular tuna will suffice.)

Veggie-Tuna Pasta Salad	
Calories per serving:	215
Fat grams per serving:	1
Fat percentage:	4%
Number of servings:	8
Serving size: approximately 1 cup	

1 tomato, medium, seeded and chopped
1 cucumber, diced
1 green onion, chopped

Cook pasta according to package directions. Drain. Transfer hot pasta immediately to a large bowl. In a separate bowl, blend cream cheese and ranch dressing. Stir in milk and dill weed. Add to pasta and toss until completely blended. Add tuna, tomato, cucumber, and green onion. Toss lightly. Cover and chill for four or more hours.

POTATOES

AuGratin Potatoes ("A" Choice)

---

12 medium potatoes,
    boiled with skin on
    (peel after cooking)
4   tablespoons butter*
6   tablespoons flour,
    whole-wheat or white
3   teaspoons salt
    pepper to taste
4   cups skim milk, heated
11/2 cups mozzarella cheese,
    part-skim, grated
    (loosely packed)

AuGratin Potatoes	
Calories per serving:	418
Fat grams per serving:	9
Fat percentage:	19%
Number of servings:	8
Serving size:	3/4 cup

Old Fashioned Goodness!

Dice cooked potatoes. Melt butter in saucepan and stir in flour, salt, and pepper. Heat and stir constantly until mixture bubbles. Gradually add milk and cook over low heat, stirring constantly until sauce boils and thickens. Stir in 2/3 cup cheese and diced potatoes. Pour into a 9 x 13 x 2 baking dish coated with nonstick cooking spray and top with rest of cheese. Bake at 375 degrees for 15 minutes or until cheese melts and browns.

Time Saving Variation:

Follow instructions above, except replace fresh potatoes with two pounds of frozen, diced potatoes. Thaw frozen potatoes thoroughly in the microwave before adding to above mixture.

*Even with 4 tablespoons of butter, this recipe is still under 20% fat!

FREEDOM RECIPES

Chicken-Chili Stuffed Potato ("A" Choice)

1	large potato
11/2	cups chicken chili, lowfat (1 can)
1/4	cup mozzarella cheese, part-skim, grated
1/2	green pepper, diced
1/4	cup onion, diced (optional)

Chicken-Chili Stuffed Potato	
Calories per serving:	714
Fat grams per serving:	11
Fat percentage:	14%
Number of servings:	1
Serving size:	1 potato

To microwave: Scrub, then prick potato in 3 or 4 places with a fork to allow steam to escape. Place on a paper towel in microwave. Microwave on high for 3 to 5 minutes. Let stand 1 minute. Add 3 to 5 extra minutes for each additional potato.

To bake: Scrub potato and prick with a fork. Bake in oven at 375 degrees for 45 to 60 minutes. Four potatoes require 1 to 11/4 hours at 375 degrees, 11/4 to 11/2 hours at 350 degrees, or 11/2 hours at 325 degrees.

Slice cooked potato down the center and top with chicken chili, cheese, green pepper, and onion. Microwave for one to two minutes until warm.

Variations: Lower-fat beef chili is a good choice. You can also melt a little part-skim mozzarella cheese or low-fat cottage cheese over the top. Fat free sour cream and some chopped chives add a tasty finishing touch.

Hash Browns ("A–" Choice with Olive Oil "B+" Choice with Butter)

4	cups potatoes, shredded (You can use frozen, pre-shredded potatoes.)
1/3	cup green onion, finely chopped
3	tablespoons olive oil or butter
1/2	teaspoons salt
1/8	teaspoon pepper

Hash Browns	
Calories per serving:	206
Fat grams per serving:	8
Fat percentage:	35%
Number of servings:	4
Serving size:	1 cup

Rinse shredded potatoes in a strainer and pat dry with paper towels. Combine potatoes, onion, salt, and pepper. In a large skillet, heat oil or melt butter. (Olive oil contains the healthiest fat. Butter gives the hash browns a richer flavor.) Pat potato mixture into skillet with a flat spatula. Cook over medium-low heat for about 9 to 12 minutes until bottom is crispy. Cut into four square sections. Turn and cook other side until crispy golden brown.

Mashed Potatoes ("A" Choice without Butter "B+" Choice with Butter)

6	medium potatoes
1/2	cup skim milk
1/4	cup butter
1/2	teaspoon salt
	dash of pepper

Mashed Potatoes	
Calories per serving with butter:	187
Calories per serving w/o butter:	121
Fat grams per serving with butter: (33% fat)	7
Fat grams per serving w/o butter: (trace%)	trace
Number of servings:	6
Serving size:	1 cup

Wash potatoes and leave skin on if you like. (The skin contains many nutrients.) Heat 1 inch water and 1 teaspoon salt to boiling. Add potatoes and cover. Heat to boiling. Cook until tender, 25 to 35 minutes. Drain, cool, and peel.

Place potatoes back in pan and warm over low heat. Mash until no lumps remain. Add milk, a little at a time, during mashing. Add butter, salt, and pepper and beat vigorously until potatoes are fluffy. Sprinkle with paprika and parsley or chives, if desired. If you choose to omit the butter, sprinkle with butter- and sour-cream-flavored sprinkles.

FREEDOM RECIPES

Minestrone Soup with Country Corn Bread

Egg Drop Soup

Perfect Potato Casserole ("A–" Choice)

1	large onion, chopped
1/3	cube butter
2	pounds potatoes, frozen, diced (Thaw unopened package slightly under warm water.)
2	10 3/4 oz. cans cream of mushroom or cream of chicken soup, lowfat
2	cups mozzarella cheese, part-skim, shredded, loosely packed

Perfect Potato Casserole	
Calories per serving:	288
Fat grams per serving:	8
Fat percentage:	25%
Number of servings:	8
Serving size:	1/2 cup

1	cup sour cream, fat free
1/2	teaspoon salt
2	cups cornflakes, crushed

In a large skillet saute onion in melted butter. Stir in potatoes, soup, cheese, sour cream, and salt. Pour into 9 x 13 x 2 baking dish coated with nonstick cooking spray. Sprinkle cornflakes over top of casserole.

Bake at 350 degrees for 30 minutes.

Veggie-Stuffed Potato ("A" Choice)

1	large potato
1 1/2	cups mixed vegetables of your choice, steamed
1/4	cup mozzarella cheese, part-skim, grated
1/4	cup cottage cheese, lowfat
4	tablespoons sour cream, fat free
	salt and pepper, (to taste)
	Molly McButter (to taste)
1	tablespoon chopped chives

Veggie-Stuffed Potato	
Calories per serving:	475±
Fat grams per serving:	6
Fat percentage:	11%
Serving size:	1 large potato

*Calories can vary depending upon the veggies used. Veggies will average about 50 to 100 calories per cup.

Cut open baked potato and stuff with vegetables, cheese, cottage cheese, and sour cream. Moderately salt and pepper to taste. (If you suffer from high-blood pressure, be very moderate with salt intake.)

Sprinkle with Molly McButter and chives to add a delicious finishing touch.

247

SANDWICHES

Bacon, Lettuce, and Tomato Sandwich ("B+" Choice)

1	tablespoon mayonnaise, fat free
1	tablespoon salad dressing, fat free
2	slices toast, whole-wheat
1/2	large tomato, sliced
2	large lettuce leaves
2	strips bacon*, cooked, lowfat (Blot with paper towels.)

As a time-saver, cook bacon in advance.

Bacon, Lettuce, and Tomato Sandwich

Calories per 1 sandwich;
Regular bacon (30% fat)	244
Turkey bacon (23% fat)	234

Fat grams per 1 sandwich;
Regular bacon:	8
Turkey bacon:	6
Number of servings:	1
Serving size:	1 sandwich

Bacon is high in saturated fat, so use it in great moderation.

Spread mayonnaise on one slice of toast and salad dressing on another slice. Then layer lettuce, tomato, and two strips of bacon onto the toast with mayonnaise. Top with the toast covered with salad dressing. Cut into triangles. Delicious!

*I have recently seen Jennie-O's turkey bacon at the grocery store with only 1/2 fat gram per piece! It's delicious and it makes this sandwich an "A" Choice! Be sure to read the labels.

Fast-Food Sandwiches ("A" & "B" Choices)

I usually order grilled chicken, turkey, or seafood sandwiches on whole-wheat or multi-grain buns. It's difficult to get 100% whole wheat, so order as close to this as you can get. I have them add a little mustard to the chicken and turkey sandwiches, or better yet, I take them home and add fat free mayonnaise and fat free salad dressing to them.

I always have extra *tomatoes, pickles,* and *onions* added to my sandwiches to increase the complex carbohydrates, fiber, vitamins, and minerals.

If you are really in the mood for a ham, roast beef, or turkey with bacon sandwich, just follow the multi-grain and extra-vegetable suggestions, and more of the extra fat may be eliminated from your body as it mixes with the additional fiber. However, if you are highly resistant to fat loss, avoid these choices and be certain to study the Restaurant Food Charts on pages 351 through 373 very carefully and regularly!

LEAN & FREE Homemade Sandwiches, Pita Pockets, and Burritos ("A" & "B+" Choices)

*Place the following ingredients on whole-wheat or other multi-grain bread, inside whole-grain or white pita pockets, or roll in **corn** tortillas in the case of a wheat allergy. Dressings include fat free or light mayonnaise, fat free salad dressing, mustard, and lowfat buttermilk dressing. Salsa and fat free sour cream are excellent on white, wheat, and corn tortillas stuffed with sandwich filling.*

Chicken Sandwich—use 3 oz. skinless, broiled or baked white meat— go heavy on all the vegetables.

Club Sandwich—one thin slice turkey, extra-lean ham, and extra-lean roast beef—add lettuce, tomatoes, pickles, and onions.

Corned Beef Sandwich—use 1 slice extra-lean corned beef—add extra vegetables and enjoy.

Ham 'n' Cheese Sandwich—buy extra-lean ham—be moderate with the meat and part-skim mozzarella cheese and extra heavy with the vegetables. Makes a great hot sandwich! (Serve with hot vegetable soup.)

Pastrami Sandwich—just remember to go heavy on the vegetables and very light on the meat. (Use 4 extra-lean thin pastrami slices per sandwich.)

249

Sandwiches Continued

Roast Beef 'n' Cheddar Sandwich—use two 1 oz. slices extra-lean luncheon meat beef slices—add vegetables of your choice after 1/4 cup grated cheddar is melted on top.

Roast Beef Sandwich—use two 1 oz. slices extra-lean luncheon meat beef slices—add mild hot peppers, pickles, lettuce, and onions.

Seafood 'n' Avocado Sandwich—mix real or imitation crab pieces with fat free mayonnaise and fat free salad dressing—half and half). Add 1/3 sliced avocado, sprouts, and tomatoes. (Avocados are high in "good" fat.)

Tuna Salad Sandwich—mix 3 oz. tuna (in water, drained) with equal parts of fat free mayonnaise and fat free salad dressing—add green peppers, onions, lettuce, tomatoes, sprouts, and chopped celery, if desired.

Turkey 'n' Provolone Cheese Sandwich—use 4 oz. lean turkey breast—add pickles, tomatoes, onions, lettuce, sprouts, and 1 ounce Provolone cheese.

Turkey Breast Sandwich—use 4 oz. lean turkey breast—skinless, broiled or baked—add pickles, tomatoes, onions, lettuce, and green peppers. This sandwich tastes great with Cranberry Sandwich Spread found on page 165. Fat free cream cheese is also very tasty.

LEAN & FREE Homemade Sandwiches, Pita Pockets* or Burritos		
	fg/cal	fat %**
• Chicken Sandwich	3/450	6%
• Club Sandwich	4/410	9%
• Corned Beef Sandwich	3/293	9%
• Ham 'n' Cheese Sandwich	6/385	14%
• Pastrami Sandwich	t/306	trace%
• Roast Beef 'n' Cheddar Sandwich	10/500	18%
• Roast Beef Sandwich	4/400	9%
• Seafood 'n Avocado Sandwich	11/450	22%
• Tuna Salad Sandwich	2/400	5%
• Turkey 'n' Provolone Sandwich	7/462	14%
• Turkey Breast Sandwich	1/362	2%
Serving size: 1 sandwich		

Pita Pockets and Burritos have approximately the same fat-gram/calorie-numbers as sandwiches.

**Read ALL luncheon meat labels to insure low percentages of fat and all-natural ingredients.*

LEAN & FREE Peanut Butter and Jelly or Jam Sandwich ("B+" Choice)

2 slices bread, whole-grain
2 tablespoons Skippy Reduced Fat Peanut Butter
2 tablespoons All Fruit Jam or jelly (Be certain to avoid artificially sweetened jams and jellies!)

Peanut Butter and Jelly or Jam Sandwiches	
Calories per serving:	400
Fat grams per serving:	12
Fat percentage:	27%
Number of servings:	1
Serving size:	1 sandwich

Spread peanut butter and All-Fruit Jam or jelly on 2 slices of bread. Place slices together and enjoy!

Special Note on Freedom: The *freedom* to continue driving an automobile comes from consistently obeying the rules of the road. The *freedom* to continue to maintain a healthy, high-energy body that is free from excess body fat comes from consistently obeying the rules of your "body." Caloric and/ or nutrient starvation is the number one signal to your body's survival system to reduce your energy level and increase your fat stores! Listen to your body, your doctor, and the LEAN & FREE LIFESTYLE. They will guide you toward optimum physical and emotional health and a lifetime free from excess body fat, hunger, and cravings!

FREEDOM RECIPES

SEAFOOD

Company Casserole ("A" Choice)

1/4 onion, chopped
1/4 cup green pepper, chopped
1 cup peas, frozen
3 103/4 oz. cans cream of mushroom, celery, or chicken soup, lowfat
11/2 soup cans skim milk
1 7 oz. can tuna, in water
6 cups cooked noodles or brown or white rice
2/3 cup mozzarella cheese, part-skim, grated
2 - 3 cups cornflakes, coarsely crushed

Company Casserole	
Calories per serving:	348
Fat grams per serving:	3
Fat percentage:	8%
Number of servings:	6
Serving size: 1 cup mixture plus 1 cup noodles	

Sauté onion, green pepper, and peas. Add soup, milk, and tuna. Heat through and serve over cooked noodles or rice. Top with cheese and cornflakes. (Kids also love "a few" crumbled potato chips on top.)

Time Saving Variation: Blend soup, peas, and tuna gently into cooked noodles. Spread in 9 x 13 x 2 glass baking dish coated with nonstick cooking spray. Top with cheese and cornflakes. Bake at 350 degrees for 25 to 35 minutes, until hot and bubbly.

Creamed Tuna on Toast ("A" Choice)

1 onion, chopped
1 103/4 oz. can lowfat cream of chicken, or lowfat cream of celery soup,
1/2 can water
1 cup skim milk
2 cans tuna, water packed, drained

Creamed Tuna on Toast	
Calories per serving:	164
Fat grams per serving:	3
Fat percentage:	16%
Number of servings:	4
Serving size: 1 cup tuna mixture	
(Whole-wheat toast adds 71 calories and a trace of fat per slice.)	

Sauté onion. Add soup, water, milk, and tuna. Cook on low heat until mixture thickens. Serve on whole-wheat toast, lowfat biscuits, or multi-grain English muffins.

Orange Roughy with Tartar Sauce ("A–" Choice)

8	5 oz. orange roughy fillets, washed well in cold water
	salt, pepper, and paprika
1/4	cup lemon juice
1/4	cup butter*, melted
1/4	cup parsley, chopped
1	lemon, sliced

Orange Roughy

Calories per serving:	254
Fat grams per serving:	8
Fat percentage:	28%
Number of servings:	8
Serving size:	one 5 oz. fillet

Place fillets on nonstick baking sheet coated with nonstick cooking spray. Sprinkle with salt, pepper, and paprika. Mix lemon juice and butter and drip over fish. Broil about 6 inches away from heat for about 10 minutes, basting once with lemon butter. Remove from broiler when fish is firm and flaky. Baste again and top with parsley and lemon slices. Serve immediately with tartar sauce (recipe below).

Butter is high in "naturally" saturated fat and is used very sparingly in this delicious "A–" recipe. This nutritious fish is high in fatty acids that can reduce LDL (bad) cholesterol. It fits nicely into a day that contains an overall fat percentage of less than 20 percent.

Tartar Sauce ("A" Choice)

1/4	cup mayonnaise, fat free
1/4	cup salad dressing, fat free (Kraft Free Miracle Whip)
1	tablespoon dill pickle, finely chopped
11/2	teaspoons parsley, chopped
1	teaspoon pimento, chopped
1 to	1/2 tablespoon onion, grated

Tartar Sauce

Calories per serving:	7
Fat grams per serving:	trace
Fat percentage:	trace
Number of servings:	10
Serving size:	1 tablespoon

253

Mix all ingredients; refrigerate until serving over the fish of your choice.

Parmesan Halibut Steaks ("A–" Choice)

4	5 oz. halibut steaks, about 3/4 inch thick
1/4	teaspoon salt
1/8	teaspoon pepper
3/4	cup dairy sour cream, fat free
1/4	cup bread crumbs, dry, whole-wheat
1/4	teaspoon garlic salt
11/2	teaspoons chives, chopped
1/8	teaspoon tarragon leaves, dried (optional)

Parmesan Halibut Steaks	
Calories per serving:	245
Fat grams per serving:	8
Fat percentage:	29%
Number of servings:	4
Serving size:	one 5 oz. fillet

1/3	cup Parmesan cheese, freshly grated (Check in the deli section of your supermarket.)
1	teaspoon paprika
3	green onions, chopped
10	cherry tomato halves (optional)

Place steaks close together in a shallow baking dish coated with nonstick cooking spray. Sprinkle with salt and pepper. Mix sour cream, bread crumbs, garlic salt, chives, and tarragon leaves together; spread over steaks and sprinkle with Parmesan cheese and paprika. Bake uncovered at 400 degrees for 15 to 20 minutes until fish is firm and flaky. Garnish with onions and cherry tomato halves.

Red Snapper ("A" Choice)

4	6 oz. red snapper fillets
1	lemon
1	tablespoon dill weed

Red Snapper	
Calories per serving:	217
Fat grams per serving:	3
Fat percentage:	12%
Number of servings:	4
Serving size:	one 6 oz. fillet

Rinse fillets. Place on a shallow baking pan sprayed with nonstick cooking spray. Squeeze fresh lemon juice over each fillet. Then sprinkle dill weed over each piece of fish. Bake at 375 degrees for 15 minutes.

Shrimp Salad ("A" Choice)

1   head lettuce, chopped
1/2   cup green onion, chopped
1   8 oz. can water chestnuts,
     drained and chopped
1   cup celery, chopped
1   10 oz. package peas, frozen
1/2   pound salad shrimp
1   cup mayonnaise, fat free
1   cup salad dressing, fat free
1/2   cup Parmesan cheese,
     grated

Shrimp Salad	
Calories per serving:	218
Fat grams per serving:	2
Fat percentage:	8%
Number of servings:	4
Serving size:	2 cups

This recipe is a time-saver if the vegetables are prepared in advanced

Layer in a 9 x 13 x 2 cake pan–lettuce, onion, chestnuts, celery, peas, and shrimp. Combine mayonnaise and salad dressing, and spread over last layer. Sprinkle Parmesan cheese moderately over the top. Cover with plastic wrap and chill overnight. Toss before serving.

SOUPS

Bean and Ham Soup or Split Pea Soup ("B+ & "A–" Choices)

Both Campbell's Chunky Bean and Ham Soup and Chunky Split Pea Soup are delicious, moderate-fat choices. I eat an entire can, two slices of whole-grain toast, and fruit for lunch. Regular bean and bacon soup is also a moderate-fat choice. (These choices are not low in sodium*.)

ECONOTIP: Mix the large, family-size cans of Campbell's Bean and Bacon or Chicken Noodle with water. Then add the Chunky soups that correspond. This is deliciously economical.

If you are closely monitoring your sodium intake, purchase soups that are low in sodium; also **make** *the delicious soups on pages 256-259.*

Campbell's Chunky Bean and Ham Soup or Split Pea Soup	
Calories per serving:	250/210
Fat grams per serving:	8/5
Fat percentage:	29%/21%
Number of servings:	2 per can
Serving size:	9.5 oz. (1/2 can)

FREEDOM RECIPES

Creamy Bean and Ham Soup ("A" Choice)

1 can 8 oz. tomato sauce
1 cup water
1 cup ham, extra-lean, cubed
1 cup onion, chopped
1 teaspoon instant beef bouillon
1 teaspoon salt
1/2 teaspoon pepper
1 clove garlic, crushed
3 medium stalks celery, cut into 1/2 inch pieces
2 15 oz. cans navy or great white northern beans, undrained

2 16 oz. cans carrots, sliced, drained
2 cups potatoes, mashed (Instant potatoes work well here.)

Creamy Bean and Ham Soup	
Calories per serving:	365
Fat grams per serving:	1
Fat percentage:	trace
Number of servings:	6
Serving size:	1 1/2 cups

Heat tomato sauce, water, ham, onion, bouillon, salt, pepper, garlic, and celery in a large kettle. Heat to boiling; reduce heat, cover, and simmer for 15 to 20 minutes until celery is tender. Stir in beans, carrots, and potatoes. Heat to boiling. Reduce heat, cover, and simmer for 10 to 15 minutes to blend flavors. If soup is too thick, add skim milk or evaporated skim milk until desired consistency is achieved.

Creamy Zucchini Soup ("A" Choice)

2 onions, chopped
1 tablespoon butter
4 tablespoons water
2 cans chicken broth, fat skimmed
11/2 cups water
4 cups zucchini, chopped
1/4 teaspoon salt
1/4 teaspoon pepper
nutmeg, dash
1 cup evaporated skim milk
2 tablespoons mozzarella cheese, part-skim, grated (optional)

Creamy Zucchini Soup	
Calories per serving: (without cheese)	100
Fat grams per serving: (without cheese)	2
Fat percentage: (without cheese)	18%
Number of servings:	6
Serving size:	approximately 1 cup
(2 Tbsp. part-skim mozzarella adds 2.5 fat grams per serving.)	

This recipe is a time-saver if the onions and zucchini are chopped in advance.

Sauté onions in butter and water. Simmer for 15 minutes. Blend in all remaining ingredients except milk and cheese. Add skim evaporated milk and slowly reheat, stirring constantly. Sprinkle moderately with cheese (optional).

256

Egg Drop Soup ("A" Choice)

4   cups chicken broth,
      fat skimmed
2   cups mixed vegetables
      (frozen peas, carrots,
      and corn)
4   green onions, chopped
1/2 cup celery, sliced
      diagonally
2   eggs, beaten

Egg Drop Soup	
Calories per serving:	85
Fat grams per serving:	2
Fat percentage:	21%
Number of servings:	8
Serving size:	3/4 cup

Bring broth to a rapid boil. Add vegetables, onions, and celery and bring to a rapid boil again. Slowly pour beaten egg into boiling soup while stirring. Cook about 2 minutes. Serve in soup cups. This soup is the perfect complement to Oriental-style entreés.

Fast and Creamy Clam Chowder ("A" Choice)

1   10   3/4 oz. can Campbell's
      Cream of Potato Soup
      (condensed)
1   cup water
1   teaspoon chicken bouillon
      granules
1/2 teaspoon lemon pepper
1/4 teaspoon garlic salt
2   tablespoons flour
1   8 oz. tub cream cheese,
      fat free
2   small cans minced clams

Fast and Creamy Clam Chowder	
Calories per serving:	138
Fat grams per serving:	2
Fat percentage:	13%
Number of servings:	4
Serving size:	approximately 1 1/3 cups

Place first seven ingredients plus juice from clams in blender and pureé. Heat in medium saucepan, stirring constantly. Remove from heat and stir in clams. Serve immediately.

Variation: Instead of adding clams, add leftover steamed vegetables and a can of cooked, lowfat chicken for delicious **Cream of Chicken Vegetable Soup.** Also, if you are trying to thicken a cream soup, pureéd steamed or canned vegetable, or instant potato flakes may work very well, depending on the type of soup you are making.

257

FREEDOM RECIPES

Lentil and Barley Soup ("A" Choice)

1	cup lentils
1	cup barley
1	can (16 oz.) tomatoes
1	cup onion, chopped
1	cup celery, sliced
3/4	cup carrots, sliced
2	tablespoons soy sauce
1/2	teaspoon pepper
1	teaspoon dill weed, dried
1	teaspoon garlic powder
10	cups chicken or beef broth or bouillon, fat skimmed

Lentil and Barley Soup	
Calories per serving:	238
Fat grams per serving:	1
Fat percentage:	4%
Number of servings:	8
Serving size:	1 cup

This recipe is a time-saver if the onions, celery, and carrots are chopped and sliced in advance.

Place all ingredients in a large saucepan. Bring to a boil. Cover and reduce heat to simmer. Cook 50 minutes, stirring occasionally. Add water if soup becomes too thick. This soup is highly nutritious and very tasty!

Minestrone Soup ("A" Choice)

1/4	cup olive oil
3	cups onions, diced
3	cups carrots, diced
2	cups celery, diced
2	cups tomatoes, canned or bottled, diced
1	16 oz. can green beans, drained
1	15 oz. can kidney beans, drained
2	cups cabbage, chopped
2	teaspoons salt
1	teaspoon white pepper
11/2	teaspoons garlic powder
3	tablespoons beef bouillon
2	tablespoons chicken bouillon

Minestrone Soup	
Calories per serving:	216
Fat grams per serving:	5
Fat percentage:	21%
Number of servings:	12
Serving size:	1 cup

11/2	teaspoons basil
2	teaspoons oregano
8	cups water
1	8 oz. can tomato sauce
1/2	cup barley
1	15 oz. can garbanzo beans, drained
1	cup macaroni, uncooked

Heat olive oil. Sauté diced onions, carrots, and, celery. Add tomatoes, green beans, kidney beans, cabbage, salt, pepper, garlic powder, beef and chicken bouillon, basil, oregano, water, tomato sauce, and barley. Simmer 45 minutes. Stir in garbanzo beans and macaroni. Simmer until macaroni is tender.

Potato, Corn, and Cheese Soup or Potato Corn Soup (with cheese = "B" Choice / without cheese = "A" Choice)

2 10¾ oz. cans Cream of Potato Soup
1/2 soup-can skim milk
1 16 oz. can creamed corn
1 cup sharp cheddar cheese, grated (optional)

Potato, Corn, and Cheese Soup or Potato Corn Soup	
Calories per serving with cheese:	201
Calories per serving w/o cheese:	128
Fat grams per serving with cheese:	8 1/2
Fat grams per serving w/o cheese:	3
Fat percentage with cheese:	38%
Fat percentage without cheese:	21%
Number of servings:	6
Serving size:	approximately 1 cup

Blend together all ingredients in saucepan. Heat on medium, stirring constantly until bubbly and cheese is melted. For thinner soup, add more milk. Delicious!

Variation: Leftover steamed, mixed vegetables or canned or frozen peas are delicious added to this soup making **Cream of Vegetable Soup.**

Zucchini Soup ("A" Choice)

8 to 10 cups zucchini, diced
2 onions, diced
1 teaspoon butter
1/2 cup ham, extra-lean, cubed
1 10 3/4 oz. can chicken broth
1 1/2 teaspoons salt
1 1/2 teaspoons seasoning salt
1 teaspoon basil leaves
1/4 teaspoon pepper

Zucchini Soup	
Calories per serving:	76
Fat grams per serving:	1
Fat percentage:	12%
Number of servings:	8
Serving size:	1 cup

This recipe is a time-saver if the zucchini, onions, and ham are diced or cubed in advance.

Dice zucchini and set aside. Sauté onions in 1 teaspoon butter. Add zucchini and all other ingredients and cook until zucchini is tender. Mix all ingredients in blender until smooth. Add water to thin as desired. Heat thoroughly. This delicious soup may be topped with lowfat croutons, 2 tablespoons of Parmesan cheese, plain nonfat yogurt, or fat free dairy sour cream.

VEGETABLES

Broccoli Casserole ("A" Choice)

2   **bunches broccoli, cut up,**
      steamed until tender

In large bowl, mix together :
1   **103/4 oz. can lowfat cream**
      of chicken or lowfat cream
      of mushroom soup
1   **cup mayonnaise, nonfat**
4   **egg whites, beaten**
1   **cup mozzarella cheese,**
      part-skim, grated
      (loosely packed)

Broccoli Casserole	
Calories per serving:	200
Fat grams per serving:	4 1/2
Fat percentage:	20%
Number of servings:	6
Serving size:	1 cup

This recipe is a time-saver if the broccoli is prepared in advance.

Fold broccoli into sauce and pour into an 9 x 13 x 2 glass baking dish coated with nonstick cooking spray. Bake in a 350 degree oven for 40 minutes. Even kids love this recipe!

*Special Note Concerning Veggie-Based Snacks: I often work with individuals who **hate** most vegetables. Yet, as they gradually add in more good foods and become more and more moderate with junk foods, their entire body chemistry begins to change, including their taste buds. They begin to not only "like" vegetables, but to "love" vegetables. They even start to **snack** on "veggie-based" foods such as soups, stews, and casseroles like the preceding Broccoli Casserole.*

Their minds are clearer and their physical stamina is greatly increased. They also develop "fat-burning", rather than "fat-storing" metabolisms. A wonderful bonus!

Cauliflower 'n' Cheddar ("B" Choice*)

For cauliflower:

Heat 1 inch salted water (1/2 teaspoon salt to 1 cup water) to boiling. Add 1 head cauliflower. Cover and heat to boiling. Cook until tender; whole, 20 to 25 minutes; florets, 10 to 12 minutes — drain. Place in 9 x 9 x 2 casserole dish or glass baking dish.

For cheese sauce:

2	tablespoons butter (be very moderate)
2	tablespoons flour
1	teaspoon dry mustard
1/4	teaspoon salt pepper, dash
1	cup evaporated skim milk
3/4	cup cheddar cheese, shredded (loosely packed)

Cauliflower 'n' Cheddar	
Calories per serving:	184
Fat grams per serving:	8
Fat percentage:	39%*
Number of servings:	6
Serving size:	1/2 cup cooked

If you omit the cauliflower cooking-time, this recipe is a time-saver.

Heat butter over low heat until melted. Blend in flour, mustard, salt, and pepper. Cook over low heat, stirring constantly, until mixture is smooth and bubbly. Remove from heat and stir in milk. Heat until boiling, stirring constantly. Boil and stir 1 minute. Gradually stir in cheese and cook over low heat until melted. Pour over cauliflower.

This 39 percent-fat recipe fits nicely into a meal that has an overall fat percentage of less than 20 percent. Remember that a "B" Choice main course or side dish is more nutritious and a better fat-loss food than a "B" Choice dessert. And it's your day's overall fat percentage that counts, not the fat percentage of each individual food choice. Some fat may actually attach to high-fiber foods you have eaten and be wasted from your body. In other words, it's more what you **add than what you **subtract** that often makes the biggest difference in your overall good health and permanent leanness.*

261

Chinese Salad Bar ("A" Choice) *EASY!*

leafy lettuce, torn
cherry tomatoes
carrots, shredded
purple cabbage, shredded
yellow cabbage, shredded
Chinese pea pods
water chestnuts
bamboo shoots
bean sprouts
celery, chopped
green onions, chopped
mandarin oranges, drained

pineapple chunks, drained
Catalina dressing, fat free
   or other fat free dressing
chow-mein noodles (optional)

Chinese Salad Bar	
Calories per serving:	150 to 350*
Fat grams per serving:	trace
Fat percentage:	trace
Serving size:	2 cups

Make individual salads with all ingredients. Just a few chow-mein noodles on top add a tasty crunch. The noodles are not extremely low in fat, so be moderate. The vegetables have little if any fat. Eat a large variety and enjoy!

Cooking Frozen Vegetables ("A" Choice)

Follow the package instructions. Remember to use only small amounts of water and save the nutritious vegetable-water for use in sauces and gravies.

One tablespoon of butter folded into 3 cups of vegetables adds 4 fat grams to each cup and makes the vegetables very flavorful and moist. Butter-flavor sprinkles can also be used. I notice that my husband, my children, and I eat a lot more cooked vegetables when a little butter or a delicious glaze is added.

Caution: Be careful with amounts. If you added 1 tablespoon of butter to *every* cup of vegetables, you would increase the fat grams to 11, mostly from saturated fat. Moderation, not excessiveness or exclusion, is the key!

Another good addition is Jennie O's extra-lean turkey bacon with 1/2 fat gram per slice. I cook it, cool it, and then cut it with scissors into little pieces and mix them into the vegetables. Kids love this idea and it's a lot lower in fat than adding butter.

FREEDOM RECIPES

Easy Cabbage Dinner ("A" Choice)

7   potatoes, cubed
1/2   head green cabbage,
      chopped
1   medium onion, chopped
1   16 oz. can corn,
      whole-kernel, drained
1/2   pound ground beef,
      extra-lean, cooked
      salt and pepper to taste

Easy Cabbage Dinner	
Calories per serving:	310
Fat grams per serving:	4 1/2
Fat percentage:	13%
Number of servings:	8
Serving size:	1 cup

This recipe may take slightly longer than 15 minutes to prepare.

Boil potatoes in small amount of water in skillet for 5 minutes. Add cabbage and onion, cooking until tender. Add remaining ingredients and warm through.

Fast-Food Salads and Potatoes ("A" Choice)

Chili or vegetable-stuffed baked potatoes with cheese and onions on top are good eating-out choices. Omit the cheese sauce and you've just turned your "B" potato into an "A" potato.

I generally order a large garden salad and then remove most of the cheese. It is very helpful to bring your own nonfat salad dressing from home because many of the dressing packets contain as many as 30 fat grams. Cottage cheese is also an excellent addition to your salad. Even regular cottage cheese, that isn't "lowfat," is much lower in fat than most salad dressings. Ask your waiter to please bring some cottage cheese on the side and bring the salad dressing on the side if it isn't low in fat. Some restaurants are now offering lowfat and fat free dressings.

Glazed Carrots, Cauliflower, and Broccoli ("B" Choice)

Vegetables:

3   cups carrot sticks, fresh
3   cups cauliflower pieces,
       fresh
3   cups broccoli pieces, fresh,
       trimmed
1/2 teaspoon salt
1   cup water, boiling

Glazed Carrots, Cauliflower and Broccoli	
Calories per serving:	126
Fat grams per serving:	7
Fat percentage:	50%*
Number of servings:	6
Serving size:	11/3 cups

Glaze:

2   teaspoons cornstarch
1   cup water, cold
4   tablespoons butter*

1   teaspoon chicken bouillon
1   tablespoon parsley flakes
1/4 teaspoon paprika

For vegetables:

Heat water and salt to boiling. Add carrots, cauliflower, and broccoli. Cover and heat to boiling. Reduce heat and simmer until stems are tender, about 15 minutes. Drain.

For glaze:

While vegetables are cooking, mix cornstarch in cold water. Melt 4 tablespoons butter in saucepan over medium heat. Pour in cornstarch mixture and chicken bouillon. Continue stirring until it is thick, clear, and completely blended.

Place vegetables in a 9 x 13 x 2 casserole dish or glass cake dish. Top with glaze. Sprinkle with parsley flakes and paprika.

*This recipe has a high fat-percentage, but it is absolutely delicious, high in fiber and nutrition, and it blends in beautifully with other "lower-in-fat" choices because it contains only 7 fat grams per every 11/3 cups. This keeps your overall day easily under 20 percent fat.

FREEDOM RECIPES

Great Green Beans ("A–" Choice)

Heat canned green beans or trim ends off of fresh green beans and heat eat in 1 inch salted water (1/2 teaspoon salt to 1 cup water) to boiling. Cook uncovered for 5 minutes. Cover and cook until tender, 10 to 15 minutes. Drain and toss with 1 teaspoon butter and 1 piece crumbled Jennie O's Turkey Bacon (one piece contains 1/2 fat gram) per 1 cup of beans. Sprinkle with butter-flavored sprinkles.

The fat grams and fat percentage in this recipe become "traces" by simply omitting the butter.

Great Green Beans	
Calories per serving:	96
Fat grams per serving:	3*
Fat percentage:	28%*
Number of servings:	4
Serving size: approximately 1 cup	

Mixed Veggie Festival ("A" Choice)

1   **package (16 oz.) mixed vegetables*, frozen**

1   **cup cottage cheese, lowfat butter- and sour-cream-flavored sprinkles**

Mixed Veggie Festival	
Calories per serving:	162
Fat grams per serving:	2
Fat percentage:	11%
Number of servings:	2
Serving size:	1 heaping cup

Cook vegetables according to package directions. Drain and place in two microwave-safe bowls. Top each with 1/2 cup lowfat cottage cheese and butter- and sour-cream-flavored sprinkles. Microwave on high for 1 to 2 minutes. (Two tablespoons of fat free dairy sour cream is delicious mixed into the cottage cheese.)

*The mixed vegetables I like best for this recipe include pinto, kidney, and garbanzo beans mixed in with the vegetables.

265

FREEDOM RECIPES

FREEDOM RECIPES

Saucy Green Beans and Almonds ("B" Choice)

2	15 oz. cans French-cut green beans, drained
1	can lowfat cream of mushroom soup
1/4	cup almonds, slivered
1/4	cup cheddar cheese, shredded (loosely packed)

Saucy Green Beans and Almonds	
Calories per serving:	139
Fat grams per serving:	6
Fat percentage:	39%*
Number of servings:	4
Serving size: approximately 1 1/4 cups	

Mix together beans, soup, and almonds. Heat thoroughly in 350-degree oven or microwave. Top with cheese.

This 39 percent-fat recipe is absolutely delicious and fits well into an overall meal and day that is under 20 percent fat. It contains only 6 fat grams in every 1 1/4 cup serving.

Short-Cut Tossed Salad ("A" Choice)
Colorful—Nutritious—Easy!

Mix together:

1	bag prepared tossed salad
1	package stir-fry vegetables, fresh (carrot slivers, onions, pea pods, broccoli, cauliflower)
1	carton cherry tomatoes, halved

Short-Cut Tossed Salad	
Calories per serving:	50 to 200±
Fat grams per serving:	trace
Fat percentage:	trace
Serving size:	1 cup

I purchase bags of prepared tossed salad that feature leafy types of lettuce because iceberg lettuce is not as nutritious as other lettuce varieties. Mix with stir-fry vegetables and cherry tomato halves. Top with lowfat or nonfat salad dressing. Crisp and delicious!

266

Purchase bags of prepared tossed salad that feature leafy types of lettuce because these lettuces have a higher nutritional value than does iceberg lettuce.

Single Vegetable Ideas ("A" Choices)

1. Corn on the cob, or creamed or regular canned corn.
2. Fresh, frozen, or canned green beans.
3. Fresh or frozen cooked peas.
4. Baked summer or winter squash.
5. Baked or mashed potatoes.
6. Steamed stir-fry vegetable mixture.
7. Steamed fresh or frozen cauliflower, broccoli, carrots, cabbage, broccoflower, etc.

These choices are all high in nutrition and very low in fat.

Special Note: Cases of regular green beans, French-cut green beans, regular corn, and creamed corn are excellent items to have in storage. Purchase them at case lot sales. Check the dates for freshness. (See the Master List—Shopping List on pages 59-61.)

Tossed Salad or Homestyle Salad Bar ("A" Choice)

Be creative and colorful! Enjoy a variety of any of the following delicious vegetables:

Lettuce—looseleaf, romaine, butterhead, etc. Enjoy purple or yellow or green cabbage, slivered carrots, diced green or yellow or red peppers, tomatoes, cauliflower, broccoli, celery, onions, cucumbers, radishes, jicama, corn, peas, sprouts, beets, mushrooms, etc. Pineapple, apples, raisins, mandarin oranges, and cottage cheese also mix well with a beautiful array of vegetables. Top with your favorite lowfat or nonfat dressing.

This recipe may or may not be a time-saver, depending on the number of vegetables you choose to cut up for your salad.

Tossed Salad	
Calories per serving:	50 to 200±
Fat grams per serving:	trace
Fat percentage:	trace
Serving size:	1 cup

267

FREEDOM RECIPES

Vegetable Pizza ("A" Choice)

2	8 oz. tubs cream cheese, fat free
2/3	cup mayonnaise, fat free
1	tablespoon dill weed
1	tablespoon onion powder
6	green onions, finely diced
2	carrots, finely grated
2	green peppers, finely chopped
1	red pepper, finely chopped
6	radishes, sliced
3	tomatoes, diced
2	cups broccoli florets

Vegetable Pizza with	
Emily's Delectable Pizza Crust	
Calories per serving:	149
Fat grams per serving:	2
Fat percentage:	12%
Number of servings:	12
Serving size:	one 21/2"
	pie-shaped slice

2	cups cauliflower florets
1	can pineapple tidbits

Mix together cream cheese, mayonnaise, dill weed, and onion powder. Spread this mixture over the top of the already-baked pizza crust below. Top with onions, carrots, peppers, radishes, tomatoes, broccoli, cauliflower, and pineapple. Serve cold. This makes a sumptuous summer-time or anytime meal!

Time-Saving Variation: Use pre-cut, fresh, stir-fry vegetables and prepare the pizza crust in advance. You may also try Boboli Pizza Crust (1/8 shell = 3 fat grams and 160 calories); or slice fresh French bread lengthwise and top with toppings of your choice such as lowfat ham, pineapple, and mushroom. These crusts make delicious "A–" Choices. (Canned, lowfat spaghetti sauce makes excellent pizza sauce.)

Emily's Delectable Pizza Crust ("A" Choice)

1	cup water, very warm
1	tablespoon yeast
1	teaspoon sugar
1	teaspoon salt

3	tablespoons "good" oil (see page 280)
21/2	cups flour, whole-wheat

Mix together all ingredients. Dough must be stiff so that it is easy to work with. Spread evenly on pizza pan or cookie sheet coated with nonstick cooking spray. Bake at 450 degrees for 8 to 13 minutes. Cool and cover with freezer wrap and freeze until you're ready to top it with your favorite toppings. Thaw before topping.

Pizza Variations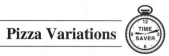

After spreading pizza dough (found on page 168) onto a pizza pan or cookie sheet coated with nonstick cooking spray, spread on your favorite lowfat pizza sauce or spaghetti sauce. Then top generously with your favorite lowfat toppings such as lowfat ham or turkey, green and red peppers, olives (sparingly as they are high in good fat), tomatoes, onions, mushrooms, pineapple tidbits, etc. Be very sparing with higher-fat toppings such as pepperoni. Their fat grams add up fast!

Bake at 450 degrees for 10 to 15 minutes. Remove from oven and sprinkle with a moderate amount of part-skim mozarella cheese. The cheese will look and taste like you've used much more than if you put it on before baking. Teenagers love this pizza!

Vegetable Relish Trays ("A" Choices)

Have fun with your relish trays. Use a variety of color, vary the selection, and take advantage of specials, buying vegetables in their individual seasons.

Quadruple-combination relish trays include:

1. Baby carrots, broccoli and cauliflower florets, and purple cabbage cut in lacy slices.
2. Raw sweet potato slices, celery sticks, sliced fresh mushrooms, and cherry tomatoes. (Tomatoes are technically a fruit, but lend themselves to a vegetable platter.)
3. Sliced cucumbers, sliced tomatoes, sliced purple cabbage, and cauliflower chunks.
4. Sliced sweet red and yellow peppers, sliced zucchini, and carrot sticks.
5. Jicama slices, green pepper slices, cherry tomatoes, and sliced sweet potatoes.
6. Snow pea pods, baby corn cobs, cherry tomatoes, and baby carrots.

Zucchini AuGratin ("A" Choice)

4   large zucchini cut in
      1/2" slices
1   onion, chopped
2   cups water, boiling
1/2   teaspoon salt
1   cup part-skim mozzarella
      cheese, shredded
1/2   cup evaporated skim milk
1/2   teaspoon salt
1/2   teaspoon pepper
2   cups bread crumbs,
      whole-wheat

Zucchini AuGratin	
Calories per serving:	242
Fat grams per serving:	5
Fat percentage:	19%
Number of servings:	4
Serving size:	1 cup

This recipe may take slightly longer than 15 minutes to prepare.

Cook zucchini with onion in boiling water and salt, covered for 5 minutes; drain. Layer zucchini mixture and cheese in 2-quart casserole. In a small bowl, blend milk, salt, and pepper. Pour milk mixture over zuccini mixture and top with finely-ground bread crumbs. Bake uncovered at 350 degrees for 30 minutes.

Zucchini Casserole ("B+" Choice) *EASY!*

2   pounds or 6 cups zucchini,
      cubed, well-drained
1/4   cup onion, chopped
1   can lowfat cream of chicken
      soup
1/2   cup dairy sour cream, fat free
1/2   cup yogurt, plain, nonfat
1   cup carrots, shredded
1   package stuffing mix with
      seasonings (lowfat corn-bread
      stuffing mix is excellent.)

Zucchini Casserole	
Calories per serving:	183
Fat grams per serving:	6
Fat percentage:	30%*
Number of servings:	10
Serving size:	1 cup

1/4   cup butter, melted
4   tablespoons water

Boil zucchini and onion 5 minutes only. Drain very well. Combine soup, sour cream, and yogurt. Stir in carrots. Combine dry stuffing mix, butter, and water. Spread half of dressing mixture in 12 x 71/2 x 2 baking dish coated with nonstick cooking spray. Spoon zucchini mixture in; pour soup mixture over the top and sprinkle rest of dressing mixture on the top. Bake at 350 degrees for 30 minutes.

*This delicious 30 percent fat casserole fits nicely into a day that has an overall fat percentage of less than 20 percent. It contains only 6 fat grams per 1 cup serving.

FREEDOM RECIPES

Deliciously-
Easy
Idea Lists

It's easy to have the ideal nutrient balance from Water, Vegetables, Grain, Protein, and Fruit at each meal when numerous ideas are at hand. Simply mix and match the following Deliciously-Easy Ideas into quick, beautiful meals full of color and variety.

Make certain to include at least one or two fruits and vegetables that are high in vitamins A and C each day. It's also a good idea to choose fruits and vegetables that have a high calcium content, especially if you suffer from a dairy allergy. Both the fruit and the vegetable idea lists contain specific information concerning these essential nutrients.

So become a kitchen artist! Fill your "paint palette" full of gorgeous greens, ravishing reds, pleasant purples, and yummy yellows. Let your hair down and have a wonderful time creating "palate-pleasing," simply delicious meals!

BREAD, GRAIN, & PASTA IDEAS

Breads, whole-grain* or part whole-grain and rolls.

Cereals, cold, whole-grain, low-sugar (See cereal lists on pages 275 - 278.)

Cereals, hot, whole-grain (oatmeal, brown rice, cracked wheat—plain or mixed with Wheat Hearts, millet, coarsely-ground brown rice, etc.)

Lowfat, whole-grain, or part whole-grain muffins.

Whole-wheat, artichoke, or regular white pasta including macaroni, spaghetti, fettuccine, etc.

Brown or white rice.

Whole-wheat, corn, or white tortillas.

Whole-grain breads, rolls, muffins, and pastas are higher in fiber and more nutritious than white, re-fined-flour products. However, part whole-grain products create less gas-trointestinal distress for people just starting out, and white-flour products, eaten occasionally, will not slow your pro-gress towards optimal health and leanness unless you are allergic to them.

Special Note: When my meals are comprised mainly of beans or potatoes, I usually go a little lighter with the grains and heavier with the dark green, yellow, and orange veg-etables.

272

BREAD AND MUFFIN RECIPES

Apple-Cinnamon Muffins . . 226
Banana Muffins 226
Better Bran Muffins 227
Big Soft Pretzels 158
Blueberry Muffins 227
Carrot Muffins 228
Cheese Muffins 228
Corn Muffins 229
Country Corn Bread 159
Cranberry Muffins 229
Cranberry-Orange Muffins 230
Date Muffins 230
Garlic-Cheese Toast 159
Marvelous Muffins 231
Oatmeal-Raisin Muffins 232
Pumpkin Muffins 233
Pumpkin-Carrot Muffins 233
Perfect Whole-Wheat Bread 160
Sourdough Starter 160
Super Cinnamon Rolls 161
Sweet Potato Muffins 234
Whole-Wheat Bread 160
Whole-Wheat Pita Bread 162
Whole-Wheat Tortillas 162
Zucchini Muffins 234
Zucchini-Pineapple-Nut Bread 163

PASTA RECIPES

Cappellino Primavera 235
Cheese-Stuffed Jumbo Shells 236
Homemade Macaroni & Cheese . . 238
Homemade Noodles 239
Luscious Lasagna 239
Packaged Macaroni & Cheese . . . 240
Salmon Pasta Salad 240
Savory Meat & Cheese Manicotti . . . 241
Spaghetti & Pasta Varieties 242
Spaghetti Salad 242
Veggie Lasagna 243
Veggie-Tuna Pasta Salad 243

BREAD SPREAD IDEAS

FOR TOAST:

Fat free cream cheese (regular or fruit-flavored).

Jams sweetened with concentrated Fruit Juices (no added sugar or artificial sweeteners).

Plain fat free cream cheese with All Fruit jam on top. (Use jams in moderation as they are very high in natural sugars.)

FOR SANDWICHES:

Fat free mayonnaise and fat free salad dressing (Kraft Miracle Whip) blended together with equal parts of each for a more balanced flavor.

Lowfat and fat free salad dressings.

BREAD SPREAD RECIPES

All Fruit Jam. 164
Apple-Raspberry Butter. 165
Cranberry Sandwich Spread. . . . 165
Honey Butter. 165
(in great moderation)

THE BUTTER / MARGARINE ISSUE

Margarine is a popular fat that is totally fabricated. When margarine first came on the market, it was not widely accepted because it looked like lard. Artificial colors and flavors were soon added. Margarine was then packaged in sticks and tubs, making it look and taste almost exactly like real butter.

Margarine is made by taking liquid vegetable fat (that is not highly saturated) and then heating it, or hydrogenating it so that it becomes solid at room temperature. This changes the oil's molecular structure, thus damaging its healthful qualities. Dr. Kummerow of the University of Illinois has shown that these unnatural fats can actually raise cholesterol levels.

Recent media reports suggest a greater link between margarine and heart disease than between butter and heart disease.

So what's the bottom line? I always use butter when margarine is called for in a recipe. I use only half the amount called for (because butter is still very high in naturally saturated fat) and I replace the other half with another liquid ingredient that enhances that particular recipe. (Examples: apple-sauce, water, fruit-juice concentrate, egg whites, milk, etc.) Preréd beans can replace *all* of the butter in cookie recipes along with enhancing the texture.

I seldom use butter on my bread, opting instead for a lower-fat choice such as fat free cream cheese and All Fruit Jam. I use it in places where nothing else will suffice.

I do not believe that *Mother Nature* would create something as delicious as butter and expect us never to taste it. *Moderation*, not excessiveness or exclusion is the key to a life filled with health, vigor, and permanently-reduced body fat.

273

BREAKFAST IDEAS

"A" or "B" Choice cold cereal with
skim or 1% milk and fruit (see
pages 275-278)

Hot cereal with skim or 1% milk and
fruit (see recipe list—right →).

Leftovers from yesterday's breakfast.

Whole-grain pancakes and fruit.

"A" CHOICE SWEETENERS FOR CEREALS AND PANCAKES

All Fruit Jam* (page 164)
Blueberries
Fruit cocktail or other canned fruit
in extra-light syrup or fruit juice.
Fruit-juice concentrates*
Fruit Syrup* (page 214)
Raisins *
Raspberries
Sliced bananas
Sliced peaches
Sliced strawberries

*Be moderate with these choices
as they are very high in natural, concentrated sugar.*

"B" CHOICE SWEETENERS

*(Not For Diabetics or Those Highly
Resistant to Fat Loss)*

Brown sugar (in moderation)
Honey (in moderation)
Maple syrup (in moderation)
Regular, sugar-sweetened jams
and jellies
Sugar (in moderation)

*Top pancakes with fruit or All
Fruit Jam and fat free or lowfat fruit-
flavored yogurt; or small amounts of
pancake syrup.*

*If you are diabetic, purchase fat
free or lowfat yogurt sweetened with
concentrated fruit juice (Alta Dena);
or sweeten your own plain nonfat yogurt with All-Fruit Jam.*

BREAKFAST RECIPES

Banana Pancakes 176
Belgian Waffles 166
Big Soft Pretzels 158
Blender Whole-Wheat
Pancakes 176
Blintzes 167
Blueberry Pancakes 177
Blueberry Streusel Coffee
Cake 189
Breakfast Burritos 167
Breakfast Fruit Compote 168
Breakfast Shake 168
Cheese Egg Scramble 175
Cinnamon-Maple Oatmeal 169
Country Corn Bread 159
Cracked Wheat, Raisin,
and Honey Cereal 169
Date Bars 191
Egg and Cheese Muffins 171
French Toast 171
Fried Eggs 172
Fruit Syrup 214
Granola 172
Granola (crunchy) 170
Granola Bars 173
Hash Browns 246
Instant Blueberry Ice Cream 194
Instant Peach Ice Cream 194
Muffins 226
Oatmeal Pancakes 177
Omelet Supreme 174
Orange Jubilee 174
Peach Pancakes 177
Perfect Whole-Wheat Bread 160
Rice 'n Honey Pudding
with Raisins 198
Super Cinnamon Rolls 161
Super Quick Pancakes 177
Three Bear Porridge
and Honey 175
Tropical Fruit Ice 201
Veggie and Cheese
Egg Scramble 175
Yogurt-Fruit Delight 219
Zucchini-Pineapple-Nut Bread . . 163

CEREAL IDEAS

"A" CEREALS	Serving Size	Fat Grams	Calories
All Bran (Kellogg's)	1.1 oz.	1/2 cup	1	80
Blueberry Fruit Wheats (Nabisco)	1 oz.	1/2 cup	0	90
Bran Flakes (Post)	1 oz.	2/3 cup	0	90
Cheerios (General Mills)	1 oz.	1 cup	2	110
Complete Bran Flakes (Kellogg's)	1.1 oz.	1 cup	0	100
Corn Flakes (Kellogg's)	1.1 oz.	1 cup	0	110
Corn Chex (Ralston)	1.1 oz.	11/4 cup	0	110
Cream of Rice (Nabisco)	1 oz.	21/2 Tb dry	0	100
Cream of Wheat (Nabisco)	1 oz.	21/2 Tb dry	0	100
Crispix (Kellogg's)	1.1 oz.	1 cup	0	110
Crispy Rice (Malt O Meal)	1.1 oz.	1 cup	0	120
Fruit & Fibre Peaches, Raisins, Almonds & Oat Clusters (Post)	1.25 oz.	2/3 cup	2	120
grape-nuts (Post)	2 oz.	1/2 cup	0	200
grape-nuts Flakes (Post)	1 oz.	3/4 cup	1	100
Great Grains Raisin Date Pecan (Kellogg's)	1.25 oz.	1/3 cup	3	140
Great Grains Double Pecan (Kellogg's)	1 oz.	1/3 cup	3	120
Kenmei Rice Bran Flakes (Kellogg's)	1.1 oz	3/4 cup	1	120
Kix (General Mills)	1.1 oz.	1 1/3 cup	1	120
Maypo Instant Oatmeal	1 oz.	1/4 cup dry	1	100
Oatmeal (Quaker)	1.5 oz. dry	1 cup cooked	3	150
Oatmeal, Instant (Quaker)	1 oz.	1 pkt.	2	100
Quaker Oat Bran (Quaker)	1.5 oz.	1/2 cup	3	150
Product 19 (Kellogg's)	1.1 oz.	1 cup	0	110
Puffed Wheat (Malt O Meal)	1/2 oz.	1 cup	0	50
Puffed Rice (Malt O Meal)	1/2 oz.	1 cup	0	60
Raspberry Fruit Wheats (Nabisco)	1 oz.	1/2 cup	0	90
Rice Chex (Ralston)	1 oz.	1 cup	0	120
Rice Krispies (Kellogg's)	1 oz.	11/4 cup	0	110
Ripple Crisp Honey Corn (General Mills)	1 oz.	3/4 cup	1	110
Rolled Oats (Buckeye)	1.5 oz.	1/2 cup dry	3	150
Shredded Wheat, Biscuit Size (Nabisco)	5/6 oz.	1 biscuit	0	80
Shredded Wheat Spoon Size (Nabisco)	1.7 oz.	1 cup	0	170
Shredded Wheat 'N Bran (Nabisco)	2 oz.	11/4 cup	1	200

Cereals that are whole-grain and contain 5 or fewer grams of sugar per serving (not including the sugars occurring naturally in fruit, which I estimate at 4 to 8 grams, depending on the amount of fruit added) are given an "A" rating. Diabetics and those who are extremely resistant to fat loss should choose cereals that have 3 or fewer grams of sugar. Hot cereals, such as oatmeal and cracked wheat, are definitely more nutritious than cold cereals, yet the convenience of cold cereal may come in very handy.

IDEA LISTS

	Serving Size		Fat Grams	Calories
Special K (Kellogg's)	1.1 oz.	1 cup	0	110
Strawberry Squares (Kellogg's)	2 oz.	1 cup	1	180
Team Flakes (Nabisco)	1 oz.	1 cup	1	110
Toasties (Post)	1 oz.	11/4 cup	0	110
Toasty O's (Malt O Meal)	1 oz.	1 cup	2	100
Total Whole Grain (General Mills)	1 oz.	3/4 cup	1	110
Wheat Chex (Ralston)	1.8 oz.	2/3 cup	1	100
Wheat, Cracked (stone-buhr)	2 oz.	1/4 cup dry	1	190
Wheat Hearts (General Mills)	1.25 oz.	1/4 cup dry	1	130
Wheaties (General Mills)	1 oz.	1 cup	1	110
Zoom Quick Wheat Cereal (Krusteaz)	1.1 oz.	1/3 cup dry	1	125

"B" CEREALS*

	Serving Size		Fat Grams	Calories
Almond Raspberry Muesli (Ralston)	2 oz.	3/4 cup	3	220
Apple Cinnamon Rice Krispies (Kellogg's)	1.1 oz.	3/4 cup	0	110
100% Bran (Nabisco)	1 oz.	1/3 cup	1	70
Banana Nut Crunch (Post)	2 oz.	1 cup	6	250
Basic 4 (General Mills)	2 oz.	1 cup	3	210
Blueberry Morning (Post)	2 oz.	11/4 cup	4	230
Bran'nola (Post)	1 oz.	1/3 cup	2	110
Double Chex (Ralston)	1 oz.	11/4 cup	0	120
Frosted Mini Wheats (Kellogg's)	2 oz.	1 cup	1	190
Fruit & Fibre Dates, Raisins, Walnuts & Oat Clusters (Post)	1.25 oz.	2/3 cup	2	120
Healthy Choice (Kellogg's)	2 oz.	11/4 cup	1	190
Honey Bunches of Oats (Post)	1 oz.	2/3 cup	2	110
Honey Bunches of Oats/Almonds (Post)	1 oz.	2/3 cup	3	120
Just Right Fruit & Nut (Kellogg's)	1.9 oz.	1 cup	2	200
King Vitaman (Quaker)	1 oz.	11/4 cup	1	110
Life (Quaker)	1.1 oz.	3/4 cup	2	120
Mueslix Crispy Blend	1.5 oz.	2/3 cup	2	120
Mueslix Golden Crunch (Kellogg's)	1.2 oz.	3/4 cup	5	210
Multi Bran Chex (Ralston)	2 oz.	11/4 cup	2	220
Multi Grain Cheerios (General Mills)	1 oz.	1 cup	1	110

*Whole-grain cereals that contain 6 to 8 grams of added sugar (not including fruit sugar) are given a "B" rating. "B" Choice cereals are more helpful for fat loss than a "B" Choice dessert. Cereals are graded more harshly because they are considered a "main course." I see fat loss with "B" Choice cereals but not "B" Choice desserts because I'm highly resistant to fat loss. Listen to **your** body and work with your individual needs.

	Serving Size		Fat Grams	Calories
Nutri Grain Almond Raisin (Kellogg's)	2 oz.	1 1/4 cup	3	200
Nutri Grain Golden Wheat (Kellogg's)	1 oz.	3/4 cup	0	100
Oatmeal Crisp with Almonds (General Mills)	2 oz.	1 cup	6	230
Oatmeal Crisp with Apples (General Mills)	2 oz.	1 cup	3	210
Quaker Oat Squares (Quaker)	2 oz.	1 cup	1	100
Raisin Nut Bran (General Mills)	2 oz.	1 cup	4	210
Raisin Squares (Kellogg's)	2 oz.	3/4 cup	1	180
Raisin Bran (Malt O Meal)	1.4 oz.	3/4 cup	2	130
Ripple Crisp Honey Bran (General Mills)	1 oz.	2/3 cup	1	100
Strawberry Muesli (Ralston)	2 oz.	1 cup	3	210
Triples (General Mills)	1 oz.	1 cup	1	110

"C" CEREALS*

(9 to 12 grams of sugar—excluding fruit sugars)

	Serving Size		Fat Grams	Calories
Almond Delight (Ralston)	1.1 oz.	1 cup	3	210
Apple Cinnamon Cheerios (General Mills)	1 oz.	3/4 cup	2	110
100% Natural Oats & Honey (Quaker)	1.5 oz.	1/2 cup	8	220
100% Natural Oats, Honey & Raisin (Quaker)	1 oz.	1/4 cup	5	120
Berry Berry Kix (General Mills)	1 oz.	3/4 cup	1	120
Bran'nola with Raisins (Post)	2 oz.	1/2 cup	3	200
Cap'n Crunch Peanut Butter (General Mills)	1 oz.	3/4 cup	3	120
Cinnamon Toast Crunch (General Mills)	1 oz.	3/4 cup	4	130
Cracklin Oat Bran (Kellogg's)	2 oz.	3/4 cup	8	230
Double Dip Crunch (Kellogg's)	1.1 oz.	3/4 cup	0	110
Frosted Bran (Kellogg's)	1.1 oz.	3/4 cup	0	100
Frosted Wheat Bites (Nabisco)	2 oz.	1 cup	0	180
Fruity Pebbles (Post)	1 oz.	3/4 cup	1	110
Golden Grahams (General Mills)	1 oz.	3/4 cup	1	120
Honey Comb (Post)	1 oz.	1 1/3 cup	0	110
Honey Nut Cheerios (General Mills)	1 oz.	1 cup	2	120
Honey & Nut Toasty O's (Malt O Meal)	1 oz.	3/4 cup	1	100

277

*When my kids want a junk-food treat, I sometimes let them choose a "C" Choice cereal which is lower in sugar, more nutritious, and much less "junky" than most candy and other junk food. I included Cracklin' Oat Bran in the "C" category instead of the "D" category because of it's high-fiber content. However, it is very high in sugar.

	Serving Size		Fat Grams	Calories
Low Fat Granola (Kellogg's)	2 oz.	2/3 cup	3	210
Nut & Honey Crunch (Kellogg's)	1.1 oz.	2/3 cup	2	120
Raisin Bran* (Kellogg's)	2 oz.	1 cup	1	170
Raisin Bran* (Post)	2 oz.	1 cup	1	190
Rice Krispies Treats (Kellogg's)	1.1 oz.	3/4 cup	2	120
Total Raisin Bran* (General Mills)	2 oz.	1 cup	2	180
Toasted Oatmeal (Quaker)	1.1 oz.	3/4 cup	1	120
Wheaties Honey Gold (General Mills)	1 oz.	3/4 cup	1	110

"D" CEREALS

*(13 or more grams of sugar–
excluding fruit or natural sugars)*

	Serving Size		Fat Grams	Calories
Alpha Bits (Post)	1 oz.	1 cup	1	130
Apple Jacks (Kellogg's)	1.1 oz.	1 cup	0	110
Cap'n Crunch (Quaker)	1 oz.	3/4 cup	2	110
Cap'n Crunch Crunch Berries (Quaker)	1 oz.	3/4 cup	2	100
Cinnamon Life (Quaker)	1.75 oz.	1 cup	2	190
Cinnamon Mini Buns (Kellogg's)	1 oz.	3/4 cup	1	110
Clusters (General Mills)	2 oz.	1 cup	5	220
Coco-Roos (Malt O Meal)	1 oz.	3/4 cup	1	115
Cocoa Krispies (Kellogg's)	1.1 oz.	3/4 cup	1	120
Cookie Crisp Chocolate Chip (Ralston)	1 oz.	1 cup	1	120
Corn Pops (Kellogg's)	1.1 oz.	1 cup	0	110
Frosted Flakes (Kellogg's)	1.1 oz.	3/4 cup	0	120
Golden Crisp (Post)	1 oz.	3/4 cup	0	110
Golden Sugar Puffs (Malt O Meal)	1 oz.	3/4 cup	0	100
Graham Chex (Ralston)	2 oz.	1 cup	2	210
Lucky Charms (General Mills)	1.1 oz.	1 cup	1	120
Marshmallow Alpha Bits (Post)	1.1 oz.	1 cup	1	130
Smacks (Kellogg's)	1.1 oz.	3/4 cup	1	110
Super Golden Crisp (Post)	1 oz.	1 cup	0	100
Tootie Fruities (Malt O Meal)	1 oz.	1 cup	1	110
Trix (General Mills)	1 oz.	1 cup	2	120

"F" CEREALS

(Avoid this list.)

	Serving Size		Fat Grams	Calories
All Bran Extra Fiber (Kellogg's) (Artificial Sweeteners)	1.1 oz.	1/2 cup	1	50
Cocoa Pebbles (Post) (Coconut and Palm Kernel Oils)	1 oz.	3/4 cup	1	120
Fiber One (General Mills) (Artificial Sweeteners)	1 oz.	1/2 cup	1	60
Fruit Loops (Kellogg's) (Coconut Oil)	1 oz.	1 cup	1	120

*Raisin bran cereals received "C" ratings because they are extremely high in natural fruit-sugar (1/4 cup = approximately 28 grams of sugar; so 1 cup = 112 grams of sugar—Wow!) Also, their flakes are generally made up of bran "only", instead of the "whole" grain.

IDEA LISTS

278

COOKING OIL AND "REAL" FOOD IDEAS

FATTY ACID COMPOSITION OF COMMON FOOD FATS

	"Bad" fats in excess	*"Good" essential fats*		
Oil	Saturated Fat	Linoleic Acid (Omega-6)	Linolenic Acid (Omega-3)	Mono-unsaturated Fat
Safflower oil	9%	78%	1%	12%
Sunflower oil	11%	69%	0%	20%
Peanut oil	13%	33%	5%	49%
Corn oil	13%	62%	0%	25%
Olive oil	14%	9%	0%	77%
Soybean oil	15%	61%	0%	62%
Canola (Rapeseed) oil	6%	31%	1%	24%
Margarine	18%	29%	5%	48%
Chicken fat	30%	22%	1%	47%
Lard	41%	12%	0%	47%
Palm oil	51%	10%	0%	39%
Beef fat	52%	3%	1%	44%
Butterfat	66%	2%	2%	30%
Coconut oil	77%	2%	15%	6%

Sources: Canola oil: data, Procter & Gamble. All others: J.B. Reeves and F.L. Weihrauch.

COLD-PRESSED OILS ARE THE MOST HEALTHFUL

The words "cold-pressed" on the label of an oil do not always ensure that the oil has not been damaged by mechanical extraction methods that expose the oil to temperatures ranging from 140 to 160 degrees. Your best bet is to look for the words "expeller-pressed" or "crude" on the label to ensure the most natural, unrefined type of oil you can buy. Check the regular oil section in your grocery store, the health food section, or your local health food store to purchase expeller-pressed oil.

279

The Best Expeller-Peressed Oils to Purchase

1. Olive oil	4. Sunflower oil
2. Peanut oil	5. Corn oil
3. Safflower oil	6. Soybean oil

Canola oil goes through a different expelling process. It is high in mono-unsaturated fats and linoleic acid but does not perform well when heated to high temperatures.

Expeller-pressed oils should be refrigerated. They do not store well for long periods of time. For long-term storage, I buy partially hydrogenated corn oils such as Mazola Corn Oil. These oils have a longer shelf life. However, they are not quite as healthful as expeller-pressed oils. If you suffer from high cholesterol, use only expeller-pressed oils.

Real Foods

Recent reports indicate a stronger link between the use of margarine and heart disease than between the use of butter and heart disease—not surprising! (See page 273 for more information.)

I always choose "real" cheese over the plastic kind with artificial ingredients that melts like a tupperware lid. I wonder what it does in my stomach?!!

I do enjoy fat free (real dairy) sour cream, fat free Ricotta Cheese, lowfat and fat free cottage cheese, and lowfat and fat free ice milk. These products are just as natural as their high-fat counterparts and taste delicious.

Mayonnaise and salad dressings are interesting issues. These products contain artificial ingredients whether you purchase the high-fat, low-fat, or fat-free varieties. So, if the product is already artificial, I use it very sparingly and choose the lowfat and fat free varieties.

I also purchase "real" eggs, never the "low-cholesterol" substitutes. I have a marvelous way of making them low-cholesterol and fat-free, the all-natural way. I throw the yolks away and use two egg whites in place of one whole egg. This is usually quite inexpensive, as well (especially at the doctor's office).

It's so nice not to be a food-fanatic. *Moderation* is the key to optimum health and leanness for life.

DESSERT AND DRINK IDEAS

Desserts and sweets, when eaten on an empty stomach, can encourage a greater rise in your blood-sugar level. Your pancreas may then release more insulin and drive the sweets into your fat cells. When desserts are eaten after full meals, they absorb more slowly into your blood stream, having less of an effect on your blood-sugar and insulin levels. And some of the fat and sugar that you've eaten may actually attach to high-fiber foods you have just eaten and be wasted from your body.

My dessert motto is this: "I can eat dessert any time, any where, any place I want it, as long as I'm completely satisfied on Water, Veggie, Grain, Protein, and Fruit first. But I'm really not that crazy about desserts."

If you are highly resistant to fat loss as I have always been, or if you are diabetic or hypoglycemic, you'll do much better if you give yourself the freedom to go with the most delicious "A" choice dessert known to humankind—FRUIT—every kind you can imagine! Check out the fruit list on pages 285 and 286 and enjoy.

DESSERT RECIPES

Apple Cake 186
Apple Cobbler 187
Applesauce Cookies 203
Applesauce Oatmeal Raisin
    Cookies 204
Blueberry Streusel Coffee
    Cake 189
Breakfast Shake 168
Cake Mix Sweet Rolls 190
Chocolate Chip Cookie 205
Chocolage Frosting 191
Date Bars 191
Fresh-Fruit Combination Trays . . 213
Fruit with Sour Cream
    Fruit Dip 212
Fruit Gelatin 214
Grandma's Marvelous
    Chocolate Velvet Cake 193
Instant Blueberry Ice Cream 194
Instant Peach Ice Cream 194
Minute Cherry Cheesecake 195
No-Sugar Date Bars 192
Oatmeal Chocolate Chip
    Cookies 206
Oatmeal Raisin Cookies 206
Orange Jubilee 174
Peach Cobbler 196
Pumpkin Cake Cookies 207
Pumpkin Pie 197
Raisin Chippers Cookies 208
Rice 'n Honey Pudding
    with Raisins 198
Strawberry Pie 199
Super Cinnamon Rolls 161
Texas Brownies 200
Tropical Fruit Ice 201
Whole-Wheat Angel Food
    Cake 202
Zucchini Nut Cookies 209
Zucchini-Pineapple-Nut Bread . . .163

DRINK IDEAS ("A+" CHOICES)

WATER* with lemon juice or
fresh lemon.
WATER with a touch of lime juice
or fresh lime.
WATER with fruit-juice ice cubes.
WATER that is bottled.
WATER with 3 or 4 Tbsp. frozen
fruit-juice concentrate stirred in.

DRINK IDEAS ("B+" CHOICES)

Fruit juice with no added sugar
or artificial sweeteners ("B+"
Choice).
Fruit juice...made with one can
concentrate, two cans water, and
one can Sprite or 7-Up ("B"
Choice—not for diabetics or those
highly resistant to fat loss).
Sparkling all-natural fruit juices
("B" Choice—not for diabetics or
those highly resistant to fat loss.)

*The less sweet your drinks are,
the better, because you'll completely
lose your taste for a lot of sweets and
your energy and blood-sugar levels
will remain more stable, thus greatly
increasing your rate of fat loss and
increasing your overall energy and
good health.*

*Filtered or bottled water is an
excellent choice if your water is im-
pure or bad tasting. Yes—actually
spend money on "healthy fat-burning" water rather than on "unhealthy," fat-storing, soda pop!*

*Special Note: If you are highly resis-
tant to fat loss, you may choose to
avoid all "B" Choice desserts and
drinks. Once your body is at its ideal
percentage of body fat, "B" Choice
drinks and desserts, in moderation,
after full satisfaction on Water,
Veggie, Grain, Protein, and Fruit,
will most likely have little affect on
the fat percentage of your new, high-
energy, healthy, fat-burning body.*

DIP, DRESSING, AND SAUCE IDEAS

DIP / DRESSING / SAUCE RECIPES

Bottled Dressings 210
Buttermilk Dressing 210
Chicken Gravy 220
Cranberry Glaze 182
Cranberry Sandwich Spread 165
Creamy Onion Dip 210
Delicious Dill Dip 211
Easy Lowfat Dressings and
    Dips 211
Glazed Carrots, Cauliflower,
    and Broccoli 264
Meat Marinade 220
Mushroom Gravy 220
Oriental-Style Sauce 221
Quick Chicken Gravy 221
Quick Spaghetti Sauce 221
Quick Turkey Gravy 222
Ranch Dip 212
Sour Cream Fruit Dip 212
Spaghetti Econo-Sauce 222
Spinach & Vegetable Dip 212
Stir-Fry Sauce 222
Taco Dressing 147
Tartar Sauce 253

DRESSINGS AND FAST FOOD SANDWICHES

I always ask for extra lettuce, tomatoes, pickles, onions, and any other veggies they might have. Then I request *no dressings*. The veggies add ample moisture to the sandwich without added dressings.

If you still desire dressing, go with mustard and/or vinegar. Ask if they have lite mayonnaise or lite ranch dressing. Then have them put a small amount on your sandwich. Or take the sandwich home and add your own fat free mayonnaise and salad dressing.

DRESSINGS AND FAST FOOD SALADS

Ask for light dressings on the side. Also lowfat cottage cheese (on the side) will add delicious flavor and moisture to your salad. You could also bring your own fat free or lowfat dressing from home. The dressing recipes in this book are delicious!

GRAVY

Corn-starch gravies are deliciously low in fat. Lowfat cream of mushroom and lowfat cream of chicken soups are also excellent on chicken, pasta, etc. I do not dilute them with milk or water. I use them in their thick, rich, concentrated form.

IDEA LISTS

283

Food-Storage Ideas
For One 2000-Plus-Calorie Adult For One Year

If you are interested in storing a one-year supply of food as insurance in the event of a financial, military, or natural disaster, the following list is ideal for you. Use this list in conjunction with the Master List on pages 59-61.

IDEA LISTS

WATER	360 gallons (30 gal./month) *(Start by storing 8 gal. per person.)*
VEGETABLES	50 lbs.— Variety of canned 50 lbs.— Variety of dried beans peas, lentils, nonfat or lowfat refried beans
GRAINS	300 lbs.— White or red wheat *(unless you're allergic to wheat— then store other grains.)* *(You will need a grinder)* 100 lbs.— Other grains—brown and white rice, oats, hard yellow popcorn, barley, millet, etc. Brown rice does not store well for long periods of time. 30 lbs.— Variety of whole-grain and white pastas
PROTEINS	85 lbs.— Nonfat dried milk *(unless allergic)* 20 lbs.— Variety of lowfat canned meats *(tuna in water, canned chicken, turkey, lean beef, etc.)* 5 lbs.— Powdered egg whites 3 to 6 lbs.— Peanut butter
FRUITS	50 to 100 lbs.— Canned fruit *(in own juice)*
FATS	20 lbs.— Vegetable oil *(See page 280.)* 3 to 6 lbs.— Butter *(frozen)*
SWEETENERS	15 lbs.— Sugar *(unless diabetic)* 15 lbs.— Honey *(unless diabetic)* 20 lbs.— Variety of canned, frozen fruit-juice concentrates *(No sugar or artificial sweeteners added)*
SALT	5 lbs.— Iodized salt

284

FRUIT IDEAS

Fruits are delicious and make an essential addition to any meal. A meal without fruit is like a winter coat without sleeves. You can just feel that something is missing. You may be full, yet you're still hunting for chocolate cake because you're not satisfied.

Fruit contains vitamins, minerals, and fiber essential for optimum health and body-fat loss. Eat at least one vitamin A and one vitamin C-rich fruit or vegetable choice every day. Aim for lots of variety and color variation to optimize nutrient benefits. Vita-

mins A and C are listed next to the appropriate fruits. Refer to page 292 for an understanding of the many health benefits related to the proper intake of vitamins A and C.

Fruit is high in natural sugar and is the least complex of the complex carbohydrates. Therefore, I eat fruits with my meals or for dessert, but not on an empty stomach. Remember to go with more canned and bottled fruits, when first starting out, if fresh fruits create gastrointestinal distress.

Fruit Ideas	High in Vitamin A or C	U.S. RDA % for average size serving
Apples		
Applesauce		
Apricots	A	60%
Avocados	C	50%
Bananas		
Blackberries		
Blueberries		
Boysenberries		
Breadfruit		
Canned or Bottled Fruit in light syrup or fruit juice		

Fruit Ideas	High in Vitamin A or C	U.S. RDA % for average size serving
Cantaloupes	A & C	180% & 150%
Casaba Melons	C	30%
Cherries		
Cranberries		
Crenshaw melons		
Currants	C	270%
Dates		
Elderberries	C	70%
Figs *(high in calcium)**		
Fruit Cocktail		
Fruit Platters		
Gooseberries	C	56%
Grapefruit	C	73%

*See italics statement at bottom of next page for more calcium information.

285

FRUIT IDEAS (CONTINUED)

Fruit Ideas	High in Vitamin A or C	U.S. RDA % for average size serving
Grapes		
Guava	C	220%
Honeydew Melon	C	57%
Kiwifruit	C	100%
Kumquats		
Lemons	C	65%
Limes	C	33%
Loganberries	C	60%
Loquats		
Lychees		
Mangos	A & C	158 & 97%
Mulberries	C	68%
Nectarines	A & C	45% & 30%
Oranges	C	110%
Papayas	A & C	49% & 130%
Passion Fruit		
Peaches	A	25%
Pears		
Persimmon	A	76%
Pineapple	C	45%
Plantains	C	62%
Plums		
Pomegranates		
Prunes		
Raisins		
Raspberries	C	40%
Rhubarb (high in calcium)*		
Star Fruit		
Strawberries	C	150%
Tangerines	C	45%
Tomatoes	A & C	35% & 70%
Watermelons	A & C	50% & 50%

FRUIT RECIPES

Fresh Fruit Combination Trays, (high in vitamins A & C) 213
Fruit Canning, (sometimes A & C). 213
Fruit Gelatin 214
Instant Blueberry Ice Cream 194
Instant Peach Ice Cream, (A) . . . 194
Pineapple & Cottage Cheese Salad (C) 215
Pineapple-Marshmallow Coleslaw (Fruit or Vegetable Choice). 216
Pineapple Orange-Banana Gelatin (C) 217
Super Citrus Salad (C) 218
Tropical Fruit Ice (C) 218
Yogurt Fruit Delight (A &/or C). 219

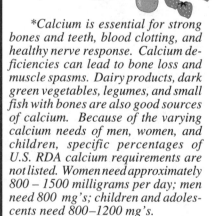

*Calcium is essential for strong bones and teeth, blood clotting, and healthy nerve response. Calcium deficiencies can lead to bone loss and muscle spasms. Dairy products, dark green vegetables, legumes, and small fish with bones are also good sources of calcium. Because of the varying calcium needs of men, women, and children, specific percentages of U.S. RDA calcium requirements are not listed. Women need approximately 800 – 1500 milligrams per day; men need 800 mg's; children and adolescents need 800–1200 mg's.

You may choose to eat foods high in calcium and take a good, doctor-recommended calcium supplement.

LEGUME IDEAS *(BEANS, PEAS, AND LENTILS)*

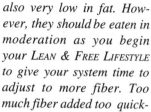

Many legumes are high in calcium and vitamin C. All are high in fiber. When a whole grain and a legume are eaten together, all of the essential amino acids are present to equal a complete protein. In other words, it's difficult to find a more "power-packed" food.

Legumes are an ideal addition to your menus. They add flavor, fiber, and tremendous nutrition. They are also very low in fat. However, they should be eaten in moderation as you begin your LEAN & FREE LIFESTYLE to give your system time to adjust to more fiber. Too much fiber added too quickly can greatly slow your progress towards health and leanness. (See the Fiber-Progression Chart on page 13.) And be certain to drink plenty of water to aid in the digestion of legumes.

Legume Ideas	High in Vitamin A or C	U.S. RDA % for average size serving
Black Beans (high in calcium)*		
Black-Eyed Peas	C**	38%
Garbanzos (high in calcuim)*		
Kidney Beans		
Lentils		
Lentil Sprouts		
Lima Beans	C**	23%
Mung Bean Sprouts		
Navy Beans (high in calcium)*		
Pinto Beans,		
Soybeans, (high in calcium)*	C**	41%
Soybean Curd (Tofu) (high in calcium)*		
Soybean Sprouts		
Split Peas		

LEGUME RECIPES

Bean and Ham Soup or
  Split-Pea Soup 265
Chicken Chili Enchiladas 255
Creamy Bean & Ham Soup 144
LEAN & FREE Nachos 256
Mexican Lasagna 145
Mixed Veggie Festival 146
Taco Salad with
  Taco Dressing 147
Tempting Tacos 148

*See italics statement at the bottom of page 286 for more calcium information.

**Refer to the bottom-left column of page 292 for a more in-depth understanding of the many health benefits related to the proper intake of vitamins A & C.

287

Main Course, Sandwich, and Side Dish Ideas

See pages 374 - 377 in the recipe indexes in the back of this book for listings of main course and side-dish recipes.

Snack Ideas

Snacking on good, veggie-based foods is an excellent way to increase fat-burning metabolism. If you are *not* hungry in between meals, and you would still like to snack to increase your metabolism, choose mainly raw, steamed, or canned vegetables. (See vegetable list on pages 291-292.) Avoid raw vegetables if they upset your stomach.

If you are hungry, go with veggie-based foods such as veggie and chicken soup, veggie and beef stew, veggie and tuna and pea casserole, veggie stir-fry, veggie-stuffed sandwiches, pita pockets, and tortillas with a little meat or cheese, etc. These veggie-based foods, left over from your meals, make excellent snacks. Then if you want to add fruit, do so, but not on an empty stomach because of the high natural sugar content. (Fruits and vegetables together DO NOT FERMENT in your system!!! They are *friends* and are delicious enjoyed together at a meal or for snacks.)

SNACK IDEAS (CONTINUED)

What Do You Do When Your Children Beg For Junk Food?

I buy them some! But I'm very moderate with amounts and I never buy "goodies" more than once a week. I completely avoid products with palm and coconut oil, and artificial sweeteners. And I make certain that the children are completely satisfied with Water, Veggies, Grain, Protein, and Fruit *first* before they even touch the goodies.

I have discovered, over the last 12 years, that if I outlaw goodies all together and talk nonstop about healthy foods, kids as well as adults completely rebel! A fun, "common-sense" issue has suddenly become a "power" issue. And nobody wins! It must be *their* decision, not mine; and the less I say, the better.

I've listed many of the "B" and "C" Choice junk foods below that I may buy for my children once a week. I am highly resistant to fat loss and therefore avoid all of them (except for a couple of tastes) if I'm intent on seeing fat loss. Because I buy these foods now and then, they lose their novel attraction and are never smuggled into the house and hidden under beds without "Mom" knowing about it. This is a liberating *addition-lifestyle*, not a shackling *subtraction diet*! Generally speaking, it matters more what you add to your eating program than what you subtract from it. Your body handles "junk" more efficiently and you won't *crave* sweets and fatty-foods at all! So kids (and husbands or wives) take heart and enjoy!

NOW AND THEN JUNK-FOOD IDEAS

Avoid this list (except * choices) if you are diabetic or highly resistant to fat loss.

1. "C" Choice cold cereals. (These are much lower in sugar than candy.)
2. Graham crackers and skim or 1% milk ("B–" Choice).
3. Lite butter popcorn* ("B+" to "A–" Choice).
4. Potato chips and tortilla chips ("C" Choices); (Baked = "A" Choice).
5. Pretzels* ("B+" Choice).
6. Reeses Peanut Butter Cups ("C" Choice).
7. Rootbeer floats with ice-milk ("B–" Choice).
8. Smores (graham crackers, chocolate, and marshmallows = "C" Choice).
9. Sprite or 7-Up ("B–" Choice).
10. Sun Chips ("B–" Choice).
11. Dried fruits, nuts, and seeds ("B" Choice).
12 Bananas on a stick, rolled in peanut butter and nuts; and chocolate shavings or coconut ("B–" Choice).

289

SOUP IDEAS

SOUP RECIPES

Bean and Ham Soup 255
Creamy Bean and Ham Soup . . . 256
Cream Zucchini Soup 256
Egg Drop Soup 257
Fast and Creamy Clam
    Chowder 257
Lentil and Barley Soup 258
Minestrone Soup 258
Potato, Corn, and Cheese Soup . . 259
Split-Pea Soup 255
Zucchini Soup 259

FOR LUNCH:

For lunch, if I don't have some homemade soup already prepared, I will often warm up a 19-ounce can of Campbell's Chunky or Home Cookin' Soup or Progresso Soup that is moderate in fat. (Eight grams of fat or less per 9 1/2 ounce serving.) I usually have a slice or two of whole-grain toast with it (topped with fat free cream cheese and All Fruit Jam). Then I add in an apple, pear, or banana. If the soup does not have lots of vegetables in it, I'll usually have half a can. Then I'll have some tossed salad or other veggies with fat free dressing or dip.

FOR DINNER:

Because I cook for a large family, I will often buy Campbell's Family Size Tomato, Chicken Noodle, Chicken and Rice, Vegetable, Vegetable Beef, and Bean with Bacon Condensed Soup. I pour the soup into a large pot and add one-half to one can of water. If I have some leftover noodles, brown rice, white rice, barley, or beans (or canned beans), I may add them if they complement the type of soup I'm making. Then I mix the family-size condensed soup with two or three cans of a Campbell's Home Cookin' or Chunky Soup that complement the condensed soup.

EXAMPLE CANNED SOUP COMBINATIONS*:

The following canned soups range between 2 and 8 fat grams per serving:

• One 26 1/2 oz. can Condensed Chicken Noodle mixed with 1/2 to 1 can water and Campbell's Chunky Chicken Noodle, Home Cookin' Chicken Noodle, Chunky Chicken Nugget, or Chunky or Home Cookin' Chicken Vegetable, etc. (Leftover noodles also make a good addition.)

• One 26 1/2 oz. can Condensed Vegetable Beef Soup with 1/2 to 1 can water and Campbell's Chunky Pepper Steak, Beef Noodle, Steak 'n Potato or Beef with Vegetables Soup (Canned kidney or pinto beans make an excellent, high-fiber addition here.)

• One 26 1/2 oz. can Condensed Bean with Bacon Soup with 1/2 to 1 can water and Campbell's Home Cookin' Bean and Ham or Chunky Bean 'n Ham Soup—deliciously hearty!

Be creative. There are many other high-fiber, lowfat soup combinations. Have fun creating your own.

*Many canned soups are high in sodium. If you suffer from high-blood pressure, you may choose to make all of your soups from scratch. This is also much less expensive. Campbell's and Progresso have some excellent lowfat, low-sodium soups that are also delicious. Read the labels carefully. (See pages 298-299 for more information on label reading.)

IDEA LISTS

VEGETABLE IDEAS

Go for the veggies first! Otherwise, we all tend to fill up on grains, proteins, and fruits, and forget the veggies. They will really help to increase your rate of fat loss. So be a little lighter with the grains (if that's all you eat) and emphasize the vegetables.

*Steamed and canned vegetables may be more easily tolerated by your system when you first begin your new LEAN & FREE LIFESTYLE. Do not stress your body with too much fiber too quickly. It will greatly **slow** your progress, not increase it.*

Vegetable Ideas	High in Vitamin A or C	U.S. RDA % for average size serving	Vegetable Ideas	High in Vitamin A or C	U.S. RDA % for average size serving
Acorn Squash	A & C	85 & 23%	Kale	A & C	118 & 134%
Alfalfa Sprouts			*(high in calcium)*		
Artichokes			Kohlrabi	C	145%
Asparagus	A &	& 25%	Leeks	C	25%
Bamboo Shoots			Lettuce, Red Leaf		
Bean Sprouts			Lettuce, Butterleaf		
Beans, Green	C	25%	Lettuce, Romaine	A & C	29 & 22%
Beans, Dry			Mushrooms		
Beets	C	27%	Mustard Greens	A & C	162 & 112%
Beet Greens	A	46%	Okra	C	30%
Broccoli	A & C	78 & 230%	Olives *(high in*		
Brussel Sprouts	C	230%	*good, cholesterol-*		
Cabbage Platter	C	30 – 70%	*fighting fat)*		
Cabbage, Green	C	60%	Onions, Yellow	C	28%
Cabbage, Purple	C	70%	Onions, Green		
(Red) *(referred*			Parsley		
to as purple or			*(high in calcium)*		
red)			Parsnips	C	25%
Cabbage, Chinese	C	30%	Pea Pods		
Cabbage, Savoy	C	60%	Peas	C	30%
Carrots	A	159%	Peppers, Hot		
Cauliflower	C	110%	Peppers, Sweet		
Celery			Green	C	160%
Collards	A & C	296 & 240%	Peppers, Sweet		
(high in calcium)			Red	C	160%
Corn, fresh	C	20%	Peppers, Sweet		
Cowpeas			Yellow	C	160%
Cucumbers					
Dandelion Greens					
Eggplant					
Endive	A	35%			
Frozen Mixed					
Vegetables	A & C	60+& 40+%			

291

VEGETABLE IDEAS (CONTINUED)

Vegetable Ideas	High in Vitamin A* or C**	U.S. RDA % for average-size serving***
Potatoes, Russet	C	52%
Potatoes, Red	C	50%
Pumpkin	A	600%
Radishes		
Rutabaga	C	70%
(high in calcium see page 286)		
Spinach	A & C	90 & 45%
Summer Squash	C	35%
Sweet Potatoes	A & C	185 & 42%
Swiss Chard	A	23%
Turnips,	C	57%
Turnip Greens		
(high in calcium see page 286)		
V–8 juice	A & C	35 & 45%
Water Chestnuts		
Watercress	A & C	35 & 45%
Winter Squash	A & C	170 & 45%
Yams	C	30%
Yellow Wax Beans	C	27%
Zucchini	C	27%

*Vitamin A is essential for the maintenance of proper vision, bone and tooth growth, reproduction, cancer prevention, and healthy, youthful-looking skin.

**Vitamin C (ascorbic acid) helps to strengthen your resistance to infection. It helps your body absorb iron, form strong scar tissue, and strengthen blood vessels. Vitamin C is also essential for collagen synthesis and beautiful, healthy skin.

292

VEGETABLES RECIPES

Broccoli Casserole
(high in vitamins A & C) 260
Cauliflower 'n Cheddar *(C)* 261
Chinese Salad Bar *(A &C)* 262
Creamy Zucchini Soup *(C)* 256
Easy Cabbage Dinner *(C)*. 263
Fast-Food Salads and Potatoes
(A & C). 263
Frozen Vegetables, Cooking
(A & C). 262
Glazed Carrots, Cauliflower,
and Broccoli *(A & C)* 264
Great Green Beans *(C)* 265
Mixed Veggie Festival
(A & C). 265
Pineapple-Marshmallow
Coleslaw *(C)* 216
Saucy Green Beans and
Almonds *(C)* 266
Short-cut Tossed Salad
(A & C). 266
Tossed Salad or Homestyle
Salad Bar *(A & C)* 267
Vegetable Pizza 268
Vegetable Relish Tray *(A & C)* . . 269
Zucchini AuGratin *(C)* 270
Zucchini Soup *(C)* 270

***If a fruit or vegetable has a percentage of the U.S. RDA recommended amount of vitamin A or C that is higher than 20 percent, I have listed it next to the item. This percentage pertains to an "average" serving size of that particular fruit or vegetable. (Examples: apples = 1; bananas = 1; grapefruit = 1/2; orange = 1; beets = 1 cup; broccoli = 1 cup; carrots = 1 cup; etc.)

Grocery Shopping and Recipe Healthification

Grocery shopping and label reading can be a real nightmare in this world of constantly-changing food items and food labels. Lowfat, fat free, lite, lively, little, luscious, ... and the list goes on and on. Let's walk through a grocery store and decipher the garble together. It can be a fun, rewarding, and healthy experience.

Changing recipes from their old, unhealthy-state into nutritious, great-tasting dishes can also be a frustrating process. But it can be done and it's actually quite easy. Read on and find out how.

Grocery Shopping and Label Reading

When making the transition from buying your usual foods to buying new, healthier foods, it is essential to have some specific guidelines. As you walk down the aisles in the grocery store, the labels seem to scream at you, "lowfat,' "low cholesterol," "sugar-free," and so on.

The question is this: What foods do you really need to buy to make your meals healthy, perfectly balanced, and moderate in fat? The following scenario should help you avoid some of the pitfalls faced by the well-meaning but novice shopper who wants to comply with the Lean & Free 2000 Plus guidelines.

Sue enters the grocery store overwhelmed with her new quest for healthier, lower-fat foods. First she enters the produce section where she purchases six large avocados. Then she picks up five cans of mixed nuts. Next she hits the deli, where she purchases some pork and beef luncheon meat. She rounds the corner to the bread section and selects some diet or light breads. The next aisle houses cereals, and she picks up some granola. Sue then tosses beef stroganoff soup into her basket. Artificially sweetened ice cream bars and yogurt come next, along with some non-dairy whipped topping. She adds a case of diet soda to the bottom of her cart, along with a bag of cheesy corn chips. A cut of prime rib and a diet fish entreé make her shopping tour complete.

Sue feels good about all the "high-protein" foods she has selected and figures that if she eats only small amounts of these foods, she should lose weight rapidly.

Examine Sue's chart on the following page.

SUE'S SHOPPING CART

6 large avocados	1 = 28 fat grams *(good fat in excess = fat-storing stress)*
5 cans mixed nuts	1 cup = 128 fat grams *(good fat in excess = fat-storing stress)*
Pork and beef luncheon meat	1 slice = 18 fat grams
Diet or light bread	contains refined flour and cellulose fiber or sawdust *(fat-storing stress)*
Granola	4 grams of cereal = 20 fat grams *(contains coconut and palm oil— highly saturated fats)*
Beef stroganoff soup	10 3/4 oz. = 16 fat grams *(fat-storing stress)*
Artificially sweetened diet ice-cream bars and yogurt	contains artificial sweeteners *(fat-storing stress)*
Non-dairy whipped topping	contains coconut and palm oil— highly saturated *(fat-storing stress)*
Diet soda	contains artificial sweeteners *(fat-storing stress)*
Cheesy corn chips	2 oz. = 20 fat grams *(fat-storing stress)*
Prime rib	4 oz. = 38 fat grams *(fat-storing stress)*
1 diet microwave sole fish entreé	24 fat grams

While Sue is shopping, Sid enters the grocery store. He fills his cart with a large variety of fresh vegetables and fruits along with a few frozen and canned fruits (in their own juice). He selects skinless turkey breast meat and part-skim mozzarella cheese at the deli. One hundred percent stone-ground whole-wheat breads, rolls, tortillas, pita pockets, and noodles (in the health-food section) come next. He steers toward whole-corn, brown-rice and whole-oat cereals to focus on variety in the grain category. (Sid chose part-whole grain and some white products when his system was first adjusting to his new, optimum-health lifestyle.)

Sid makes certain to check the cereal box labels and stay under seven grams of sugar per cereal serving for himself and three grams for his diabetic brother, unless the additional sugar occurs naturally in the fruit (raisins, dates, etc.). He also makes certain to avoid all tropical oils such as palm and coconut oil. He tosses in Campbell's Chunky Vegetable Beef Soup and Bean and Ham Soup. Sid rounds the corner to the dairy section, where he selects regular fruit nonfat yogurt (light sugar or fruit-juice sweetened). Skim and 1% milk goes on the bottom of the cart. He also picks premium light ice milk because he doesn't like the fat free kind. He adds three cans of tuna in water and some fat free salad dressing and mayonnaise. Sid tops off his cart with some fresh strawberries he spotted at the front of the store. Let's examine Sid's chart on the following page.

GROCERY SHOPPING / RECIPE
HEALTHIFICATION

SID'S SHOPPING CART

Large variety of fruits and vegetables	1 = trace (t) of fat grams to 2 fat grams *(loaded with complex carbohydrates and fiber)*
Skinless turkey breast	2 oz. = 4 fat grams
Part-skim mozzarella cheese	2 oz. = 10 fat grams
100% stone-ground whole-wheat breads, rolls, tortillas, pita pockets, noodles, and cracked-wheat bread	1 serving = trace to 2 fat grams *(loaded with complex carbohydrates and fiber)*
Whole-corn, brown-rice and whole-oat cereals	1 serving = trace to 2 fat grams
Vegetable beef soup	9.5 oz. = 2 fat grams
Bean and ham soup	8 oz. = 4 fat grams
Nonfat yogurt—sugar- and/or fruit-juice sweetened	8 oz. = 0 fat grams
skim and 1% milk	1 cup = trace of fat up to 3 fat grams
Premium light ice milk	4 oz. = 4 fat grams
Tuna in water	3 oz. = 2 fat grams *(good fat)*
Nonfat mayonnaise and salad dressing	1 oz. = 0 fat grams *(Not a highly nutritious choice, but good used in moderation. Try mixing the mayo and salad dressing together— half and half—in salads and sandwiches.)*

Notice that Sid does not avoid all fats, meats, and dairy products. He uses them as the condiment or garnishment for his meals. Just because *a lot* is bad doesn't mean that *none* is better. *Moderation* is the whole key to the LEAN & FREE ULTIMATE WELLNESS, WEIGHT CONTROL LIFESTYLE!

Sid focuses on complex carbohydrates. He is energetic and healthy and never struggles with excess body fat as Sue does. Sid eats 3,500 to 4,500 calories a day. Sue averages around 1,400 calories a day.

Sid also knows how to read labels and avoid excess fat-storing stress. Let's take a look at how he does it.

297

Label Reading*

Sid picks up two cans of Campbell's Cream of Mushroom Soup, one regular type and one Healthy Request, that read 99% fat-free. The labels read as follows:

(Regular) Cream of Mushroom Soup	
Serving Size	4 oz. condensed (8 oz. as prepared)
Servings per container	23/4
Calories	100
Protein (grams)	2
Carbohydrates (grams)	8
Fat (grams)	7
Polyunsaturated (grams)	4
Saturated (grams)	2
Cholesterol	less than 5 mg/serving
Sodium	870 mg/serving

Healthy Request Cream of Mushroom Soup	
Serving Size	4 oz. condensed (8 oz. as prepared)
Servings per container	23/4
Calories	60
Protein (grams)	1
Carbohydrates (grams)	9
Fat (grams)	2
Cholesterol	less than 5 mg/serving
Sodium	480 mg/serving
Potassium	410 mg/serving

GROCERY SHOPPING / RECIPE HEALTHIFICATION

Many new labels now include percentages of fat, cholesterol, sodium, and carbohydrate based on a 2,000 calorie diet. The fat percentage is based on a **30 percent-fat diet which assumes that 67 fat grams is an ideal number for you. Therefore, if a food has 18 fat grams per serving, this would equal 28 percent of your total fat intake for the day. If this seems confusing to you, you're not alone. Simply follow the fat-gram/calorie-guidelines laid out in the Introduction of this book; and follow the menus and recipes. All of the calculating is already done!*

Sid simply reads that in a four-ounce serving, he will receive seven fat grams and 870 milligrams of sodium in the regular soup and only two fat grams and 480 milligrams of sodium in the Campbell's Healthy Request Soup.

Now the only question is taste. (Personally, I'd buy the regular soup if I found the new version to be quite distasteful.) Sid compared the two soups and found that if he used the Healthy Request Soup in a casserole, he couldn't tell the difference.

If Sid wants to figure out the soup's fat percentage, all he needs to do is multiply the number of fat grams in a serving by 9 (9 calories in one gram of fat) and divide that number by the number of calories in a serving.

Regular Example	Healthy Request Example
7 fat grams x 9 calories = **63 fat calories** 63 fat calories out of 100 calories = **63% fat**	2 fat grams x 9 calories = **18 fat calories** 18 fat calories out of 60 calories = **30% fat**

Keep in mind that even if Sid decided he didn't like the second soup and went with the first soup, he would still be getting only seven fat grams in a half a cup of condensed soup or one cup of prepared soup. Added into a meal plan loaded with complex carbohydrates, that is not a lot of fat. It will not create a large increase in his total fat percentage for the day, although by itself it has a high percentage of fat and sodium.

Many people begin making their own lowfat cream soups. This works well for some folks, but for others it becomes very frustrating. They then drop their entire healthy eating program and revert back to coffee and donuts.

Don't be an extremist. Eat what you like and what is good for you. Be daring and get excited as your whole body chemistry changes, including your taste buds. And, if you really don't like it, don't buy it. There's so much room for flexibility with LEAN & FREE, it's amazing. And remember to read the labels. Just because it says "lowfat" or "lite"

299

or 95% fat free doesn't necessarily mean it's a healthy choice. Check for artificial sweeteners and other fat-storing stressors. (See your LEAN & FREE 2000 PLUS book pages 18 – 36.)

With new food label government regulations in effect, label reading is becoming less confusing. Calories from fat are even being included. But if you are confused by the mathematics just explained, or you just don't want to be bothered with it, simply follow all of the 1,000's of choices built into the delicious LEAN & FREE MENUS and enjoy! The math has already been done for you.

De-Junk Your Kitchen

Sue meets Sid at the grocery store. Sue is so grateful to Sid for teaching her how to shop that she invites him home for tofu filled, sesame seed donuts. He explains to her that everything she eats doesn't have to be some strange "health food". "In fact," Sid continues, "you'll do a lot better if you'll relax, fill your kitchen full of good, basic food and avoid the weird stuff."

Sid then helps Sue throw out a few things in her kitchen cupboards like the chips, the diet soda, the artificial sweetener packets, and the pastries.

They both then go to work filling Sue's cupboards and her refrigerator with hearty, "normal" foods that they have chosen following the LEAN & FREE shopping lists. And they never "overfill" the refrigerator, thus avoiding food spoilage.

Sue and Sid make a very happy, healthy, lean, and de-stressed couple. And even when their eating and exercise habits are less than perfect, they never gain much weight or body fat back. Sid has now lost 11 pounds and 5 inches in his waist, and Sue has lost 26 pounds and reduced from a size 14 to a 6. So why don't they gain much back when they're lax? Because they have developed fat-burning bodies through eating abundantly, rather than fat-storing bodies through dieting. And they follow the only THREE HARD-FAST RULES of the LEAN & FREE Lifestyle.

THE LEAN & FREE
THREE HARD-FAST RULES

1. **Never Skip Meals!!!**
2. **Eat Dessert or junk** *after* **a full W.V.G.P.F. meal, never on an empty stomach!**
3. **Never let more than** *one day* **go by without exercising gently and aerobically for at least 20 minutes.**

So even when Sid and Sue eat too much sugar and fat, because they follow these three easy rules, their bodies don't gain enormous amounts of weight and size. Sid and Sue are never in a fat-storing-state brought on by caloric and/or nutrient starvation. Therefore, their bodies are better able to *spend* excessive fat and sugar calories for energy rather than storing them as fat.

When Sid and Sue become serious about perfecting their LEAN & FREE LIFESTYLE again, they give the program one 200 percent week "effort-wise", and then it's easy again. It takes only ONE week to fall away from fat-burning "A" habits, and only ONE hard-fast week to gear back into them. And then it's easy again. Remember that next time you get frustrated. Trust your body and follow the program. You can be LEAN & FREE from the worry of ever getting fat again for life!

RECIPE HEALTHIFICATION
HOW TO MAKE YOUR FAVORITE
RECIPES DELICIOUSLY LEAN & FREE

Throughout this book I have repeatedly said that eating an abundance of healthy food is critical to becoming healthy and lean. But, if you're like many people, the mere thought of "eating healthy" may bring to mind tasteless, bland meals that become boring and dissatisfying very quickly. And they starve your body of essential calories and nutrients.

I cannot tell you how many times I have been disappointed by so-called healthy recipes that tasted more like rubber than food. I felt that I'd almost rather be fat than be doomed to eat like that. Who wants to live the rest of their life eating lousy-tasting food? I certainly don't! LEAN & FREE eating is a total pleasure, not a chore.

In this section I'll explain how to make your recipes healthier *without* sacrificing taste—how to enhance them, not destroy them. My definition of *modification* is "to make less." And, as you already know, there is nothing "less" about the LEAN & FREE 2000 PLUS LIFESTYLE. You've learned that you need to eat *more good food,* move *more,* and create *more* positive thoughts about your body so you can avoid triggering your survival system to store excess fat.

So, instead of "modification," I have chosen the term "healthification" and named this section "Recipe Healthification." Recipe healthification is simply the process of making familiar, tasty recipes more healthy by reducing fat, sugar, and salt; increasing complex carbohydrates, fiber, and overall nutrient value; and balancing solids and liquids.

One of your goals in this program is to maintain a protein intake of 10 to 15 percent of your total calories, increase your intake of complex carbohydrates to 65 to 80 percent, and optimize your intake of fat at the 10- to 20-percent level. (This is all done for you in the LEAN & FREE menus.) This doesn't mean you eliminate fat. In fact, the more food you eat, the more fat grams you should consume. For instance, at 2,000 calories per day, 15 percent dietary fat is 33 fat grams. But at 3,000 calories per day, 50 fat grams is only 15 percent. That's 50 grams of fat you should eat every day for greater health, energy, supple skin, and optimal leanness. If, on the other hand, you're on a restricted diet of 1,000 calories per day, and you are consuming 15 percent fat, you can eat only 17 fat grams—a particularly difficult task because on a 1,000-calorie diet, your survival system is triggering cravings for fats and sweets.

When I "healthify" recipes, I never sacrifice flavor or appeal. My goal is always to add and enhance nutritional value *and* flavors.

For instance, unless you suffer from diabetes or are highly resistant to fat loss, there is no need to eliminate *all* refined sugar from your eating program. The key is to be moderate and eat "real desserts" for dessert. Mix sugar with more complex foods (make whole-grain cookies, not white-flour cookies) and save sugary foods until you've eaten to comfortable satisfaction on water, vegetables, grain, protein, and fruit. If you've already eaten plenty of complex, high-fiber foods, sweets are much less likely to be stored as fat; and you'll also probably eat much less of them because you will not crave sweets when your body is completely calorically and nutritionally satisfied. If you are diabetic or highly resistant to fat loss, choose only "A" Choice desserts when you are intent on seeing fat loss, and be very moderate with these choices.

You should be excited to know that about 90 percent of the recipes in your home can be healthified. Exceptions are recipes like a buttermint recipe, which calls for sugar, butter, and oil of peppermint—pretty tough to healthify. So, I eat to full satisfaction, then treat myself to two or three buttermints once in a great while, without any worry or guilt when I'm coasting and am not into weekly inch loss.

Most recipes can be easily healthified by following four simple rules:

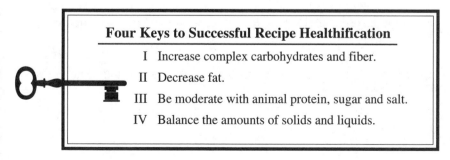

Four Keys to Successful Recipe Healthification

I   Increase complex carbohydrates and fiber.

II Decrease fat.

III Be moderate with animal protein, sugar and salt.

IV Balance the amounts of solids and liquids.

303

Let's take a look at each of these four rules and see how easy they are to implement.

I. Increase Complex Carbohydrates and Fiber

1. Make whole grains, legumes, vegetables and fruits the center of your meal.

2. Purchase 100 percent stone-ground, whole-wheat flour, breads, pancakes, waffles, and pita pockets. Buy whole-wheat, whole-corn, and white pasta and tortillas. Artichoke pasta is also wonderfully tasty and very complex. It is blond, and it looks and tastes almost exactly like regular white pasta. I've never found anyone who could tell the difference. (Remember to go with part whole grains for several months or a year or more to allow your system to adjust.) Most of these foods can be found in the regular or health-food section of larger grocery stores. Ask your grocer. Many times they will order these items for you if they don't already stock them. And remember, white pasta and rice will probably not slow your progress if you're eating plenty of other high-nutrient foods.

3. Purchase a wheat grinder. After wheat has been ground for three days, it loses approximately 80 percent of its nutrition. (A grinder is a big money saver. K-Tec stores carry excellent, relatively inexpensive grinders.)

4. Have cracked wheat and brown rice in the fridge. Microwave a bowl full with milk, honey, and cinnamon, and you have a wonderful, complex, nutritious snack if you're hungry. And include veggies with your snack. If you aren't hungry and you want to snack to increase your metabolism, snack *only* on veggie-based foods.

5. Generally eat the whole fruit and vegetable rather than just its juice where most of the fiber has been extracted (three oranges = eight ounces of orange juice). Juices are much better than soda pop, however, and are also very good for people with systems that are highly sensitive to more complex foods. But remember, by deleting the fiber you have increased the concentration of natural sugar along with its ability to be stored more easily in your fat cells.

6. Gradually add beans and peas into your eating program. (Examples: chili, split-pea soup, bean soup, refried beans with little or no fat added, etc.)

7. Oat bran and wheat bran are good, but whole oats and whole wheat are much better!

II. Decrease the Fat

1. Use skim or 1 percent milk. Buy lowfat (2 percent fat) cottage cheese unless you prefer dry-curd cottage cheese. Purchase skim yogurt and lowfat or nonfat (all natural) cheeses and ice-milk and lowfat or nonfat frozen yogurt instead of ice cream. (LEAN & FREE "Instant Ice Cream" is wonderful.) Use evaporated skim milk instead of cream or half and half.

2. Decrease the oil in recipes by one half or more. (Be certain to add an equal amount of liquid elsewhere.) You can replace the oil in many muffin, cookie, and cake recipes with mashed or pureed fruits such as mashed, extra-ripe bananas, applesauce, or pureed peaches. You can also replace all of the oil or butter in a cookie recipe with twice the amount of pureéd beans. And replace half of the oil or butter in a cake or muffin recipe with twice that amount of pureéd beans. Simply purchase a can of white beans and finely pureé them in your blender. You may need to add 1 to 3 tablespoons of water or liquid you drained from the canned beans to achieve the consistency of thick wall-paper paste or creamed shortening and sugar. The beans make the end product even moister and more delicious than the oil or butter makes it. (Example: If cookies call for 1/2 cup butter, omit and use 1 cup pureéd beans. If a cake calls for 1/2 cup oil, use 1/4 cup "good" oil and 1/2 cup pureéd beans. Delicious!)

3. Use non-stick pans, non-stick cooking sprays, and paper muffin cups.

4. Use two egg whites to replace one whole egg in recipes. Throw out five to nine fat grams with the yolk, depending on the size of the egg, as the whites contain just a trace of fat. Egg substitutes contain up to eight fat grams per serving and are generally more expensive than following this simple method. Or use powdered egg whites for an economical, "no-waste" alternative. (Check health food or food-storage stores for powdered egg whites.

5. When making omelets, use one whole egg and two egg whites.

6. Use butter or light margarines very sparingly. Butter is 100 percent natural and it's 100 percent fat! Margarines, however, are being linked to more heart disease than butter because of the trans-fatty acids

that are created through the process of making liquid-fat, solid at room temperature. This process, known as hydrogenation, actually damages the fat, making it more harmful to the body than butter fat, according to recent studies reported in the media. (See page 273 for more information.)

7. Use fat-free mayonnaises and salad dressings. If you don't like the fat-free kind, try the lowfat varieties.

8. Try mixing equal parts of Kraft Free Mayonnaise and Kraft Free Miracle Whip for a delightful dressing for coleslaw, tossed salad, and tuna salad or sandwiches.

9. Fry in very small amounts of "good" oil, (see page 280), low-sodium soy sauce, non-stick cooking spray, bouillon, water, etc.

10. Skin poultry *before* you cook it to prevent the fat in the skin from absorbing into the poultry.

11. Cook extra-lean hamburger in a microwave-safe colander with a dish underneath it in the microwave. Rinse meat under hot water twice during cooking time and break the meat into small pieces. This will help drain off and rinse away excess fat. Or, put a spoon under your hamburger frying pan to tip it to one side. Keep the fat at the bottom and the meat at the top to avoid fat absorption. Then, rinse the meat in hot water.

12. Buy white, skinless chicken and turkey meat and small amounts of extra-lean red meat.

13. Be very moderate with "health foods" such as nuts, seeds, avocados, and olives. They are loaded with "healthy" fat. If you would like to increase your body-fat percentage, or "bulk up" in a healthful manner, eat more of these.

14. Use soft fat-free cream cheese and Smuckers' Simply Fruit Spread on bread in place of butter. (Be moderate with fruit spread as it is high in *natural* sugar. Yet it is a much more healthy choice than regular jam or jelly.)

15. Use Campbell's "Healthy Request" lower-in-fat Cream of Chicken and Cream of Mushroom soups for gravies and casseroles. They are delicious mixed with fat free sour cream and/or fat free cream cheese on stroganoff-type dishes.

16. Make cornstarch gravies, or refrigerate your regular gravies and skim the fat off the top after they cool and harden.

GROCERY SHOPPING / RECIPE
HEALTHIFICATION

17. Be very moderate with all fried foods, cream soups, and cream sauces unless you have healthified the food's recipes. (Add thickness to homemade cream soups with pureéd vegetables, instant potato flakes and evaporated skim milk.)

18. Use light whipped cream in moderation and fat free sour cream. Avoid whipped toppings and sour-cream substitutes that contain palm or coconut oil. These oils are even more highly saturated than lard.

19. Use cold- or expeller-pressed unsaturated oils. (See pages 279-280.)

20. Be very moderate with high-fat corn chips, potato chips, crackers, movie-type popcorn with hydrogenated oils, and related snack items. Purchase *baked* tortilla chips and light-butter popcorn.

III. Be Moderate with Animal Protein, Sugar, and Salt
Animal Protein

1. Replace one half of the ground beef in a recipe with cracked or bulgur wheat. Flavor the mixture with bouillon, onion soup mix, low-fat cream of mushroom or chicken soup, etc.

2. Use lowfat ground turkey in some recipes to replace higher-fat ground beef.

3. Be aware that dark chicken and turkey meat with skin can be higher in fat than extra-lean beef. Be moderate with all meat, not just beef. Beef sometimes gets an undeserved bad rap.

4. Use more beans and vegetables to replace half of the meat in appropriate dishes.

5. Eat fish at least once or twice per week as it contains omega-3 fatty acids that can help reduce your risk of high blood cholesterol. Tuna in water is a good choice.

Sugar

1. Replace sugar with frozen fruit-juice concentrates such as Dole Pineapple, Apple, Orchard Peach, Mountain Cherry, Country Raspberry, Orange, Pine-Orange-Banana, Welch's White Grape Juice, etc. Try mixing pineapple and apple-juice concentrate to complement hard-to-match flavors. (Make certain

307

the frozen juice concentrate you choose is void of added sugar and artificial sweeteners.)

If you are diabetic, use fruit-juice concentrates exclu sively and check with your local health food store to see if they carry, or can order, "Fruit Sweet," by Wax Orchards, a won derful combination of three neutral, complementary fruit flavors. (For "Fruit Sweet" recipes and information, send several stamps to: Wax Orchards, 22744 Wax Orchard Rd., SW, Vashon, WA 98070.)

2. Dried fruits such as raisins and dates are a good natural sweetener when added in moderation to cookies, cakes, and cereals. Eating them in large quantities is not recommended, as they are very high in natural sugar.

3. Use pureéd fresh fruit, Smuckers' Simply Fruit Spread, and lowfat fruit yogurt on your whole-grain pancakes, waffles, and French toast. Or be very sparing with regular syrup. (Avoid syrup if you are diabetic, hypoglycemic, or highly resistant to fat loss.)

4. Virtually eliminate soda pop. Drink water and occasionally fruit juice and very occasionally carbonated fruit juice. Veg etable juice is a good choice, but not as good as the whole veggie.

5. Buy fresh fruits or fruits packed in their own juice or very light syrup. Rinse off the light syrup in a colander.

6. When canning fruit, use 1/8 to 1/4 cup sugar to one quart fruit. If you are diabetic, use 1/4 cup fruit-juice concentrate to one quart fruit.

7. Avoid *ALL* artificial sweeteners!

Salt

If you suffer from high blood pressure:

1. Take the salt off of the table.
2. Cut the salt by one-half in recipes.
3. Avoid foods such as many canned soups and stews that are high in sodium.
4. Use low-sodium soy sauce.
5. Drink six to twelve eight-ounce glasses of water per day. (but no more than 20).
6. Exercise regularly.

If you *do not* suffer from high blood pressure:

1. Drink six to twelve eight-ounce glasses of water per day.
2. Exercise regularly.
3. Be moderate with salt (sodium) intake.

IV. Balance the Amounts of Solids and Liquids

1. If you decrease the solid ingredients in a recipe, find appropriate ingredients to increase or balance out the recipe. (Example: if you decrease the meat in a recipe by 1 cup, increase the vegetables in the recipe by 1 cup.)

2. If you decrease the liquid ingredients in a recipe, find appropriate ingredients to increase to balance out the recipe. (Example: If you decrease the oil in a recipe by 1/2 cup, you may decide to increase another appropriate ingredient such as water, applesauce, skim milk, fruit-juice concentrate, etc., by 1/2 cup. Or add twice that amount of puréed white beans.)

Now that you can see how easy it is to follow the four keys to recipe healthification, let's healthify the following three recipes.

Betty Crocker Chicken or Turkey A´ La King

Regular Recipe:	Healthification Example:
1 can (6 oz.) sliced mushrooms, drained (reserve 1/4 cup liquid)	Just over 1 1/2 cans (10 oz.) sliced mushrooms, drained (reserve 1/2 cup liquid)
1/2 cup diced green pepper	1 cup diced green pepper
1/2 cup butter or margarine	1/4 cup butter
1/2 cup Gold Medal flour	1/2 cup whole-wheat flour
1 teaspoon salt	1/2 teaspoon salt
1/4 teaspoon pepper	1/4 teaspoon pepper
2 cups light cream	2 cups skim evaporated milk
1 3/4 cups chicken broth (fat is not skimmed off the top)	1 3/4 cups chicken broth (refrigerate and skim fat off the top)
2 cups cubed cooked chicken or turkey	1 cup cubed, cooked, pre-skinned white chicken or turkey
1 jar (4 oz.) pimiento, chopped	1 jar (4 oz.) pimento, chopped
Toast cups (next recipe)	Toast cups (next recipe)

Betty Crocker Toast Cups

Toast Cups	Healthification Example:
Heat oven to 375°. Trim crusts from thinly sliced fresh bread; spread with soft butter or margarine. Press buttered side down into muffin cups. Bake 12 minutes or until lightly toasted.	Follow original recipe, except use whole wheat bread and a very sparing amount of butter. Spray muffin tin with cooking spray to prevent sticking.

Notice how easy it was to employ the four keys to recipe healthification in the Chicken a la King recipe:

I. Increase complex carbohydrates:
    A. Increased mushrooms by 4 oz.
    B. Increased green pepper by 4 oz.
    C. Use whole-wheat flour instead of white flour.
II. Decrease fat:
    A. Decreased butter by 1/4 cup (cut it in half) = minus 46 fat grams.
    B. Use skim evaporated milk instead of 2 cups light cream = minus 74 fat grams.
    C. Skimmed chicken broth (if applicable) = minus 5 fat grams.
III. Be moderate with animal protein, sugar, and salt:
    A. Decreased salt by 1/2 teaspoon. (I must admit, I don't always follow this step. I don't suffer from high blood pressure, and 1/2 teaspoon isn't very much in an eight-serving recipe.)
    B. Decreased meat by 1 cup (be certain to use white meat and skin it before cooking it or buy it that way) = minus 104 fat grams.
IV. Balance the amounts of solids and liquids.

PERFECT	A. Solid increases:	4 oz. mushrooms
BALANCE		4 oz. green pepper
	B. Solid decreases:	8 oz. chicken or turkey
PERFECT	C. Liquid increases:	1/4 cup mushroom liquid or water
BALANCE	D. Liquid decreases:	1/4 cup butter

We have now followed the four keys to successful recipe healthification. The result will contain a whopping 229 fewer fat grams than the original product. It is higher in complex carbohydrates, healthier, and absolutely delicious.

GROCERY SHOPPING / RECIPE
HEALTHIFICATION

Let's look at how the following recipe follows the four keys to successful recipe healthification:

Coffee Cake	Healthification Example:
3/4 cup butter or margarine, softened	6 tablespoons butter, softened
1 1/2 cups sugar	3/4 cup sugar
3 eggs	6 egg whites
1 1/2 teaspoons vanilla	1 1/2 teaspoons vanilla
3 cups Gold Medal flour	3 cups whole-wheat flour
1 1/2 teaspoons baking powder	1 1/2 teaspoons baking powder
1 1/2 teaspoons soda	1 1/2 teaspoons soda
1/4 teaspoon salt	1/4 teaspoon salt *(because it is such a small amount)*
1 1/2 cups dairy sour cream	1 3/4 cups fat free sour cream
Filling:	**Filling:**
1/2 cup brown sugar *(packed)*	1/4 cup brown sugar (not packed)
	1/2 cup chopped dates
1/2 cup finely chopped nuts	1/4 cup finely chopped nuts
1 1/2 teaspoons cinnamon	1 1/2 teaspoons cinnamon

I. Increase complex carbohydrates:
    A. Use whole-wheat flour instead of white flour.
    B Add chopped dates (more complex than sugar for added sweetness).

II. Decrease fat:
    A. Decreased butter from 3/4 cup to 3/8 cup = minus 46 fat grams.
    B. Change 3 eggs to 6 egg whites = minus 17 fat grams. (This decreases the fat and balances the liquid.)
    C. Change 1 1/2 cups dairy sour cream to 1 1/2 cups fat free sour cream = minus 72 fat grams.
    D. Decrease chopped nuts from 1/2 cup to 1/4 cup = minus 17 fat grams.

III. Be moderate with animal protein, sugar and salt.
    A. Decrease brown sugar from 1/2 cup to 1/4 cup, adding chopped dates for sweetness.

311

IV. Balance the amounts of solids and the liquids.

PERFECT **BALANCE** }	A. Solid increases:	1/2 cup chopped dates
	B. Solid decreases:	1/4 cup brown sugar
		1/4 cup nuts

PERFECT **BALANCE** }	C. Liquid increases:	3 more egg whites
	D. Liquid decreases:	3 egg yolks

As you can see, by following the four keys to successful recipe healthification, it is easy to make your recipes delicious while making them much healthier and leaner. We just decreased the fat in this coffee-cake recipe by 152 fat grams. Wow! It also makes you feel quite creative and satisfied that you are performing a much-needed service for yourself and others who enjoy your cooking.

It takes no great skill or magic to drench a recipe in butter and sugar. The test of a truly great cook is to make something taste great and be good for you at the same time.

To get a quick, easy start on eating healthy foods, just refer to the many fast and delicious LEAN & FREE recipes and combine them with the perfect nutrient balance contained in each one of the menus. You may also find great fun in healthifying your own favorite recipes, so make a goal to healthify one of your own recipes each week. Healthifying recipes helps keep you personally involved in the process of transforming your body from a fat-storing warehouse to a fat-burning machine.

GROCERY SHOPPING / RECIPE
HEALTHIFICATION

Guidelines for Those with Special Needs

GUIDELINES FOR THOSE WITH SPECIAL NEEDS

In my work with thousands of students of the LEAN & FREE LIFESTYLE, I have seen many physical and emotional health problems vastly improve and in many cases disappear completely, as these students incorporated the principles of the program into their daily lives. You can find many examples of these transformations in the Success Stories beginning on page 176 of you LEAN & FREE 2000 PLUS book. Read them again and again as a source for your own confidence and inspiration. You'll also hear from many people with special needs on your Support Group Video tapes that can serve to greatly enhance your knowledge of your new lifestyle as well as your vision of yourself as a lean, healthy, and happy individual.

Recently, a woman told me that she was having a hard time with the program because, she said, "I have such a difficult time actually believing that I can lose fat without *abusing* my body." As we talked further, I discovered that she didn't have any of the new video tapes and had only skimmed the book. Her understanding of the LEAN & FREE program, on a scale from one to ten, was only a "one." I see this problem repeatedly. People assume they already understand this program because they're familiar with all of the *diet* programs out there that scream that they aren't really diets. Yet hidden in the subtext of each is caloric and nutrient starvation. It's not unusual to see a so-called "health expert" whose hair has fallen out and whose skin looks like shoe leather—and isn't that a good indication that what they're teaching you is wrong!? You *must study* LEAN & FREE and *live* its principles *every day* if you want to establish faith in your own body and in its responses to nurturing, nourishment, and lack of caloric and/or nutrient starvation. This program is light years ahead of "quick-fix" diet programs. Every element of it is vastly different! And even if you study those differences, if you don't continue studying and reinforcing this new information, you may threaten your progress. That little crevice of LEAN & FREE knowledge you're carving into your brain will be obscured and swallowed up by the *Grand Canyon* of diet falsehoods you've been learning all your life.

So give yourself the FREEDOM to live, love, and be happy by adequately preparing yourself—continue studying and reaffirming the LEAN & FREE principles until they are an integral part of your nature. You can then, finally get on with your life.

An important part of your self-affirmation lies in the ability to overcome obstacles, many of which are self-imposed, even though they may seem beyond your control. These obstacles often stem from fears and doubts based on physical handicaps or illnesses that people feel will interfere with their ability to follow the program. To help you overcome those doubts, I will briefly discuss some of the physical and emotional health problems that many LEAN & FREE students have brought to my attention. Many of these subjects are discussed much more fully in your LEAN & FREE 2000 PLUS book and on the tapes. Let me emphasize the fact that this information can in no way serve as a substitute for the advice you should be seeking from your physician for these special health needs and disorders. I am not a doctor. But I am a very informed woman who for many years has researched the most effective eating and exercise habits. When I could not find the answers to my own problems, organized in a complete, sensible, livable way, I began to formulate them myself. I never planned to design a program for the public. It simply developed naturally because the need was so great and because so many people began asking me to share this knowledge with them.

My advice is simple: *listen* to your doctor; *listen* to this program; and then really learn to trust and *listen* to your body. It already knows what you need. All you have to learn to do is correctly interpret its signals to you. And LEAN & FREE, along with your personal physician, can teach you how.

Now let's briefly explore some of the special physical and emotional conditions to which this program can be adapted, and which, in many cases, can be alleviated by its principles.

315

ALLERGIES

Wheat and dairy food allergies are very common in our culture. If you are allergic to a specific food, it's essential that you avoid it. It can threaten your health and signal your body that there is a threat to your survival, thus encouraging it to store fat. Specific allergy tips given on page 11 (and throughout the menus and recipes) include good food substitutes for wheat and dairy products. You may also try lactaid or acidophilus supplements (ask advice from your doctor or pharmacist) to help combat a lactase enzyme deficiency in the small intestine. Such deficiencies can create a milk-sugar (lactose) intolerance. If you are allergic to both the sugar and the protein in milk, you will need to completely avoid dairy products and take a calcium supplement. To provide yourself with protein at breakfast, choose protein foods from the lunch and dinner menus, in place of milk or yogurt.

Also check with your local book stores for cookbooks that deal with your particular food intolerance. (Examples: Wheat-Free Cooking, Milk-Free Cooking, Gluten-Free Cooking, etc.)

Work with your doctor when dealing with hay fever and any allergies. You may find that as you closely adhere to the LEAN & FREE optimum wellness lifestyle, your immune system becomes stronger and your allergies lessen and, in some cases, clear up completely. (See LaRane's story on page 205 in your LEAN & FREE 2000 PLUS book.)

Amenorrhea: *See page 335.*

ANOREXIA, BULIMIA, AND CHRONIC DIETING / STOMACH-STAPLING SURGERY
Where Do You Start?

If you have an eating disorder, or have made the mistake of having your stomach stapled, your first essential step is to seek professional help. The second step is to begin recording your eating patterns. Write down exactly what you eat (or are unable to eat) on a typical day. If vomiting is one of the symptoms of your disorder, record how many times you vomit each day. The next step is to very gradually increase the amounts of good healthy food you eat. The key word here is *gradually*. If you increase these foods too rapidly they can place extreme physical stress on your body, which will trigger it to store fat. Too rapid an increase can also be very dangerous to your health. Remember that your goal is to get *well* physically and emotionally, and that goal is achieved through knowledge and gradual change. To obtain that knowledge you must study the LEAN & FREE program intensively every day. Then slowly begin to implement that new knowledge. Your body will begin talking to you again. It will send signals of hunger, fullness, energy, and contentment. Just give it time.

The following is an example of how one woman very gradually changed her eating habits and began to enjoy good, healthy food again. We'll call this person "Jeanine." Jeanine was anorexic when she began the program, so anorexic that she even had trouble swallowing. Fear of fat interfered with every attempt she made to take a bite of food. Even plain water tasted bitter to her. Yet each time Jeanine looked at her withered hands, or found herself crying uncontrollable for hours at a time, she determined that she had to change. Her first step was to seek professional help for eating disorders and depression. Her next step was to begin eating very small balanced meals throughout the day.

317

Jeanine's Starter Meals

Breakfast
- Water: 3 to 8 ounces bottled water *(if tap water tastes bitter)*
- Grain: 1/4 to 1/2 cup Cream of Wheat hot cereal with 1/2 teaspoon of honey
- Protein: 1/4 to 1/2 cup skim milk
- Fruit: 1 to 2 slices of orange *(1/2 inch thick each)*

Snack
- Water: 3 to 8 ounces
- Veggie: 1 to 2 baby carrots *(Or steamed or canned veggies if raw veggies upset your stomach.)*

Lunch
- Water: 3 to 8 ounces
- Veggie: 1 to 2 baby carrots
- Grain: 1/4 to 1/2 slice bread *(part-whole-grain)*
- Protein: 1 to 2 tablespoons tuna in water mixed with fat free mayonnaise *(Put tuna on bread.)*
- Fruit: 1 to 2 small slivers of apple

Snack
- Water: 3 to 8 ounces
- Veggie: 2 to 3 green beans

Dinner
- Water: 3 to 8 ounces
- Veggie: 2 to3 green beans
- Grain: 1/4 to 1/2 small blueberry muffin *(part whole-grain)*
- Protein: 1/4 to 1/2 cup nonfat fruit yogurt
- Fruit: *(blueberries in muffin)*

Snack
- Water: 3 to 8 ounces
- Veggie: 1 to 2 celery sticks *(Or steamed or canned veggies if raw veggies upset your stomach.)*

Exercise
- 3 minutes/3 times a day
- *Drink* 3 to 8 ounces cool water *while exercising.*

Jeanine's beginning exercise was this: She would sit, play gentle music on her recorder, and perform simple arm movements. She would move her arms very slowly in and out, in and out; then up and down, up and down. The movements were very gentle; the arms were bent at the elbows.

SPECIAL NEEDS

As Jeanine's body and mind developed more strength, stamina, and balance, she very gradually increased the amounts of food she was eating. She threw away her scale and monitored her progress instead by how she felt and looked.

Today Jeanine is a high-energy, vivacious, and attractive woman who leads a happy, fulfilled life. She looks fifteen years younger than she did in her anorexic state. Her menstrual cycle is once again regular. She eats like a normal person. Her entire life is back in balance.

If you suffer from an eating disorder, have been a chronic dieter, or have had your stomach stapled, it's time to get excited! You've found the answers you've been seeking. Take advantage of the knowledge you're being offered: Study! Study! Study! And be gentle and kind to your body. Listen to its signals, for it will talk to you. You'll develop faith in it and in how it works with you, instead of against you. Take these steps and you too can have a lean, high-energy, beautiful body. And you'll be eating like a healthy, normal person for the rest of your life. You CAN do this—it will work for YOU!

See Charlene's, Karla's, and Lisa's success stories on pages 184, 192, and 194 in your LEAN & FREE 2000 PLUS book concerning eating disorders. Carefully study Carol Ann's and Janelle's stories on pages 179 and 181 of your LEAN & FREE 2000 PLUS book if you've had stomach stapling or bypass surgery.

ARTHRITIS AND MUSCULAR DISORDERS

As an arthritis sufferer, or as an individual suffering from muscular disorders, you may find that ideal gentle exercises* for you will include walking hip deep in water, gentle walking in place, and the twenty minute extra-gentle or low-level movements on your *Enjoying the Freedom* aerobics tapes. Remember to work closely with your doctor and physical therapist. Counsel with them regularly concerning the type, intensity, and amount of exercise you perform.

Refer to pages 90 and 91 in your LEAN & FREE 2000 PLUS book for more exercise suggestions for arthritic sufferers.

Stay with mainly "A" Choice desserts, "A" and "B" Choice main courses, and follow the LEAN & FREE menus completely. The moderate fat, salt, and protein intake, increase in fiber, and precise nutrient balance will gradually improve your sense of well-being. As your body increases in health, strength, and vitality, an optimal percentage of body fat may then follow.

Work closely with your doctor to monitor your need for pain medication. Many LEAN & FREE students have noticed a marked decrease in their need for medication. Some now require no medication at all and can move more freely and easily than they've been able to for years. (See Patty's story on page 193 in your LEAN & FREE 2000 PLUS book.)

Remember you are nourishing, nurturing, and rebuilding your entire body. While caloric and nutrient starvation bears down and destroys muscles and other body tissues, LEAN & FREE rebuilds and strengthens, muscle and body tissue. And since muscle "curves" and fat "hangs,' which would you prefer? Curves of course!

BACK, LEG, KNEE, AND FOOT PROBLEMS

Work closely with your doctor and physical therapist to monitor your need for pain medications, muscle-relaxants, and exercises specifically designed for your needs. Then you may want to try the greatest muscle-relaxant I've ever discovered—a quality calcium supplement. Such supplements have enabled me to feel like a completely different person, and I've suffered severe lower-back and upper-back pain since I was eleven years old! Now I take between 800 and 1,500 milligrams of quality calcium every day —the recommended dosage for women. I generally take the lower dose, because I get some calcium from my food. But if I'm feeling added tension in my back, I increase the dosage of my supplement with no fear of developing kidney stones or calcium deposits because I drink 8 to 12 glasses of water every day and take a *quality* supplement.

I have had many students who received marked relief from back, leg, knee, ankle, and foot problems by adhering to the following three steps:

1. Take 800 to 1,500 milligrams of a *quality* calcium supple
   ment each day.
2. Follow the LEAN & FREE menus to a tee.
3. Follow the exercise guidelines given on page 319 for
   arthritis sufferers, and then gradually increase your level of
   exercise intensity as your body strengthens and increases in
   stamina.

Remember, this program is not a quick solution for annoying symptoms—you're building a new healthier, fat-burning body for life!

BREAST FEEDING

The process of breast-feeding may promote an accelerated rate of fat loss in your body *if* you're fully satisfying your body's caloric and nutritional needs. However, if you are slightly "under-eating," not balancing your meals, and not keeping your daily fat intake at about 20%, your body may perceive a threat of starvation that affects not one, but two people. Therefore, your body may decide to begin storing fat for *two* people, or it may simply retain the extra fat it may already have stored during pregnancy.

Three Water/Veggie/Grain/Protein/Fruit meals, plus three good-sized "veggie plus other food" snacks, are an excellent way to feed your baby, feed your lean muscle, and starve your fat!

If your calorie requirement for comfortable satisfaction when *not* nursing is 1,800 to 2,500 calories, your calorie requirement *while* nursing could easily be 1,000 calories more than that, especially if you don't supplement your baby with other food.

When my babies reached about 18 pounds (which occurred when they were about six months old—I had big babies!), my caloric intake averaged about 3,800 a day. *I* was never full, but my babies were. They were very healthy and happy and I couldn't keep *my* weight on—for a brief period, I actually got a little too thin. But if I didn't eat enough, and didn't completely follow the LEAN & FREE *nutrient-balance* guidelines, I would be stuck with a couple of sizes to lose.

321

Occasionally, there is a complication that requires an adjustment in this plan. For instance, one of my children had severe stomach aches. He would scream and stiffen from the pain all day long. He weighed only twelve pounds when he was five months old. My child's doctor suspected a dairy allergy and had me omit all dairy products from my own diet. My baby's stomach aches and his mucous-filled cough immediately stopped; his complexion went from white to rosy; and in one month he gained five pounds. I proceeded to nurse this child for 18 months. During the last six months, I added a lot of good solid foods to his diet, and a few dairy products to mine. He could tolerate a few dairy products "through me" after he was a year old.

At twelve years old, this child is still allergic to dairy products, but he does tolerate small amounts of them (with acidophilus added). I believe he tolerates them better because I nursed him and introduced dairy products gradually into his diet.

Bulimia: *See page 317.*

CANCER

As you study the American Cancer Society guidelines, you will recognize immediately that they are based on plain common sense. They include:

- Increase fiber in your diet.
- Decrease fat, especially saturated fat.
- Stop smoking.
- Exercise regularly.
- Get an adequate supply of vitamins and minerals in your diet.
- Avoid excessive exposure to sun and always wear sun screen.

The LEAN & FREE program shows you specifically how to incorporate each of these guidelines into your everyday life and how to avoid *over doing it* by introducing too much fiber, too fast, or too much exercise too suddenly. In addition, it offers you food that truly tastes wonderful because you haven't completely eliminated good, essential fats. Finally, you won't *crave* fats and sweets because you're neither calorically nor nutritionally deprived. You are free to *eat* and enjoy life!

CHILDREN

The health and leanness rules are basically the same if you are 2 or 92 years old, 100 pounds overweight, or anxious to gain a little weight.

Study the "A" and "B" main course, side dish, and dessert recipes in this book. Unless your children are resistant to excess body-fat loss, you may want to keep their fat in the 20 to 30% range (mostly from "good" fat choices). You may, if you like, provide good "B" Choice desserts for them more often than you do for yourself if you're resistant to excess fat loss. It is easy to design meals that suit the specific needs of both you and your children. For instance, if we have homemade pizza at our house, I might put a little more cheese on the children's side of the pizza and even a few slices of pepperoni. On my side of the pizza, I would be more moderate with cheese, leave off the pepperoni, and load on the veggie toppings. Once in a while, I buy the children *regular* tortilla chips while I buy the *baked* variety for my husband and myself. And sometimes I will fix the children ice-milk shakes and my husband and myself *Instant Ice Cream* shakes made with fruit juice concentrate and fruit. Have fun with your family meals, be flexible, and *enjoy the freedom* LEAN & FREE offers! (See Corine's story on page 187 of your LEAN & FREE 2000 PLUS book. Also notice the pictures pages 55 and 132 of this same book.)

Chronic Dieting: *See page 317.*

CHRONIC FATIGUE / DEPRESSION / SEASONAL AFFECTIVE DISORDER (SAD)

Chronic fatigue, depression, and Seasonal Affective Disorder are three ailments that require the advice of your doctor. As you read through the Success Stories beginning on page 176 of your LEAN & FREE 2000 PLUS book, you will be introduced to numerous individuals who have seen marked improvements in these areas as they followed the program's guidelines. The increase in endorphins (the "feel good" hormones) along with the general increase in health, energy, and lean muscle tissue that occurs with LEAN & FREE, contributes greatly to relief from these ailments. Furthermore, a sense of service to others and a renewed sense of purpose in life—focus of LEAN & FREE—can make a tremendous difference to your state of mind and emotional well-being.

Seasonal Affective Disorder can also be treated with special full-spectrum lights. (Ask your doctor which are best.) These can be installed throughout your home. In severe cases, a change in location to a place with a year-round-sunny climate may be very helpful. For immediate relief, when you start to feel that cloudy, dark mood descending, make certain to exercise (gentle aerobics) for at least 20 minutes; if you don't feel like cooking, eat three balanced Grab 'n' Go meals each day; and take life one day at a time or even each hour at a time. Being happy for one hour at a time is a realistic, attainable goal for almost everyone. (Watch your Support Group tapes weekly to help boost your mood, strengthen your understanding of LEAN & FREE principles, and renew your own faith in yourself!)

When I have been completely overwhelmed by life or overcome with grief or frustration, I take the following five steps every day:

1. Eat three W.V.G.P.F. meals.
2. Exercise gently and aerobically for 20 minutes.
3. Practice Positive Body Talk *(See page 51 in your LEAN & FREE 2000 PLUS book.)*
4. Lose myself in service to others.
5. *Take life one day or one hour at a time!*

There is one more element that, in good conscience, I can't omit. I keep a prayer in my heart at all times.

CHRONIC SORE THROATS

If you suffer from sore throats, see your doctor and get your sore throat treated. Then ask him or her about the following approach for keeping well:

1. Carefully follow the LEAN & FREE menus.
2. Exercise aerobically 20-60 minutes, 3–6 days each week.

3. Some individuals may benefit from taking a quality multi-vitamin mineral supplement that includes vitamin C.

4. Make certain to eat at least one citrus fruit or another fruit or vegetable high in vitamin C, each day.

5. Get adequate sleep (generally 7 to 8 hours a night—sometimes 9). Retire early and arise early.

I was once a "walking sore throat," until I learned to follow these six steps. I find if I don't include vitamin C in my routine, I get sick much more often, as do many of the people I work with. But don't overdo it! Even though vitamin C is water soluble, excesses of *any* vitamin or mineral are not advisable. Be moderate and consult your physician.

CONSTIPATION / DIARRHEA

Relief from constipation and even some forms of diarrhea may be a benefit enjoyed from the optimum nutrition outlined in this book. If the problem persists, see your doctor and continue working with him or her until the problem is alleviated. (Read John's story on page 196 in your LEAN & FREE 2000 PLUS book.)

Depression: *See page 323.*

DIABETES / HYPOGLYCEMIA

Throughout this entire book, there are specific instructions and information for individuals suffering from diabetes. If this applies to you, read each page of this book very carefully and highlight the sections that pertain to diabetes.

Depending on the severity of hypoglycemia, an individual with this malady should follow the same basic guidelines as a diabetic:

1. Eat smaller meals often. Eat six or more a day, never allowing more than 2 or three hours between meals. This maintains an even blood-sugar level and a high fat-burning metabolism. Veggie-based leftovers make excellent small meals and snacks

325

SPECIAL NEEDS

(for example, vegetable beef soup, chicken veggie stir-fry, chicken broccoli casserole, and veggie-stuffed sandwiches, pita, and tortillas—with a little meat.)

2. Eat fruit with your meals, but not on an empty stomach, as fruit has a high natural sugar content. Eat the whole fruit with all of its fiber; it's more nutritious and has less impact on your blood-sugar level than fruit juice.

3. Save the fruit-juice concentrate for sweetening your desserts. Always eat dessert *after* a full Water/Veggie/Grain/Protein/Fruit meal, and *never* on an empty stomach. Choose the "A" Choice fruit-juice-sweetened desserts in this book. They are delicious! Avoid concentrated sugars and completely avoid all artificial sweeteners! (Refer to the artificial sweetener information on page 27 of your LEAN & FREE 2000 PLUS book).

4. Eat to comfortable satisfaction. Don't starve and don't stuff.

5. Exercise gently and aerobically 20 to 60 minutes, three to six days per week.

If you are interested in excellent health, steady blood-sugar levels, and a strong immune system, but do not need to lose excess body fat, an excellent exercise regimen would be as follows. Every other day do one of the following:

- Twenty minute portion of "Enjoying the Freedom" aerobics video—excellent for fat loss but also for general fitness, yet non-strenuous enough to prevent stress and injury.

- Twenty minutes on an excellent cross-training aerobic machine*, while watching the morning or evening news.

- Five minutes dancing in place (using "Enjoying the Freedom" movements), five minutes on aerobics machine; five minutes dance; five minutes aerobics machine while watching your favorite television show (for a total of 20 minutes).

- Twenty minutes of brisk outdoor walking, if you enjoy it and the weather permits.

*See page 90 in your LEAN & FREE 2000 PLUS book for recommendations.

If you desire excess body fat loss, do one of the following six days a week:

- Twenty to sixty minutes of "Enjoying the Freedom."
- Twenty minutes on aerobics machine.
- Sixty minutes on aerobics machine and aerobic dance combined.
- (Optional:) Floor exercises and light weight lifting. They don't burn fat but they firm and tighten the muscle under the fat. Aerobic all-over-body exercises do BOTH.

6. Avoid getting over-tired. Retire and arise early, to provide yourself with 7 to 9 hours of sleep a night (the optimum hours for most people).

By following these six easy guidelines, many LEAN & FREE students, working closely with their doctors and dieticians, have been able to decrease markedly their insulin intake. Doctors and dieticians support this program and recommend LEAN & FREE for their patients every day.

Finally, refer to your first "Dana—I Need to Know" Support Group Video. Steve very gradually increased his calories, until they were almost triple those of the initial diet he'd been put on. His energy level also tripled, and his need for insulin was reduced by half.

Don't fall into the trap of thinking that the fewer calories you ingest, the less insulin you'll need. This may be true in the short-run. However, in the long-run, the major factor in minimizing your need for added insulin is the overall good health of your body. I've worked with women who never had a problem with excess body fat in their lives until they got stuck on a 1,200 calorie diet to control their adult-onset diabetes. Then almost immediately, their energy levels were cut in half, their skin began to age rapidly, and their hips expanded. Don't starve yourself! Work with your doctor and listen to your body. It knows what you need. (Carefully study Joseph's, Clarise's, and Marsha's success stories on pages 187, 191, and 202 of your LEAN & FREE 2000 PLUS book.)

Diarrhea: *See page 325.*

Gastrointestinal Distress: *See page 337 .*

Hair Problems: *See page 333.*

327

HEADACHES

First, consult a doctor to determine the cause and treatment for your headaches.

I have worked with many people whose headaches were caused by caloric and nutrient starvation, and/or the use of artificial sweeteners. Such sweeteners have been linked to additional symptoms such as loss of memory, dizziness, inability to think clearly, fainting, and grand mal-seizures. A woman student I once taught stood up after four weeks of class and announced: "I've had loss of memory, dizziness, seeing stars, and fainting spells for one year. I'm only 35, but I thought I had Alzheimer's or a tumor on my brain, as did my doctor. My CAT scan revealed nothing; It's been four weeks since I had a diet pop or even a stick of diet gum. All of my symptoms are gone. My mind is back. No fainting—no fogginess; I feel wonderful!"

Many headaches can be avoided by following the exact same guidelines I described in the previous section on DIABETES / HYPOGLYCEMIA. Follow those guidelines closely as you work with your doctor.

Heart Disease: *See page 329.*

HIGH BLOOD PRESSURE

If you don't already suffer from high blood pressure, and you follow the LEAN & FREE program to the letter, chances are very good that you'll never have this problem. If you already suffer from high blood pressure, work closely with your physician and follow the LEAN & FREE program exactly, making certain to adhere to the following special guidelines:

1. Drink 8 to 16 8-ounce glasses of water a day (do not drink soft water or soda pop).
2. Avoid high-sodium foods, including many canned soups and chips (make your own soups or purchase low-sodium varieties).
3. Gently exercise (low-level "Enjoying the Freedom") for 20 to 60 minutes, three to six days a week.

4. Study portions of the LEAN & FREE optimum health program every day and follow it carefully!

Many LEAN & FREE students have completely freed themselves from high blood pressure problems after following this program faithfully for just a few months. For many people, the biggest initial problem isn't excessive sodium or salt; it's a deficit of good balanced calories, water and gentle exercise. A healthy, fat-burning, hydrated body handles a little extra sodium much more efficiently than an unhealthy, fat-storing, dehydrated body. So live the LEAN & FREE lifestyle every day!

HIGH CHOLESTEROL AND HEART DISEASE

Work closely with your doctor and follow the basic optimum health guidelines of the Lean & Free program. Study the numerous Success Stories in your LEAN & FREE 2000 PLUS book to form a vision of yourself as a lean, healthy, energetic person with an optimal cholesterol level and a strong heart. Basic guidelines include these:

1. Follow the LEAN & FREE menus carefully.
2. Follow the LEAN & FREE exercise guidelines completely.
3. Practice *Positive Body Talk* everyday.
4. Provide yourself with adequate sleep.
5. Study portions of the LEAN & FREE program every day!

I have seen many people whose cholesterol levels have dropped dramatically in very short periods of time, when they began to follow this program. They are often people who previously tried reducing the fat in their diet and increasing their fiber and exercise, with no positive results. One 66-year-old woman told me: "My husband eats poorly and does not exercise. I do just the opposite, and I have high cholesterol while he doesn't. So I did what my doctor said. I cut my fat more, increased fiber more, and exercised more, but, I guess because I didn't know how to put it all together, in six months my cholesterol rose from 276 to 285. Now, after one month with LEAN & FREE, which helped me understand how to balance my eating, it's already down to 220. I didn't have all the pieces of the puzzle before. Now the whole thing fits together. It's so easy. It feels right and it just makes sense."

Put all the pieces together as this woman did, and use your Success Planners. They are very effective and can make all the difference between success and failure when it comes to body fat, cholesterol levels, and a healthy heart.

HIGH RESISTANCE TO FAT LOSS AND WOMEN EXPERIENCING MENOPAUSE*

Many women past the age of menopause wonder if they are *too old* to lose excess body fat. Absolutely not! See a physician to monitor your possible need for estrogen replacement. In excess, estrogen may encourage fat storage; but if deficient, it can result in osteoporosis or bone loss and increased risk of heart disease and strokes, as well as thinning and wrinkling of the skin.

The biggest frustration I see in women experiencing menopause is that they are often more resistant to fat loss than before (or after) menopause. This is because their bodies are experiencing profound changes. Many of these women were not born with fat-loss-resistant bodies (as I was), so they become scared, anxious, and frustrated with their bodies.

If this describes you, you need to slow down, relax, and enjoy your new LEAN & FREE LIFESTYLE. If you stay with it and continue to nurture, nourish, and gently move your body, you will see remarkable changes. Permanent fat loss becomes a reality, not just a dream.

Follow all of the guidelines for high resistance to fat loss that I include throughout the introduction, menus, and recipes, including these:

1. Follow the LEAN & FREE menus faithfully, making certain to always include Water, Veggie, Grain, Protein, and Fruit.

*Many women who are currently experiencing menopause find that their bodies are more resistant to fat loss. Other individuals are "born" with highly-resistant bodies. Still others develop high resistance to fat loss through years of dieting, meal skipping, and junk-food eating. Regardless of the reason for fat-loss resistance, the guidelines in this section may significantly increase a highly-resistant person's rate of fat loss.

2. Choose only "A" Choice, fruit-juice-sweetened desserts, and be moderate with them, including them *only after* comfortable satisfaction on water, vegetables, grain, protein, and fruit.
3. Eat smaller meals more often, snacking on veggie-based snacks (six smaller meals are ideal).
4. Remember to go a little lighter on the grains and heavier on the veggies, if you have a tendency to do the opposite.
5. Keep your fat intake at 10–15% of your overall calories (or 20% if you do not need to lose excess body fat).
6. Avoid almost all concentrated sugars (like candy) and of course ALL artificial sweeteners, like the plague!
7. Never go more than four to five hours without eating some good veggie-based foods.
8. Exercise aerobically for 20–60 minutes, six days a week.
9. Practice Positive Body Talk everyday!
10. Picture yourself as a lean, healthy, high-energy person.
11. Lose yourself in service to others (this can be as simple as a smiling, happy attitude with your family or co-workers).
12. Use your Success Planners *every day*!
13. Listen to your LEAN & FREE audio or video tapes everyday to motivate, inspire, and teach you correct guidelines.
14. Take life just *one day at a time*.

You can do this...it *will* work for *you*! There's nothing to procrastinate. Both LEAN & FREE and life are fun exciting *journeys*, not destinations. If you aren't happy today, becoming healthy and lean won't make you any happier. So get excited, go for it, and give it 200 percent just for today!

Hypoglycemia: *See page 325.*

Infertility: *See page 335.*

Knee Problems: *See page 320.*

Leg Problems: *See page 320.*

Menopause: *See page 330.*

Morbid Obesity

If you have more than 100 pounds to lose, work closely with your doctor, and follow this program diligently. Make certain not to *starve* yourself, either calorically or nutritionally. And listen to Marie's story on your first Support Group tape.

It is very upsetting to me when I see the messages in television programs about extreme obesity. Such obesity is almost always blamed on one thing—*over eating*, brought on by *emotion* and *lack of self-control*. I heartily disagree. (Read "The Myth of Food Addiction" beginning on page 209 of your Lean & Free 2000 Plus book.)

1. They are calorically and/or nutritionally starved because...
2. They have dieted and/or skipped meals all of their lives in a futile attempt to lose weight and therefore...
3. Their bodies crave fats and sweets. Fats and sweets are stored more easily in fat cells than any other foods offering optimum protection against starvation. The craving and binge behaviors of obese people are therefore *physical*, not *emotional* in most instances! As soon as these people begin following the Lean & Free menus, (usually within only one to two weeks),their cravings are gone!

As you have read in your Lean & Free 2000 Plus book, numerous studies indicate that overall, even with binges taken into account, obese people eat fewer calories than lean people, and the difference in activity levels doesn't even begin to account for the difference in calorie intake!

So please, follow these menus. Feed your body, and **study—study—study**! The information in this program is completely different from any you have heard before. Finally—you are *free*. Knowledge is the key to that freedom. Let go of the guilt and learn. Once your mind catches the vision of Lean & Free, it's only a matter of time before your body follows!

Oh yes, and don't forget your "Enjoying the Freedom" aerobics video. Start with just five minutes on the extra-gentle level. If standing is too difficult, do the arm movements while sitting, or while reclining, propped up. Good luck! You have found the answers—now *you* can succeed!

Muscular Disorders: *See page 319.*

Osteoporosis/Premature Aging/Skin and Hair Problems

Recently, I read in the newspaper of a study on the effects of a well-balanced 1,000 to 1,200 calorie diet, combined with aerobic exercise, on young, premenopausal women aged 18 to 38. The expected outcome was an increase in bone-mass. But the result was quite the opposite—a 3% bone-mass loss! Just imagine what repeated low-calorie dieting can do.

As you study the Body Composition Chart on page 45 of your LEAN & FREE 2000 PLUS book, you'll make an exciting and relieving discovery. Lean muscle, body hydration, and increases in bone mass occur when you *feed* your body. Feed it to be naturally lean, high-energy, and healthy, and don't starve it to be temporarily and artificially skinny (and low-energy, and fatigued).

Remember that you want a beautiful, curvy, dense body, not a withered, saggy, and soft body. If someone asked you: "Would you rather be a size 12 and 120 pounds, or a size 6 and 135 pounds," which would you choose?

SPECIAL NEEDS

Dieting Can:	**LEAN & FREE Can:**
• Decrease bone mass	• Increase bone mass
• Decrease *curvy* muscle mass	• Increase *curvy* muscle mass
• Decrease body hydration	• Increase body hydration
• Increase wrinkles, saggy skin, dry hair, and hair loss.	• Help prevent wrinkles, saggy skin, dry hair, and hair loss.
• Greatly increase risk of disease, stress, and premature aging.	• Greatly decrease risk of disease, stress, and premature aging.

333

I truly believe that by following the principles of LEAN & FREE, we will get about as close to the fountain of youth as we can get.

PHYSICAL HANDICAPS

Work closely with your doctor and therapist in devising an exercise program that meets your individual needs. Learn to listen to your body as you follow the principles of the LEAN & FREE program. If your ability to move is greatly limited, your caloric needs will be less than if you were more mobile. Eating small meals often can help greatly to increase your energy level and accelerate your metabolism. Be careful to satisfy your hunger and energy needs. Cutting calories below your level of comfortable satisfaction or going way beyond this level can reduce your energy and your ability to think clearly, and increase your excess fat stores.

Be creative with your exercise and gently move the areas of your body that function well (for many people this may be the arms). Do the arm movements following the extra-gentle level on your "Enjoying the Freedom" aerobics video if your doctor and physical therapist give you the "go-ahead." If both your upper and lower body are handicapped, start out with deep slow breathing for five minutes, three times a day. This, along with your perfectly balanced LEAN & FREE eating can help greatly to increase the overall good health of your body and decrease excess body fat.

PMS

Pre-menstrual Syndrome is a condition linked to abnormal seratonin metabolism. It requires the advice and assistance of a doctor. LEAN & FREE can be a great benefit to you in your efforts to manage this problem. Make certain to:

1. Follow closely the LEAN & FREE menus, taking care to avoid foods to which you are allergic.
2. Exercise 20 to 60 minutes with your LEAN & FREE aerobics videos and excellent cross-training aerobic machines* at least every other day.
3. Practice *Positive Body Talk* every day.
4. Take life just one day at a time.

See page 90 in your LEAN & FREE 2000 PLUS book for recommendations.

The increase in endorphins, energy, and overall health can make a remarkable difference and improvement in your PMS symptoms and discomfort. (Study the many LEAN & FREE Success Stories in your LEAN & FREE 2000 PLUS book, including Jane's story on page 176.)

PREGNANCY / INFERTILITY / AMENORRHEA

Work closely with your doctor. If you are nauseated the first three to four months, eat very small amounts of good food frequently, and drink plenty of water throughout the day. It is best to eat dry food and do not take solids and liquids together. If your doctor gives the okay, exercise gently three to six days per week for 20 minutes, taking care not to over-heat (this greatly helped my own nausea during pregnancy).

Continue with good LEAN & FREE eating habits and take the supplements recommended by your doctor. Many women on the LEAN & FREE program experience inch loss in their arms, legs, face, and neck throughout their healthy pregnancies, inch loss they didn't experience before the program, even though they were already exercising. (See Toni's story on page 197 of your LEAN & FREE 2000 PLUS book.)

Women with infertility and amenorrhea problems (loss of menstruation) have also been greatly helped by LEAN & FREE principles as they totally avoid caloric, nutrient, physical, and emotional starvation. They often develop the wellness sufficient to signal their bodies that they can now support two lives, not just one, Study Lisa's story on page 194 of your LEAN & FREE 2000 PLUS book. Lisa's husband now refers to this program as the "Eat and Get Pregnant!" program.

Work closely with your doctor regarding your infertility problem. LEAN & FREE is definitely not a cure-all. However, it is true that we are made up of exactly what we eat, and our entire body chemistry changes for the better when we eat the LEAN & FREE way.

Premature Aging: *See page 333.*

Seasonal Affective Dissorder (SAD): *See page 323.*

Self-Esteem: *See page 337.*

Senior Citizens

Isn't it nice to know that the rules are basically the same if you are 2 or 92 years old? My grandfather will be 93 this year, and he is a perfect example of the benefits of the Lean & Free principles. He had a massive heart attack thirty years ago and was not expected to live. Grandpa gradually began incorporating many of the common-sense, livable principles you are learning in this program. Today he still drives, plays pool twice a week, exercises six days a week for 20 to 30 minutes (including lying on the floor and touching his toes behind his head 20 times, and men's push-ups). He eats like a horse and yet says he would love to "gain" a little weight. Grandpa said to me the other day, "My only complaint is, I don't quite have the energy I did in my 80's." Grandpa was told two months ago by his doctor that he had the body of a 65-year-old man. (I might add that his mind is extremely alert, as well.) This is especially amazing, since one-third of his heart is nonfunctioning.

Grandma, at 89, also does very well. She is extremely active mentally, but arthritis is slowing her down physically. The only Lean & Free guidelines that she has not adhered to are regular exercise (she is a very hard worker, but work is not aerobic) and avoidance of soda pop. In her words, "I'd rather be dead than give up my cola!" Well, for 89, I would say she is doing pretty well.

Stay active, maintain a sense of purpose in life, lose yourself in service, and follow *all* of the Lean & Free eating, exercise, and positive-thinking guidelines. Here's to a happy, healthy life and glowing golden years! (Study Luann's, Gib's, Kyle's, Janet's, and Renee's success stories in your Lean & Free 2000 Plus book. These people are all 60 or over.)

Skin Problems: *See page 333.*

SPECIAL NEEDS

STOMACH ACHES / GASTROINTESTINAL DISTRESS

These conditions are often brought on by adding too much fiber to your eating program too quickly (see the *Fiber Progression Chart* on page 13. Adding foods you are allergic to can also cause discomfort as can infrequent eating. (Never go more than four to five hours without eating.) Stuffing or eating beyond the point of comfortable satisfaction can cause distress and pain as well.

Legumes are not tolerated well by some people and can often be a cause of stomach distress. If you have this problem, try taking *Beano* drops* (ask your pharmacist for them) and drink more water when you have chili, split-pea soup, bean soup, etc.

Gastrointestinal problems can have numerous other causes. If symptoms persist, see your doctor immediately.

Stomach Stapling Surgery: *See page 317.*

STRESS CONTROL/SELF-ESTEEM

You have found a large part of the solution right here. The entire LEAN & FREE LIFESTYLE is about *stress control* and *self-esteem*. This program could be renamed, "The Ultimate Self-Esteem/Stress Control Lifestyle"! Dutifully follow every element of this program and chances are strong that your life will even out. You will become your own best friend. Meanwhile, take life just *one day at a time*! Have faith in yourself and tell yourself every day what a remarkable, intelligent, priceless, human being you are—the kind everyone wants to have as a personal friend—especially you! And remember— complete your Success Planners every day to ensure optimum physical and emotional health, *and* stress control.

*Beano drops are a natural food enzyme that aids in the digestion of complex carbohydrates such as whole grains, legumes, vegetables, and fruits.

337

WEIGHT GAIN AS A GOAL

Invariably, at the end of my seminars, someone will ask me what to do to gain weight, or to *muscle-up* a bit. This is what I say:

1. Follow the LEAN & FREE menus, increasing your fat intake (from good fats) to 20–30% by eating more fish, nuts, seeds, avocados, and olives—all high in good cholesterol-fighting fat.

2. Monday, Wednesday, and Friday, do 20 minutes of gentle, yet vigorous aerobic exercise to strengthen your heart, lungs, and immune system and to increase muscle tissue. Tuesday, Thursday, and Saturday do 20 minutes of gentle body-lifting or weight-lifting exercises (work with a professional). Work gradually up to heavier weights and fewer repetitions. This can encourage your muscles to harden and your body to "bulk up" with beautiful, lean muscle.

3. Retire and rise early, getting seven to eight hours of sleep nightly, to maximize growth and repair of muscle tissue.

4. Remember to drink plenty of good, pure water.

5. Avoid foods that are high in sugar. Sugar seems to encourage bodies that are highly resistant to fat-loss to increase fat stores. Ironically, it seems to do just the opposite to bodies that are highly resistant to weight gain. They lose even more weight. Optimum health is followed by the ideal percentage of body fat whether that percentage needs to increase or decrease.

These five guidelines can help you bulk up in a healthy manner while you continue to share meals with the rest of your family. Simply add more cheese, nuts, seeds, avocados, and olives next time you have a salad or potato bar. And appreciate that wonderful, healthy body you are maintaining and enjoying for life!

Food Evaluation Charts and Recipe Indexes

A fat-gram/calorie book, with 10,000 or more foods listed, makes an excellent addition to your nutrition library. Condensed Fat-Gram/Calorie Evaluation Charts are also an essential tool. The next eleven pages contain about 550 of the most commonly-eaten foods, especially those recommended in the LEAN & FREE 2000 PLUS program. These charts offer an invaluable guide to a wonderful world of delicious, wholesome food. Also listed are numerous foods that are best consumed in moderation or, in some cases, avoided completely.

Also included are detailed Restaurant-Food Charts with "A" and "B" ratings. ("C," "D," and "F" ratings are not listed because all three of these categories should be avoided.) You will find examples of fast-food and restaurant-food meals on pages: 17, 18, 21, 23, 24, 25, 26, 54, 56, 64, 67, 70, 79, 85, 90, 97, 103, 113, 115, 119, 121, 125, 127, 131, 133, and 137.

Easy-to-use Fat-Calorie Percent Charts come next, followed by Topical and Alphabetical Recipe Indexes for your convenience.

Fat Gram / Calorie Evaluation Charts

	Serving Size	Fat Grams	Calories		Serving Size	Fat Grams	Calories
ALFALFA				Ground, regular;			
Sprouts	1 cup	tr.*	40	cooked medium	3 oz.	18	244
ALMONDS				T-bone steak;			
Blanched, slivered,				choice, raw	4 oz.	30	348
whole or sliced	1 oz.	15	170	**BEEF DISHES**			
APPLES				**Canned**			
Canned				Stew with vegetables	1 cup	7	186
Applesauce,				Quick & Delicious			
sweetened	1/2 cup	tr.	97	Beef Stew			
Applesauce,				(LEAN & FREE)	1 cup	4	238
unsweetened	1/2 cup	tr.	53	**BEETS**			
Fresh, medium	1	tr.	81	**Canned**			
(Tree Top)	6 oz.	0	90	Diced (Libby)	1/2 cup	0	35
Frozen, not prepared	6 oz.	1	349	**BLUEBERRIES**			
APRICOTS				**Fresh**	1 cup	1	82
Canned, with skin				**BREAD**			
& light syrup	3 halves	tr.	54	(see also *BAGELS,*			
Fresh	3	tr.	51	*MUFFINS*)			
ASPARAGUS				Whole wheat	1 slice	tr.	71
Fresh, cooked	1/2 cup	tr.	22	Cracked wheat			
AVOCADOS	1/2	14	153	(Pepperidge Farm)	1 slice	1	70
BACON				French	1 slice	tr.	75
(see also *BACON*				Honey Wheat Berry			
SUBSTITUTES)				(Roman Meal)	1 slice	1	66
Oscar Mayer; Cooked	1 strip	3	35	Pita, whole wheat,	1 pocket		
Turkey Bacon				regular size	(2 oz.)	2	150
(Butterball)	1 strip	2	30	Rye, Jewish, seeded	1 slice	1	80
Canadian bacon	2 slices	4	86	White	1 slice	1	70
BACON				Whole wheat 100%	1 slice	1	75
SUBSTITUTES				**BROCCOLI**			
Oscar Mayer; Cooked	1 strip	5	54	**Fresh,**			
Breakfast Strips				raw, chopped	1/2 cup	tr.	12
Lean 'n Tasty Pork;				whole; cooked	1/2 cup	tr.	23
cooked				**BRUSSEL SPROUTS**			
(Oscar Mayer)	1 strip	5	54	**Fresh,**			
Sizzlean	1 strip	4	50	cooked	1/2 cup	tr.	30
BAGELS				**BUTTER**			
Cinnamon & Raisin				(see also *BUTTER*			
(Sara Lee)	1	2	240	*BLENDS, BUTTER*			
BAKING POWDER				*SUBSTITUTES,*			
Calumet	1 tsp.	tr.	3	*MARGARINE*)			
BAKING SODA				**Regular**	1 Tbsp.	11	100
Arm & Hammer	1 tsp.	0	0	1 pat	1 tsp.	4	36
BAMBOO SHOOTS,				1 stick	4 oz.	92	813
Sliced	1 cup	1	25	**Whipped**	1 tsp.	13	27
BANANAS,				**BUTTER BLENDS**			
Fresh	1	tr.	105	Honey-Butter	1 Tbsp.	5	34
BEANS				**BUTTER**			
Barbecue Beans,				**SUBSTITUTES**			
(Campbells)	7 7/8 oz.	4	250	(see also *BUTTER*			
Cut Green Beans	1/2 cup	0	20	*BLENDS,*			
Four Bean Salad				*MARGARINE*)			
(Hanover)	1/2	0	80	Butter Buds	1 oz.	0	12
Kidney Beans	1/2	0	120	Butter Buds			
Pork & Beans in				Sprinkles	1/2 tsp.	0	4
Tomato Sauce	8 oz.	3	240	Molly McButter			
Refried Beans				All Natural			
(no fat added)	1/2 cup	tr.	45	Butter Flavor			
BEEF				Sprinkles	1/2 tsp.	0	4
Canned				Molly McButter			
Corned Beef	1 slice (21g)	3	53	Natural Sour			
Fresh				Cream & Butter			
Chuck arm pot roast,				Flavor Sprinkles	1/2 tsp.	0	4
lean only, choice;				**CABBAGE**			
braised	3 oz.	9	199	**Fresh**			
Ground, extra-lean;				green, shredded,			
cooked medium	3 oz.	14	213	raw	1/2 cup	tr.	8

Tr. = A trace of fat. *(Less than one fat gram.)*

FAT GRAM / CALORIE

Item	Serving Size	Fat Grams	Calories
Red, shredded, raw	1/2 cup	tr.	10
Red, shredded; cooked	1/2 cup	tr.	16
CANADIAN BACON			
Oscar Mayer	1 slice	1	35
CANTALOUPE			
Cubed	1 cup	tr.	57
CARROTS			
Canned			
sliced	1/2 cup	0	20
Fresh			
cooked	1/2 cup	0	35
raw	1 cup	0	35
CASHEWS			
dry roasted	1 oz.	13	160
CAULIFLOWER			
Fresh			
cooked	1/2 cup	tr.	15
raw	1/2 cup	tr.	12
CELERY			
diced; cooked	1/2 cup	tr.	11
raw	1 stalk	tr.	6
CEREAL			
(Cereals are listed in A,B,C, and F categories on pages 275 through 278)			
CHEESE (4 oz. grated, "loosely packed" cheese = 1 cup) (see also *COTTAGE CHEESE, CREAM CHEESE*)			
Cheddar	1 oz.	9	110
Colby	1 oz.	9	110
Monterey Jack	1 oz.	9	110
Mozzarella, low moisture, part-skim	1 oz.	5	79
Mozzarella, whole milk	1 oz.	6	90
Parmesan, grated	2 Tbsp.	3	46
Provolone	1 oz.	7	100
Ricotta, fat free	1/4 cup	0	45
Swiss	1 oz.	8	110
CHERRIES			
Canned			
Sweet in water	1/2 cup	tr.	57
Juice, Mountain Cherry Pure & Light	6 oz.	tr.	87
CHESTNUTS			
roasted	1 oz.	tr.	70
roasted	1 cup	3	350
CHICKEN (see also *CHICKEN DISHES*)			
Canned			
Chunk Premium, White (Swanson)	2.5 oz.	2	90
Chunk White & Dark (Swanson)	2.5	4	100
Fresh			
Breast, meat only, roasted	1/2 breast (3 oz.)	3	142
Dark meat with skin; roasted	(5.9 oz.)	26	423
Dark meat without skin; roasted	1 cup	14	286
Light meat with skin; roasted	1/2 chicken (4.6 oz.)	14	293
Lt. meat without skin;	1 cup	6	242
CHICKEN DISHES			
Canned			
Chicken Stew (Chef Boy-ar-dee)	7 oz.	5	140
CHILI			
Chicken Chili (Hormel)	7.5 oz.	3	200
Mixed Vegetarian with beans (Health Valley)	4 oz.	6	120
CHIPS (see also *POPCORN, PRETZELS, SNACKS*)			
Corn Chips (Health Valley)	1 oz.	11	160
Potato Chips	10 chips	7	105
Tortilla:			
Doritos, Cool Ranch	1 oz.	7	140
Nacho Cheese	1 oz.	7	140
Nacho Cheese, Light	1 oz.	4	120
CHOCOLATE (see also *COCOA, ICE CREAM TOPPINGS*)			
Chocolate Flavored Chips (Bakers)	1/4 cup	9	196
Real Semi-Sweet Chocolate Chips (Bakers)	1/4 cup	14	201
CLAMS			
Canned			
meat only	1 cup	3	236
COCOA (see also *CHOCOLATE*)			
Mix			
Hershey's Cocoa	1/3 cup	4	120
COCONUT			
Angel Flake, Bag (Bakers)	1/3 cup	8	116
CORN			
Canned			
Cream Style (Libby)	1/2 cup	0	80
Whole Kernel (Libby)	1/2 cup	1	80
Frozen, 1 ear on the cob; cooked	(2.2 oz.)	tr.	59
CORNSTARCH			
Argo	1 Tbsp.	tr.	30
COTTAGE CHEESE			
Lowfat Land O' Lakes,	4 oz.	2	100
Regular	1/2 cup	5	109
CRAB			
Canned			
Blue	1 cup	2	133

FAT GRAM / CALORIE

341

	Serving Size	Fat Grams	Calories
CRACKERS			
Grahams (Nabisco)	2	1	60
Wheat Thins	8	3	70
CRANBERRIES			
Canned			
Sauce			
Jellied, Old			
Fashioned, (S&W)	1/4 cup	0	90
Fresh			
chopped	1 cup	tr.	54
CREAM			
(see also *SOUR CREAM, SUBSTI- TUTES, WHIPPED TOPPING*)			
Half & Half	1 Tbsp.	2	20
Half & Half	1 cup	28	315
Heavy whipping	1 Tbsp.	6	52
Light, whipping	1 Tbsp.	5	44
Whipped			
Heavy whipping	1 cup	44	411
Light whipping	1 cup	37	345
CREAM CHEESE			
Light Reduced Fat			
Philadelphia Brand Light Cream cheese product	1 oz.	5	60
with chives & onion	1 oz.(2Tbsp.)	9	100
with strawberries	1 oz.	8	90
with pineapple	1 oz.	8	90
CROUTONS			
Croutettes (Kellogg's)	1 cup	tr.	144
CUCUMBERS			
Raw	1 cup	tr.	39
DATES			
Dried, chopped	1 cup	1	489
DIPS			
Creamy Onion Dip (LEAN & FREE)	2 Tbsp.	1	40
Delicious Dill Dip (LEAN & FREE)	2 Tbsp.	1	40
Ranch Dip (LEAN & FREE)	2 Tbsp.	1/2	35
Sour Cream Fruit Dip (LEAN & FREE)	2 Tbsp.	1	52
Spinach-Vegetable Dip (LEAN & FREE)	1/2 cup	tr.	87
EGGS			
(see also *EGG DISHES*)			
Lowered Cholesterol (Full Spectrum Farms)	11 g.	1	60
Fried with butter	1	6.4	83
Raw	1	5.6	79
White only	1	tr.	16
Yoke only	1	5.6	63
EGG DISHES			
(see also *EGGS*)			
Omelets, (LEAN & FREE)	5' x 6'	10	254
Egg Scramble, (LEAN & FREE)	1 cup	10	289

	Serving Size	Fat Grams	Calories
FAT			
(see also *BUTTER, BUTTER BLENDS, BUTTER SUBSTI- TUTES, MARGAR- INE, AND OIL*)			
Crisco	1 Tbsp.	12	110
Beef fat; cooked	1 oz.	20	193
Chicken fat, raw	1 oz.	22	201
Lard	1 Tbsp.	13	115
Pork fat	1 oz.	21	200
Shortening, lard, & vegetable oil	1 Tbsp.	13	115
Turkey fat	1 Tbsp.	13	115
FISH			
(see also *INDIVI- DUAL NAMES*)			
Frozen			
Light Recipe Lightly Breaded Fish Fillet (Gorton's)	1 fillet	7	170
Today's Catch Fish Fillets (Van De Kamp's)	5 oz.	4	100
Value Pack Fish Sticks(Gorton's)	4 sticks	11	210
FLOUR			
All-Purpose (Gold Medal)	1 cup	1	400
Medium Rye (Pillsbury Best)	1 cup	2	400
Whole Wheat (Gold Medal)	1 cup	2	390
FRENCH TOAST			
French Toast (LEAN & FREE)	2 slices	1	191
French toast (regular)	1 slice	14	270
FRUIT DRINKS			
Frozen			
White Grape Juice; as prepared (Seneca)	6 oz.	0	110
Ready-To-Use: Grape	6 oz.	0	94
Ready-To-Use: Orange	6 oz.	0	94
FRUIT, MIXED			
(see also *INDIVIDUAL NAMES*)			
Canned			
Fruit Cocktail in Juice (Dole)	1/2 cup	tr.	56
Tropical Fruit Salad in Juice (Dole)	1/2 cup	tr.	62
FRUIT JUICES			
Cherry, Mountain Cherry (Dole)	6 oz.	0	87
Orange	6 oz.	0	90
Orange-Grapefruit	1 cup	tr.	107
Peach, Orchard Peach (Dole)	6 oz.	0	90

342

Many types of fish contain amega 3 fatty acids, which help to increase HDL levels (good cholesterol) and decrease LDL levels (bad cholesterol). Make certain to avoid deep-fried fish choices, which can be high in fats that can increase not only body fat but also triglyceride and LDL levels. Enjoy baked, broiled, and canned fish choices.

	Serving Size	Fat Grams	Calories
Pineapple Pink Grapefruit (Dole)	6 oz.	tr.	101
Pineapple-Orange-Banana (Dole)	6 oz.	tr.	90
Raspberry, Country Raspberry (Dole)	6 oz.	0	87
GELATIN			
Mix			
dry, unsweetened	1 Tbsp.	tr.	23
GRAPES			
Fresh	10	tr.	36
GRAPEFRUIT			
Fresh	1/2 medium	0	50
GRAVY			
Canned			
Beef (Franco-American)	2 oz.	1	25
Chicken Giblet (Franco-American)	2 oz.	2	30
Mushroom (Franco-American)	2 oz.	1	25
Turkey (Franco-American)	2 oz.	2	30
Dry			
Brown; as prepared	1/4 oz.	0	15
Home Style; as prepared	1/4	0	15
GREEN BEANS			
Canned			
Cut Premium Blue Lake (S&W)	1/2 oz.	0	20
French Natural Pack, (Libby)	1/2 oz.	1	20
HADDOCK			
Frozen			
Today's Catch, Haddock (Van De Kamp's)	5 oz.	0	110
HALIBUT			
Fresh			
Atlantic & Pacific; cooked	3 oz.	4	199
HAM			
(see also *LUNCHEON MEATS & COLD CUTS*)			
Boneless			
Oscar Mayer Breakfast Ham, water added	1 slice (43 g.)	2	52
HAMBURGER			
(see *BEEF*, Ground)			
HONEY	1 Tbsp.	0	60
HONEYDEW MELON			
Cubed	1 cup	tr.	60
ICE CREAM AND FROZEN DESSERT			
Chocolate Ice Milk (Borden)	1/2 cup	2	100
Cookies 'n Cream on a stick	1 bar	15	220

	Serving Size	Fat Grams	Calories
Instant Blueberry Ice Cream (Lean & Free)	1 1/2 cups	3	224
Instant Peach Ice Cream (Lean & Free)	1 1/2 cups	3	176
Orange Sherbet	1/2 cup	1	110
Peach Fruit & Cream, (Chiquita)	1 bar	1	80
Pina Colada Fruit 'n Juice Bars (Dole)	1 bar	tr.	90
Pineapple Sorbet (Dole)	4 oz.	tr.	120
Raspberry Fruit & Yogurt Bars	4 oz.	tr.	120
Strawberry Banana Fruit & Cream	1 bar	2	80
Strawberry Banana Fruit & Juice Bars	1 bar	1	50
Vanilla Ice Cream (Land O'Lakes)	1/2 cup	7	140
Vanilla Ice Milk (Borden)	1/2 cup	2	90
Vanilla Ice Milk, Soft serve	1 cup	5	223
ICE CREAM CONES & CUPS			
Comet Cups	1	0	20
Comet Sugar Cone	1	0	40
ICE CREAM, NON-DAIRY			
Mocha Mix Neapolitan	1/2 cup	7	130
ICE CREAM TOPPINGS			
Hot fudge topping (nonfat)	1 Tbsp.	0	70
Swiss Milk Chocolate Fudge Topping (Smucker's)	2 Tbsp.	1	140
JAM JELLY/ PRESERVES			
All Fruit Jams			
All flavors, Simply Fruit Spread (Smucker's)	1 tsp.	0	16
Blueberry Fruit Spread (Pritikin Foods)	1 tsp.	0	14
Peach Fruit Spread (Pritikin Foods)	1 tsp.	0	14
All Fruit Jams (Lean & Free)	2 Tbsp.	tr.	32
JICAMA,			
Raw—sliced	1 cup	tr.	50
JUICE			
(see *FRUIT JUICES*)			
KIDNEY BEANS			
Canned			
Red, kidney	1 cup	1	216
KIWIFRUIT	1	tr.	46
KETCHUP	1 Tbsp.	0	6
LEMON JUICE			
(Seneca)	1 Tbsp.	0	6

	Serving Size	Fat Grams	Calories
LENTILS			
Canned			
cooked	1 cup	tr.	258
LETTUCE			
Iceberg	1 leaf	tr.	3
Romaine; shredded	12 cup	tr.	4
LOBSTER			
Frozen			
Northern; cooked	1 cup	1	142
Home Recipe;			
Newburg	1 cup	27	485
LUNCHEON MEATS/			
COLD CUTS			
(see also *CHICKEN*			
HAM, TURKEY)			
Carl Budding Beef	1 oz.	2	40
Oscar Mayer			
Corned Beef	1 slice	tr.	16
Oscar Mayer			
Honey Loaf	1 slice	1	32
Oscar Mayer			
Pastrami	1 slice	tr.	16
Oscar Mayer			
Smoked Beef	1 slice	tr.	14
MARGARINE			
Reduced Calorie			
Blue Bonnet	1 Tbsp.	6	50
Fleischmann's	1 Tbsp.	6	50
Kraft Spread	1 Tbsp.	6	50
Regular			
Blue Bonnet	1 Tbsp.	11	100
Fleischmann's	1 Tbsp.	11	100
Parkay	1 Tbsp.	11	100
MARSHMALLOW			
Campfire (Borden)	21 g.	0	40
Miniature (Kraft)	10	0	18
MAYONNAISE			
(see also			
MAYONNAISE-			
TYPE SALAD			
DRESSING)			
FAT FREE			
Kraft Free Nonfat			
Mayonnaise			
Dressing	1 Tbsp.	0	12
Reduced Calorie			
Best Foods Light	1 Tbsp.	5	50
Regular			
Best Foods Real	1 Tbsp.	11	100
Best Foods Real	1 cup	175	1570
MAYONNAISE-TYPE			
SALAD DRESSINGS			
(see also			
MAYONNAISE)			
Fat Free			
Kraft Free Miracle			
Whip Nonfat			
Dressing	1 Tbsp.	0	12
Regular			
Miracle Whip Salad			
Dressing	1 Tbsp.	7	70
Delicious Buttermilk			
Dressing (LEAN &			
FREE)	2 Tbsp.	1	42
MELONS			
(see also *INDIVI-*			
DUAL NAMES)			

	Serving Size	Fat Grams	Calories
Frozen			
Melon balls	1 cup	tr.	55
MEXICAN FOOD			
(see also *CHIPS,*			
DINNER, SNACKS)			
Canned			
Enchilada Sauce, hot	1 oz.	0	12
Enchilada sauce,			
mild	1 oz.	0	12
Picante salsa	1 oz.	0	10
Red taco sauce,			
mild	2 Tbsp.	0	10
Frozen			
3 Chicken Enchiladas			
(El Charrito)	11 oz.	13	440
Shredded Beef			
Enchilada with Rice			
& Corn, Mexican			
Classic (Van De			
Kamp's)	14.75 oz.	15	490
Tortillas, corn	2	1	95
Tortillas, flour	2	4	170
Home Recipe			
Taco salad	1 cup	20	292
Taco Salad			
(LEAN & FREE)	11/2 cup	10	247
Mix			
Taco meat seasoning,			
mild	1 oz.	1	90
Taco meat seanoning,			
mild; as prepared			
with ground beef	3 oz.	12	180
MILK			
(see also			
CHOLOLATE,			
COCOA)			
Canned			
Carnation			
Evaporated	1/2 cup	10	170
Carnation			
Evaporated; Lowfat	1/2 cup	3	110
Carnation			
Evaporated,			
Skimmed	1/2 cup	tr.	100
Carnation			
Sweetened,			
Condensed	1 oz.	3	123
Eagle Sweetened			
Condensed	1/3 cup	9	320
Pet Lite Evaporated,			
Skimmed	1/2 cup	0	100
Dried			
Carnation Nonfat			
Dry; as prepared			
with water	8 oz.	tr.	80
Buttermilk,			
Sweet Cream	1 Tbsp.	tr.	25
Liquid, Low-fat			
1%	1 cup	3	102
2%	1 cup	5	121
Lactaid	1 cup	0	102
Buttermilk	1 cup	2	99
Whey, sweet	1 cup	1	66
Liquid, Regular			
Goat milk	1 cup	10	168
Human milk	1 oz.	14	21
Whole, 3.3% fat	1 cup	8	150

	Serving Size	Fat Grams	Calories
Liquid, Skim			
Skim	1 cup	tr.	86
Non-Fat Solids added	1 cup	tr.	90
MINERAL WATER			
Bottled			
Artesian	7 oz.	0	0
MOLASSES			
Brer Rabbit, Dark	1 Tbsp.	0	60
MOUSSE			
Chocolate Mousse, No Bake Dessert; as prep (Jell-O)	1/2 cup	5	141
MUFFINS			
(LEAN & FREE) (see pages 226 through 234)			
MUFFIN MIXES			
Corn Muffin; as prepared (Dromedary)	1	4	120
Wild Blueberry; as prepared (Duncan Hines)	1	3	110
Oat Bran Raisin (Health Valley)	2 oz.	3	140
MUSHROOMS			
Canned			
Mushrooms (Libby)	1/4 cup	0	35
Fresh			
Raw; sliced	1/2 cup	tr.	9
MUSTARD			
Grey Poupon Dijon	1 Tbsp.	1	18
Kraft Pure Prepared	1 Tbsp.	0	4
NECTARINES			
Fresh	1	tr.	67
NOODLES			
(see also **PASTA DINNERS**)			
Canned			
Chow mein noodles	1/2 cup	5	228
Dry			
Chow mein noodles (La Choy)	1/2 cup	8	150
Egg Noodles (Creamette)	2 oz.	3	221
Noodles & Sauce, Beef as prep (Lipton)	1/4 pkg.	2	128
Ramen Noodles with Chicken Flavoring; as prepared (La Choy)	1/2 pkg.	7	190
Spinach Egg Noodles	2 oz.	2	209
Whole Wheat Lasagna Noodles	2 oz. dry	2	210
Whole Wheat Spaghetti Noodles, cooked	1 cup	tr.	200
NUTS, Mixed			
(see also **INDIVIDUAL NAMES**)			
Mixed Nuts, Dry Roasted (Planters)	1 oz.	15	170
OATS	1 oz.(1/3 cup)	2	100

	Serving Size	Fat Grams	Calories
OIL			
(see also **FAT**)			
Crisco	1 Tbsp.	14	120
Coconut	1 Tbsp.	14	120
Corn	1 Tbsp.	14	120
Cottonseed	1 Tbsp.	14	120
Mazola	1 Tbsp.	14	120
Mazola No Stick Spray	2.5 sec spray	1	6
Olive	1 Tbsp.	14	119
Palm	1 Tbsp.	14	120
Planters Peanut	1 Tbsp.	14	120
Puritan (canola)	1 Tbsp.	14	120
Rapeseed (canola)	1 Tbsp.	14	120
Safflower	1 Tbsp.	14	120
Soybean	1 Tbsp.	14	120
Sunflower	1 Tbsp.	14	120
Sunflower	1/4 cup	54	482
Sunflower	1/2 cup	109	964
Sunflower	1 cup	218	1927
Wheat germ	1 Tbsp.	14	120
ONION			
Fresh			
Chopped	1 cup	tr.	48
OLIVES			
Canned			
Ripe, Pitted, Large (S&W)	8 small	3	30
ORANGES			
Fresh	1	tr.	62
Frozen			
Orange Juice Prepared	1 cup	tr.	112
Canned			
Mandarin oranges in light syrup	1 cup	tr.	125
ORIENTAL FOOD			
Canned			
Chun King Divider Pak Beef Chow Mein	7 oz.	2	100
Chicken Chow Mein	8 oz.	4	120
Pork Chow Mein	7 oz.	4	120
Shrimp Chow Mein	7 oz.	2	100
La Choy Beef Pepper Oriental	3/4 cup	2	90
La Choy Chow Mein, Beef	3/4 cup	1	60
Chicken	3/4 cup	2	70
Shrimp	3/4 cup	1	45
Sweet & Sour Oriental with Chicken	3/4 cup	2	240
Choy Mein Noodles	1/2 cup	5	228
Chow Mein with Chicken	1 cup	tr.	95
Chow Mein with Pork (LEAN & FREE)	1 cup	8	302
Sweet and Sour Chicken (LEAN & FREE)	3/4 cup	4	396
Frozen			
Birds Eye Chinese Style Stir-Fry Vegetable	1/2 cup	tr.	36

	Serving Size	Fat Grams	Calories
Birds Eye Chow Mein Style International Recipe	1/2 cup	4	89
Chun King Imperial Chicken	13 oz.	1	294
Chun King Szechuan Beef	13 oz.	2	331
La Choy Shrimp Chow Mein	2/3 cup	1	70
Shrimp Egg Roll	3 small	2	80
Fresh & Lite Beef Broccoli	11 oz.	7	290
Fresh & Lite Sweet & Sour Chicken	10 oz.	4	280
PANCAKES			
Krusteaz Whole Wheat & Honey Pancake Mix	three 4" pancakes	1	215
Krusteaz Buckwheat Pancake Mix	three 4" pancakes	3	215
LEAN & FREE (see pages 176 and 177)			
PANCAKE/WAFFLE SYRUP			
(see also *SYRUP*)			
Karo Pancake Syrup	1 Tbsp.	0	60
Log Cabin Syrup, Buttered	1 oz.	tr.	106
PASTA			
(see also *NOODLES, PASTA DINNERS, PASTA SALAD*)			
Dry			
Elbow macaroni	2 oz.	1	210
Lasagna jumbo	2 oz.	1	210
Lasagna, Whole Wheat	2 oz.	1	170
Ribbon Pasta, Whole Wheat (Pritikin Foods)	2 oz.	2	220
Spaghetti, regular & thin	2 oz.	1	210
Whole Wheat (Health Valley)	2 oz.	1	170
Cooked			
Macaroni	1 cup	1	155
Egg Noodles	1 cup	2	200
PASTA DINNERS			
(see also *PASTA SALAD*)			
Chef•Boy•ar•dee ABC's & 1,2,3's in sauce	7.5 oz.	1	160
Beef Ravioli	7 oz.	5	180
Cheese Ravioli in Beef & Tomato Sauce	7.5 oz.	3	200
Chicken Ravioli	7.5 oz.	4	180
Dinosaurs in Spaghetti Sauce with Cheese Flavor	7.5 oz.	1	155
Macaroni Shells in Tomato Sauce	7.5 oz.	1	150

	Serving Size	Fat Grams	Calories
Franco-American PizzO's	7.5 oz.	2	170
Spaghetti-O's	7 3/8 oz.	2	170
Mama Leone's Pasta Supreme Mini Lasagna	7.5 oz.	1	170
Dry Mix			
Chef•Boy•ar•dee Spaghetti Dinner with Mushroom Sauce	7.9 oz.	1	210
Lipton Pasta & Sauce Cheddar Broccoli with Fusilli; as prepared	1/2 cup	2	137
Creamy Garlic; as prepared	1/2 cup	tr.	144
Herb Tomato; as prepared	1/2 cup	tr.	130
PASTA SALAD			
Frozen			
Italian Pasta Salad (Hanover)	1/2 cup	0	60
Oriental Pasta Salad (Hanover)	1/2 cup	0	80
PEACHES			
Canned			
halves in own juice	1 cup	tr.	109
Fresh	1	tr.	37
Juice			
Pure & Light (Dole)	6 oz.	tr.	102
PEANUT BUTTER			
Jif Creamy	2 Tbsp.	16	190
Jif Crunchy	2 Tbsp.	16	190
Skippy Creamy	2 Tbsp.	17	190
Skippy Creamy	1 cup	135	1540
PEANUTS			
Dry roasted	1 oz.	14	170
PEARS			
Canned,			
halves in own juice	1 cup	tr.	123
halves in light syrup	1 cup	tr.	144
Fresh	1	0	98
PEAS			
Canned			
green	1/2 cup	tr.	61
Dried			
split; cooked	1 cup	1	231
Frozen			
Chinese Pea Pods (Chun King)	6 oz.	0	8
PECANS			
halves, dried	1 cup	73	721
PECTIN			
Sure-Jell Fruit Pectin	1/4 pkg.	0	38
PEPPERS			
Canned			
green & red, sweet, chopped	1/2 cup	tr.	13
PICKLES			
Vlasic Bread & Butter Sweet Butter Chips	1 oz.	0	30
Kosher Dill Spears	1 oz.	0	4

	Serving Size	Fat Grams	Calories
PIE			
(see also *PIE CRUST*)			
Frozen			
Banquet			
Apple	3.33 oz.	11	250
Cherry	3.33 oz.	11	250
Lemon	2.33 oz.	9	170
Peach	3.33 oz.	11	245
Pumpkin	3.33 oz.	8	200
Strawberry	2.33 oz.	9	170
Mix			
Jell-O			
Banana Cream; as			
prepared with	1/6 of		
whole milk	8" pie	3	107
Coconut Cream; as			
prepared with	1/6 of		
whole milk	8" pie	5	115
Lemon; as prepared	1/6 of		
	8" pie	2	180
Royal			
Key Lime Pie			
Filling; as prepared	1/2 cup	3	160
Real Cheese Cake			
(No Bake)	1/8 pie	9	280
PIE CRUST			
(see also *PIE*)			
Frozen			
Mrs. Smith's	1/8 of 9 5/8"		
Pie Shell	Shell	8	130
Pet-Ritz			
Deep Dish	1/6 shell	8	130
Graham Cracker	1/6 shell	6	110
Home Recipe	1 9" pie	60	900
PINE NUTS			
Pignolia, dried	1 Tbsp.	5	51
PINEAPPLE			
Canned			
All Cuts in Juice			
(Dole)	1/2 cup	tr.	70
Crushed	1 cup	tr.	140
Fresh			
diced	1 cup	tr.	77
Frozen			
juice	1 cup	tr.	139
PINTO BEANS			
Canned	1 cup	tr.	186
PIZZA			
Frozen			
Canadian-style bacon	1 pizza		
	9.25 oz.	26	550
Croissant Pastry			
Deluxe			
(Pepperidge Farm)	1 pizza	27	520
Cheese	1/7 of 10"	4	140
Mix			
Chef•Boy•ar•dee			
2 Complete Cheese			
Pizzas	3.16 oz.	5	210
Sauce			
Ragu			
Pizza Quick Sauce,			
Chunky Style	3 Tbsp.	2	45
Pizza Quick Sauce,			
with Mushrooms	3 Tbsp.	2	40

	Serving Size	Fat Grams	Calories
PIZZA WHEELS			
(LEAN & FREE) see			
page 152			
PLUMS			
Canned			
purple, in own juice	3	tr.	55
Fresh	1	tr.	36
POPCORN			
(see also *CHIPS,*			
PRETZELS,			
SNACKS)			
Jiffy Pop, Microwave			
Butter Flavor; as			
prepared	4 cups	7	140
Air Popped	1 cup	tr.	30
Microwave light			
butter flavor	3 cups	3	80
POT PIE			
Beef (Banquet)	7 oz.	29	439
Chunky Chicken			
(Swanson)	10 oz.	33	580
Hungry-Man Turkey			
(Swanson)	16 oz.	38	690
POTATOES			
(see also *CHIPS*)			
Fresh Baked, Flesh			
& Skin	1(6.5 oz.)	tr.	220
Cheddar Browns			
(Ore-Ida)	3 oz.	2	90
Hash Browns,			
shredded (Ore-Ida)			
(uncooked)	3 oz.	tr.	70
Tater Tots (uncooked)			
(Ore-Ida)	3 oz.	7	140
Tater Tots, Microwave			
(uncooked) (Ore-Ida)	2 oz.	9	200
Mix			
Mashed, not prepared	1/3 cup	0	70
Potato Salad,			
Classic Idaho,			
as prepared (Lipton)	1/2 cup	tr.	94
Potato Salad,			
German, as			
prepared (Lipton)	1/2 cup	tr.	99
Potatoes & Sauce			
AuGratin as			
prepared (Lipton)	1/2 cup	tr.	108
Beef & Mushroom,			
as prepared			
(Libby)	1/2 cup	tr.	95
Cheddar Bacon, as			
prepared (Lipton)	1/2 cup	1	106
Cheddar Broccoli,			
as prepared			
(Lipton)	1/2 cup	1	104
Chicken Flavored			
Mushroom, as			
prepared (Lipton)	1/2 cup	tr.	90
Italiano, as			
prepared (Lipton)	1/2 cup	2	107
Nacho, as prepared			
(Lipton)	1/2 cup	1	103
Scalloped, as			
prepared (Lipton)	1/2 cup	2	102
POTATO STARCH			
Potato starch	1 cup	0	570

FAT GRAM / CALORIE

	Serving Size	Fat Grams	Calories
PRETZELS (see also *CHIPS, POPCORN, SNACKS*)			
Twist, tiny	14 pieces	1	109
PRUNES			
Dried	10	tr.	201
Juice	1 cup	tr.	181
PUDDING			
Mix			
Banana Cream Instant (Jell-O)	1 pkg. (3.6 oz.)	tr.	360
Butterscotch (Jell-O)	1 pkg. (3.6 oz.)	tr.	364
Chocolate (Jell-O)	1 pkg. (3.5 oz.)	1	346
Chocolate Tapioca Americana (Jell-O)	1 pkg. (3.5 oz.)	2	378
French Vanilla, Instant (Jell-O)	1 pkg. (3.5 oz.)	tr.	360
PUMPKIN			
Canned	1/2 cup	1	40
RADISHES			
Fresh, raw	10	tr.	7
RAISINS			
California seedless	1/2 cup	0	250
RASPBERRIES			
Fresh, red	1 cup	1	61
Frozen, red			
Whole in Lite Syrup (Birds Eye)	1/2 cup	tr.	99
Juice, Pure & Light (Dole)	6 oz.	tr.	87
RICE			
Brown, cooked	1/2 cup	tr.	90
Birds Eye Rice & Peas with Mushrooms	2/3 cup	tr.	108
Birds Eye Spanish Style International Rice	1/2 cup	tr.	111
White			
Long Grain, cooked	2 oz.	0	61
RICE CAKES			
7 Grain Rice Cakes (Pritikin Foods)	1	0	35
ROUGHY			
Orange, raw	3 oz.	6	107
SALAD (see also *PASTA SALAD*)			
Home Recipe			
Chef	1.5 cups	28	386
Tossed	1 cup	tr.	32
SALAD DRESSING			
Buttermilk Farm Style; as prepared (Good Seasons)	1 Tbsp.	6	58
Ready-To-Use-Reduced Calorie			
Bacon & Tomato (Kraft)	1 Tbsp.	2	30
Buttermilk Creamy (Kraft)	1 Tbsp.	3	30
Thousand Island (Kraft)	1 Tbsp.	2	30

	Serving Size	Fat Grams	Calories
SALMON			
Canned			
Pink (Bumble Bee)	3 oz.	7	137
Fresh, steak	3.5 oz.	15	220
SAUSAGE			
Polish (Oscar Mayer)	1 (2.7 oz.)	20	229
Vienna, canned, beef & pork	1 sausage	4	45
SCALLOPS			
Frozen			
Lightly Breaded Scallops (King & Prince)	3.5 oz.	tr.	120
SCONES			
Home recipe	1 (1/4 oz.)	6	130
SHRIMP			
Canned	1 cup	3	154
Frozen			
Fried Shrimp (Mrs. Paul's)	3 oz.	11	200
Gourmet Hand Breaded Shrimp Round (King & Prince)	3.5 oz.	tr.	150
Shrimp Pimavera (Mrs. Paul's)	11 oz.	4	240
Shrimp Scampi (Gorton's)	1 pkg.	24	350
Home recipe			
Breaded & Fried	3 oz.	10	206
SNACKS (nutritious) (see also *CHIPS, NUTS, MIXED, POPCORN, PRETZELS*)			
Cheddar Lites (Health Valley)	2 oz.	2	40
Cheddar Lites with green onion (Health Valley)	2 oz.	1	40
Wheat Snax (Estee)	1 oz.	1	110
SNAPPER			
Cooked	1 fillet (6 oz.)	3	217
SODA			
Apple Sparkling (Welch's)	12 oz.	0	180
Root Beer (Hire's)	6 oz.	0	90
Sprite	6 oz.	0	71
SOLE			
Frozen			
Au Natural Sole Fillets (Mrs. Paul's)	4 oz.	2	90
Today's Catch, Baby Sole (Van De Kamp's)	5 oz.	1	100
SOUP			
Canned, **Ready-To-Serve**			
Bean with Ham, Chowder (Hormel Micro-Cup, Hearty)	9.5 oz.	3	191
Bean with Ham (Campbell's Chunky Old Fashioned)	9.5 oz.	8	250

	Serving Size	Fat Grams	Calories
Beef (Campbell's Chunky)	9.5 oz.	4	170
Beef Hearty (Campbell's Home Cookin')	9.5 oz.	3	130
Chicken (Campbell's Chunky Old Fashioned)	9.5 oz.	4	150
Chicken Barley (Progresso)	9.5 oz.	3	120
Chicken Broth	1 cup	1	39
Chicken with Noodles (Campbell's Home Cookin')	9.5 oz.	3	120
Campbell's Chunky Chicken w/ Rice	9.5 oz.	4	140
Chicken Vegetable	9.5 oz.	6	170
Chili Beef	9.75 oz.	6	260
Clam Chowder, Manhattan	9.5 oz.	4	150
Pea, Split with Ham	9.5 oz.	5	210
Pepper Steak	9.5	3	160
Campbell's Chunky Steak and Potato	9.5 oz.	4	170
Campbell's Home Cookin'; Lentil, Garden	9.5 oz.	3	130
Lentil Hearty (Campbell's Home Cookin')	9.5 oz.	1	150
Vegetable Beef (Campbell's Old Fashioned)	9.5 oz.	5	160
Canned, Condensed and Prepared According to Directions			
Campbell's			
Bean with Bacon	8 oz.	4	120
Beef,	8 oz.	2	80
Chicken Broth and Noodles	8 oz.	2	35
Chicken, Cream of	8 oz.	7	110
Mushroom, Cream of	8 oz.	7	100
Potato, Cream of	8 oz.	3	70
Tomato	8 oz.	2	90
Healthy Request			
Bean with Bacon	8 oz.	4	140
Cream of Chicken, prepared	8 oz.	2	70
Cream of Chicken, condensed	10 3/4 oz.	5.5	193
Cream of Mushroom, condensed	10 3/4 oz.	5.5	165
Cream of Mushroom, prepared	8 oz.	2	60
Vegetable	8 oz.	2	90
Chicken Noodle	8 oz.	2	60
Tomato	8 oz.	2	90
SOUR CREAM			
(see also SOUR CREAM SUBSTITUTES)			
Fat Free	1 Tbsp.	0	10
Lowfat	1 cup	0	160
Lean Cream (Land O' Lakes)	1 Tbsp.	1	20
Regular			
Sour Cream	1 Tbsp.	3	26
Sour Cream	1 cup	48	493
SOUR CREAM SUBSTITUTES			
Imitation, nondairy	1 cup	45	479
SPAGHETTI SAUCE			
(see also PIZZA, TOMATO)			
Bottled			
Chef Boy·ar·dee			
Meatless	4 oz.	3	90
w/Ground Beef	4 oz.	3	90
w/Mushrooms	4 oz.	2	70
Econo-Sauce (LEAN & FREE)	3/4 cup	tr.	62
Ragu Chunky Garden style, Extra Tomatoes, Garlic, and Onions	4 oz.	2	80
Ragu Homestyle with Mushrooms	4 oz.	2	70
SPINACH			
Fresh			
cooked	1/2 cup	tr.	21
Chopped, raw	1/2 cup	tr.	6
SQUASH			
(see also ZUCCHINI)			
Fresh			
Acorn, cubed, baked	1/2 cup	tr.	57
Summer, all varieties, raw, sliced	1/2 cup	tr.	13
STRAWBERRIES			
Fresh	1 cup	tr.	45
STUFFING/ DRESSING			
Mix			
Chicken (Stove Top)	1/2 cup	9	181
Corn Bread (Pepperidge Farm)	1 oz.	1	110
Herb Seasoned (Pepperidge Farm)	1 oz.	1	110
SUGAR			
Brown	1 cup	0	836
Powdered	1 cup	0	493
White, granulated	1 cup	0	770
SUNFLOWER SEEDS			
(Planters)	1 oz.	14	160
SWEET POTATOES			
Canned			
In syrup	1/2 cup	tr.	106
Mashed	1/2 cup	tr.	233
Fresh			
(baked in skin)	3.5 oz.	tr.	118
SYRUP *(see also PANCAKE/ WAFFLE SYRUP)*			
Maple	2 Tbsp.	0	110
TANGERINE			
Fresh	1	tr.	37

FAT GRAM / CALORIE

349

	Serving Size	Fat Grams	Calories
TOMATO			
(see also PIZZA, SPAGHETTI SAUCE)			
Canned			
Stewed Tomatoes (S&W)	1/2 cup	0	35
Red, whole	1 cup	tr.	47
Tomato paste	1/2 cup	1	110
Tomato sauce	1 cup	tr.	74
Fresh	1	tr.	30
Juice	6 oz.	tr.	32
TORTILLAS			
Corn	1	0	45
Taco shell	1	2	50
Flour	1	2	85
Taco salad shell	1	12	200
Whole wheat	1	2	93
TROUT			
Rainbow, cooked	1 fillet (2.1 oz.)	3	94
TUNA			
Canned			
Chunk Light in Oil (Bumble Bee)	3 oz.	15	200
Chunk Light in Water (Bumble Bee)	3 oz.	2	90
TURKEY			
Canned			
Turkey with broth	1/2 can (2.5 oz.)	5	116
Fresh			
Ground Lean 90% Fat Free; cooked (Louis Rich)	3.5 oz.	9	183
Dark meat with skin, roasted	3.6 oz.	11	222
Dark meat without skin, roasted	1 cup	10	260
Light Meat with skin, roasted	4.8 oz.	10	260
Light meat without skin, roasted	1 cup	4	215
Ready-To-Use			
Breast, Honey Roasted (Louis Rich)	1 slice (2.9 g.)	tr.	29
Breast, Oven Roasted (Louis Rich)	1 oz.	tr.	30
TURNIPS			
Fresh			
cubed, raw	1/2 cup	tr.	18
VANILLA EXTRACT			
Pure	1 tsp.	0	10
VEGETABLES, Mixed			
(see also INDIVIDUAL VEGETABLES)			
Frozen			
Brussels Sprouts, Cauliflower & Carrots, Farm Fresh Mixtures (Birds Eye)	3/4 cup	tr.	40
Chinese Style Stir-Fry Vegetable (Birds Eye)	1/2 cup	tr.	36
VINEGAR			
Apple cider	2 Tbsp.	0	4
WAFFLES			
Frozen Ready-To-Use			
Raisins, Bran & Whole Grain Nutri-Grain (Eggo)	1	5	130
WATER CHESTNUTS			
Water Chestnuts (La Choy)	1/4 cup	tr.	16
WATERMELON			
cubed	1 cup	tr.	50
WHEAT			
Durum	1 cup	5	650
Hard red	1 cup	3	628
Hard white	1 cup	3	656
Soft white	1 cup	3	571
Bulgur, cooked	1 cup	tr.	152
Sprouted	1 cup	1	214
WHIPPED TOPPING			
(see also CREAM)			
Cool Whip (non-dairy)	1 Tbsp.	tr.	11
Dream Whip as prepared	1 Tbsp.	tr.	9
YEAST			
Baker's Dry, Active	1 pkg. (7 g.)	tr.	20
YOGURT			
Regular			
Fruit, lowfat	1 cup	3	232
Fruit, nonfat	1 cup	0	200
Plain, lowfat	1 cup	3.5	144
Plain, skim milk	1 cup	tr.	127
Vanilla, lowfat	1 cup	3	194
Vanilla, nonfat	1 cup	0	180
Frozen			
Mixed Berries On-a Stick (Dannon)	1 bar	1	50
Vanilla (Colombo)	4 oz.	2	99
ZUCCHINI			
Fresh			
Sliced; cooked	1/2 cup	tr.	14
Sliced, raw	1/2 cup	tr.	9

FAT GRAM / CALORIE

SPECIAL NOTICE

*These charts have been especially fine-tuned for your optimal health needs. They will heighten your awareness of foods you should eat abundantly and foods you should avoid or eat in moderation. These lists contain the vast majority of foods you'll be eating, so study them **very** carefully.*

RESTAURANT-FOOD EVALUATION CHARTS

"A" = Optimum Health and Fat-Loss Choice

"B" = Coasting Choice *(Avoid "B" Choice desserts such as lowfat shakes and frozen yogurt if you are diabetic or resistant to fat loss.)*

No Rating = "C", "D", or "F" = Fat-Storing, Marginal to Poor Health Choices. *(These choices are not rated because you should be avoiding **all three** categories.)*

Ratings are based on the fat, cholesterol, fiber, complex carbohydrate protein, sugar, and overall nutrient content of the foods listed. Many "B" Choices can be advanced to "A" Choices by omitting such items as butter, mayonnaise, oil, cheese, and sour cream, and by asking for additional vegetables (tomatoes, pickles, onions, sprouts, green peppers, etc.) and whole-grain bread or buns, if available.

Many restaurants change their menus frequently. To keep a current fat gram/calorie listing of the foods offered by your favorite restaurants, request this information from them at least once a year and then highlight those foods that fall into "A" and "B" categories. Refer to these lists often to keep you on the fat-burning, high-energy track and out of the fat-storing low-energy trenches.

		Serving Size	Fat Grams	Calories	Fat %
ARBY'S					
	Junior Roast Beef	3.1 oz.	10.8	233	42%
	Regular Roast Beef	5.5 oz.	18.2	383	43%
	Beef 'n Cheddar	6.9 oz.	26.5	508	47%
	Bacon 'n Cheddar Deluxe	8.1 oz.	31.5	512	55%
	Super Roast Beef	9.0 oz.	28.3	552	46%
B–	Hot Ham 'n Cheese Sandwich	6.0 oz.	14.2	355	36%
A	Light Roast Turkey Deluxe	6.8 oz.	6	260	21%
	Fish Fillet Sandwich	7.8 oz.	27	526	46%
	Philly Beef 'n Swiss	7 oz.	25.3	467	49%
A	Light Roast Chicken Deluxe	6.8 oz.	7	276	23%
	Chicken Club Sandwich	8.4 oz.	27	503	48%
A	Tossed Salad with Low-Calorie Italian Dressing	5.3 oz.	0.3	25	11%
A	Baked Potato, Plain	8.5 oz.	1.9	240	7%
	Deluxe Baked Potato	12.3	36.4	621	53%

351

		Serving Size	Fat Grams		Fat Grams	Calories	Fat %
B–	Broccoli & Cheddar Baked Potato	12 oz.	1		17.9	417	39%
	Superstuffed Potato Mushroom & Cheese Baked Potato	12.3 oz.	1		26.7	515	47%
	Superstuffed Potato, Butter/Sour Cream	11 oz.	1		25.2	463	49%
	French Fries	2.5 oz.		1 order	13.2	246	48%
	Potato Cakes	3 oz.	1		12	204	53%
	Vanilla Shake	11 oz.	1		11.5	330	31%
	Chocolate Shake	12 oz.	1		11.6	451	23%
B–	French Dip	5.4 oz.	1		15.4	368	38%
B–	Arby Q	6.7 oz.	1		15.2	389	35%
	Grilled Chicken Deluxe	8.1 oz.	1		19.9	430	42%
B	Grilled Chicken Barbeque	7.1 oz.	1		13.1	386	31%
B	Turkey Sub	9.7 oz.	1		19	486	35%
B	Roast Chicken Salad	14 oz.	1		7.2	204	32%
B	Light Roast Beef Deluxe	6.4 oz.	1		10	294	31%
	BIG BOY'S (JB'S)						
A	Baked Potato	med.	1		0.2	163	1%
B	Frozen Yogurt		1		0.0	72	0%
B–	Breast of Chicken	Dinner	1		13	349	34%
B–	Cajun Chicken	Dinner	1		13	349	34%
B+	Cajun Cod	Dinner	1		12	364	30%
A	Chicken 'n Vegetable Stir-Fry	Dinner	1		14	562	22%
B+	Cod, Baked or Broiled	Dinner	1		12	364	30%
	Cod Dijon, Baked or Broiled	Dinner	1		18	427	38%
A	Spaghetti Marinara	Dinner	1		6	450	12%
A	Vegetable Stir-Fry	Dinner	1		10	408	22%
B+	Pitas (sandwich only) Breast of Chicken with Mozzarella		1		13	404	29%
A	Turkey Pita		1		5	224	20%
	Soups & Salads						
A	Cabbage Soup	bowl	1		0.5	43	10%
A–	Chicken Breast Salad with Dijon (includes 1/2 pita bread)		1		11	391	25%
A	Dinner Salad		1		0.2	19	9%

	Serving Size	Fat Grams	Calories	Fat %
BURGER KING				
B– Hamburger	103 g.	1	10	260	35%
Cheeseburger	115 g.	1	14	300	42%
Whopper Sandwich	270 g.	1	38	630	54%
Double Whopper	351 g.	1	55	860	58%
Double Whopper					
with Cheese	375 g.	1	63	950	60%
Whopper Jr	133 g.	1	19	330	52%
Whopper with Cheese	294 g.	1	46	720	58%
BK Big Fish Sandwich	255 g.	1	43	710	55%
B BK Broiler Chicken					
Sandwich	154 g.	1	10	280	32%
(Add extra veggies and					
no sauce = 4 fat grams,					
220 calories, and 16%					
fat = "A" Choice.)					
Chicken Sandwich	229 g.	1	42	700	54%
Chicken Tenders	90 g.	6 pieces	13	236	50%
Chef Salad	273 g.	1	9	178	46%
A– Chunky Chicken Salad	258 g.	1 salad	4	142	25%
Onion Rings	97 g.	1 order	19	339	50%
French Fries					
(medium salted)	116 g.	1 order	20	372	48%
A Salad Bar *(typical)*					
without Dressing		1	0	28	0%
Garden Salad without					
Dressing	223 g.	1	5	95	47%
Salad Dressing		1 pkg.	23-26	260-280	80–84%
B– Reduced Calorie Italian					
Salad Dressing	30 g.	1 pkg.	1	15	60%
Bacon, Egg, Cheese					
Croissan'wich	118 g.	1	23	353	59%
Sausage, Egg, Cheese					
Croissan'wich	159 g.	1	40	534	67%
Ham, Egg, Cheese					
Croissan'wich	144 g.	1	22	351	56%
French Toast Sticks	141 g.	1 order	27	440	55%
B– Vanilla Shake	284 g.	1	6	310	17%
B– Chocolate Shake	284 g.	1	7	320	20%
Dutch Apple Pie	113 g.	1	15	308	44%
CARL JR.'S					
Famous Star Hamburger		1	38	610	56%
Super Star Hamburger		1	53	820	58%
Hamburger		1	14	320	39%
B– Happy Star Hamburger		1	8	220	33%

RESTAURANT-FOOD
EVALUATION CHARTS

353

		Serving Size	Fat Grams	Calories	Fat %
A	Charbroiler BBQ Chicken Sandwich	1	6	310	17%
	Charbroiler Chicken Club Sandwich	1	29	570	46%
A	Santa Fe Chicken Sandwich	1	13	540	22%
A	Teriyaki Chicken Sandwich	1	6	330	16%
A–	California Roast Beef 'n Swiss	1	8	360	20%
	Fillet of Fish Sandwich	1	30	560	48%
	Hot Dog with Chili	1	23	510	41%
B–	Fiesta & Cheese Potato	1	23	550	38%
	Broccoli & Cheese Potato	1	31	590	47%
	Bacon & Cheese Potato	1	43	730	53%
B–	Sour Cream & Chive Potato	1	19	470	36%
	Cheese Potato	1	36	690	47%
A	Lite Potato	1	1	290	3%
	French Fries, Regular	1 order	20	420	43%
	Zucchini	1 order	23	390	53%
	Onion Rings	1 order	26	520	45%
B	Chicken Salad-To-Go	1	8	200	36%
	Garden Salad-To-Go	1	3	50	54%
B–	Reduced-Cal French Dressing	2 tbsp.	2	40	45%
	House Dressing	2 oz.	11	110	90%
	Soups:				
B–	Cream of Broccoli	1 order	6	140	39%
	Boston Clam Chowder	1 order	8	140	51%
A	Old Fashioned Chicken Noodle	1 order	1	80	11%
	Hot Cakes with Margarine *(Syrup not included)*	1 order	24	510	42%
	Sausage	1 patty	18	190	85%
	Bacon	2 strips	4	45	80%
	Hashed Brown Nuggets	1 order	17	270	57%
A–	Bran Muffins	1	7	310	20%
B–	Shakes	reg. size	7	350	18%

354

CHICK-FIL-A

		Serving Size	Fat Grams	Calories	Fat %
A–	Chick-Fil-A Sandwich, with bun*	5.8 oz.	1	8.5	360	21%
	Chick-Fil-A Nuggets	4 oz.	8 pieces	15	287	47%
A–	Chargrilled Chicken Deluxe Sandwich*	1	4.9	266	17%

These sandwiches would recieve "A" ratings if they were served on whole- or part whole-grain buns.

		Serving Size		Fat Grams	Calories	
A	Chargrilled Chicken Garden Salad		1	3.1	148	19%
A–	Chargrilled Chicken Sandwich*		1	4.8	258	17%
B	Chick-n-Q Sandwich		1	14.7	409	32%
A	Grilled 'n Lites		2 skewers	1.8	97	17%
A	Hearty Breast of Chicken Soup	17.5 oz.	large	9	432	19%
	Chicken Salad Sandwich *(wheat bread)*	5.7 oz.	1	26	449	52%
	Chicken Salad Plate	11.8 oz.	1	18.7	291	58%
	Chicken Salad Cup	4 oz.	1	28	309	82%
	Cole Slaw		1 cup	14	175	72%
	Potato Salad		1 cup	15	198	68%
B	Carrot-Raisin Salad		1 cup	5	116	39%
A	Tossed Salad *(with lite Italian dressing)*		1	1.2	43	11%
	Waffle, Potato Fries	3 oz.	regular	14	270	47%
	Icedream	4.5 oz.	1 serving	5	134	34%
B–	Lemon Pie		1 slice	5	329	14%
B–	Fudge Brownies with nuts	2.8 oz.	1	5	369	12%
COLOMBO						
B–	Lowfat Frozen Yogurt	4 fl. oz.	1 serving	2	99	18%
B	Lite Nonfat Frozen Yogurt**	4 fl. oz.	1 serving	0	95	0%
DAIRY QUEEN						
B–	Single Hamburger		1	13	310	38%
	Double Hamburger		1	25	460	49%
	Double with cheese		1	34	570	54%
	Hot Dog		1	16	280	51%
B–	Fish Sandwich		1	16	370	39%
A–	Grilled Chicken Sandwich		1	8	300	24%
	Chicken Breast Fillet		1	20	430	42%
	All White Chicken Nuggets	99 g.	1 order	18	276	59%
	Cone, vanilla		regular	4	140	26%
B–	Mr. Misty		small	0	250	0%
B	Yogurt Cone, Vanilla		regular	0	180	0%
	DQ Sandwich		1	4	140	26%
	Dilly Bar		1	13	210	56%
	Chocolate Shake		regular	14	540	23%

This sandwich would receive an "A" rating if it were served on a whole- or part-whole-grain bun.

**Make certain that none of the foods you choose contain artificial sweeteners.*

355

		Serving Size	Fat Grams	Calories	Fat %
	Heath Blizzard		36	820	40%
B	BREEZES *(Basic calories*		trace+	200+	trace%+
	and fat grams change	small	0+	100+	0%+
	depending on what you	medium	0+	150+	0%+
	add. Breezes are made	large	0+	200+	0%+
	with nonfat frozen yogurt.)				
	DENNY'S				
	Bacon	1 slice	4	48	75%
	Bacon Swiss Burger		52	819	57%
A–	Bagel, Plain		1	240	4%
A–	Beef Barley Soup	1 bowl	0.1	17	5%
B	Biscuit		7	217	29%
	BLT *(bacon, lettuce, and*				
	tomato sandwich)		34	492	62%
	Blueberry Muffin		14	309	41%
A	Carrots	3 oz. 1 bowl	0.1	17	5%
	Catfish (entree only)		48	576	75%
	Cheese Soup	1 bowl	22	309	64%
B	Chef Salad		20.3	492	37%
	Chicken, Fried				
	(entree only)	4 pieces	29.6	463	58%
A	Chicken, Grilled				
	(entree only)		3.9	192	18%
	Chicken Fried Steak				
	(entree only, no gravy)	2 pieces	14.6	252	52%
A–	Chicken Noodle Soup	1 bowl	3.3	105	28%
A	Chicken Salad *(no shell)*		4	207	17%
A–	Chicken Sandwich, Grilled		12	439	25%
B–	Chicken Strips	4 oz.	10	240	38%
	Chili	8 oz.	15	238	57%
B–	Cinnamon Roll		14	450	28%
	Clam Chowder	1 bowl	14.2	235	54%
B	Club Sandwich		20	590	31%
	Coleslaw	1 cup	9.5	119	72%
A	Corn	3 oz.	0.8	63	11%
	Country Gravy	1 oz.	8	140	51%
	Denny Burger		37.4	629	54%
B	Egg (no added fat or salt)		6	80	68%
	Eggs Benedict		35.6	658	49%

356

		Serving Size	Fat Grams	Calories	Fat %
A–	English Muffin, Plain	2 halves	1	150	6%
	French Fries	4 oz.	15.8	303	47%
	French Toast	2 slices	56	729	69%
A	Green Beans	3 oz.	0.1	13	7%
	Grilled Cheese Sandwich		29	454	57%
	Guacamole	1 oz.	6.2	60	93%
	Ham Slice		6.8	156	39%
	Hamburger Steak *(entree only)*		53.8	669	73%
A	Hashed Browns	4 oz.	2	164	11%
	Liver with Bacon & Onions *(entree only)*	2 slices	14.5	334	39%
A	Mashed Potatoes	4 oz.	0.4	74	5%
	Mozzarella Sticks	1 slice	6.7	88	69%
	New York Steak		36	582	56%
	Omelet, Denver		27	567	43%
	Onion Rings	3 rings	15	258	52%
A–	Pancakes*, plain	2	4	272	13%
	Patty Melt		47	761	56%
A	Peas	3 oz.	0.2	40	5%
A	Potato, Baked	1 medium	0.1	180	1%
	Potato Soup	1 bowl	13.3	141	85%
	Ranch Dressing	2 tbsp.	11	104	95%
A	Rice Pilaf	1/3 cup	2.3	89	23%
	San Fran Burger		48	872	50%
	Sausage	1 link	10	113	80%
	Shrimp, Fried *(entree only)*	5 shrimp	15	230	59%
A	Split Pea Soup	1 bowl	4.9	231	19%
B+	Stir-Fry *(entree only)*		10.9	328	30%
	Stuffing	1/2 cup	9	180	45%
B–	Super Bird		24	625	35%
B–	Taco Salad *(no shell)*		20	514	35%
B	Top Sirloin Steak *(entree only)*		6.3	223	25%
	Tortilla Shell, Fried		30	439	62%
	Tuna Salad		17.8	340	47%
A–	Turkey *(entree only, no gravy)*	6 slices	14.4	505	26%
	Veggie Cheese		20	350	51%
B–	Waffle		10.4	261	36%

RESTAURANT-FOOD
EVALUATION CHARTS

*These pancakes would receive an "A" rating if they were whole grain or part-whole grain. Be **very** moderate with butter and syrup.*

		Serving Size		Fat Grams	Calories	Fat %
DOMINO'S PIZZA*						
B	Cheese Pizza *(large)* 12"	5.5 oz.	2 sl.	10	360	25%
B–	Pepperoni Pizza *(large)* 12"	5.5 oz.	2 sl.	15	410	33%
B–	Deluxe Pizza *(small)* 12" includes: sausage, pepperoni, onion, green pepper, mushrooms	5.5 oz.	2 sl.	23	540	38%
B+	Veggie Fest 12"	5.5 oz.	2 sl.	13	390	30%
GODFATHER'S PIZZA*						
B+	Original Pizza: Cheese Pizza—mini	79 g.	1/4 of whole	4	190	19%
B	Original Cheese Pizza— large, Hot Slice	156 g.	1/8 of whole	11	370	27%
	Combo Pizza— large, Hot Slice	241 g.	1/8 of whole	24	550	39%
B	Thin Crust: Cheese Pizza—small	75 g.	1/6 of whole	6	180	30%
B	Thin Crust: Cheese Pizza—large	96 g.	1/10 of whole	7	228	28%
	Thin Crust: Combo Pizza—large	152 g.	1/10 of whole	16	336	43%
B–	Stuffed Pie: Cheese Pizza—small	124 g.	1/6 of whole	11	310	32%
	Stuffed Pie: Combo Pizza—large	216 g.	1/10 whole	26	521	45%
GOLDEN CORRAL						
	Sirloin	104 g.	5 oz.	14	230	55%
	Ribeye	146 g.	reg.	35	450	70%
	Sirloin Tips with onions & peppers	233 g.	1 serv.	13	290	40%
A–	Golden Grilled Chicken	118 g.	1 serv.	5	170	26%
	Golden Fried Chicken Fillets	155 g.	1 serv.	19	370	46%
	Golden Fried Shrimp	87 g.	1 serv.	12	250	43%
A	Baked Potato	219 g.	1	2	220	8%
B	Texas Toast	49 g.	1 serv.	6	170	32%

*If I am interested in fat loss, most pizza choices greatly slow down or halt my progress, probably because I often eat six or more pieces. Eating a large bowl of chicken vegetable soup. 2 slices of whole-grain toast, and a big bowl of fresh fruit before I eat the pizza is the only way I eat fewer than three pizza slices. "Willpower" has never been **my** answer! Eating more **good** food is **always** my answer.*

RESTAURANT-FOOD EVALUATION CHARTS

	Serving Size	Fat Grams	Calories	Fat %
HARDEE'S				
B– Hamburger	99 g. 1	10	260	35%
Cheeseburger	112 g. 1	14	300	42%
Big Deluxe	216 g. 1	30	500	54%
Bacon Cheeseburger	219 g. 1	39	610	58%
Mushroom 'n Swiss	186 g. 1	27	490	50%
B– Regular Roast Beef	126 g. 1	11	280	35%
B– Hot Ham 'n Cheese	149 g. 1	12	330	33%
Fisherman's Fillet	207 g. 1	21	470	40%
B– Turkey Club				
(Request no bacon or				
mayonnaise for an				
"A" Choice = 6 f.g.				
and 260 cal.)	208 g. 1	16	390	37%
B Chicken Fillet	173 g. 1	13	370	32%
Frisco Burger	1	47	730	58%
Frisco Chicken	1	41	680	54%
Frisco Club	1	42	670	56%
A– Grilled Chicken Breast				
Sandwich	1	9	310	26%
B– Turkey Club	1	16	390	37%
A Ham Sub	1	7	370	17%
B– Roast Beef, regular	1	11	280	35%
A Roast Beef Sub	1	5	370	12%
A Combo Sub	1	6	380	14%
A Turkey Sub	1	7	390	16%
Hot Dog	119 g. 1	16	290	50%
B– Chicken Stix	6 pieces	9	210	39%
Fried Chicken:				
Breast	1	19	340	50%
Leg	1	8	152	47%
Thigh	1	26	370	63%
Wing	1	13	205	57%
Garden Salad	1	12	184	59%
A Side Salad	1	0	20	0%
Chef Salad	1	13	214	55%
Coleslaw	4 oz.	20	240	75%
A Fat Free French Dressing	1 pkg.	0	0	0%
A Fat Free Italian Dressing	1 pkg.	0	0	0%
B+ Grilled Chicken Salad				
w/o dressing	1	4	120	30%

359

		Serving Size	Fat Grams	Calories	Fat %
	Potato Salad, small	5 oz.	19	260	66%
A	Mashed Potatoes	4 oz.	0	70	0%
	French Fries, regular	1 order	11	230	43%
	Crispy Curl Fries	1 order	16	300	48%
	Rise 'n Shine Biscuit	83 g.	18	320	51%
	Sausage & Egg Biscuit	150 g.	31	490	57%
	Ham Biscuit	106 g.	16	320	45%
	Ham, Egg Biscuit	138 g.	19	370	46%
	Cinnamon 'n Raisin Biscuit	80 g.	17	320	48%
	Canadian Rise 'n Shine Biscuit	161 g.	27	470	52%
	Frisco Breakfast Sandwich		20	430	42%
B–	Blueberry Muffin		17	400	38%
B–	Oatbran Raisin Muffin		16	410	35%
A–	Bagel, plain		3	200	14%
A–	Breadstick		4	150	24%
A–	Pancakes, plain	1 order	2	280	6%
	Big Country Breakfast Sausage	274 g.	57	850	60%
	Big Country Breakfast, Ham		33	620	48%
B+	Orange Juice*	6 oz.	tr	140	trace%
	Apple Turnover	91 g.	12	270	40%
	Big Cookie Treat	49 g.	13	250	47%
B–	Cool Twist Cone, Chocolate	118 g.	4	180	20%
B–	Cool Twist Cone, Vanilla	118 g.	4	180	20%
	Chocolate Shake	326 g.	10	390	23%
JACK-IN-THE-BOX					
B–	Hamburger	103 g.	11	267	37%
	Cheeseburger	113 g.	14	315	40%
	Jumbo Jack with Cheese	242 g.	40	677	53%
	Ultimate Cheeseburger	280 g.	69	942	66%
A–	Club Pita without sauces	179 g.	8	277	26%
	Chicken Supreme	231 g.	39	641	55%
	Pizza Pocket	497 g.	28	497	51%
	Moby Jack	137 g.	25	444	51%
	Fish Supreme	228 g.	27	510	48%
	Hot Club Supreme	213 g.	28	524	48%
B–	Sirloin Steak Dinner	334 g.	27	699	35%
B–	Chicken Strip Dinner	321 g.	30	689	39%

*Orange juice is a much better choice than soda pop. However, because most of the fiber has been removed and fruit juice is high in natural sugar, it receives a "B+" rating. The best choice would be to order water and bring a **whole** fruit from home.*

	Serving Size		Fat Grams	Calories	Fat %
Shrimp Dinner	301 g.	1	37	731	46%
Taco Salad	358 g.	1	31	503	55%
Pasta and Seafood Salad	417 g.	1	22	394	50%
Side Salad	111 g.	1	3	51	53%
Buttermilk House Dressing	35 g.	1 pkg.	36	362	90%
Bleu Cheese Dressing	35 g.	1 pkg.	22	262	76%
B– Reduced Calorie French Dressing	35 g.	1 pkg.	4	80	45%
Super Taco	135 g.	1	17	288	53%
Cheese Nachos	170 g.	1	35	571	55%
Supreme Nachos	338 g.	1	45	787	51%
A Fajita Pita	175 g.	1	7	278	23%
A– Chicken Fajita Pita	189 g.	1	8	292	25%
French Fries	68 g.	regular	17	351	44%
Chicken Strips	125 g.	4 piece	13	285	41%
Shrimp	84 g.	10 piece	16	270	53%
Supreme Crescent	146 g.	1	40	547	66%
Hash Browns	62 g.	1	11	156	63%
Mayo-Onion Sauce	21 g.	1 pkg.	15	143	94%
Mayo-Mustard Sauce	21 g.	1 pkg.	13	124	94%
Hot Apple Turnover	119 g.	1	24	410	53%
Cheesecake	99 g.	1	18	309	52%
B– Vanilla Shake	317 g.	1	6	320	17%
B– Chocolate Shake	322 g.	1	7	330	19%
B Pancake Platter	231 g.	1	22	612	32%

KENTUCKY FRIED CHICKEN

	Serving Size		Fat Grams	Calories	Fat %
B+ Rotisserie Gold Chicken (white quarter w/o skin)	117 g.	1	5.9	199	27%
Rotisserie Gold Chicken (dark quarter w/o skin)	117 g.	1	12.2	217	51%
Center Breast, Original Recipe	103 g.	1	14	260	48%
Drumstick, Original Recipe	57 g.	1	9	152	53%
Center Breast, Extra Crispy	118 g.	1	19	330	52%
Hot Wings	135 g.	6 pieces	33	471	63%
Center Breast Hot and Spicy	126 g.	1	22	360	55%
Kentucky Nuggets	95 g.	6	18	284	57%
Chicken Sandwich	166 g.	1	27	482	50%
Chicken Little's Sandwich	47 g.	1	10	169	53%

RESTAURANT-FOOD EVALUATION CHARTS

361

		Serving Size	Fat Grams	Calories	Fat %
	Buttermilk Biscuits	61 g.	1	12	220	49%
A–	Breadstick*	33 g.	1	3	110	25%
A–	Sourdough Roll*	47 g.	1	2	128	14%
	Corn Bread	56 g.	1	13	228	51%
A	Mashed Potatoes with Gravy	120 g.	1	1	70	13%
	Crispy Fries	71 g.	1 order	11	210	47%
	Corn-on-the-Cob	151 g.	1 (1/2 cob)	12	222	49%
	Cole Slaw	90 g.	1	6	114	47%
	Potato Salad	125 g.	1	11	180	55%
A–	Green Beans	102 g.	1	1	36	25%
A	BBQ Beans	110 g.	1	2	132	14%
A–	Vegetable Medley Salad	114 g.	1	4	126	29%
A	Garden Salad	87 g.	1	0	16	0%
	Italian Dressing	28 g.	1	1	15	60%
	Ranch Dressing	28 g.	1	18	170	95%
	Macaroni Salad	108 g.	1	17	248	62%
	Pasta Salad	108 g.	1	8	135	53%
	Macaroni and Cheese	114 g.	1	8	162	44%
B+	Mean Greens	111 g.	1	2	52	35%
A	Red Beans and Rice	112 g.	1	3	114	24%
	Potato Wedges	92 g.	1 order	9	192	42%
A	Garden Rice	107 g.	1	1	75	12%

LITTLE CEASARS PIZZA

			Fat Grams	Calories	Fat %
B–	Baby Pan! Pan!, Cheese & Pepperoni		1	22	525	38%
A–	Crazy Bread*		1 piece	1	98	9%
A	Crazy Sauce		1 order	1	63	14%
	Slice! Slice!, Cheese & Pepperoni		1 slice	31	756	37%
B	Cheese, Medium Round		2 slices	10	308	29%
B	Cheese, Medium Square		2 slices	12	370	29%
B–	Cheese & Pepperoni, Medium Round		2 slices	14	336	38%
B–	Cheese & Pepperoni, Medium Square		2 slices	16	402	36%
	Antipasto Salad, no dressing		1 small	5	96	47%
	Greek Salad, no dressing		1 small	5	85	53%
	Ham & Cheese Sandwich		1	27	553	44%

362

This breadstick and roll would receive an "A" rating if they were made from whole or part-whole grains.

		Serving Size	Fat Grams	Calories	Fat %
	Italian Sandwich		1	35	615	51%
A	Tossed Salad, no dressing	1 small	1	37	24%
	Tuna Sandwich		1	31	610	46%
B	Turkey Sandwich		1	17	450	34%
	Veggie Sandwich *(Request no dressing for an "A–" Choice.)*		1	47	784	54%

MCDONALD'S

		Serving Size	Fat Grams	Calories	Fat %
B–	Hamburger	106 g.	1	9	250	32%
	Cheeseburger	119 g.	1	13	300	39%
	Quarter Pounder	166 g.	1	20	400	45%
	Quarter Pounder w/Cheese	191 g.	1	27	490	50%
	Big Mac	215 g.	1	27	490	50%
	Fillet-O-Fish	141 g.	1	18	370	44%
B–	McLean Deluxe with Cheese	219 g.	1	14	370	34%
B+	McGrilled Chicken Sandwich *(Order extra tomato, pickle, and onion, and no sauce for an "A" Choice.)*	240 g.	1	12	400	27%
B–	Chicken Fajitas	82 g.	1	8	190	38%
	Chicken McNuggets	109 g.	6	15	270	50%
	French Fries	68 g.	sm. order	12	220	49%
B+	Orange Juice	6 oz.		0	80	0%
	Chef Salad	265 g.	1	9	170	48%
B	Garden Salad	189 g.	1	2	50	36%
A–	Chunky Chicken Salad	255 g.	1	4	150	24%
A–	Side Salad	106 g.	1	1	30	30%
B–	Croutons	11 g.	1 pkg.	2	50	36%
	Bacon Bits	3 g.	1	1	15	60%
	Dressings:					
	Blue Cheese	1 pkg.		21	240	79%
	Ranch	1 pkg.		21	230	82%
	1000 Island	1 pkg.		16	230	63%
B–	Lite Vinaigrette	1 pkg.		2	50	36%
	Red French Reduced-Calorie	1 pkg.		8	160	45%
B–	Egg McMuffin	135 g.	1	11	280	35%
	Scrambled Eggs	100 g.	1	10	140	64%

		Serving Size	Fat Grams	Calories	Fat %
	Pork Sausage	43 g.	1	15	160	84%
A–	English Muffin w/butter	58 g.	1	4	170	21%
	Hash Brown Potatoes	53 g.	1	7	130	48%
	Biscuit	75 g.	1	13	260	45%
	Biscuit with Sausage	118 g.	1	28	420	60%
	Biscuit with Sausage and Egg	175 g.	1	34	520	59%
	Biscuit with Bacon, Egg and Cheese	153 g.	1	26	440	53%
	Sausage McMuffin	135 g.	1	20	350	51%
	Sausage McMuffin with Egg	159 g.	1	25	430	52%
	Apple Pie	84 g.	1	15	280	48%
B	Vanilla Lowfat Frozen Yogurt Cone	84 g.	1	1	110	8%
B–	Vanilla Shake	480 g.	1	5	310	15%
B–	Chocolate Shake	480 g.	1	6	350	15%
B–	Strawberry Shake	480 g.	1	5	340	13%
B–	Strawberry Sundae	172 g.	1	1	210	4%
B–	Hot Fudge Sundae	168 g.	1	3	240	11%
B–	Hot Caramel Sundae	174 g.	1	3	270	10%
	McDonaldland Cookies		1 box	9	290	28%
	Chocolate Chip Cookies		1 box	15	330	41%
B+	Hot Cakes with Butter&Syrup*	174 g.	1 order	9	410	20%
	Apple Danish	105 g.	1	16	360	40%
A–	Apple Bran Muffin**	75 g.	1	0	180	0%
	Hot Cheese Danish	105 g.	1	22	400	50%
	Cinnamon Raisin Danish	110 g.	1	22	430	46%
	Raspberry Danish	105	1	16	390	37%
OLIVE GARDEN						
A–	Breadstick *(Wonderful!)*		1 plain	0	30	0%
A	Minestrone Soup *(Delicious)*		1 bowl	1	80	11%
B–	Capellini Primavera	lunch	1 serv.	13	290	40%
A–	Venetian Chicken	dinner	1 serv.	8	290	25%
B+	Raspberry Sorbet		1 serv.	0	160	0%

Be very moderate with butter and syrup. The pancakes, by themselves, rate an "A–". They would rate an "A" if they were made from whole-wheat flour.

**Because I do not have the sugar-content information on these muffins, I cannot give them a solid "A" rating.*

		Serving Size		Fat Grams	Calories	Fat %
PIZZA HUT						
B–	Thin-n-Crispy Pizza, Cheese	med.	2 slices	17	398	38%
	Thin-n-Crispy Pizza, Pepperoni	med.	2 slices	20	413	44%
	Thin-n-Crispy Pizza, Supreme	med.	2 slices	22	459	43%
B-	Hand Tossed Pizza, Cheese	med.	2 slices	20	518	35%
	Hand Tossed Pizza, Pepperoni	med.	2 slices	23	500	41%
	Hand Tossed Pizza, Supreme	med.	2 slices	26	540	43%
	Pan Pizza:					
B–	Cheese	med.	2 slices	18	492	33%
	Pepperoni	med.	2 slices	22	540	37%
	Supreme	med.	2 slices	30	589	46%
	Personal Pan Pizza: *(whole pizza)*					
	Pepperoni		1 pizza	29	675	39%
	Supreme		1 pizza	28	647	39%
PONDEROSA						
	Fish, baked, Bake 'R Broil	5.2 oz.	1	13	230	51%
	Fish, Broiled:					
A	Halibut	6.0 oz.	1	3	170	16%
B+	Roughy	5.0 oz.	1	5	139	32%
A	Salmon	6.0 oz.	1	3	192	14%
B+	Swordfish	5.9 oz.	1	10	271	33%
A	Trout	5.0 oz.	1	4	228	16%
A	Chicken Breast	5.5 oz.	1	2	98	18%
	Chopped Steak	5.3 oz.	1	22	296	67%
	Kansas City Strip	5 oz.	1	6	138	39%
B–	New York Strip, Choice	8 oz.	1	11	304	33%
	Porterhouse, Choice	16 oz.	1	31	640	44%
	Ribeye, Choice	6 oz.	1	14	282	45%
B–	Sirloin Tips, Choice	5 oz.	1	8	197	37%
B	Steak Kabbobs *(meat only)*	3 oz.	1	5	153	29%
A	Teriyaki Steak	5 oz.	1	3	174	16%
	T-Bone, Choice	10 oz.	1	18	444	36%
	Chicken Wings		2 pieces	9	213	38%
PRETZELMAKER						
A–	Plain Pretzel*		1	1.4	363	3%
A–	Original Pretzel*		1	3.4	402	8%
B	Cinnamon Pretzel		1	6.4	498	12%

These pretzels would receive an "A" rating if they were made from whole grains.

RESTAURANT-FOOD EVALUATION CHARTS

365

	Serving Size	Fat Grams	Calories	Fat %
RED LOBSTER*				
Catfish	5 oz.	1	15	220	61%
B+ Atlantic Cod	5 oz.	1	6	150	36%
B+ Broiled Flounder	5 oz.	1	6	150	36%
B+ Grouper	5 oz.	1	6	150	36%
B+ Haddock	5 oz.	1	6	160	34%
A– Halibut	5 oz.	1	6	180	30%
B– Atlantic Ocean Perch	5 oz.	1	9	180	45%
B Red Rockfish	5 oz.	1	6	140	39%
B+ Red Snapper	5 oz.	1	6	160	34%
B– Coho Salmon**	5 oz.	1	14	240	53%
B– Atlantic Salmon**	5 oz.	1	17	230	67%
A– Shrimp	1 oz.	6 large	2	90	20%
A Sauce	1 oz.	1	0	30	0%
A– Chilled Shrimp (in the shell)	6 oz.	1 serv.	2	130	14%
B– Grilled Chicken and Shrimp	4 oz. chicken 10 shrimp		20	490	37%
B– Broiled Fish Fillet Sandwich	4 oz.	1	9.6	230	38%
A– Grilled Chicken Sandwich	4 oz.	1	10	340	26%
Orange Roughy	5 oz.	1	15	220	61%
B+ Walleye Pike	5 oz.	1	6	170	32%
B Mahi-Mahi	5 oz.	1	6	160	34%
Ocean Perch	5 oz.	1	9	180	45%
Swordfish	5 oz.	1	9	150	54%
B– Sea Bass	5 oz.	1	8	180	40%
B Lemon Sole	5 oz.	1	6	160	34%
Rainbow Trout	5 oz.	1	14	220	57%
Snow Crab Legs	1 lb.	1	11	200	50%
A– Maine Lobster	1 1/4 lb.	1	5	200	23%
A Rock Lobster	1 tail	1	5	250	18%
B+ Grilled Shrimp, skewers		20 pieces	9	290	28%
B Chicken Breast, Grilled	4 oz.	1	6	170	32%
SHONEY'S				
All American Burger		1	32.6	501	59%
A Baked Fish, light		1	1.4	170	7%
A Baked Potato	10 oz.	1	0.3	264	1%
B+ Charbroiled Chicken		1	6.1	198	28%
B Charbroiled Chicken Sandwich		1	17	451	34%
A– Charbroiled Shrimp		1 serv.	3	138	20%

RESTAURANT-FOOD EVALUATION CHARTS

*Even though many of Red Lobster's fish choices rate a "B" because of their fat percentage, their fat gram numbers are low and fit nicely into a day that has an overall fat percentage of 10 to 20 percent. Fish also contains good," cholesterol-fighting fat.

**Salmon contains fatty acids essential for reducing LDL's (bad Cholesterol) and raising HDL'S (good cholesterol). Request "broiled" salmon with no added butter or oil to reduce the fat grams.

		Serving Size	Fat Grams	Calories	Fat %
	Chicken Fillet Sandwich		1	21.2	464	41%
	Chicken Tenders		1 serv.	20.4	388	47%
	Country Fried Steak		1	27.2	449	55%
B–	French Fries		1 serv.	7.5	189	36%
B–	French Toast Sticks		1	2.9	69	38%
A–	Grecian Bread		1 slice	2.2	80	25%
A	Green Salad (includes 9oz. fresh vegetables and low-cal dressing)		1	0.6	63	9%
	Half-o-Pound Dinner		1	34.4	435	71%
A–	Hawaiian Chicken		1 serv.	6.2	221	25%
	Hot Fudge Sundae		1	22	451	44%
B+	Lasagna		1 serv.	9.8	297	30%
	Liver & Onions		1 serv.	22.9	411	50%
	Onion Rings		1 ring	3.1	52	54%
A–	Pancakes*		1	0.1	41	2%
A–	Rice	3.5 oz.	1 serv.	3.7	137	24%
	Shrimper's Feast		1 serv.	22.2	383	52%
	Sirloin	6 oz.	1	24.5	357	62%
	Slim Jim		1	23.9	484	44%
A	Soups, Lightside, averaged		1 cup	1.7	73	21%
B+	Spaghetti Dinner		1 serv.	16.3	496	30%
	Strawberry Pie		1 slice	16.7	332	45%
SKIPPER'S						
A	Baked Potato	6 oz.	1	0	145	0%
	Beverages:					
	Coke Classic	12 oz.	1	0	144	0%
	Diet Coke	12 oz.	1	0	2	0%
B+	Milk (lowfat–2%)	12 oz.	1	7.5	181	37%
B–	Root Beer	12 oz.	1	0	154	0%
B–	Sprite	12 oz.	1	0	142	0%
	Chicken Tenders (fried)	2.5 oz.	1	6	130	42%
B	Clam Chowder:					
	Cup	6 oz.	1	3.5	100	32%
	Pint	12 oz.	1	7	200	32%
	Clams (fried)	4 oz.	1 order	41.5	495	75%
	Coleslaw	5 oz.	1 order	27	289	84%
	Corn Muffin	2 oz.	1	5	91	49%

367

*These pancakes would receive an "A" rating if they were made from whole grains.

	Serving Size		Fat Grams	Calories	Fat %
Fish:					
A– Baked with margarine & seasonings *(Butter would be better!)*	4.4 oz.	1 piece	3	147	18%
B– Captain's Cut	2.6 oz.	1 piece	7	160	39%
English Style	2.4 oz.	1 piece	12	187	58%
French Fries	3.5 oz.	1 order	12	239	45%
A Green Salad	4 oz.	1	0	24	0%
B– Jell-O	2.75 oz.	1	0	55	0%
Margarine	0.5 oz.	1	6	50	100%
Root Beer Float	12 oz.	1	10	302	39%
Sauce:					
A Cocktail	Tb.	1	0	20	0%
A Ketchup	Tb.	1	0	17	0%
Tartar *(original)*	Tb.	1	7	65	97%
Shrimp:					
Cajun *(fried)*	4 oz.	1 order	21	342	55%
Jumbo *(fried)*	.65 oz.	1 piece	2.39	51	42%
Original *(fried)*	4 oz.	1 order	13	266	52%
Salad Dressing:					
Reduced-Calorie Italian	2 oz.	1	12	120	90%
Hidden Valley Ranch	2 oz.	1	23	189	100%
SUBWAY*					
Cold Cut Combo Sub, Italian Roll	12"	1	40	853	42%
B– Cold Cut Combo Sub, Honey Wheat Roll	12"	1	41	883	42%
Cold Cut Combo Salad		1	37	506	65%
Spicy Italian Sub, Italian Roll	12"	1	63	1,043	54%
Spicy Italian Sub, Honey Wheat Roll	12"	1	64	1,073	54%
Spicy Italian Salad		1	60	896	60%
BMT Sub, Italian Roll	12"	1	55	982	51%
BMT Sub, Honey Wheat Roll	12"	1	57	1,011	50%
BMT Salad		1	52	635	74%
B+ Subway Club Sub, Italian Roll	12"	1	22	693	29%

RESTAURANT-FOOD
EVALUATION CHARTS

Remember to ask for extra vegetables, a whole-grain bun, and a large water. Subway sandwiches are rated higher than other sandwiches with similar fat percentages because of their increased fiber and nutrients from abundant fresh vegetables and whole-grain buns.

Grade	Item	Serving Size		Fat Grams	Calories	Fat %
A–	Subway Club Sub, Honey Wheat Roll	12"	1	23	722	29%
	Subway Club Salad		1	19	346	49%
	Tuna Sub, Italian Roll	12"	1	72	1,103	59%
	Tuna Sub, Honey Wheat Roll	12"	1	73	1,132	58%
	Tuna Salad		1	68	756	81%
	Seafood & Crab Sub, Italian Roll	12"	1	57	986	52%
	Seafood & Crab Sub, Honey Wheat Roll	12"	1	58	1,015	52%
	Seafood & Crab Salad		1	53	639	75%
	Seafood & Lobster Sub, Italian Roll	12"	1	53	944	50%
	Seafood & Lobster Sub, Honey Wheat Roll	12"	1	54	974	50%
	Seafood & Lobster Salad		1	49	587	74%
	Meatball Sub, Italian Roll	12"	1	44	918	43%
	Meatball Sub, Honey Wheat Roll	12"	1	45	947	43%
B–	Steak & Cheese Sub, Italian Roll	12"	1	32	765	37%
B–	Steak & Cheese Sub, Honey Wheat Roll	12"	1	33	711	41%
A–	Turkey Breast Sub, Italian Roll	12"	1	19	645	27%
A	Turkey Breast Sub, Honey Wheat Roll	12"	1	20	674	27%
	Turkey Breast Salad		1	16	297	48%
B	Roast Beef Sub, Italian Roll	12"	1	23	689	30%
B+	Roast Beef Sub Honey Wheat Roll	12"	1	24	717	30%
	Roast Beef Salad		1	20	340	52%
B+	Ham & Cheese Sub, Italian Roll	12"	1	18	643	25%
A–	Ham & Cheese Sub, Honey Wheat Roll	12"	1	22	673	29%
	Ham & Cheese Salad		1	18	296	54%
B+	Veggies & Cheese Sub, Italian Roll	12"	1	17	535	29%

RESTAURANT-FOOD EVALUATION CHARTS

369

	Serving Size	Fat Grams	Calories	Fat %
A– Veggies & Cheese Sub, Honey Wheat Roll	12"	1	18	565	29%
Veggies & Cheese Salad		1	14	188	66%
Pepsi Cola	12 oz.	1	tr.	157	trace%
Diet Pepsi	12 oz.	1	tr.	8	trace%
Caf. Free Diet Pepsi	12 oz.	1	tr.	8	trace%
B– Lemon-Lime Slice	12 oz.	1	tr.	150	trace%
B– Mandarin Orange Slice	12 oz.	1	tr.	173	trace%
Mountain Dew	12 oz.	1	tr.	168	trace%
A+! Water	12 oz.	1	0	0	0%

TACO BELL

	Serving Size	Fat Grams	Calories	Fat %
B Bean Burrito*		1	14	381	33%
Beef Burrito		1	21	431	44%
Double Beef Burrito Supreme		1	22	440	45%
Tostada*		1	11	243	41%
Soft Taco Supreme		1	16	272	53%
Chicken Soft Taco*		1	10	213	42%
Burrito Supreme		1	22	440	45%
B– Combination Burrito*		1	16	407	35%
Taco		1	11	183	54%
Cinnamon Twists		1 order	8	171	42%
Ranch Dressing		1 pkg.	25	236	95%
Guacamole		1 serv.	2	34	53%
Taco Salad *(with shell)*		1	61	905	61%
Taco Salad *(without shell)**		1	31	680	41%
Mexican Pizza		1	37	575	58%
Pintos & Cheese*		1 order	9	190	43%
Nachos		1 order	18	346	47%
Nachos Supreme		1 order	27	367	66%
Taco Supreme		1	15	230	57%
Soft Taco		1	12	225	48%
Fajita Steak Taco	142 g.	1	11	235	42%
Fajita Steak Taco *(with sour cream)*	163 g.	1	15	281	48%
Fajita Steak Taco* *(with guacamole)*	163 g.	1	13	269	43%
Chicken Fajita*	135 g.	1	10	226	40%
Chicken Burrito*	160 g.	1	12	334	32%

370

Request without sour cream or cheese to turn these "B" and "C" Choices into "A" and "B" Choices. Then add fat free sour cream and lowfat or fat free shredded cheese at home. (Four tablespoons of shredded cheddar cheese contain approximately 5 fat grams and 4 tablespoons of regular sour cream contain 12 fat grams. Whoa!)

		Serving Size	Fat Grams	Calories	Fat %
TACO TIME					
	Chicken Taco Salad	1	31	571	49%
	Tostado, Meat	1	22	409	48%
	Veggie Salad *(without dressing)**	1	17	357	43%
	Side Salad *(without dressing)**	1	7	106	59%
A	Mexican Brown Rice	1	2	160	11%
	Refritos	1 order	18	378	43%
B+	Chicken Soft Taco*	1	12	390	28%
B	Veggie Burrito* *(I order this without cheese and sour cream all the time ="A" Choice.)*	1	20	535	37%
	Taco	1	13	218	54%
	Soft Flour Taco*	1	19	416	41%
B–	Crisp-Bean Burrito*	1	17	391	39%
	Crisp-Meat Burrito	1	20	393	46%
B–	Soft Combo Burrito*	1	24	550	39%
B–	Soft Bean Burrito*	1	21	547	35%
	Soft Meat Burrito*	1	26	552	42%
	Tostado Delight, Meat	1	30	560	48%
	Taco Cheese Burger	1	30	589	46%
	Taco Salad*	1	21	447	42%
	Casita Burrito	1	32	602	48%
	Empanada, Cherry	1	9	250	32%
	Crustas	1 order	15	373	36%
	Mexi-Fries	1 order	17	266	58%
TCBY (YOGURT)					
B–	TCBY—all flavors	4.5 oz.	1	3	130	21%
B	TCBY Nonfat—all flavors**	4 oz.	1	0	110	0%
VILLAGE INN					
A	Cinnamon Raisin French Toast	1 serv.	16	809	17%
A	Turkey & Vegetable Scrambled Sensation	1 serv.	19	726	24%
A	Low Cholesterol Fruit & Nut Pancakes *(Wonderful!)*	1 serv.	19	936	18%

371

*See italics statement at bottom of page 370.

**TCBY nonfat yougurt would be an "A" Choice dessert if it were sweetened with naturally concentrated fruit juices (as in LEAN & FREE Instant Ice Cream) instead of sugar. Then it would be an ideal dessert for diabetics and those highly resistant to fat loss (in moderation–after a balanced meal, of course).

		Serving Size	Fat Grams	Calories	Fat %
A	Fresh Veggie Omelette *(Delicious!)*		18	701	24%
A–	Mushroom & Cheese Omelette		18	680	24%
A–	Chicken & Cheese Omelette		19	715	24%
WENDY'S					
	Single Hamburger on White Bun with everything	219 g. 1	23	440	47%
	Big Bacon Classic	287 g. 1	36	640	51%
B	Jr. Hamburger	117 g. 1	9	270	30%
B–	Jr. Cheeseburger	129 g. 1	13	320	37%
	Jr. Bacon Cheeseburger	170 g. 1	25	440	51%
	Jr. Cheeseburger Deluxe	179 g. 1	20	390	46%
B–	Chicken Sandwich, breaded	208 g. 1	20	450	40%
A	Chicken Sandwich, grilled	177 g. 1	7	290	22%
	Chicken Club Sandwich	220 g. 1	25	520	43%
A	Plain Baked Potato	284 g. 1	0	310	0%
B	Bacon & Cheese Potato	380 g. 1	18	530	31%
A–	Broccoli & Cheese Potato *(no cheese = 4 f.g., 370 cal., and 10% fat = "A" Choice)*	411 g. 1	14	460	27%
B–	Cheese Potato	383 g. 1	23	560	37%
B–	Chili & Cheese Potato *(no cheese = "B+")*	139 g. 1	24	610	35%
A	Sour Cream & Chives Potato	314 g. 1	6	380	14%
	French Fries:				
	Small	3.2 oz. 1 order	12	240	45%
	Medium	4.6 oz. 1 order	17	340	45%
	Biggie	5.6 oz. 1 order	20	420	43%
	Chicken Nuggets	94 g. 6 pieces	20	280	64%
A	Barbecue Sauce	1	tr.	50	trace%
B+	Sweet & Sour Sauce	1	tr.	45	trace%
A	Sweet Mustard	1	1	50	18%
A–	Chili	227 g. 8 oz. small	6	190	28%
		340 oz. 12 oz. large	9	290	28%
	Taco Salad	510 g. 1 prepared	30	580	47%
A	Taco Sauce	1 pkg.	tr.	10	trace%

		Serving Size	Fat Grams	Calories	Fat %
	Pick-up Window Salad (Side Salad)	155 g. 1	3	60	45%
	Garden Salad (take out)	271 g. 1	6	110	49%
B	Grilled Chicken Salad	338 g. 1	8	200	36%
	Deluxe Garden Salad	271 g. 1	6	110	49%
B–	Caesar Side Salad	89 g. 1	5	110	41%
	Salad Dressings: (1 ladle = 2 Tbsp.)				
	Bleu Cheese	25 g. 2 Tbsp.	19	180	95%
	Celery Seed	28 g. 2 Tbsp.	7	100	63%
	French Style	28 g. 2 Tbsp.	11	120	83%
	Golden Italian	28 g. 2 Tbsp.	7	90	70%
	Ranch	28 g. 2 Tbsp.	10	90	100%
	1000 Island	28 g. 2 Tbsp.	13	130	90%
	Oil	14 g. 1 Tbsp.	14	130	97%
A	Wine Vinegar	15 g. 1 Tbsp.	tr.	0	trace%
	Reduced Calorie Dressings:				
A	French, fat free	28 g. 2 Tbsp.	0	35	0%
	Italian*	28 g. 2 Tbsp.	3	40	68%
	Ranch*	28 g. 2 Tbsp.	5	60	75%
	Frosty Dairy Dessert**				
	Small	243 g. 12 oz.	10	340	26%
	Medium	324 g. 16 oz.	13	460	25%
	Large	405 g. 20 oz.	17	570	27%
	Chocolate Chip Cookie	64 g. 1	13	280	42%

*Put lots of moist veggies and cottage cheese on your salad. Then be extremely moderate with these dressings. Better yet, use the fat free French dressing or bring your own fat free or lowfat dressing from home.

**I must confess, I do order a Frosty every now and then. Frostys sit on the fence between a "B–" and a "C+" Choice dessert because of their combination of being high in sugar and containing more than 20 percent fat. (I never have a Frosty on an empty stomach.) They definitely do not accelerate fat loss, but they are a fun, "very-tasty" treat once in a great while!

RESTAURANT-FOOD EVALUATION CHARTS

FAT-CALORIE PERCENT CHARTS

Find the calorie number across the top of the chart with your right index finger and find the number of fat grams along the left side with your left index finger. Follow your right finger down and your left finger across to the right. The number your fingers meet on indicates the percentage of fat in that particular food.

INDIVIDUAL FOOD CALORIES

FAT GRAMS	10	20	30	40	50	60	70	80	90	100	110	120	130	140	150	160	170
1	90	45	30	23	18	15	13	11	10	9	8	8	7	6	6	6	5
2	100	90	60	45	36	30	26	23	20	18	16	15	14	13	12	11	11
3		100	90	68	54	45	39	34	30	27	25	23	21	19	18	17	16
4			100	90	72	60	51	45	40	36	33	30	28	26	24	23	21
5				100	90	75	64	56	50	45	41	38	35	32	30	28	26
6					100	90	77	68	60	54	49	45	42	39	36	34	32
7						100	90	79	70	63	57	53	48	45	42	39	37
8							100	90	80	72	65	60	55	51	48	45	42
9								100	90	81	74	68	62	58	54	51	48
10									100	90	82	75	69	64	60	56	53
11										99	90	83	76	71	66	62	58
12										100	98	90	83	77	72	68	64
13											100	98	90	84	78	73	69
14												100	97	90	84	79	74
15													100	96	90	84	79
16														100	96	90	85
17															100	96	90
18																100	95
19																	100

INDIVIDUAL FOOD CALORIES

FAT GRAMS	180	190	200	210	220	230	240	250	260	270	280	290	300	310	320	330
1	5	5	5	4	4	4	4	4	3	3	3	3	3	3	3	3
2	10	9	9	9	8	8	8	7	7	7	6	6	6	6	6	5
3	15	14	14	13	13	12	12	11	11	10	10	9	9	9	8	8
4	20	19	18	17	16	16	15	14	14	13	13	12	12	12	11	11
5	25	24	23	21	20	20	19	18	17	17	16	16	15	15	14	14
6	30	28	27	26	25	23	23	22	21	20	19	19	18	17	17	16
7	35	33	32	30	29	27	26	25	24	23	23	22	21	20	20	19
8	40	38	36	34	33	31	30	29	28	27	26	25	24	23	23	22
9	45	43	41	39	37	35	34	32	31	30	29	28	27	26	25	25
10	50	47	45	43	41	39	38	36	35	33	32	31	30	29	28	27
11	55	52	50	47	45	43	41	40	38	37	35	34	33	32	31	30
12	60	57	54	51	49	47	45	43	42	40	39	37	36	35	34	33
13	65	62	59	56	53	51	49	47	45	43	42	40	39	38	37	35
14	70	66	63	60	57	55	53	50	48	47	45	43	42	41	39	38
15	75	71	68	64	61	59	56	54	52	50	48	47	45	44	42	41
16	80	76	72	69	65	63	60	58	55	53	51	50	48	46	45	44
17	85	81	77	73	70	67	64	61	59	57	55	53	51	49	48	46
18	90	85	81	77	74	70	68	65	62	60	58	56	54	52	51	49
19	95	90	86	81	78	74	71	68	66	63	61	59	57	55	53	52
20	100	95	90	86	82	78	75	72	69	67	64	62	60	58	56	55
21		99	95	90	86	82	79	76	73	70	68	65	63	61	59	57
22		100	99	94	90	86	83	79	76	73	71	68	66	64	62	60
23			100	99	94	90	86	83	80	77	74	71	69	67	65	63
24				100	98	94	90	86	83	80	77	74	72	70	68	65
25					100	98	94	90	87	83	80	78	75	73	70	68
26						100	98	94	90	87	84	81	78	75	73	71
27							100	97	93	90	87	84	81	78	76	74
28								100	97	93	90	87	84	81	79	76
29									100	97	93	90	87	84	82	79
49										100	96	93	90	87	84	82
50											100	96	93	90	87	85
51												99	96	93	90	87
52												100	99	96	93	90
53													100	99	96	93
54														100	98	95
55															100	98
56																100

FAT / CALORIE % CHARTS

INDIVIDUAL FOOD CALORIES

	340	350	360	370	380	390	400	410	420	430	440	450	460	470	480	490	500
1	3	3	3	3	2	2	2	2	2	2	2	2	2	2	2	2	2
2	5	5	5	5	5	5	5	4	4	4	4	4	4	4	4	4	4
3	8	8	8	7	7	7	7	7	6	6	6	6	6	6	6	6	5
4	11	10	10	10	9	9	9	9	9	8	8	8	8	8	8	7	7
5	13	13	13	12	12	12	11	11	11	10	10	10	10	10	9	9	9
6	16	15	15	15	14	14	14	13	13	13	12	12	12	11	11	11	11
7	19	18	18	17	17	16	16	16	15	15	15	14	14	14	13	13	13
8	21	21	20	10	19	19	18	18	18	17	17	16	16	15	15	15	14
9	24	23	23	22	21	21	20	20	19	19	18	18	18	17	17	17	16
10	26	26	25	24	24	23	23	22	21	21	20	20	20	19	19	19	18
11	29	28	28	27	26	25	25	24	24	23	23	22	22	21	21	20	20
12	32	31	30	29	28	28	27	26	26	25	25	24	23	23	23	22	22
13	34	33	33	32	31	30	29	29	28	27	27	26	25	25	24	24	23
14	37	36	35	34	33	32	32	31	30	29	29	28	27	27	26	26	25
15	40	39	38	36	36	35	34	33	32	31	31	30	29	29	28	28	27
16	42	41	40	39	38	37	36	35	34	33	33	32	31	31	30	29	29
17	45	44	43	41	40	39	38	37	36	36	35	34	33	33	32	31	31
18	48	46	45	44	43	42	41	40	39	38	37	36	35	34	34	33	32
19	50	49	48	46	45	44	43	42	41	40	39	38	37	36	36	35	34
20	53	51	50	49	47	46	45	44	43	42	41	40	39	38	38	37	36
21	56	54	53	51	50	48	47	46	45	44	43	42	41	40	39	39	38
22	58	57	55	54	52	51	50	48	47	46	45	44	43	42	41	40	40
23	61	59	58	56	54	53	52	50	49	48	47	46	45	44	43	42	41
24	64	62	60	58	57	55	54	53	51	50	49	48	47	46	45	44	43
25	66	64	63	61	59	58	56	55	54	52	51	50	49	48	47	46	45
26	69	67	65	63	62	60	59	57	56	54	53	52	51	50	49	48	47
27	71	69	68	66	64	62	61	59	58	57	55	54	53	52	51	50	49
28	74	72	70	68	66	65	63	61	60	59	57	56	55	54	53	51	50
29	77	75	73	71	69	67	65	64	62	61	59	58	57	56	54	53	52
30	79	77	75	73	71	69	68	66	64	63	61	60	59	57	56	55	54
31	82	80	78	75	73	72	70	68	66	65	63	62	61	59	58	57	56
32	85	82	80	78	76	74	72	70	69	67	65	64	63	61	60	59	58
33	87	85	83	80	78	76	74	72	71	69	68	66	65	63	62	61	59
34	90	87	85	83	81	78	77	75	73	71	70	68	67	65	64	62	61
35	93	90	88	85	83	81	79	77	75	73	72	70	68	67	66	64	63
36	95	93	90	88	85	83	81	79	77	75	74	72	70	69	68	66	63
37	98	95	93	90	88	85	83	81	79	77	76	74	72	71	69	68	67
38	100	98	95	92	90	88	86	83	81	80	78	76	74	73	71	70	68
39		100	98	95	92	90	88	86	84	82	80	78	76	75	73	72	70
40			100	97	95	92	90	88	86	84	82	80	78	77	75	73	72
41				100	97	95	92	90	88	86	84	82	80	79	77	75	74
42					99	97	95	92	90	88	86	84	82	80	79	77	76
43					100	99	97	94	92	90	88	86	84	82	81	79	77
44						100	99	97	94	92	90	88	86	84	83	81	79
45							100	99	96	94	92	90	88	86	84	83	81
46								100	99	96	94	92	90	88	86	84	83
47									100	98	96	94	92	90	88	86	85
48										100	98	96	94	92	90	88	86
49											100	98	96	94	92	90	88
50												100	98	96	94	92	90
51													100	98	96	94	92
52														100	98	96	94
53															99	97	95
54															100	97	95
55																100	99
56																	100

375

RECIPE TOPICAL INDEX

Color pictures of menus and recipes are found following pages 22, 46, 70, 94, 142, 166, 182, 198, 222, and 246.

The large bold numbers below indicate the page numbers the recipes are located on. The smaller italic numbers indicate selected "menu" pages where the recipe is featured.

BEANS / LEGUMES

Bean Burritos	**24**
Chicken-Chili Enchiladas *45, 49, 77,* **144**
Chilighetti	*18,* **29**
LEAN & FREE Nachos	*94,* **145**
Mexicali Salad	**31**
Mexican Lasagna	*79,* **146**
Taco Salad with Taco Dressing	**147**
Tempting Tacos	*30, 57, 109,* **148**

BEEF / PORK

Beef Fajitas	*100,* **149**
D'Ann's Delicious 15 Minute Beef Stroganoff	*41, 46, 57,* **150**
Enchilada Casserole	*42, 46, 132,* **151**
Pigs in a Blanket	**29**
Pizza Wheels	*55,* **152**
Porcupine Meatballs	*44, 102* **153**
Pork Chow Mein	*72, 97, 102,* **154**
Quick, Delicious Beef Stew	*28, 73, 106,* **155**
Roast Beef	**155**
Shepherd's Pie	*47,* **156**
Sloppy Joes	*49, 138,* **156**
Stew in a Bun	**28**
Taco Casserole	*44, 48,* **157**

BREAD

Big Soft Pretzels	*40, 45, 106, 118,* **158**
Country Corn Bread	*39, 71, 130, 139,* **159**
Emily's Delectable Pizza Crust	**268**
Garlic Cheese Toast	*43, 90, 114,* **159**
Perfect Whole-Wheat Bread	*58, 120,* **160**
Sourdough Starter	**160**
Super Cinnamon Rolls	*40, 56,* **161**
Whole-Wheat Pita Bread	**162**

Whole-Wheat Tortillas	**162**
Zucchini-Pineapple-Nut Bread	*56, 137,* **163**

BREAD SPREADS

All Fruit Jam	**164**
Apple-Raspberry Butter	*67,* **165**
Cranberry Sandwich Spread	**165**
Honey Butter	**165**
Jam Variations	**164**
Store Variety Jams, Jellies, Syrups	**166**

BREAKFAST FOODS

Belgian Waffle	*28, 38, 95, 113,* **166**
Blintzes	*30,* **167**
Breakfast Burrito	**167**
Breakfast Fruit Compote	*36, 84, 132,* **168**
Breakfast Shake	*39,* **168**
Cinnamon-Maple Oatmeal	*39, 101, 136,* **169**
Cracked Wheat, Raisin, and Honey Cereal	*37, 95, 102,* **169**
Crunchy Granola	*37, 76,* **170**
Egg & Cheese Muffins	*40, 119,* **171**
French Toast	*38, 57, 121,* **171**
Fried Eggs	*39, 67, 97, 127,* **172**
Granola	*39,* **172**
Granola Bars	*112,* **173**
Hash Browns	*42, 113,* **246**
Omelet Supreme	*103, 113,* **174**
Orange Jubilee	*85, 90,* **174**
Three Bear Porridge and Honey	*40, 106,* **175**
Veggie and Cheese Egg Scramble or Cheese Egg Scramble	*31, 71, 133,* **175**

LEAN & FREE PANCAKES

Banana Pancakes   66, 130, **176**
Blender Whole-Wheat
   Pancakes–*Key Recipe*   39, **176**
Blueberry Pancakes   115, **177**
Oatmeal Pancakes   40, **177**
Peach Pancakes   35, 39, 94, **177**
Super Quick Pancakes   20, 85, **177**

CHICKEN / TURKEY

Baked Chicken Breasts   66, **178**
BBQ Chicken   48, 137, **178**
Chicken and Rice   32, **179**
Chicken Bake   **179**
Chicken Broccoli Casserole 22, 42, 46, **180**
Chicken Casserole   **180**
Chicken Divan   85, **181**
Chicken Fajitas   35, 46, 141, **149**
Chicken Veggie Stir-Fry   50, 101, **181**
Cranberry-Glazed Turkey
   Breast   73, 88, **182**
Crock-Pot Chicken   119, **182**
Easy Chicken 'n' Dumplings 30, 43, **183**
Hawaiian Haystacks   34, 43, 48, 133, **183**
Pineapple-Lime Chicken   49, 115, **184**
Sweet and Sour Chicken   **184**
Teriyaki Chicken   **185**
Turkey Fajitas   **149**

DESSERT / COOKIES

Apple Cake   102, **186**
Apple Cobbler –*Key Recipe* 76, 83, **187**
Apple-Raspberry Bars   **188**
Blueberry Streusel Coffee Cake 126, **189**
Cake-Mix Sweet Rolls– *Key Recipe* **190**
Chocolate Frosting   **191**
Date Bars   77, **191**
Date Bars–No-Sugar Style   79, **192**
Ginger Snap Pie Crust   **197**
Grandma's Marvelous
   Chocolate Velvet Cake   **193**
Instant Blueberry Ice Cream
   Key Recipe   29, 71, **194**
Instant Peach Ice Cream 29, 55, 130, **194**

Minute Cherry Cheesecake   106, **195**
Peach Cobbler   136, **196**
Pumpkin Pie, (Chiffon)   88, **197**
Rice 'n' Honey Pudding   77, **198**
Strawberry Pie   82, **199**
Texas Brownies   90, **200**
Tropical Fruit Ice   **201**
Whole-Wheat Angel
   Food Cake   78, 96, **202**

LEAN & FREE COOKIES

Applesauce Cookies   **203**
Applesauce Oatmeal Raisin Cookies **204**
Chocolate Chip Cookies   118, **205**
Oatmeal Raisin Cookies or Oatmeal
   Chocolate Chip Cookies   **206**
Pumpkin Cake Cookies   **207**
Raisin Chippers   **208**
Zucchini-Nut Cookies   **209**

DIPS / DRESSINGS

Bottled Dressings   **210**
Buttermilk Dressing   58, 138, **210**
Cranberry Sandwich Spread   **165**
Creamy Onion Dip   94, **210**
Delicious Dill Dip   73, 79 **211**
Easy Lowfat Dressings
   and Dips   29, 118, **211**
Ranch Dip   44, 120, **212**
Sour Cream Fruit Dip   94, 133, **212**
Spinach and Vegetable Dip   **212**
Taco Dressing   **147**

FRUIT

All Fruit Jam   55, 132, **164**
Fresh Fruit Combination
   Trays   133, **213**
Fruit Canning   **213**
Fruit Gelatin   42, 127, **214**
Fruit Syrup   **214**
Juice   **215**
Juice Popsicle *(Variation)*   **215**
Pineapple and Cottage Cheese
   Salad   47, 73, **215**

RECIPE INDEXES

Pineapple-Marshmallow
  Coleslaw   *100, 112,* **216**
Pineapple-Orange-Banana
  Gelatin   *115,* **217**
Super Citrus Salad   **218**
Tropical Fruit Ice   *97, 138,* **201**
Yogurt Fruit Delight   *29, 131,* **219**

GRAVY / SAUCE

Chicken Gravy   **220**
Meat Marinade   **220**
Mushroom Gravy   *66, 96, 102,* **220**
Oriental-Style Sauce   **221**
Quick Chicken Gravy   **221**
Quick Spaghetti Sauce   *90,* **221**
Quick Turkey Gravy   *73, 88,* **222**
Spaghetti Econo-Meat Sauce
  (Variation)   **222**
Spaghetti Econo-Sauce   *49, 67,* **222**
Stir-Fry Sauce   **222**
Tartar Sauce   *131,* **253**

MISCELLANEOUS

Brown Rice Cooking Hints   *101,* **223**
Buying Pizza Out   **223**
Chinese Take-Out   **224**
Fresh Cranberry Relish   **224**
Light Butter Popcorn   *119,* **225**
Microwaved Brown Rice   **225**

MUFFINS

Apple-Cinnamon Muffins   *72, 73,* **226**
Banana Muffins   *79, 118,* **226**
Better Bran Muffins   *40, 44, 97,* **227**
Blueberry Muffins   *44, 48, 58, 106,* **227**
Carrot Muffins   **228**
Cheese Muffins   *96, 106,* **228**
Corn Muffins   *89,* **229**
Cranberry Muffins   **229**
Cranberry-Orange Muffins   *89,* **230**
Date Muffins   **230**
Marvelous Muffins –
  Key Recipe   *35, 43, 46, 82, 136,* **231**

Minute Muffins   **232**
Oatmeal Raisin Muffins   *40,* **232**
Pumpkin-Carrot Muffins   *88,* **233**
Pumpkin Muffins   **233**
Sweet Potato Muffins   *126,* **234**
Zucchini Muffins   *78, 115, 132,* **234**

PASTA

Cappellino Primavera   *83,* **235**
Cheese-Stuffed Jumbo Shells *47,* **236**
Chilighetti   **29**
Chili Skillet   *41, 46, 89, 94, 150,* **237**
Company Casserole   *118,* **252**
D'Ann's Delicious 15 Minute
  Beef Stroganoff   **150**
Homemade Macaroni
  and Cheese   *42, 47, 65, 121,* **238**
Homemade Noodles   *96,* **239**
Luscious Lasagna   *43, 48, 71,* **239**
Mushroom Stroganoff *(Variation)*   **150**
Packaged Macaroni and Cheese **240**
Salmon Pasta Salad   *102,* **240**
Savory Meat and Cheese
  Manicotti   *32, 36, 45, 50, 106,* **241**
Spaghetti and Pasta Varieties *90,* **242**
Spaghetti Salad   *43, 47,* **242**
Veggie Lasagna   *84,* **243**
Veggie -Tuna Pasta Salad   *56,* **243**

POTATOES

AuGratin Potatoes   *58, 131,* **244**
Chicken-Chili Stuffed
  Potato   *22, 28, 45,* **245**
Hash Browns   *71,* **246**
Mashed Potatoes   *73, 88,* **246**
Perfect Potato Casserole   *48, 112,* **247**
Sour Cream & Chives
  Baked Potato   **31**
Veggie-Stuffed Potato   *72,* **247**

SALADS

Chinese Salad Bar   *72, 97,* **262**
Fast-Food Salads and Potatoes **263**
Mexicali Salad   *266,* **31**

Pineapple and Cottage Cheese
  Salad   *31, 139,* **215**
Salmon Pasta Salad   **240**
Short-Cut Tossed Salad   *28, 58,* **266**
Shrimp Salad   **255**
Spaghetti Salad   *114,* **242**
Super Citrus Salad   *118,* **218**
Tossed Salad or Homestyle
  Salad Bar   *42, 138,* **267**
Veggie-Tuna Pasta Salad   **243**

SANDWICHES

Bacon, Lettuce and Tomato
  Sandwich   *114,* **248**
Chicken Sandwich   *41,* **249**
Club Sandwich   *41, 96,* **249**
Corned Beef Sandwich   *41, 89,* **249**
Fast-Food Sandwiches   **249**
Ham 'n' Cheese Sandwich *24, 41, 130,* **249**
LEAN & FREE Burritos   **249**
LEAN & FREE Homemade
  Sandwiches   **249**
LEAN & FREE Peanut Butter
  and Jelly or Jam Sandwich *20, 95,* **251**
LEAN & FREE Pita Pockets   **249**
Pastrami Sandwich   *41,* **249**
Roast Beef 'n' Cheddar
  Sandwich   *41,* **250**
Roast Beef Sandwich   **250**
Seafood 'n' Avocado Sandwich *41, 77,* **250**
Tuna Salad Sandwich   *31, 71, 126,* **250**
Turkey 'n' Provolone Cheese
  Sandwich   *41, 106,* **250**
Turkey, Cream Cheese, and
  Cranberry Sandwich   **24**
Turkey Breast Sandwich   *41,* **250**

SEAFOOD

Company Casserole   **252**
Creamed Tuna on Toast *24, 65, 91,* **252**
Orange Roughy with
  Tartar Sauce   *82, 112,* **253**
Parmesan Halibut Steaks   *58, 96,* **254**

Red Snapper   *31, 78, 131,* **254**
Shrimp Salad   *120,* **255**

SOUPS

Bean and Ham Soup   *25, 50, 94,* **255**
Cream of Chicken Vegetable
  Soup *(Variation)*   **257**
Creamy Bean and Ham Soup   **256**
Creamy Zucchini Soup   **256**
Egg Drop Soup   *72, 97,* **257**
Fast and Creamy Clam
  Chowder   *36, 44, 91, 130,* **257**
Lentil and Barley Soup   *96,* **258**
Minestrone Soup   *35, 46,* **258**
Potato, Corn, and Cheese Soup   **259**
Potato Corn Soup   *25, 44, 106,* **259**
Split Pea Soup   *78,* **255**
Zucchini Soup   *49, 114,* **259**

VEGETABLES

Broccoli Casserole   *31,* **260**
Cauliflower 'n' Cheddar   *78,* **261**
Chinese Salad Bar   **262**
Cooking Frozen Vegetables   **262**
Easy Cabbage Dinner   *136,* **263**
Emily's Delectable Pizza Crust   **268**
Fast-Food Salads and Potatoes   **263**
Glazed Carrots, Cauliflower,
  and Broccoli   *115,* **264**
Great Green Beans   *88, 106,* **265**
Mexicali Salad   **31**
Mixed Veggie Festival *32, 70, 91, 130,* **265**
Pizza Variations   **269**
Saucy Green Beans
  and Almonds   *137,* **266**
Short-Cut Tossed Salad   **266**
Single Vegetable Ideas   **267**
Tossed Salad or
  Homestyle Salad Bar   *32,* **267**
Vegetable Pizza   *108,* **268**
Vegetable Relish Trays   **269**
Zucchini AuGratin   *127,* **270**
Zucchini Casserole   *139,* **270**

379

RECIPE INDEXES

RECIPE ALPHABETICAL INDEX

A

All Fruit Jam 164
Angel Food Cake, Whole-Wheat 202
Apple Cake 186
Apple-Cinnamon Muffins 226
Apple Cobbler–*Key Recipe* 187
Apple-Raspberry Bars 188
Apple-Raspberry Butter 165
Applesauce Cookies 203
Applesauce Oatmeal Raisin
  Cookies 204
AuGratin Potatoes 244
AuGratin, Zucchini 270

B

Bacon, Lettuce, and Tomato
  Sandwich 248
Baked Chicken Breasts 178
Baked Potato, Sour Cream
  and Chives 31
Banana Muffins 226
Banana Pancakes 176
Banana, Pineapple-Orange Gelatin 217
BBQ Chicken 178
Bars, Apple-Raspberry 188
Bars, Date 191
Bars, Date, No-Sugar Style 192
Bars, Granola 173
Bean and Ham Soup, Creamy 256
Bean Burritos 24
Beans, Great Green 265
Beef Fajitas 149
Beef, Roast 155
Beef Stew, Quick, Delicious 155
Beef Stroganoff, D'Ann's
  Delicious 15 Minute 150

Belgian Waffles 166
Better Bran Muffins 227
Big Soft Pretzels 158
Blender Whole-Wheat
  Pancakes – *Key Recipe* 176
Blintzes 167
Blueberry, Ice Cream,
  Instant – *Key Recipe* 194
Blueberry Muffins 227
Blueberry Pancakes 177
Blueberry Streusel Coffee Cake 189
Bottled Dressings 210
Bread, Country Corn 159
Bread, Whole-Wheat, Perfect 160
Bread, Whole-Wheat Pita 162
Bread, Zucchini-Pineapple-Nut 163
Breakfast Burrito 167
Breakfast Fruit Compote 168
Breakfast Shake 168
Broccoli Casserole 260
Broccoli, Cauliflower, and
  Carrots, Glazed 264
Broccoli, Chicken Casserole 180
Brownies, Texas 200
Brown Rice Cooking Hints 223
Brown Rice, Microwaved 225
Bun, Stew in a 28
Burrito, Breakfast 167
Burritos, Bean 24
Butter, Apple-Raspberry 165
Butter, Honey 165
Buttermilk Dressing 210
Buying Pizza Out 223

C

Cabbage Dinner, Easy 263
Cake, Apple – *Key Recipe* 186
Cake, Blueberry Streusel Coffee 189

RECIPE INDEXES

Cake-Mix Sweet Rolls– *Key Recipe* 190
Cake, Whole-Wheat Angel Food 202
Canning, Fruit 213
Cappellino Primavera 235
Carrot Muffins 228
Carrots, Cauliflower, and Broccoli, Glazed 264
Casserole, Broccoli 260
Casserole, Chicken 180
Casserole, Company 252
Casserole, Perfect Potato 247
Casserole, Zucchini 270
Cauliflower 'n' Cheddar 261
Cauliflower, Carrots, and Broccoli, Glazed 264
Cheese and Egg Muffins 171
Cheese Egg Scramble 175
Cheese, Garlic Toast 159
Cheese Muffins 228
Cheese-Stuffed Jumbo Shells 236
Cheesecake, Minute Cherry 195
Chicken 'n' Dumplings, Easy 183
Chicken and Rice 179
Chicken Bake 179
Chicken, Baked Breasts 178
Chicken, BBQ 178
Chicken Broccoli Casserole 180
Chicken Casserole 180
Chicken-Chili Enchiladas 144
Chicken-Chili Stuffed Potato 245
Chicken, Crock-Pot 182
Chicken Divan 181
Chicken Fajitas 149
Chicken Gravy 220
Chicken, Pineapple-Lime 184
Chicken Sandwich 249
Chicken, Sweet and Sour 184
Chicken, Teriyaki 185
Chicken Vegetable Soup, Cream of *(Variation)* 257
Chicken Veggie Stir-Fry 181

Chilighetti 29
Chili Skillet 237
Chinese Salad Bar 262
Chinese Take-Out 224
Chocolate Chip Cookies 205
Chocolate Frosting 191
Chow Mein, Pork 154
Cinnamon Maple Oatmeal 169
Cinnamon Rolls, Super 161
Clam Chowder, Fast and Creamy 257
Club Sandwich 249
Cobbler, Apple – *Key Recipe* 187
Cobbler, Peach 196
Coffee Cake, Blueberry Streusel 189
Coleslaw, Pineapple-Marshmallow 216
Company Casserole 252
Cookies, Applesauce 203
Cookies, Applesauce Oatmeal Raisin 204
Cookies, Chocolate Chip 205
Cookies, Oatmeal Chocolate Chip 206
Cookies, Oatmeal Raisin 206
Cookies, Pumpkin Cake 207
Cookies, Raisin Chippers 208
Cookies, Zucchini Nut 209
Corn Bread, Country 159
Corn Muffins 229
Corned Beef Sandwich 249
Cottage Cheese and Pineapple Salad 215
Country Corn Bread 159
Cracked Wheat, Raisin, and Honey Cereal 169
Cranberry-Glazed Turkey Breast 182
Cranberry Muffins 229
Cranberry-Orange Muffins 230
Cranberry Relish, Fresh 224
Cranberry Sandwich Spread 165
Cranberry Sandwich, Turkey, Cream Cheese, and 24
Creamed Tuna on Toast 252

Cream of Chicken Vegetable
 Soup *(Variation)* 257
Creamy Bean and Ham Soup 256
Creamy Onion Dip 210
Creamy Zucchini Soup 256
Crock-Pot Chicken 182
Crunchy Granola 170

D

Date Bars 191
Date Bars—No-Sugar Style 192
Date Muffins 230
Delicious Dill Dip 211
Dip, Creamy Onion 210
Dip, Delicious Dill 211
Dip, Ranch 212
Dip, Sour Cream Fruit 212
Dip, Spinach and Vegetable 212
Dressing, Buttermilk 210
Dressings and Dips, Easy
 Lowfat 211
Dressings, Bottled 210

E

Easy Cabbage Dinner 263
Easy Chicken 'n' Dumplings 183
Easy Lowfat Dressings and Dips 211
Econo-Meat Sauce, Spaghetti 222
Econo-Sauce, Spaghetti 222
Egg and Cheese Muffins 171
Egg Drop Soup 257
Egg Scramble, Cheese 175
Egg Scramble, Veggie and Cheese 175
Eggs, Fried 172
Emily's Delectable Pizza Crust 268
Enchilada Casserole 151
Enchiladas, Chicken-Chili 144

F

Fajitas, Chicken, Beef, or Turkey 149
Fast and Creamy Clam Chowder 257
Fast-Food Salads and Potatoes 263
Fast-Food Sandwiches 249
French Toast 171
Fresh Cranberry Relish 224
Fresh Fruit Combination Trays 213
Fried Eggs 172
Frosting, Chocolate 191
Fruit, All, Jam 164
Fruit Canning 213
Fruit Compote, Breakfast 168
Fruit, Fresh Combination Trays 213
Fruit Gelatin 214
Fruit Ice, Tropical 201
Fruit Syrup 214
Fruit, Yogurt Delight 219

G

Garlic Cheese Toast 159
Gelatin, Fruit 214
Gelatin, Pineapple-Orange-
 Banana 217
Ginger Snap Pie Crust 197
Glazed Carrots, Cauliflower,
 and Broccoli 264
Grandma's Marvelous
 Chocolate Velvet Cake 193
Granola 172
Granola Bars 173
Granola, Crunchy 170
Gravy, Chicken 220
Gravy, Mushroom 220
Gravy, Quick Chicken 221
Gravy, Quick Turkey 222

Great Green Beans 265
Green Beans and Almonds,
    Saucy 266
Green Beans, Great 265

H

Halibut Steaks, Parmesan 254
Ham 'n' Cheese Sandwich 249
Hash Browns 246
Hawaiian Haystacks 183
Homemade Macaroni and
    Cheese 238
Homemade Noodles 239
Homemade Sandwiches, Pita
    Pockets, and Burritos,
    LEAN & FREE 249
Honey Butter 165

I

Instant Blueberry Ice Cream–
    Key Recipe 194
Instant Peach Ice Cream 194

J

Jam, All Fruit 164
Jams, Jellies, Syrups,
    Store Variety 166
Jam Variations 164
Juice 215
Juice Popsicles *(Variation)* 215
Jumbo Shells, Cheese-Stuffed 236

K

Key Recipe – Apple Cobbler 187
Key Recipe – Blender Whole-
    Wheat Pancakes 176
Key Recipe – Cake-Mix Sweet
    Rolls 190
Key Recipe – Instant Blueberry
    Ice Cream 194
Key Recipe – Marvelous
    Muffins 231

L

Lasagna, Luscious 239
Lasagna, Mexican 146
Lasagna, Veggie 243
LEAN & FREE Homemade
    Sandwiches, Pita Pockets,
    and Burritos 249
LEAN & FREE Nachos 145
LEAN & FREE Pancakes 176
LEAN & FREE Peanut Butter
    and Jam or Jelly Sandwich 251
Lentil and Barley Soup 258
Light Butter Popcorn 225
Luscious Lasagna 239

M

Macaroni and Cheese, Packaged 240
Macaroni and Cheese, Homemade 238
Manicotti, Savory Meat and Cheese 241
Marinade, Meat 220
Marvelous Muffins – *Key Recipe* 231
Mashed Potatoes 246
Meat Marinade 220
Meatballs, Porcupine 153

383

RECIPE INDEXES

Mexicali Salad	31
Mexican Lasagna	146
Microwaved Brown Rice	225
Minestrone Soup	258
Minute Cherry Cheesecake	195
Minute Muffins	232
Mixed Veggie Festival	265
Muffins, Apple-Cinnamon	226
Muffins, Banana	226
Muffins, Better Bran	227
Muffins, Blueberry	227
Muffins, Carrot	228
Muffins, Cheese	228
Muffins, Corn	229
Muffins, Cranberry	229
Muffins, Cranberry-Orange	230
Muffins, Date	230
Muffins, Egg and Cheese	171
Muffins, Marvelous –*Key Recipe*	231
Muffins, Oatmeal Raisin	232
Muffins, Pumpkin	233
Muffins, Pumpkin-Carrot	233
Muffins, Sweet Potato	234
Muffins, Zucchini	234
Mushroom Gravy	220
Mushroom Stroganoff *(Variation)*	150

N

No-Sugar Style, Date Bars	192
Noodles, Homemade	239
Nut Bread, Zucchini-Pineapple	163

O

Oatmeal Chocolate Chip Cookies	206
Oatmeal, Cinnamon-Maple	169
Oatmeal Pancakes	177
Oatmeal Raisin Cookies	206
Oatmeal Raisin Muffins	232

Omelet Supreme	174
Orange Jubilee	174
Orange, Pineapple, Banana Gelatin	217
Orange Roughy with Tartar Sauce	253
Oriental-Style Sauce	221

P

Packaged Macaroni and Cheese	240
Pancakes, Banana	176
Pancakes, Blender Whole-Wheat – *Key Recipe*	176
Pancakes, Blueberry	177
LEAN & FREE Pancakes	176
Pancakes, Oatmeal	177
Pancakes, Peach	177
Pancakes, Super Quick	177
Parmesan Halibut Steaks	254
Pasta Varieties, Spaghetti and	242
Pasta, Salmon, Salad	240
Pastrami Sandwich	249
Peach Cobbler	196
Peach Pancakes	177
Peanut Butter and Jelly or Jam Sandwich, LEAN & FREE	251
Perfect Potato Casserole	247
Perfect Whole-Wheat Bread	160
Pie, Pumpkin	197
Pie, Strawberry	199
Pigs in a Blanket	29
Pineapple and Cottage Cheese Salad	215
Pineapple-Lime Chicken	184
Pineapple-Marshmallow Coleslaw	216
Pineapple-Orange-Banana Gelatin	217
Pita Bread, Whole-Wheat	162
Pita Pockets, LEAN & FREE	249
Pizza, Buying Out	223

RECIPE INDEXES

Pizza Wheel Variations   152
Pizza, Vegetable   268
Pizza Wheels   152
Popcorn, Light Butter   225
Porcupine Meatballs   153
Pork Chow Mein   154
Porridge, Three Bear, and
    Honey   175
Potato, Baked, Sour Cream
    and Chives   31
Potato, Chicken-Chili Stuffed   245
Potato, Corn, and Cheese Soup   259
Potato Corn Soup   259
Potato, Perfect Casserole   247
Potato, Veggie-Stuffed   247
Potatoes and Salads, Fast-Food   263
Potatoes, AuGratin   244
Potatoes, Hash Browns   246
Potatoes, Mashed   246
Pretzels, Big Soft   158
Pudding, Rice 'n' Honey   198
Pumpkin Cake Cookies   207
Pumpkin-Carrot Muffins   233
Pumpkin Muffins   233
Pumpkin Pie   197

Q

Quick Chicken Gravy   221
Quick, Delicious Beef Stew   155
Quick Turkey Gravy   222
Quick Spaghetti Sauce   221

R

Raisin Chippers   208
Ranch Dip   212
Raspberry, Apple Butter   165
Red Snapper   254

Relish, Fresh Cranberry   224
Relish Trays, Vegetable   269
Rice, Brown, Cooking Hints   223
Rice 'n' Honey Pudding   198
Roast Beef   155
Roast Beef Sandwich   250
Roast Beef 'n' Cheddar
    Sandwich   250
Rolls, Cake-Mix, Sweet
    Key Recipe   190

S

Salad Bar, Chinese   262
Salad, Mexicali   31
Salad, Pineapple and Cottage
    Cheese   215
Salad, Salmon Pasta   240
Salad, Short-Cut Tossed   266
Salad, Shrimp   255
Salad, Spaghetti   242
Salad, Super Citrus   218
Salad, Tossed or Homestyle,
    Salad Bar   267
Salad, Veggie-Tuna Pasta   243
Salads and Potatoes, Fast-Food   263
Salmon Pasta Salad   240
Sandwich, Bacon, Lettuce,
    and Tomato   248
Sandwich, Chicken   249
Sandwich, Club   249
Sandwich, Corned Beef   249
Sandwiches, Fast-Food   249
Sandwich, Ham 'n' Cheese   249
Sandwiches, Homemade,
    LEAN & FREE   249
Sandwich, Pastrami   249
Sandwich, Peanut Butter and
    Jelly or Jam, LEAN & FREE   251
Sandwich, Roast Beef   250
Sandwich, Roast Beef 'n'
    Cheddar   250

RECIPE INDEXES

Sandwich, Seafood 'n' Avocado   250
Sandwich, Tuna Salad   250
Sandwich, Turkey Breast   250
Sandwich, Turkey, Cream
    Cheese, and Cranberry   24
Sandwich, Turkey 'n'
    Provolone Cheese   250
Sauce, Oriental-Style   221
Sauce, Quick Spaghetti   221
Sauce, Spaghetti Econo-   222
Sauce, Spaghetti Econo-Meat   222
Sauce, Stir-Fry   222
Sauce, Tartar   253
Saucy Green Bean and Almonds   266
Savory Meat and Cheese
    Manicotti   241
Seafood 'n' Avocado Sandwich   250
Shake, Breakfast   168
Shepherd's Pie   156
Short-Cut Tossed Salad   266
Shrimp Salad   255
Single Vegetable Ideas   267
Sloppy Joes   156
Soft Pretzels, Big   158
Soup, Bean and Ham   255
Soup, Bean and Ham, Creamy   256
Soup, Cream of Chicken
    Vegetable (Variation)   257
Soup, Creamy Zucchini   256
Soup, Potato Corn   259
Soup, Potato, Corn, and Cheese   259
Sour Cream and Chives Baked
    Potato   31
Sour Cream Fruit Dip   212
Sourdough Starter   160
Spaghetti and Pasta Varieties   242
Spaghetti Econo-Meat Sauce   222
Spaghetti Econo-Sauce   222
Spaghetti Salad   242
Spaghetti Sauce, Quick   221
Spinach and Vegetable Dip   212
Spread, Cranberry Sandwich   165
Starter, Sourdough   160
Stew in a Bun   28

Stew, Quick, Delicious Beef   155
Stir-Fry, Chicken Veggie   181
Stir-Fry Sauce   222
Store Variety Jams, Jellies,
    Syrups   166
Strawberry Pie   199
Stroganoff, Beef, D'Ann's
    Delicious 15 Minute   150
Super Cinnamon Rolls   161
Super Citrus Salad   218
Super Quick Pancakes   177
Sweet and Sour Chicken   184
Sweet Potato Muffins   234
Sweet Rolls, Cake-Mix   190
Syrup, Fruit   214
Syrups, Jams, Jellies,
    Store Variety   166

T

Taco Salad with Taco Dressing   147
Taco Casserole   157
Taco Dressing   147
Tacos, Tempting   148
Tartar Sauce   253
Tempting Tacos   148
Teriyaki Chicken   185
Texas Brownies   200
Three Bear Porridge and Honey   175
Toast, Creamed Tuna on   252
Toast, Garlic Cheese   159
Tortillas, Whole-Wheat   162
Tossed Salad or Homestyle
    Salad Bar   267
Trays, Fresh Fruit Combination   213
Tropical Fruit Ice   201
Tuna, Creamed, on Toast   252
Tuna Salad Sandwich   250
Tuna, Veggie, Pasta Salad   243
Turkey Breast,
    Cranberry-Glazed   182
Turkey, Cream Cheese,
    and Cranberry Sandwich   24

Turkey Fajitas 149
Turkey 'n' Provolone Cheese
    Sandwich 250
Turkey Breast Sandwich 250

V

Vegetable Pizza 268
Vegetable Relish Trays 269
Vegetable Soup, Cream of
    Chicken (Variation) 257
Vegetables, Cooking Frozen 262
Veggie and Cheese Egg
    Scramble or Cheese Egg
    Scramble 175
Veggie Festival, Mixed 265
Veggie Lasagna 243
Veggie-Stuffed Potato 247
Veggie-Tuna Pasta Salad 243

W

Waffles, Belgian 166
Whole-Wheat Angel
    Food Cake 202
Whole-Wheat Bread, Perfect 160
Whole-Wheat Pita Bread 162
Whole-Wheat Tortillas 162

Y

Yogurt Fruit Delight 219

Z

Zucchini AuGratin 270
Zucchini Casserole 270
Zucchini Muffins 234
Zucchini-Nut Cookies 209
Zucchini-Pineapple-Nut Bread 163
Zucchini Soup 259

Special Note: *All topics found in the recipe section of this book from pages 144 to 270 are included in these indexes. This includes topics such as "Buying Pizza Out," "Fast-Food Sandwiches," "Bottled Dressings," etc.*

LEAN & FREE™ LECTURE SERIES
Live Acceleration Course on Eight Audio Cassettes

Let Dana personally take you through her time-tested eight steps to a LEAN & FREE™ life! Learn how to nourish your body back to health and leanness. You'll discover how to *LIVE LEAN – NOT EXTREME™* and how to personalize the LEAN & FREE™ program to your individual needs.

LEAN & FREE™ COMPUTERIZED DETAILED PLANNER
What An Advancement!

This program will simplify your entire LEAN & FREE™ detailed planner. Type in breakfast, lunch and dinner, and it figures all the fat grams, calories, and fat percentages for you! It will also calculate and file your personal recipes. what simplicity and freedom!

LIVING LEAN – NOT EXTREME™
9-SESSION FAT-BURNING ACCELERATION™ COURSE
Live Course Taught by Dana!

In Dana's highly personalized Fat-burning Acceleration Course, you'll learn how to feed your entire family delicious, healthy, five and 10 minute meals, while staying on a tight budget and time schedule. You may see extraordinary improvements in those with diabetes, high cholesterol, chronic fatigue, high blood pressure, fibro myalgia, and other special health needs. Average weekly inch loss is one to five overall inches.

PERSONALIZED ONE-ON-ONE TELEPHONE COUNSELING
Talk with a LEAN & FREE™ Counselor Each Week by Appointment

Fax or mail homework assignments to your counselor weekly. You and your counselor will then set weekly goals and fine tune your health and inch-loss habits. This is a highly effective, personalized course. You do the fun, simple assignments, and you see great results!

******THE OPTIMAL ACCELERATION PACKAGE******
Maximum Success and Value!

Special Bonus: When you combine your LEAN & FREE™ Library with an Eight- or 16-Session Phone Counseling Acceleration Course or Live Acceleration Course, you receive the $79.95 Lecture Series and Study Guide FREE! This special bonus is only included here because either Acceleration Course, in combination with the Library, promotes the most rapid, permanent success for students. If you want the OPTIMUM PACKAGE for success, this is it – AN ACCELERATION COURSE PLUS THE LEAN & FREE™LIBRARY!

To **ORDER** these breakthrough LEAN & FREE LIFESTYLE™ products, call **1-800-554-DANA** or 801-546-3262 or write:

Danmar Health Corporation
505 North Kays Drive
Kaysville, Utah 84037